Alternative Beta Strategies and Hedge Fund Replication

Lars Jaeger

with Jeffrey Pease

John Wiley & Sons, Ltd

Other Wiley Editorial Offices

John Wiley & Sons Inc., 111 River Street, Hoboken, NJ 07030, USA

Jossey-Bass, 989 Market Street, San Francisco, CA 94103-1741, USA

Wiley-VCH Verlag GmbH, Boschstr. 12, D-69469 Weinheim, Germany

John Wiley & Sons Australia Ltd, 42 McDougall Street, Milton, Queensland 4064, Australia

John Wiley & Sons (Asia) Pte Ltd, 2 Clementi Loop #02-01, Jin Xing Distripark, Singapore 129809

John Wiley & Sons Canada Ltd, 6045 Freemont Blvd, Mississauga, Ontario, L5R 4J3 Canada

Wiley also publishes its books in a variety of electronic formats. Some content that appears in print may not be
available in electronic books.

Library of Congress Cataloging-in-Publication Data

Jaeger, Lars.
  Alternative beta strategies and hedge fund replication / Lars Jaeger.
      p. cm.
  Includes bibliographical references and index.
  ISBN 978-0-470-75446-7 (cloth : alk. paper)   1. Hedge funds.   I. Title.
  HG4530.J327 2008
  332.64′524–dc22

                                                              2008022826

British Library Cataloguing in Publication Data

A catalogue record for this book is available from the British Library

ISBN 978-0-470-75446-7

Typeset in 10/12pt Times by Aptara Inc., New Delhi, India

Alternative
Beta Strategies and Hedge Fund Replication

"It was around early 2002 when Lars Jaeger and I started exchanging ideas about distinguishing between hedge fund alphas and hedge fund betas as different sources of performance. Hitherto, most hedge fund return models were rooted in performance attribution literature. The notion of a rule-based approach to investing into a portfolio of hedge fund strategies, such as investable hedge fund indices, was not much more than a germ of an idea. Lars' seven-year journey, from embracing the concept of alternative beta to persuading the investment community that this represents an efficient avenue for achieving hedge fund-like returns, is a tour de force. This book offers the reader valuable insight into the thinking behind this landmark development in hedge fund research."

Bill Fung, Visiting Research Professor of Finance, Hedge Fund Research Centre, London Business School.

About the author

LARS JAEGER holds a PhD degree in theoretical physics from the Max-Planck Institute for Physics of Complex Systems, Dresden. He studied physics and philosophy at the University of Bonn, Germany, and École Polytechnique, Paris. After his post-doctorate studies in Dresden, Lars began his finance career as a quantitative researcher on econometric and mathematical modeling of financial markets at Olsen & Associates AG in Zurich. He subsequently joined the Hedge Fund group of Credit Suisse Asset management, where he was responsible for risk management and quantitative strategy analysis. Lars is a founding partner of saisGroup, an investment firm specializing on alternative investment strategies which in 2001 merged with Partners Group, where he is now a partner heading the group "Alternative Beta Strategies". Lars holds the CFA charter and is a certified Financial Risk Manager (FRM). He is the author of numerous research publications and the books *Risk Management of Alternative Investment Strategies*, published in 2002 with Financial Times Prentice Hall, *The New Generation of Risk Management for Hedge Funds and Private Equity* (ed.) published by Euromoney in 2003, and *Through the Alpha Smokescreen: A guide to hedge fund return sources*, published by Institutional Investors (2005). Lars lives with his wife and three children near Zurich, Switzerland.

To my children, Anika Mai, Kira Anh, and Talia Linh

For other titles in the Wiley Finance Series
please see www.wiley.com/finance

Contents

Preface

The increased academic and nonacademic effort in modeling and understanding hedge fund return sources has finally reached Wall Street. A new buzzword is out and has quickly captured the imagination of product providers and investors alike: 'hedge fund replication'. In the broadest sense, replicating hedge fund strategies means replicating their return sources and corresponding risk exposures. However, there is still no coherent picture of what hedge fund replication means in practice, what its premises are, how to distinguish different approaches, and where this can lead us to. In this book I will try to change that.

Because investors must understand return sources to achieve replication, I will present them in considerable detail. Thus the early chapters of this book cover some of the same, though updated, ground as two of my earlier books: *Risk Management in Alternative Investment Strategies* (2002) and *Through the Alpha Smokescreen: A Guide to Hedge Fund Return Sources* (2005). The discussion of replication techniques and their practical application, however, is entirely new.

How this book is different

As hedge funds grow, so does the number of books about them. But it has taken a long time to see a first handbook dedicated to the topic of replicating hedge fund strategies. This is in part because the financial community is only now coming around to the view that hedge fund replication is possible. As far as I know, this is the first book on the topic. It uniquely focuses on replication, explaining along the way the return sources (and systematic risks) that make replication possible. If you wish to understand the background of the new discussion on hedge fund replication and how to derive the returns of many hedge fund strategies at much lower cost, to differentiate the various underlying approaches, or simply to understand in greater detail how hedge fund replication can improve your own investment process into hedge funds, you have come to the right place.

Who needs it?

Anyone who wants to understand hedge funds and the new hedge fund replication discussion can benefit from this book. It is aimed at financial professionals who work with or allocate assets to hedge funds. But it will also be helpful to traditional asset managers, financial analysts, consultants, regulators, legal authorities, advisors, financial journalists, and students. Because I examine a wide range of strategies, even hedge fund experts are likely to learn something new.

What do you need to know first?

All you need to benefit from this book is a basic knowledge of financial markets. To serve a broad audience, I have minimized the math and defined any technical jargon. On the way, I will also explain what hedge funds really are and detail how different strategies derive their returns. In the process I hope to dispel popular misperceptions of hedge funds as either a magic money machine or a scam. If you understand the fundamentals of these three things: traditional investment vehicles such as equity, fixed income, foreign exchange and commodities; plain vanilla derivatives such as options and futures; and the core principles of modern portfolio theory – then you are good to go.

What is in the book

This book is divided into three parts: Hedge Fund Background; Return Sources; and Replication Techniques.

The first part consisting of Chapters 1 and 2 – Hedge Fund Background – provides a short course in what hedge funds actually are and how they operate. It will arm you with the background knowledge you will need to absorb the rest of the book. Chapter 2 is an overview of the hedge fund industry and its recent developments. It also dispels common myths and misperceptions about hedge funds.

Armed with this background, the Return Sources part illuminates, unsurprisingly, the sources from which hedge funds derive their returns. Most importantly this section shows that the majority of hedge fund returns derive from systematic risk exposure rather than manager 'alpha'. Chapter 3 describes the individual hedge fund strategies in some detail, while Chapter 4 examines their past performance characteristics. Chapter 5 discusses the background of the capital markets theory and explains the economic reasons for hedge fund returns. Hedge fund managers and veterans might choose to skip ahead, but both the Background and Return Sources parts will be useful if you are either new to hedge funds, or simply want a refresher before heading into new territory.

The third part – Replication Techniques – is the beating heart of this book. It presents both conventional and emerging approaches to replicating hedge fund returns. Chapter 6 presents the first generation of hedge fund replications products, and points out the pitfalls of the linear factor model approach that underlies them. Chapters 7 and 8 introduce alternative approaches to hedge fund replication, designed to overcome some of the problems of previous models, and also discuss the limitations of hedge fund replication. Chapter 9 is a practical guide for using your new replication knowledge to construct optimal portfolios. You will learn about a new 'core–satellite' investment approach, which optimizes returns and costs by integrating sector allocation and manager selection. This chapter is especially useful for the fund-of-funds manager.

With hedge fund replication going mainstream, investors are given a choice among several different views and approaches. But despite its immense importance, there is not yet a book out which gives readers clear guidance on this topic. This is what motivated me to write this book.

This book represents untold hours of effort by many persons other than myself, and I would like to thank everybody who helped me to complete this work. The first person I owe gratitude is my dear wife, Julie, who provided love, understanding and support throughout many hours of writing. Secondly, I owe particular gratitude to Jeffrey Pease, my brother-in-law, who spent countless hours editing and rewriting the manuscript. Without him, the book would not be in the form and language presented here. Furthermore, I would like to acknowledge my colleagues and partners at Partners Group, who were the joint architects of many of the ideas presented in this book, particularly Michel Jacquemai for numerous years of collaboration, Dr Stephan Müller for valuable support and ideas on the topic as well as in the implementation of these ideas into a real-world trading environment, and Björm Imbjerowic for helping on some calculations presented.

Finally, I thank my editor at Wiley, Pete Baker, for his enthusiastic support of this book and for assistance in editing and reviewing the manuscript. Despite the extensive support I received, I take responsibility for any mistakes, misrepresentation, or omissions in the book.

Dr Lars Jaeger
September 2008

1
Breaking the Black Box

This is a handbook for replicating the returns of hedge funds at considerably lower cost. Once thought to be impossible, hedge fund replication is fast becoming a buzzword in the finance community – driven by the growing realization that most hedge fund returns come from risk premiums rather than manager alpha. Not since the emergence of index funds have so many people gotten active about being 'passive'!

However, the term 'hedge fund replication', while catching the imagination of investors and product providers, is also a source of confusion. What is it that we want to replicate: the past time series properties of past hedge fund returns, the distributional properties of the past hedge fund performance, or maybe the economic sources of hedge fund returns? This book will shed some light on this legitimate question.

Because replication means modeling beta-driven returns, it requires a thorough understanding of hedge return sources and their associated risks. So I will pave the way for replication by first reviewing what hedge funds really are (and aren't), and explaining the return sources of common strategies. By opening the black box of hedge funds, I also hope to dispel two conflicting but popular misconceptions. Hedge funds as a class are neither magic money machines nor scams but simply innovative investment vehicles whose characteristics can, in most cases, be understood, analyzed, modeled, and duplicated. I hope to help you do just that.

1.1 NEW POPULARITY, OLD CONFUSION

Not so long ago, the investment industry did not need to worry what people thought about hedge funds – because most people did not think about them at all! Hedge fund managers operated with little scrutiny and disclosed very little of their strategies. As recently as 10 years ago, hedge funds were limited to a few very wealthy individuals. These super-rich generally accepted high fees and a 'black box' lack of transparency as the fair tribute to the hedge fund wizards, and their apparently market-proof returns. So investors with millions at stake left the wizards alone to work their magic. No wonder that average people, if they had even heard of hedge funds, thought of them as mystical money machines for the rich.

That old world is gone – blown apart by huge success and a few truly spectacular failures. Hedge fund investment volume has multiplied fifteenfold in as many years. An investment once limited to the wealthy has been democratized. Even many staid institutional investors now see hedge funds as an essential element of their portfolios. This mainstreaming has fueled such unprecedented growth that hedge funds are today the fastest growing 'asset class' in the investment world. Some researchers even hail hedge funds as a 'new paradigm in asset management',[1] and more and more investors see them as a necessary element of their overall portfolio.

Now the bad news. Despite all of this growth and acclaim, in the popular imagination the very term 'hedge fund' carries a whiff of scandal. Some European politicians went so far as

---

[1] See, for example, the introduction to A. Ineichen, *Absolute Returns* (2002), *Asymmetric Returns* (2007).

to brand hedge fund managers as 'locusts'.[2] The popular business press heavily covered such high-profile fund meltdowns as Long Term Capital Management in 1998, Amaranth Capital in 2006, or Peleton Capital in 2008. In these stories hedge funds are often portrayed as a scam, the likely cause of the next investment bubble, or even a threat to the very architecture of the global capital markets.

What accounts for these wildly differing views of hedge funds? If they are successful enough to draw ever more investment, why do so many people view them so negatively? Certainly the extraordinarily rich compensation hedge fund managers receive – successful fund managers are among the richest of Wall Street billionaires – causes some jealousy. And some even refer to hedge funds as a 'compensation scheme rather than an asset class'. But there is more at work here. The press and public also periodically criticize the compensation and perks of traditional industry CEOs or investment managers as well. But the tone of coverage of a Jack Welch or Warren Buffet is more often admiring than critical; and the basic premise that a GE or Berkshire Hathaway should exist at all is not questioned. Why does there seem to be a special circle of purgatory reserved for those who make their living in hedge funds?

The answer is that most investors, business writers, and even many investment managers outside the hedge fund arena simply do not know how hedge funds make money. And hedge fund managers' traditionally low transparency has only aggravated this problem. Hedge funds draw such heated debate because they have produced both extraordinary gains and spectacular losses by means that most people simply do not understand well enough.

1.2   THE CHALLENGES OF UNDERSTANDING HEDGE FUNDS

Hedge funds are by nature challenging to understand. They are both diverse and technically complex involving techniques that the average investor is not entirely familiar with, such as spread strategies, leverage, and short selling, and investing in a variety of different asset classes and instruments at the same time. To make matters worse, hedge fund strategies evolve quickly, so they are changing even as investment professionals struggle to understand them. But these innate challenges have been exacerbated by an artificial one: lack of transparency.

Unfortunately, understanding of hedge funds has been hampered by many hedge fund managers' unwillingness to disclose details of their strategies. But besides the complexity in the specifics of a hedge fund strategy, the investor can make a simple statement: misunderstanding and myth flourish in darkness. So this 'black box' approach on the part of hedge fund managers has perpetuated myths about hedge funds, both positive and negative. Many investors still incorrectly regard hedge funds as an 'asset class' that generates returns by mysterious means. Without visibility into actual return sources, investors could only judge these successful managers by their past returns. But the hedge fund battlefield is now littered with the bodies of secretive and once-stellar funds such as LTCM, Quantum, Tiger, Niederhoffer, Beacon Hill, Amaranth, Basis Capital, and very recently in 2008[3] such names as Drake Management,

---

[2] A term used by some German politicians (originally applied by the former leader of the German Social Democrats, Franz Münterfering, however, to private equity managers). The popular press usually does not distinguish between private equity and hedge funds although these two investment types are very different in their nature.

[3] Every author has his own time frames in which he writes his books: I happened to finish this book in early 2008, a period in which the industry is about to experience a shake-out that could easily become its largest in history.

Peleton Partners, or Carlyle Capital – all of which failed spectacularly, even as they were supposed to offer market-neutral returns.

But greater transparency is being forced on the industry. These very public failures occurred at just the time when hedge funds broadly expanded their investor base to include institutional investors bearing fiduciary responsibilities. These investors require a better understanding of hedge funds in order to overcome the negative perceptions created by these high-profile disasters, and allocate capital to them. Institutional investors in particular insist on a credible and understandable answer to the question of 'How do hedge funds earn returns?' This level of disclosure provides risk-averse investors with the knowledge they need to protect their stakeholders from the next great hedge fund disaster. And only transparency about return sources will allow hedge funds to be universally regarded as a legitimate asset class.

1.3 LEAVING ALPHAVILLE

Traditionally hedge funds were thought to derive their returns from manager 'alpha': superior expertise and information that allowed wizard-like fund managers to safely take advantage of market inefficiencies. Recent hedge fund returns challenge this notion.

Ironically the surge in capital flows and increased institutional investment to hedge funds come at a time when hedge fund managers have provided only mediocre returns: returns which are significantly below their historical means. In the seven-year period from early 2001 to 2007, hedge fund performance averaged only 300–400 basis points per annum above the risk-free rate. This seems quite anemic compared with the prior seven years' average of 800–1000 bps above the risk-free rate.[4]

Furthermore, despite the claim of market-neutrality, hedge funds as a group have clearly not escaped the losses in times of global stock market distress. In fact periods of weak hedge fund performance coincide with the most severe equity downturns: October 2005, May/June 2006, February/March 2007, July/August 2007, March 2008. We must now admit that today the average hedge fund portfolio has shown a substantial correlation with the broad equity markets.

Falling returns and increased correlations to the global equity markets naturally lead investors to ask about hedge fund return sources and risk exposures, before allocating capital to them. But even more importantly, it leads investors to ask why the hedge fund managers receive such high fees. Further, can at least some hedge fund returns be duplicated at lower cost?

In the quest to understand and even replicate hedge funds, academics and investors have started to unravel the mystique of hedge fund returns. Shining light into the 'black box' reveals an 'inconvenient truth': the majority of hedge fund returns stem from risk premiums rather than market inefficiencies – in other words, from 'beta' rather than 'alpha'. In still other words, hedge fund managers earn most of their returns the same way as every other investment manager. They take systematic risks.

This is not to say that alpha doesn't exist, only that it is far rarer than previously believed. The search for alpha in hedge funds must begin with understanding their betas, the latter constituting an important – if not the most important – source of their returns. This insight has finally caught wider attention. The question that is changing the industry is this: isn't it possible to construct suitable benchmarks for hedge funds on the basis of an analysis of the underlying systematic risk factors? If so, why not render these models into an investable format?

---

[4] Based on Hedge Fund Research data. The result does not change significantly if we consider other indices.

1.4 THE BEAUTY OF BETA

The attraction of alpha, if it can be found, is obvious. Who would not want to take advantage of market imperfections and superior information if possible? The charms of beta are more mundane, but also more abundant. The general attraction of beta – be it traditional or alternative – is that it can be systematically described, modeled, and replicated. The particular charm of hedge funds' beta is that it can provide investors with new systematic sources of return which are not highly correlated to traditional risk premia and thus provide efficiency enhancement to their overall portfolio. And the attraction of applying replication techniques to hedge fund profiles can be summarized in one short word: fees! If beta (in alternative form, see below) accounts for 80% of hedge fund returns, and replication can make savings of approximately 2% in management fees and 20% in performance fees, then approximately 2.5% to 3.5% p.a. of total fees can be eliminated. Assuming a gross performance of 9% to 18% on the manager level and roughly 1.5% fees for the replication, this is a dramatic saving against a typical fund of funds' total fee burden.

But as they say in TV commercials: wait, there's more. Replication techniques can also save another layer of fees. In traditional funds of funds, the performance of individual managers is not netted before they are paid their individual performance fees. In other words, the investor participates only 80% with the winning managers, but 100% with the losers.[5] Hedge fund replication saves these asymmetric performance fees or (as I would like to refer to them) 'diversification costs', which range from 0.4% to 0.8% per annum in a typical hedge fund portfolio.

Financing costs for leverage impose a third, even less transparent fee layer onto a traditional fund of funds. Inevitably some hedge funds employ external leverage, while others such as CTAs retain extra cash. As there is no way of netting the collateral across different hedge funds, the fund of funds investor pays the financing spread to the prime broker. Leverage financing comes in at around Libor plus 60–80 bps while the credit on cash yields roughly Libor minus 20 bps. This spread is lost to the investor in the form of lower returns. Replication products avoid this cost simply by trading futures and options on margin. The leverage cost or cash credit of each strategy is correctly allocated. Netting the collateral across the various replicated strategy sectors saves the investor 40–80 bps p.a. – a 'fee retrocession' that comes right out of the pocket of the prime broker, or does not find its way there in the first place.

1.5 ALTERNATIVE VERSUS TRADITIONAL BETA

The hypothesis that drives replication is that the majority of hedge funds' returns stem from beta rather than alpha. However, hedge fund beta and traditional beta are often very different. While both are the result of exposure to systematic risks in global capital markets, the beta in hedge fund returns can be significantly more complex than traditional beta. We shall therefore refer to this beta as 'alternative beta' (or synonymously 'hedge fund beta').

Unlike traditional beta, extracting alternative beta requires nonconventional techniques, including short selling, leverage and the use of derivatives. These techniques are often directly used to characterize hedge funds, because hedge funds are among the few market participants allowed to employ them. This grants hedge funds a somewhat exclusive access to alternative

---

[5] Performance fees can be seen as a free option given to the hedge fund manager. A portfolio of single options on the various underlyings is surely more expensive than an option on the overall portfolio.

beta returns. So we will label these methods 'hedge fund techniques', to contrast them with the conventional long only 'buy and hold' investment techniques employed to extract traditional beta. Alternative betas extracted by hedge funds include: various equity style factors, such as small cap versus large cap, value versus growth, and momentum; event risk premia; exposure to volatility (vega risk); commercial hedging demand premia in the global futures markets; and various types of spread positions, such as those employed in FX (foreign exchange) and interest rate carry strategies.

Since alternative beta is so complex, it's no surprise that much of what is now understood to be alternative beta was once thought to be alpha. This hidden beta was disguised as manager alpha simply because earlier models were not sophisticated enough to account for it any other way. The good news for investors is that this is changing. New modeling approaches capture more alternative beta, and set the stage for a revolution.

1.6   THE REPLICATION REVOLUTION

So can investors directly access these beautiful beta characteristics? Can hedge funds be modeled, and those models turned into investments. I propose that the answer is a strong, though qualified, 'Yes.' While there is by definition no way to model and replicate alpha – since alpha indicates superior information about market inefficiencies – returns derived from risk premia (beta) can indeed be replicated. The lure of replication is that it allows investors to optimize their portfolios with cheaper beta, and pay higher fees only for justifiably expensive true alpha. Since some returns that were once thought to be alpha-driven have now been revealed as unaccounted beta, fund managers will be increasingly under pressure to prove they deliver the alpha that justifies their rich compensation. Had he been an investor rather than an attorney, Johnny Cochran[6] might have rhymed, 'If beta explains it away, you should not pay!'

In the Winter 2005 edition of the *Journal of Alternative Investments*, I published an article entitled 'Factor modelling and benchmarking of hedge funds: Can passive investments in hedge fund strategies deliver?' The models introduced in this article were not a major innovation on other previously published articles. Academic research had introduced a variety of different models – mostly based on linear factors and regressions – to explain hedge fund returns. But the article did deal with a truly new question: Can we turn these well-known academic models into trading models and thus replicate hedge fund returns?

This was timely because the effort to model and understand hedge fund return sources has now, a couple of years later, finally reached Wall Street. The new buzzword (actually words) 'hedge fund replication' is quickly capturing the imagination of product providers and investors alike. Several product providers have either launched, or at least announced their intention to launch what they call 'passive hedge fund products' or 'hedge fund clones'. The underlying claim is that we can represent hedge fund-like returns at significantly lower fee levels to the investors.[7] So this is an opportune time to examine to what extent 'passive hedge fund products' are possible.

---

[6] For those not familiar with the recent US legal history: Johnny Cochran was the lawyer who defended O. J. Simpson in his murder trial. He became famous for using rhymes in his defence speeches. 'If it does not fit, you must acquit,' he said famously after the glove used as evidence against O. J. did not fit him.

[7] See the first article in the *Financial Times* on this topic from November 20 2006, 'Replication is the new buzz word'.

I have not been shy in the past about publicly expressing the 'return source hypothesis' that hedge funds make returns primarily by assuming risks and earning risk premia. If true, this means that hedge fund managers are in fact earning most of their returns in the same fashion as other investors, albeit at a higher level of complexity, across a wider spectrum of risk factors and with a greater degree of freedom from regulatory constraints.[8] This contention flies in the face of the alpha mystique the industry has sometimes used to market itself. But it is wholly consistent with, and in fact is the very heart of, hedge fund replication.

I hope that my previous books have validated this hypothesis, but this one goes further. Building on the return source hypothesis, it shows how investors can harness the beta-driven nature of most hedge fund strategies to reap lower-cost returns. I believe replication strategies based 'alternative beta' will become an important element in investors' hedge fund portfolios. And they may even change the landscape of the hedge fund industry.

1.7   FULL DISCLOSURE

Every human being has their biases and vested interests. The best an author can do is to disclose them, so here are mine: I am a participant as well as an observer in the 'hedge fund replication' movement. In 2004 I started a fund jointly with my colleagues at Partners Group: The 'Partners Group Alternative Beta Strategies' fund was the first of its kind and pioneered the idea of extracting the generic risk premia across the global capital markets, and thus to provide a cost-efficient alternative to traditional hedge funds. It has now been running for more than three and a half years. My involvement in the fund means of course that I have a commercial interest in hedge fund replication;[9] but it also means that I have been intimately involved with testing out the ideas presented here, pioneering many of them. I am proud that its underlying hypothesis has by now found numerous followers, including the larger Wall Street investment banks. That is the last mention you will read of this, my specific fund product, in this book.

But now let's get started!

---

[8] From this perspective it is actually doubtful whether hedge funds constitute a new 'asset class' as many protagonists of the industry proclaim.

[9] The reader should let his own judgment guide him on how to judge on solid arguments and commercial interest. I strongly believe that the strength and validity of an argument is independent of who states it. In particular, the person expressing the argument might or might not have a commercial or another type of interest in having a wide spectrum of people following the argument. The validity is independent thereof.

2

What Are Hedge Funds, Where Did They Come From, and Where Are They Going?

In order to elaborate on hedge fund return sources and replication techniques, we will first need to define what a hedge fund is and give a brief overview of the universe of hedge fund strategies. This chapter will give the reader the necessary background on hedge funds, including an understanding of where this industry came from and where it stands today. As it happens, defining what constitutes a hedge fund is quite tricky.[1] Nevertheless, before plunging into the discussion of hedge fund return sources and hedge fund replication, we must define the hedge fund universe, discuss some basic characteristics and developments of the industry (this chapter), and describe the individual strategies together with their empirical risk and return characteristics (next two chapters). Only then can we make sense of the details in later chapters. The advanced reader might want to progress to Chapter 5 right away (but may find interesting bits and pieces in this and the next two chapters).

2.1 CHARACTERISTICS OF HEDGE FUNDS

The term 'hedge fund' denotes a very heterogeneous collection of different investment strategies. The confusion many people have around hedge funds starts with the lack of any precise formal or legal definition of the term. What makes a hedge fund different from other types of investment? In the world of animals, the term 'guinea pig' describes a popular pet that is not from Guinea, and is not a pig. In the financial world, the term 'hedge fund' is not much more precise. Hedge funds include a heterogeneous collection of investment strategies that do not always hedge, and are almost never structured as funds.

A very common, but nevertheless not very explanatory, description is that hedge funds seek 'absolute returns'. In other words, the goal of hedge funds is often said to be to generate performance independent of prevailing market conditions. The notion of 'absolute returns' means that a hedge fund manager and a traditional equity or bond fund manager have different goals. Typically, the traditional fund manager seeks *relative* returns; in excess of defined benchmarks. For example, an equity mutual fund manager will seek to beat the performance of stock indices. If that manager achieves 15% return in a year when a market index returns 10%, and then loses 5% in a year the market lost 10%, she is said to have had two good years. In contrast, the hedge fund manager cares only about absolute returns. If she achieves 15% growth in year one, and 5% loss in year two, she has had one good year followed by a bad one. Since only absolute returns matter, hedge fund managers use investment strategies designed

---

[1] I sometimes find myself during dinner and cocktail party conversations struggling to provide a concise answer when asked for a short *and* comprehensive explanation of the essence of hedge funds.

to yield positive returns regardless of prevailing underlying market conditions. Because hedge funds have absolute performance targets and are not measured against any broad market index, they are also referred to as 'skill-based investment strategies'.[2]

The notion of 'absolute return' has some important implications on how a hedge fund manager defines risk. 'Absolute returns' come with 'absolute risk'. This is in contrast to most traditional equity and bond (long-only) managers who measure risk relative to a benchmark and quantify it correspondingly by the so-called 'tracking error'. The latter define risk as only the 'active risk' element in the portfolio introduced by the manager's choice of deviation from her benchmark. The exclusion of the 'passive risk', i.e. the 'beta risk' of the broad market, leaves the largest risk source in a traditional portfolio unconsidered. The traditional manager has neither the incentive nor the means to manage passive risk.[3] That risk is 'managed' (i.e. determined) by the market itself. In contrast the hedge fund manager has strong incentives to keep the total risk of the investment under control. Because of a hedge fund's focus on absolute returns, the first priority of the manager is capital preservation. Hedge funds make consistency and stability of absolute returns, rather than magnitude, their key priorities. A good hedge fund manager follows strict risk controls and concentrates on very particular risks, which he understands and for which he has good experience. He then actively hedges away unwanted and uncontrolled risk such as the risk of broad equity market downturns. That does not, however, mean that hedge funds hedge away all risks in the portfolio. Certain risks (albeit those that might be unrelated to traditional equity or interest rate risks) almost always remain in the portfolio as I will highlight in later chapters.

One can thus argue that it is the notion of active total risk management that sets hedge funds apart from traditional investment techniques. For 'hedge fund risk management' the risk-neutral position is cash rather than a benchmark as for passive investing and correspondingly 'passive risk management'.[4] Hedge funds have a way to manage the downside risk of an investment, i.e. they have some contingency – or exit – plan if something goes surprisingly wrong.

If hedge fund managers seek absolute returns, how do they go about it? The flippant but accurate answer is: in any way they can. The idea of absolute returns offers the only fully inclusive definition of hedge funds precisely because managers are free to seek those returns through a wide variety of different strategies. Hedge fund managers traditionally have enormous flexibility to invest in a wide spectrum of instruments, including equity, fixed income, currencies, commodities, and their derivatives. These instruments are used to execute a wide variety of directional and nondirectional trading strategies with few constraints. However, despite the large flexibility in their investment styles, the majority of the managers actually have a specific skill-set or experience which they apply to a rather limited range of instruments and markets. Most hedge fund managers are strongly specialized in specific niche strategies. But collectively those niches form the broadest and most heterogeneous universe of investment strategies in the world of finance. If you know that a colleague is an equity mutual

---

[2] Although almost all hedge fund strategies declare absolute and market-independent returns as their goal, the degree of compliance with this goal varies strongly across the different strategies.

[3] The end investor's definition of risk, however, is total risk as this is what determines the influence on the terminal level of his wealth.

[4] Risk measured against a benchmark can yield to the counterintuitive effect that an increase of the cash allocation in a portfolio at the expense of a lower stock allocation can lead to a higher risk in the portfolio. A traditional 'relative' money manager's first goal is to not perform worse than the benchmark, even when the benchmark loses 50%.

fund manager, you know that person is investing in a portfolio of stocks. However, knowing that someone is a hedge fund manager does not tell you much about what specific investment strategy that person is pursuing.

Despite these disparate strategies, hedge funds do have some important characteristics in common besides the pursuit of absolute returns. Since I will be devoting the next chapter to specific hedge fund strategies, let us focus for now only on general characteristics the great majority of hedge fund strategies have in common:

- absolute performance targets (as previously discussed);
- application of leverage through borrowing or investments on margin;
- application of short selling techniques for individual securities as well as entire markets or market segments;
- application of derivative instruments, either for the purpose of hedging or for taking leveraged directional positions;
- significant investment by the manager in his/her own strategy and performance-based compensation.

This last characteristic is important because it aligns the hedge fund manager's interest with those of the investors. In addition to a performance-based fee (which usually accounts for a significant part of the overall compensation scheme to the managers), many managers allocate a significant amount of their personal net worth to their own funds in an attempt to demonstrate their commitment to achieve high returns and to assume an appropriate share of the risk.

It is the employment of leverage which causes many investors to view hedge funds as 'high risk' investments. However, not all hedge fund strategies are highly leveraged. Long/Short Equity strategies, for example, do not use much leverage (and may still be risky), while on the other hand, some Relative Value strategies such as Fixed Income Arbitrage may leverage up to 10 times and more the investment amount (and may still display relatively low volatility).

Hedge fund managers obtain leverage through two means: borrowing and margin investment. In the first case the hedge fund manager simply borrows additional capital from his prime broker to obtain a higher exposure to her investment ideas. Secondly, the employment of derivatives enables the hedge fund manager to seek an investment exposure beyond her notional capital as she does not have to collateralize the entire notional position.

Hedge funds are distinctly different from traditional funds in the freedom managers have to sell securities short. Hedge fund managers use short selling as an efficient way to express their negative views and 'bet on losers' while taking long positions in securities they perceive to be the future 'winners'. Further, short selling serves them to hedge out unwanted risks. A hedge fund manager who believes in her stock-picking skills but does not believe she has an edge in market timing, uses 'shorts' to decrease exposure to broad market fluctuations.

An alternative way to hedge against unwanted risks is to use derivatives. The global derivatives markets have grown increasingly complex and have enabled various investors to obtain very specific risk and payout profiles. In traditional investment, most derivative engagements are performed to reduce unwanted risk. However, hedge funds may use derivatives as instruments of speculation as well. It is the occasional well-publicized failure of this type of speculation that has given the general public the notion that derivatives are innately risky, even though this is not the case if we consider the industry as a whole. In fact, hedge fund managers often use derivatives to both increase and reduce risk, hedging out certain unwanted risks while systematically increasing exposure to other wanted risks.

Hedge funds are typically organized as limited partnerships or limited liability companies and are often domiciled offshore for tax and regulatory reasons.[5] They are generally exposed to few regulatory constraints, and many hedge fund managers are not registered with regulatory agencies.[6] An exception is the strategy sector Managed Futures in which the managers are mostly registered with the National Futures Association (NFA) as 'commodity trading advisors' (CTAs) or 'commodity pool operators' (CPOs).[7] In 2005, the Securities and Exchange Commission (SEC) attempted to change the regulatory framework of hedge funds so that hedge fund management companies would have to register with the SEC. The courts struck down these efforts. Many management companies register anyway, perhaps because they believe that registration gives them credibility, especially with institutional investors. Note that hedge funds in which US pension funds invest must have registered management companies under the US Act.

By now the reader will recognize the inherent inaccuracy of applying the term 'hedge fund' to this heterogeneous and dynamic collection of investments. Since hedge fund managers are generally free to seek returns as they see fit, hedge funds almost never serve to provide a zero-risk investment. In many cases hedge fund strategies are rather designed to isolate specific risks to which the manager wishes to be exposed in compensation for expected returns. Most commonly, this is referred to as a 'risk premium'. We note that *hedge* funds do not always *hedge*. Likewise, since most hedge *funds* are actually organized as limited partnerships or limited liability corporations, they are not, strictly speaking, *funds*. However, it is this characteristic of isolating in certain risks while isolating out others that gives some truth to the term 'hedge' for hedge funds. Indeed, the very first hedge funds were equity investment strategies where the manager reduced his exposure to adverse downward movements in the broad market by combining long and short stock positions (the Jones model, see below). Additionally, investors can use hedge funds to provide a hedge (or more precisely a diversification) for other portfolio investments that are more directly exposed to the risk of broad market downturns.

Generally hedge funds are investment strategies that have a clear concept of risk and performance attribution. In some cases they add some small excess returns which are uniquely manager-skill-based to the return mix offered to investors; in other cases they seek expected returns for exposure to certain risks or lower liquidity. As discussed above hedge funds are putting capital at risk where they see their fortunes to be skewed to the upside, while hedging out as much as possible the undesired part of the randomness on the downside. They often do so in niches in which they possess a special expertise and unique skill-set. Without features like short selling or leverage, which are typically part of the hedge fund structure, this would simply not be possible.

---

[5] See the article 'A primer on hedge funds' by W. Fung and D. Hsieh for more details of hedge funds' legal and regulatory issues. A good coverage of regulatory issues for hedge funds is given by S. Lhabitant in his book *Hedge Fund Myths*, Wiley (2002).

[6] In the United States, investment advisors with less than 15 clients do not have to register with the Securities and Exchange Commission under the Investment Advisers Act of 1940. The management company in the case of a hedge fund has few clients – only the funds it manages. Consequently, the management company does not have to register with the SEC under the traditional interpretation of 'clients'.

[7] It should be noted that, as part of the institutionalization of the hedge fund industry, an increasing number of hedge fund managers register themselves with regulatory agencies such as the SEC in the USA or the Financial Services Authority (FSA) in the UK.

Since hedge funds can be used to seek risk as well as to reduce it, some in the field prefer the term 'Alternative Investment Strategies'.[8] However, for better or worse, the term hedge fund is historically established. So I will continue to use that term in its broader modern meaning throughout this book.

2.2   HEDGE FUNDS AS AN ASSET CLASS

The question of whether hedge funds constitute an asset class by themselves, or only extend the range of investment strategies within existing asset classes, is mostly a matter of perspective. Strictly speaking, hedge funds are not a separate asset class because hedge fund managers do not trade any particular new assets or instruments. Instead they execute alternative investment strategies using a set of existing instruments.

Why then do investors increasingly consider hedge funds as a separate 'alternative' class in their asset allocation process? Because for the practical investor, asset classes are identified as much by the purpose they serve in a portfolio, as by the identity of the instruments themselves. Hedge funds serve a different purpose in a portfolio from more straightforward investments, even though some of the same instruments may be contained in both the hedge fund and traditional components of the portfolio. So while a purist could argue that hedge funds are not a distinct asset class, because they do not invest in a separate set of assets, the practical investor or portfolio manager often treats them as a separate class for the different purpose they serve in her global portfolio.

2.3   TAXONOMY OF HEDGE FUNDS

Due to the complexity and heterogeneity within the industry there is an ongoing debate about how to categorize the hedge fund universe.[9] In the broadest sense, hedge funds are a subset of the global alternative investment universe, which includes all investments beyond traditional bond and equity investments. Figure 2.1 provides an overview of the alternative investment universe and embeds hedge funds in it.

There have been numerous professional and academic attempts to resolve the question of strategy definition and classification for hedge funds. These attempts include sophisticated statistical techniques such as clustering based on 'sum of square minimization'[10] and asset-based style factor models.[11] Partly as a result of these studies, as well as managers' own classifications and 'brand name' marketing by financial organizations, more or less widely

---

[8] As I did myself in one of my previous books, *Risk Management in Alternative Investment Strategies* (2002), or more recently A. Ineichen does in *The Critique of Pure Alpha* (2005).

[9] A discussion of the characteristics of hedge fund strategies (including their historical return properties) and a hedge fund classification scheme is presented by A. Ineichen in 'In Search of Alpha', October 2000 (updated and extended version 'The Search for Alpha Continues', September 2001, and the book *Absolute Returns*, 2002, by the same author).

[10] See the paper 'Hedge funds with style' by S. Brown and W. Goetzmann (2003) and references therein.

[11] See the following papers: 'Asset-based hedge fund styles and portfolio diversification', by W. Fung and D. Hsieh (2001); 'Characteristics of risk in risk arbitrage' by M. Mitchel, T. Pulvino (2001); 'The risk in hedge fund strategies: Theory and evidence from trend followers' by W. Fung and D. Hsieh (2001). A good summary of asset-based style factors can be found in the following publication: W. Fung, D. Hsieh, 'The risk in hedge fund strategies: alternative alphas and alternative betas', in *The New Generation of Risk Management for Hedge Funds and Private Equity Investment*, ed. by L. Jaeger (2003).

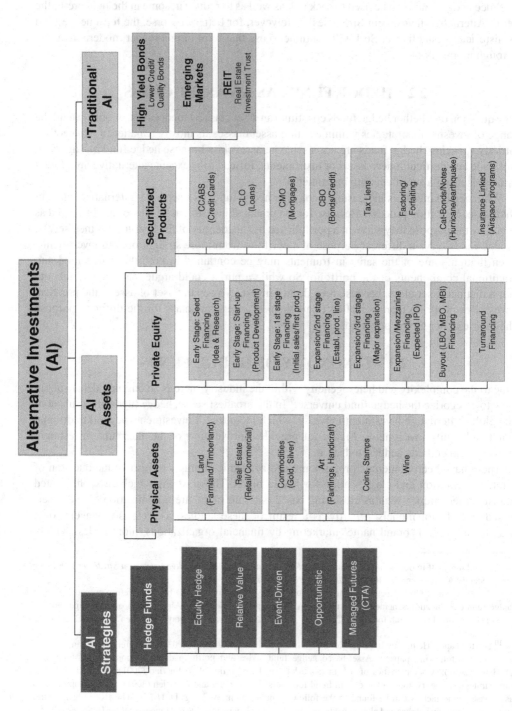

Figure 2.1 Hedge funds in the universe of alternative investments

accepted general classification schemes have emerged. Figure 2.2 presents a classification scheme that is probably very close to the industry's consensus. An important differentiating factor between the different strategies is the degree of directional trading. While the returns of Equity Hedge and Opportunistic strategies depend strongly on financial markets' directions, Relative Value strategies earn returns largely independent of those. The 'Equity Hedged' strategies, Long/Short Equity, Equity Market Neutral, and Short Selling, are strategies with a varying degree of directional bias to equity markets. 'Relative Value' strategies (Convertible Arbitrage, Fixed Income Arbitrage, Volatility Arbitrage, Capital Structure Arbitrage) in contrast capitalize on various 'spread' relationships and arbitrage opportunities in equity and fixed income markets employing various 'arbitrage' techniques to benefit from changing spread relationships between similar or related instruments.[12] Relative Value strategies are 'market neutral' (or 'non-directional') in that they do not have any directional dependency on the underlying financial markets. 'Event Driven' strategies (Distressed Securities, High Yield Credit, Spin-offs, Merger Arbitrage, and private placement arbitrage strategies under Regulation D of the US Securities Act) capitalize on the occurrence of special events such as mergers, spin-offs, distress or additional (often complex) financing rounds that impact the valuation of particular securities. 'Opportunistic' strategies describe a more heterogeneous class of strategies that take position according to the manager's perception of macroeconomic situations and corresponding profit opportunities. The most prominent strategy in this sector is Global Macro, attempting to benefit from the anticipated price movements across liquid global capital markets using a top-down approach that concentrates on forecasting how global macroeconomic and political events affect the valuations of financial instruments. I also include the growing class of multi-strategy hedge funds in this category. Finally, 'Managed Futures' programs (also called 'commodity trading advisors', CTAs) are investment strategies which assume long and short positions in exchange-traded derivatives, in particular futures and options on commodities and 'financials' (equity, fixed income, and foreign exchange).

In contrast to some classification schemes used by index providers, I do not classify hedge funds operating in Emerging Markets as a separate hedge fund category. Hedge funds with a focus on Emerging Markets can easily be classified in one of the sectors presented, as they trade along the same principles as their colleagues in the developed markets. Most of them operate with a Long/Short Equity or Global Macro strategy, while Fixed Income Arbitrage strategies in emerging markets have started to emerge more recently. Emerging Markets have for long displayed too many constraints and restrictions for hedge funds to operate their strategies properly. Specifically, short selling possibilities are limited and most derivatives markets do not display the necessary liquidity. It is therefore no surprise that most Emerging Markets equity hedge funds have come with a strong long bias and often emerged out of a previous long-only focus. That being said, however, we can observe an increased engagement of hedge funds employing their full spectrum of techniques in emerging markets in recent years.

---

[12] Unfortunately, the term 'arbitrage' as used within the hedge fund community is a misnomer. It does not refer to its original meaning, which is a risk-less trading profit above the risk-free rate of return. Here the term 'arbitrage' is used with the same meaning as 'relative value trading': buy an undervalued instrument and simultaneously sell an overvalued instrument and benefit from the probable (and statistically expected) reversion of their 'fair value'. But of course, this is by no means free of risk. The spread (mis-valuation) can become larger which leads to losses in the trading positions. This misuse of the word 'arbitrage' by the hedge fund community can lead to rather amusing oxymorons such as the term 'risk arbitrage' (another expression for 'merger arbitrage'), which literally translates into 'risky risk-free profit'.

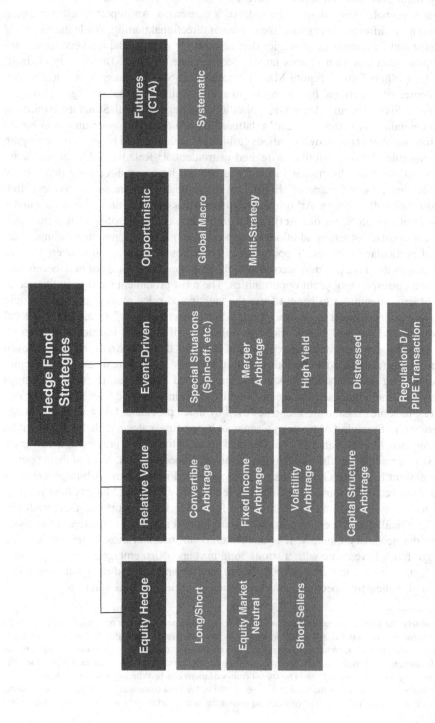

Figure 2.2 The universe of hedge fund strategies

A quick word on funds of hedge funds: the number and variety of multi-manager hedge fund investment products ('fund of funds') is growing as rapidly as hedge funds themselves, experiencing a fifteenfold increase since the early 1990s. Setting up appropriate hedge fund portfolios and selecting the best hedge fund managers requires an experienced expert with knowledge, infrastructure and relationships in the hedge fund industry. An important value added of funds of funds is the extra level of security created by continuous monitoring of managers and corresponding risk management. Many investors now invest in funds-of-hedge-funds, rather than in individual hedge funds. A fund of funds is basically a hedge fund that invests in individual hedge funds and monitors these investments, thereby providing investors with a diversified portfolio of hedge funds, risk management services, and a way to share the due diligence costs with other investors. The compensation of fund of funds managers also has a fixed fee (typically 1%) and a performance fee (typically 10% above a hurdle rate). In 2006, 30% or more of funds invested in hedge funds were managed by funds of funds.[13]

2.4   MYTHS, MISPERCEPTIONS, AND REALITIES ABOUT HEDGE FUNDS

The discomfort some investors and much of the general public feel with hedge funds is fed by the roots of historical secrecy and the branches of persistent myths that secrecy has produced. Some of these myths are obviously false and easily exposed. Others are more subtle and pernicious because they still play a significant role in how the hedge funds industry markets itself to investors. Furthermore, the secrecy that has in the past surrounded hedge funds makes them very vulnerable to myths. Secrecy fuels misinformation, because accurate information is not available. So while media coverage of fraud in an Enron or Parmalat only slightly affected the broad public view on equity investments (but rather had a strong impact on the business practice of financial intermediaries such as investment banks), fraud in the Manhattan Fund or the failure of LCTM, Amaranth, Basis Capital (and most recently Peleton) has caused the business press and the public to be sceptical of all hedge funds.

So, on the principle that more information is the best cure, let's examine the most persistent myths about hedge funds and attempt to dispel them.

(1) Hedge fund strategies are impossible for ordinary investors to understand and inherently operate on a 'black box' basis

Actually, in their basic principles hedge fund strategies are not very difficult to understand. However, they may be very complex in the details of the individual hedge fund's strategy implementation, the complexity of the traded (derivative) instruments, the nuances of the hedging, the daily execution, the manager's specific balance between isolating certain risks and consciously taking other risks, i.e. the specific risk profile.

In the past hedge fund managers themselves and their marketers were guilty of propagating this myth. The idea that these strategies were too complex for investors to understand lent a certain mystique and magic to hedge funds. And it discouraged investors from monitoring fund managers too closely. This may have seemed advantageous to managers at one time, but it is now a liability. As hedge funds become more 'mainstream' investment vehicles they will

---

[13] W. Fung, D. Hsieh, N. Naik, T. Ramadorai, 'Hedge funds: performance, risk and capital formation' (2007).

have to move away from the mysterious and secretive 'magic black box' image. This belief has for long been based on the claim that only these outrageously smart managers are able to execute the complex underlying trading strategies, and nobody else is able to understand or follow them anyway, and interfering with them only narrows their return potential. But the mystique of Nobel Prize genius did not save Long Term Capital Management, so this claim now rings false. The new investor base, in particular institutional investors, do not believe that hedge fund managers should be left alone with the investors' money.

The degree of resistance against disclosure of positions and transactions to independent (and confidential) third parties in the hedge fund industry is surprising insofar as hedge funds are often considered as the outsourced activities of proprietary trading operations of investment banks. Many of today's hedge fund strategies actually operate very similarly to investment banks' trading desks which often have been running these strategies for years and decades. But within these institutions truly independent risk management is today an essential element of trading operations.[14] One of the fundamental principles of modern risk management is: separate the traders from the risk managers (and compensate the latter independently of the trading P&L). So, if similar trading activities are put under such intense risk management scrutiny, why should hedge funds not be understood, monitored, and controlled by third parties (e.g. by independent funds of funds)?[15]

(2) Hedge funds generate their returns from market inefficiencies

The returns of hedge funds are very often described as the result of market inefficiencies, i.e. anomalies in the market price of a particular asset compared to its (however determined) 'fair value'. Indeed hedge funds are broadly thought to hold risk-factor-neutral portfolios, unfettered by short sales constraints and leverage controls, promising their investors absolute returns. In the language of the 'efficient market hypothesis', hedge funds are regarded as 'ultimate arbitrageurs'. But a deeper understanding of hedge funds reveals that hedge fund returns are much more than just the result of public financial markets not pricing assets correctly. Wall Street just does not very often offer a 'free lunch'. Since educated investors know this, they are rightly suspicious of the idea that there are such large market inefficiencies which are waiting to be exploited feeding a strongly growing multi-trillion-dollar investment industry with persistent returns.

In asset pricing theory language, excess return that does not correspond to extra (systematic) risk is referred to as 'alpha' and corresponds to the manager's ability to 'beat the market'. The two principal ways of generating alpha are market timing and security selection (and thirdly 'best execution'). At the same time, hedge fund managers expose themselves to systematic risks and can earn corresponding risk premia. Broadly speaking, a risk premium is a compensation for being exposed to systematic risk. The distinction between 'systematic' and 'unsystematic' (or 'idiosyncratic') risk is an important fundamental of modern asset pricing theory. The former refers to risks that cannot be diversified away by the entire set of investors, such as

---

[14] The fact that risk management sometimes fails in investment banks as the recent (early 2008) disclosures of the French investment bank Société General showed, only makes the claim for their necessity stronger.

[15] The discussion about issues of transparency is covered in more detail in L. Jaeger, *Risk Management in Alternative Investment Strategies* (2002); see also L. Jaeger, *Peering into the Black Box* (2002); L. Jaeger, 'Monitor transparency' (2002); and L. Jaeger, 'Risk management and transparency in the construction and monitoring of a fund of hedge funds portfolio' (2003).

the risk of economic shifts or broad market developments (e.g. declines of equity markets or general credit spread widening), while the latter describes specific developments affecting the investment instruments held in isolation (e.g. a company bankruptcy or negative earning outlook leading to a decline of a particular company's stock). According to capital asset pricing theories, exposure to systematic risks is rewarded with expected excessive return, the risk premium. Asset pricing theory also refers to these returns as 'beta returns'. In contrast, nonsystematic risks, that can be diversified by the investors, do not yield expected excess return and should therefore be avoided.

Hedge fund replication builds on the premise that a large part of the return sources of hedge funds are risk premia and outlines what the underlying systematic risks are. Nevertheless market inefficiencies, once they occur, can offer superior returns to those who are capable of exploiting them. They occur mostly in markets where information does not flow freely, as is often the case in less liquid and smaller markets (which, however, bear their own risks – mostly related to limited liquidity, as the events since the summer of 2007 have served investors as a valuable reminder). The resulting opportunities are usually temporary and quickly disappear when spotted by other investors. Market practitioners and academics often consider the returns of hedge funds as the best argument against the 'efficient market hypothesis'. But it is generally not easy to isolate the alpha from the beta in hedge fund returns. And in some cases it is not just difficult to separate alpha from beta, but it is already quite troublesome to distinguish the two (albeit in most cases the exercise of trying to do so itself increases the understanding of a particular hedge fund). Perceived price anomalies and apparent arbitrage opportunities can be, and often are, related to systematic risks and corresponding risk premia the investor is not directly aware of.[16] The distinction between market inefficiencies and risk premia as a particular source of hedge fund returns is not always as clear as it seems.

For now we can live with a rather simple scheme which will become more clear later in the book: if the specific return is available only to a handful of investors and the scheme of extracting it cannot be simply specified by a systematic process, then it is most likely real alpha. If it can be specified in a systematic way, but it involves nonconventional investment techniques such as short selling, leverage and the use of derivatives (techniques which are often used to specifically characterize hedge funds), then it is possibly beta but in an alternative form (we will refer to it as 'alternative beta'), which is often sold as alpha, but is not real alpha. If it does not require these special 'hedge fund techniques', then it is 'traditional beta'.

For certain strategies (in particular Relative Value and arbitrage strategies), some argue that hedge fund investing is like writing a disaster put option: due to attractive premia received for writing the put, the risk-adjusted returns are above average in normal market environments, but large losses can result from rare extreme market events, when the put ends up deep in the money. Hedge funds outperformed stock markets in all financial disaster periods during the

---

[16] One example from the traditional world of equity investing is the fact that stocks with high book to price value (BV/PV) – so called value stocks – have outperformed other stocks significantly in past years. An argument raised by E. Fama and K. French is that investors pursuing a strategy of buying high BV/PV stocks provide 'recession insurance' or 'distress insurance' to other investors, see E. Fama, K. French, 'The cross section of expected stock returns', *Journal of Finance*, 47, no. 2, p. 427 (June 1992). Another example is the outperformance of 'momentum stocks'. While some claim that the outperformance of recent winners is a market inefficiency (under-reaction of investors to news), others believe it is a risk premium (e.g. related to the enhanced liquidity needs associated with these stocks). The academic discussion about the success of value and momentum investing is ongoing; see also the discussion in Chapter 5.

last decades, except in August/September 1998 (the Russian debt crisis) and in the summer of 2007 (the sub-prime debt crisis). The situations in the summer of 1998 and in 2007 are now broadly referred to as 'hedge fund crises' and constitute the two most adverse market moves for hedge funds in the last two decades and therefore an illustrative example of losses due to numerous hedge funds' 'short option' type of exposure.

(3) Hedge funds are speculative in nature and short-term in outlook

This is a clear misperception about the nature and characteristics of hedge funds. In most cases the opposite is actually the truth: hedge funds base their decision largely on fundamental analysis and numerous information sources. By assessing the underlying parameters of a potential trade very carefully and weighing the risk against the expected return, hedge fund managers only take a particular position when they are convinced that the odds of winning are strongly in their favor. While detractors liken hedge funds to gambling in a casino, properly structured hedge funds are more like the bank in the casino. The probability distribution for the outcome of each of their trades is on their side. This is the opposite of speculation. Hedge fund investing is based on the rational evaluation of numerous possible trading decisions and taking those positions that have the most promising outcome, i.e. the most favorable probability distribution in the judgment of the hedge fund manager. In performing this evaluation hedge managers analyze both long-term factors, such as earning prospects and management quality for an investment in a stock, and short-term ones such as price momentum.[17]

(4) Hedge funds are high-risk investments

Like many myths, this one springs from misapplication of several facts: (a) Hedge fund managers use derivatives, which are widely – though wrongly – perceived as by nature risky and speculative instruments. (b) There have in the past been some high-profile and well-documented investment disasters. (c) Hedge funds have traditionally been both less transparent and less regulated than other investments

To dispel this myth, we must separate these three verifiable facts from their incorrect interpretations. Hedge funds do indeed use derivatives. But most fund managers use them to *decrease* risk, rather than to take directional bets. Derivatives provide a cost-efficient way to offload certain types of risk the hedge fund manager is not willing to take and thus to define more precisely the desired risk profile of a trade or a portfolio. Yes, there have been large and well-publicized failures or outright frauds in hedge funds, just as there have been in banks, manufacturing companies, and just about every other sort of entity one could think of (the memories of the Enron and WorldCom disasters have surely not yet faded away entirely). Does this mean that it is risky to invest in the stock of any manufacturing corporation? Yes and no. Investing in any single stock is risky. Investing in a diversified equity portfolio helps lower that risk. Likewise, investing in a single hedge fund is indeed risky, just as any investment is. But investing in a diversified hedge fund portfolio is surely much less risky than investing in a diversified equity portfolio.

---

[17] This does not contradict the fact that hedge fund managers generally have and use great short-term flexibility in taking and liquidating positions.

Human beings subjectively perceive something less familiar as riskier, whether it is or not. So investments that are not understood look risky. Likewise, more familiar investments are often considered to be less risky than they actually are. Back in early 2000 investors viewed an internet stock with little cash flow and negative current earnings trading at multiples of several hundreds to (already inflated) expected future earnings as not a risky investment. In part this was because they read so much about these companies and the bull market in the paper that they felt comfortable with the investment. Another example would be the investment in US residential real estate which after decades of price appreciation looked like there was no downside risk. Both perceptions were strongly corrected. But compare those volatile stocks and real estate investments with an investment with expected volatility and maximal drawdowns in single digits such as hedge funds.

One additional note on risk relates to the discussion at the beginning of this chapter. Most hedge fund managers operate rather conservatively with respect to risk, but they view risk differently than traditional fund managers. The first principal for a hedge fund manager is the protection of the principal capital. Thereby, for hedge fund managers risk is always defined as absolute risk which puts them in contrast to most traditional types of investment which define risk as relative to a specific benchmark. For a traditional equity fund manager, an investment might be considered as low risk if its expected deviation from the benchmark like the Dow Jones Industrial Average, the so called 'tracking error', is small. But on an absolute basis the risk may actually be very high, since the investment could track the Dow right into the tank. This important difference in defining risk (absolute versus relative risk) actually makes hedge funds inherently more conservative than investing in traditional investment funds.

The fact represents the most valid concern. The hedge fund industry has made its own troubles here by refusing until recently to disclose how it generates returns. While hedge fund managers may indeed need greater freedom to operate than traditional fund managers, increased transparency and independent third-party risk management will surely help to further improve the risk profile as well as investors' perceptions about hedge investing. Transparency is essential if the hedge fund industry is to continue its rapid growth and be unambiguously recognized as a legitimate investment class.

For the prudent investor, a detailed understanding of the various hedge fund strategies, thorough due diligence by the individual hedge fund managers, and systematic third-party monitoring and risk management can eliminate much of the risks and many of the problems people associate with hedge funds.

(5) Hedge funds are highly leveraged (and leverage is bad)

Leverage is one of the most misperceived characteristics of hedge funds. In fact most hedge fund managers use much less leverage than outsiders would guess. About one-third of hedge funds use no leverage at all, almost half use leverage between $1\times$ and $2\times$, and only a minority of less than one-fourth use leverage higher than $2\times$.[18] The reader should compare this with the leverage factors employed by most house owners (about $5\times$) or financial institutions ($7–10\times$).

Even in funds that do use high leverage, that leverage does not necessarily make the fund excessively risky. Leverage can be very helpful for achieving the desired risk–return profile of a strategy. For example, a hedge fund may execute extremely low-risk trades with very small

---

[18] Van Hedge Study (2003), published on the Van Hedge Website: http://www.vanhedge.com

expected returns. Since there is a cost to every trade, leverage may be required to make the returns of each trade large enough to be worth making the transaction at all. But a leveraged multiple of a very small risk can still be small. Leverage alone is not a very useful measure of risk. A high leverage factor does not necessarily imply unacceptable high risk, and neither does a low leverage factor always mean low risk. A bad and risky trade made unleveraged is still a bad and risky trade. It is important to understand implications of leverage rather than stick to a rigid no-leverage policy.

(6) Hedge funds offer no economic value

This myth is related to myth number (2). As we state in the hypothesis underlying the entire book, most hedge fund returns derive from risk premia which makes them not much different from other agents in financial markets. Most hedge funds are long-term in nature and largely base their decision-making process on fundamental analysis. This actually increases market efficiency.

In reality, hedge funds often act to counter price changes that are not based on fundamentals, such as irrational earning expectations. Further they are often the first to act when fundamentals change, and therefore support the fair valuation of securities. This reduces the likelihood of less-informed investors purchasing securities at overvalued prices and selling them at undervalued prices. Perhaps the accounting problems of US firms in 2001–2003 would have been discovered earlier if more market participants focused not only on picking winners, but also on identifying losers like Enron and WorldCom. Countries with restrictions on short selling often experience much more severe market disruptions when overvalued securities finally correct to fair value. The increase of market efficiency provided by hedge funds may come at the price of higher short-term volatility, but with the benefit of lower long-term volatility and fairer prices. One must realize that market volatility, if it reflects true information, is good and desirable.

Hedge funds also provide the market with liquidity, for otherwise-illiquid assets. This leads to corporations being able to raise more capital at lower cost. Two examples illustrate this statement:

- The emergence of convertible securities in recent years has given firms an additional option for raising capital and has reduced their overall cost of capital. The support of hedge funds was crucial to the expansion of the convertible securities market, and 60–70% of new convertible issues are now bought by hedge funds.
- Hedge funds that specialize in distressed securities make a significant contribution towards reintegrating troubled companies back into the economic cycle and reducing the financial 'cost of failure'.

(7) Hedge funds cause, or worsen, financial crises

During the credit crisis that started in the summer of 2007 and had not yet reached its peak at the time of writing, another popular myth was dispelled, namely the myth that speculators operating as hedge funds are the main threat to the architecture of global capitalism. 'It was not the hedge funds that blew up the financial world, it was the banks!' is a statement I overheard at a dinner table discussion among hedge fund investors. Indeed the hedge fund industry as a whole escaped large losses in the credit crisis (I should say, so far – I completed the book in early 2008).

Banking regulators are concerned that hedge funds may create risks to financial institutions. Hedge funds create exposures for financial institutions, ways of borrowing from them, and making securities transactions, and by being counterparties in derivatives trades. Because of leverage, a hedge fund might experience problems if its assets experience a sharp drop and/or the market for these assets lacks liquidity so that the fund cannot exit its positions (often the combination of the two occurs). The collapse of a hedge fund could have far-reaching implications if the fund is large enough. When the Long Term Capital Fund lost more than $4 billion in the late summer of 1998, the Federal Reserve Bank of New York organized a rescue by private banks to avoid possible widespread damage from a possible disorderly liquidation or bankruptcy of the fund. Addressing these concerns one can say that brokers and banks have greatly improved their systems to evaluate their exposures to hedge funds in recent years (also as a consequence of their experience with LTCM in 1998). Derivatives contracts are much better designed for defaults than they were in the past. The debacle at the hedge fund Amaranth, for example, in late 2006 had only a trivial impact on the markets. And in the credit crisis that started in 2007 this myth was further dispelled. Again, it was the banks that posed the largest threats, e.g. the collapse of Bear Stearns in March 2008.

It is often stated that short selling by hedge funds exacerbates stock market crashes. However, there is much evidence that short selling and other activities of hedge funds contribute to market efficiency and thereby help to guard against the development of 'boom and bust' scenarios in financial markets. Not only were hedge funds not the cause of past stock market turmoils (such as in 2000–2003 or in 2007/2008), they actually play a critical role in maintaining market efficiency and stability by helping to counter unrealistic security valuations. However, there are market segments in which hedge funds play an increasingly large role. In those segments, a combination of leverage, illiquidity, and misevaluations, can indeed worsen a situation of market stress.

Hedge funds because of their short selling techniques provide important economic value to financial markets and the economy as a whole.[19] This conclusion is supported by the official position of the SEC in the USA, which in 2007 decided to abandon short selling restrictions like the 'uptick rule', as did the Financial Services Authority (FSA) in the UK. In a 2003 paper,[20] the FSA states that short selling 'is a legitimate investment activity which plays an important role in supporting efficient markets. It accelerates price corrections in overvalued securities; supports derivatives trading and hedging activities; and facilitates liquidity and trading opportunities'. Finally, the European Central Bank mentions in their *Financial Stability Review* of December 2004 that 'hedge funds contribute to the liquidity and efficient functioning of financial markets': 'Hedge funds contribute to the price discovery process by arbitraging away price differences for the same risk across markets', they take risks 'more regulated financial institutions are usually reluctant to be exposed to', and they 'lower market volatility . . . as they are willing to put their capital at risk in volatile market conditions'.[21]

---

[19] The following two publications investigate the influence of hedge funds on financial markets in more detail: W. Fung, D. Hsieh, 'Measuring the market impact of hedge funds' (2000); S. Brown *et al.*, 'Hedge funds and the Asian currency crisis' (2000).

[20] *FSA Newsletter*, 'Short selling – feedback on DP17' (April 2003), available on http://www.fsa. gov.uk/pubs/discussion/fs_newsletter.pdf

[21] *Financial Stability Review of the European Central Bank*, p. 123 (December 2004).

However, one must note that while they still represent rather small assets invested worldwide, hedge funds account for a disproportionately high amount of global trading behavior due to their higher average trading frequency that comes with active investing. In fact, some estimate that hedge funds today account for roughly half of the trading volume on the New York and London stock exchanges.[22] Furthermore, hedge funds represent a significant part of the daily trading volume in some particular financial instruments. They account, for example, for around 70–90% of the global trading in convertible bonds. Thus hedge funds can indeed have a disproportionate effect in particular market segments. Further, while hedge funds are generally believed to enhance liquidity and increase efficiency in the global capital markets their strategies can sometime entail crowded trades to the extent that many hedge funds (plus proprietary trading desks of investment banks) use similar ideas and spot similar relatively narrow opportunities. The Bank of England states in its June 2004 report that 'a combination of leverage, relatively illiquid products, and a model based approach to valuation and trading may in the event of material asset price shifts, exacerbate stressed conditions'.[23] And indeed even equity markets experienced some extreme dispersion in stock price behavior due to crowded trades taken by so-called 'quant funds', hedge funds that employ computer models to take long and short equity positions. The unusual price fluctuations and consequent losses of quant funds in August 2007 were a rather new experience for hedge fund investors and stock market participants alike.

2.5 A SHORT HISTORY OF HEDGE FUNDS

The origins of some strategies within the hedge fund universe date from well before the term 'hedge fund' entered the investment vocabulary. The large consolidation wave in the railway, oil, and financial industry in the late part of the nineteenth century created an attractive environment for speculation and arbitrage on mergers. Convertible Arbitrage type of strategies were particularly attractive and performed well in the years 1929–1932 during the stock market crash. Short Selling and Distressed Securities investing have existed since the late nineteenth century (and possibly before that). However, these investment activities were largely pursued as isolated trading activities by individuals.[24] The systematic application of these strategies within a fund vehicle offered to third-party investors is a relatively modern phenomenon and emerged in the early 1950s.[25]

As previously mentioned, the name 'hedge fund' is misleading, as hedge funds can be and often are leveraged rather than hedged. The name derives historically from one specific active investment strategy where the manager tried to reduce the exposure to adverse moves in the broader equity market by combining long and short stock positions. In this original meaning, the hedge fund managers buys stocks that he believes to be undervalued, and in order to reduce the exposure to the broad equity market, he then sells certain other stocks short which he considers to be overvalued. In other words, he hedges his long position by the short positions, hence the name 'hedge' fund. This strategy – today called 'Long/Short

---

[22] J. Anderson, 'As lenders, hedge funds draw insider scrutiny', *New York Times*, October 16 2006.

[23] *Financial Stability Review of the Bank of England*, p. 52 (June 2004).

[24] See the book by Edwin Lefevre, *Reminiscences of a Stock Operator* (1923) for more details.

[25] See the book by T. Caldwell and T. Kirkpatrick, *A Primer on Hedge Funds* (1995) for a more detailed outline of the history of the hedge fund industry.

Equity' – is also referred to as the 'Jones model' after A. W. Jones who first exercised this strategy in 1949. Today the Long/Short Equity strategy constitutes only a subset of the hedge fund universe, albeit the largest one. A. W. Jones experienced phenomenal investment success with his strategy outperforming all 'traditional' money managers by a wide margin in the 1950s and 1960s. His success finally caught wider public attention,[26] which coincided with the start of a first hedge fund boom in the late 1960s. However, this boom died off quickly during the equity bust years in the early 1970s. Around the same time in the late 1960s another 'original' hedge fund strategy emerged – 'Global Macro'. The Global Macro strategy entails taking sophisticated bets on probable future price moves with a much smaller element of 'hedging'. Global Macro managers take their (rather concentrated and often leveraged) positions in individual securities or markets largely according to their own macroeconomic judgment. The Global Macro strategy is directly connected with two names that for many years became synonymous with hedge fund investing: Julian Robertson and George Soros.[27] Both showed high returns over almost three decades and gained wide public attention through an article about Julian Robertson's fund in *Institutional Investors* magazine in the mid-1980s,[28] and through the drop of the British pound out of the European Currency System in 1992, which, as it is widely believed, was caused by George Soros' 'Quantum' hedge fund.[29]

Excursion: Tiger Management[30]

Tiger Management was started by Julian Robertson in 1980, compounding an average return of >30% p.a. and assets under management of USD 23 billion at the peak in October 1998. Robertson's core investment strategy was value-driven, bottom-up stock picking. With growing assets, Tiger started to focus increasingly on Global Macro (implemented views based on the aggregation of micro-data, at the peak the company had around 180 employees to perform detailed analyses). In 1998, Tiger was hit on a few of these macro bets (Russian default, Japanese yen), and decided to refocus on bottom-up stock picking. As 'value'-based stock picking strategies had a hard time at the end of the 1999/2000 tech bubble, the manager faced heavy redemptions, putting even more pressure on the positions held. In March 2000, at the peak of the bubble, Robertson closed his funds and retired, stating that he 'did not understand the market anymore'. Robertson is still managing his own money (rather successfully as industry hearsay states), approximately USD 2 billion. There is a considerable number of so-called 'Tiger cubs', who started their own (usually very successful) hedge funds afterwards.

---

[26] Interestingly this did not happen until the mid-1960s with an article about the Jones strategy in *Fortune Magazine*: C. Loomis, 'The Jones nobody keeps up with', *Fortune Magazine*, p. 237 (April 1966).

[27] Ironically, both of these hedge fund veterans had to cease their trading almost in the same week in March 2000, after having both been around since the late 1960s. George Soros is today running his Quantum Endowment Fund in a much different (and more conservative) setting, and Julian Robertson has left the public investment scene.

[28] J. Rohrer, 'The red hot world of Julian Robertson', *Institutional Investors*, May 1986, p. 86.

[29] An interesting history of hedge funds is presented in T. Caldwell, T. Kirkpatrick, 'Introduction: the model for superior performance', in *A Primer on Hedge Funds* (1995); and in J. Lederman, R. Klein, *Hedge Funds: Investment and Portfolio Strategies for the Institutional Investor* (1995).

[30] See also D. Strachmann, *Julian Robertson – A Tiger in the Land of Bulls and Bears* (2004).

Excursion: Soros fund management

Soros started his hedge fund in 1969. The Quantum Endowment Fund had assets of about USD 22 billion at its peak in 1998. In contrast to Tiger, the fund was not closed down in 2000, but had massive losses in March/April 2000 (down −32%) and underwent significant restructuring, after having generated an average annual return of 36% since inception. The drawdown was caused mainly because after staying on the sidelines/being positioned against technology throughout most of the equity market bubble in 98/99, they finally jumped on the bandwagon in mid-1999 (which at first helped them in Q4 1999). In Q1 2000, when the technology sell-off started, the fund was still heavily overloaded with tech stocks; the decision to double up the most promising tech positions after the first decline in April 2000 did not help a lot. They lost most of the external assets and key people by April 2000. Soros continues to manage his own money and allocates to a few outside managers. But he became more broadly known as an author, capitalism critic, and humanitarian.

In 1948, Richard Donchian created 'Futures, Inc.', the first futures-based investment program in commodity markets and pioneered a technical trading method today known as 'trend following'. The use of futures and options predates most equity markets,[31] but it was not until the early 1970s that the use of futures and other derivatives started to emerge in the context of systematic portfolio management.[32] Around this time, 'managed futures' strategies were more broadly developed by what today are referred to as 'commodity trading advisors' (CTAs). In 1965, Dunn and Hagitt started trading commodity futures using technical trading systems. This same team later offered the first offshore commodity pool in 1973. The first boom in Managed Futures investment programs occurred with the introduction of financial futures in 1972 and the increasing availability of computing power starting in the decade of the 1970s. Most of these programs were based on technical trading, such as trend-following and other pattern-recognition techniques. Compared to the modest returns of stocks in the 1970s, Managed Futures strategies offered both attractive returns and low correlation to the stock markets. In the 1970s, Managed Futures strategies were considered a separate class of investment from hedge funds, based on the simplistic notion that they were limited to trading futures contracts and were registered with and regulated by the CFTC (Commodity Futures Trading Commission) and the NFA (National Futures Association). Today this distinction has become somewhat blurred. CTAs also often trade in OTC securities markets, while hedge funds also use futures as essential risk management tools. In fact, many hedge funds such as, for example, Long Term Capital Management are or were registered with the CFTC.

In the last 15 years, many new hedge fund strategies have emerged. This already heterogeneous universe has become even more so. The two main categories of these newer hedge fund strategies are Relative Value and Event Driven. Both of these strategies display impressive risk–return characteristics, even when compared to those of more established hedge fund strategies. However, they generate their returns from very different investment concepts than the Long/Short Equity, Managed Futures, or Global Macro strategies. Relative Value

---

[31] Aristotle tells the story of Thales of Miletus performing an option-like trade on olives about 2500 years ago; see Aristotle *The Politics*, Cambridge University Press (1988), p. 16.

[32] Actually, systematic portfolio management itself in today's understanding, i.e. diversified investing, did not emerge before the 1960s.

strategies seek out 'arbitrage' opportunities in the market and take opposite positions in very similar and closely related instruments (e.g. a long position in a convertible bond and a short position in the underlying stock). They attempt to avoid any correlation at all to the markets in which they operate. Event Driven strategies capitalize on special events that impact the value of specific securities. Two examples of Event Driven strategies are Distressed Securities and Merger Arbitrage. The fact that returns are generated by specific events make this strategy less dependent on fluctuations in the overall capital markets.

The hedge fund industry was hit by two major blows in the 1990s, but recovered strongly in the following decade. Rising interest rates in 1994 hurt the then-prevalent Global Macro strategies. Then another hedge fund crisis followed the Russian bond default and the liquidation of LTCM in 1998. But the industry not only recovered but expanded. The years since 1998 are now being referred to as the 'institutionalization phase'. Hedge funds prospered and looked increasingly attractive in the equity bear market that followed the bursting of the 'New Economy' bubble. Today the hedge fund industry is developed enough to be considered as an asset class in itself by most investors. On the demand side, institutional investors are increasingly interested in the risk–reward characteristics of hedge funds. In uncertain markets, the low correlation of hedge funds to traditional asset classes make them especially attractive to these investors. On the supply side, the hedge fund industry has been and will continue to be a lure for the brightest talents in finance. The smartest finance professionals and most promising investment ideas are attracted to an industry that offers the greatest flexibility for the implementation of investment and hedging strategies together with the highest level of compensation. Many experienced traders including those who were laid off as financial institutions decreased their proprietary trading operations have started hedge funds of their own. This movement is one source of the increased number and range of different hedge fund products. But the dynamic evolution of the global financial market itself also creates new opportunities for innovative investment strategies. For example, the Capital Structure Arbitrage strategy did not exist until there was a large and liquid market in credit derivatives. A final contributor to the increased supply of hedge funds is that most large banks and financial institutions began offering a range of hedge fund investments. Banks have adopted hedge funds as a new and increasingly profitable business segment. Today, nearly all large financial institutions offer hedge fund products to their clients.

I hear many protagonists of the industry say that hedge funds have started a new revolution in asset management. What does that mean? In the late 1960s/early 1970s Wall Street experienced a first revolution: the introduction of quantitative portfolio management tools and paradigms such as Markowitz's optimization, Sharpe's Capital Asset Pricing Models, Fama's Efficient Market Hypothesis, and Black and Scholes' option pricing theory. That revolution introduced the concept of benchmark-driven investment. Modern asset management emerged out of these paradigms of quantitative asset pricing and portfolio optimization. It has today become commoditized. Many investors consider active management as fruitless, and 'benchmark hugging' the best way for portfolio and risk managers to keep their jobs at best. Hedge fund managers offer the financial community a new refresher in active return generation, total risk management, and the customization and optimization of risk–return profiles.

It is ironic that hedge funds are re-entering the mainstream of finance, when they were once ruled out of the regulatory frame of the developed financial markets. They were the first to exploit the full range of instruments and techniques modern financial capitalism offers to customize and optimize the risk–return profile for their investors. But they were forced to register offshore in order to do so.[33] But with increasing mainstream acceptance, regulators and lawmakers have started to allow them to re-enter the developed investment market and offer their products to a wider public.

2.6 THE HEDGE FUND INDUSTRY TODAY

Recent years have seen the continuation of unparalleled growth in hedge funds, in terms of asset inflow as well as number of funds. Figure 2.3 displays this growth. Ironically the bear equity market period of 2000–2003 as well as occasional periods of market distress in the subsequent bull market from 2003 to 2007 coincided with unprecedented hedge fund underperformance (relative to their historic average, not relative to equity markets). The poor performance of hedge funds during stressful market conditions forces us to critically reassess the notion that 'hedge funds are uncorrelated to traditional asset classes'. We cannot deny the fact that today the average hedge fund portfolio displays a substantial correlation with the broad equity markets, and periods of low performance are part of hedge fund investing as for any other investment.

Today the term 'hedge fund' rather inaccurately describes a much broader universe of strategies than when the term was created. In general, hedge funds can be said to isolate very particular risks that they are willing to assume and reduce or 'hedge' other unwanted risk factors out of their investment exposure. But the degree and quality of 'hedging' varies strongly across different strategies. Some strategies, e.g. Global Macro, do not usually hedge overall exposure to the market (market risk), as they bet on changes in some macroeconomic variables of an entire country or region, often with significant leverage. These strategies usually seek to benefit from absolute price moves of single instruments or sectors. Many other hedge fund strategies, however, do seek to hedge against most risk factors (such as broad equity market risk) while they seek exposure to certain particular risks (e.g. Equity Market Neutral strategies). In their efforts they often try to anticipate relative differences in the price developments of related instruments and take out any exposure to the broad markets.

At the beginning of the 1990s the largest strategy in terms of assets under management and asset inflow was the Global Macro strategy. This changed considerably in the following 10 years. Today Global Macro strategies manage only around 10% of all hedge fund assets, while Long/Short Equity has become the dominant strategy sector. Figure 2.4 displays the developments of the relative allocation sizes to the different hedge fund strategies over the last 12 years, and Figure 2.5 displays how assets are invested in the different sectors in 2007 indicated by the Circle areas being proportional to industry allocation (average of HFRX, MSCI, CS/Tremont/TASS). It shows that Long/Short Equity is the dominant sector with about one-third of all hedge fund assets invested in this strategy followed by Event Driven (around 20%) and Global Macro (around 10%). Convertible Arbitrage, Fixed Income Arbitrage, Equity Market Neutral and Managed Futures each take between 5% and 8%. Other strategies fall into the low single-digit percentage range. Another about 13–15% of the amount invested in hedge

---

[33] A note on the issue of hedge fund regulation: There are increasing calls for the establishment of a hedge fund regulation scheme that would be enforced by international monetary agencies. I believe an efficient risk management and control structure established by the industry itself is surely preferable to a rigid set of regulations imposed by national or international regulatory authorities.

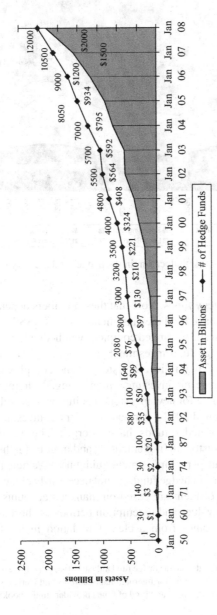

Figure 2.3 The development of the hedge fund industry

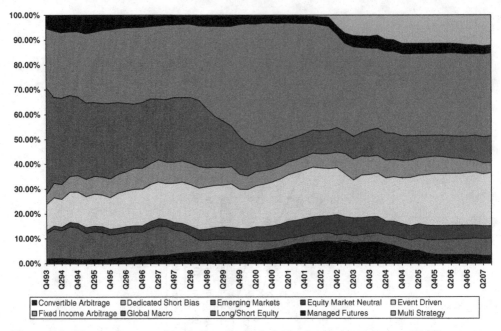

Figure 2.4   The development of asset allocation in the hedge fund industry (source: TASS)

funds is invested in multi-strategy funds. Note that these numbers depend on the classification scheme chosen. In this case I have used the classifications by TASS Research.[34]

Along with the rapid growth and expanded complexity of hedge funds has come the increasing prevalence of pooling hedge fund investments in a portfolio or fund of funds managed by a specialist fund manager. They relieve investors of the complex task of strategy sector allocation, manager due diligence and investment monitoring.[35] Therefore, investing in a fund of funds is often the chosen route for new investors, institutional as well as private.[36]

More recently – starting around 2003 – various providers of investable hedge fund indices, based on selected portfolios of hedge funds, have emerged. These claim to provide reliable investment tools and to aid investors in implementing and monitoring hedge fund investments by providing objective and transparent investment guidelines. We note that these indices have actually proven that investments in hedge funds do not necessarily come with low transparency and limited liquidity as most of them are based on managed accounts and some even come with daily published net asset values and redemption periods as short as one week. However, while index-based investing comes from a clear foundation in the traditional investment

---

[34] TASS is one of the largest data providers in the hedge fund industry. Two other large data providers in the industry are Hedge Fund Research (HFR) and the Centre for International Securities and Derivatives Markets (CISDM).

[35] See the various contributions by hedge fund and fund of funds providers in the book by S. Jaffer, *Fund of Funds* (2003).

[36] For a detailed discussion of the value added of fund of funds, see also the contribution by A. Ineichen, 'The search for alpha continues: Do fund of hedge fund managers add value?' (2001). A. Ineichen also discusses the different features and characteristics of fund of funds in great detail. A more recent discussion about fund of funds is provided in the book S. Jaffer (ed.), *Fund of Hedge Funds*, Euromoney (2003).

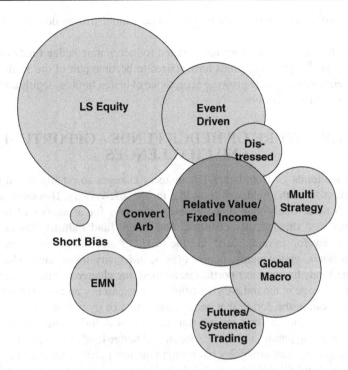

Figure 2.5 The relative size of the individual hedge fund strategies. Circle areas are proportional to industry allocation (average of HFRX, MSCI, CS/Tremont/TASS).

universe, this approach is yet unproven in the realm of absolute return oriented hedge funds. Today's investable hedge fund indices are severely challenged by their theoretical and structural shortcomings as well as significant implementation issues.[37] In fact, many investors have come to believe that the offered investable hedge fund indices offer no equivalent representative or attractive investment case.

And even more recently, several institutions have announced their intention to launch so-called 'passive hedge fund products' or, as they have more recently been referred to, 'hedge fund clones'. The underlying claim is that we can represent hedge-fund-like returns at significantly lower fee levels to the investors.[38] This trend is the main topic of this book and will be discussed extensively in the following chapters.

Today hedge funds are a fast-growing, multi-billion-dollar industry. Hedge Fund Research estimates there is currently (i.e. 2007/2008) $2000–2500 billion invested with approximately 10 000 hedge fund programs worldwide, the vast majority of which are based in the USA and Europe. Hedge fund managers have become important players in the world's financial markets, accounting for a significant part of the daily trading volume in some financial instruments. The industry continues to enjoy a strong double-digit annual asset growth rate, and therefore constitutes today one of the most dynamic and fastest-growing areas in modern

---

[37] I will discuss these in detail in a later chapter.
[38] See article in the *Financial Times* November 20 2006 'Replication is the new buzz word'.

finance. Many experts expect the industry to become a multi-trillion-dollar industry in just a few years.

Prestigious educational institutions have started to incorporate hedge funds into their educational curriculum,[39] and hedge funds have started to become part of the academic research agenda. This trend underlines the growing acceptance of hedge funds as legitimate investments by academics as well as investors.

2.7   THE FUTURE OF HEDGE FUNDS – OPPORTUNITIES AND CHALLENGES

Where will hedge funds go from here? The industry changes so rapidly that it is extremely difficult to predict what the field will look like in just a few years. However, steady strong growth is much more likely than a 'boom–bust' scenario for a number of reasons. First, the investor base has dramatically changed. The hedge fund industry has developed and will continue to develop towards satisfying the needs of institutional investors (private and public pension funds, endowments, family offices, university trusts, etc.) who now realize how well hedge funds fit into their portfolios. Second, the change in investor base is forcing a corresponding change in the industry's attitude to transparency and investment liquidity, as more investors question the notion that hedge funds must be by nature opaque and secretive. Better investor understanding and greater transparency will add to the credibility of hedge funds with the investing public. Third, the spectrum of hedge funds has expanded dramatically and continues to do so. New strategies have joined the most prominent strategies of the past, Long/Short Equity and Global Macro. The heterogeneity of hedge funds provides internal diversification and protection for the industry from a fallout due to sudden and unforeseen events. Fourth, increased interest on the part of (comparably risk-averse) institutional investors together with some well-publicized 'investment accidents' has led to the recognition that hedge fund risks have to be more systematically addressed. As a result, risk management techniques have become much more sophisticated. The 'cowboy mentality' of hedge funds has given way to investment managers who are better and more professional risk managers, and thus more credible in the eyes of the investor.

With continued asset growth and compelling and unique risk–return attributes, hedge fund investing appears destined to be recognized as a legitimate element of global asset management. Many authors have demonstrated the advantages of including hedge funds in a traditional portfolio.[40] The 'magic' of hedge funds is thus rooted in well-known portfolio theory and diversification into orthogonal risk factors. The traditional 'balanced portfolio' (i.e.

---

[39] The industry has even started to develop its own education program, analogous to the CFA Institute's well-respected 'Chartered Financial Analyst' (CFA) program: the CAIA program ('Chartered Alternative Investment Analyst'), see www.caia.org for more details.

[40] There are several empirical studies illustrating the return and risk characteristics of hedge funds and showing the benefits of hedge funds in traditional portfolios. Please refer to the following original studies: 'The risk in hedge fund strategies: alternative alphas and alternative betas' by W. Fung and D. Hsieh (2003); *The Benefits of Hedge Funds* by T. Schneeweiss and G. Martin (2000); *Understanding Hedge Fund Performance: Research Results and Rules of Thumb for the Institutional Investor* by T. Schneeweiss *et al.* (2001); 'Empirical characteristics of dynamic trading strategies: the case of hedge funds' by W. Fung and D. Hsieh; *In Search of Alpha* by A. Ineichen (2000); 'The performance of hedge funds: risk return, and incentives' by C. Ackermann *et al.* (1999); 'On taking the "alternative" route: the risks, rewards, and performance persistence of hedge funds' by V. Agarwal and N. Naik (2000); 'Hedge fund performance: 1990–2000: Do the money machines really add value?' by G. Amin and H. Kat (2001); 'On the performance of hedge funds' by L. Bing (1999); 'Hedge fund performance: 1990–1999' by L. Bing (2001); 'Hedge fund performance and

a combination of stocks and bonds) includes only two general return sources, that is the equity risk premium and (interest rate) term structure risk premium. As I will discuss in the coming chapters, hedge funds provide investors the access to new alternative 'risk premia' and thus additional return sources. These come with risks less correlated to the traditional risk premia. One can go further and state that from a global asset allocation perspective, a portfolio without hedge funds must be suboptimal. The investor is forgoing substantial additional return, which would come with low, or no, incremental risk to the overall portfolio. In summary, the real benefits from hedge funds come not necessarily from accessing today's star traders (who may be and often are next year's 'fallen stars'), but from the persistent benefits of alternative risk premia. The power of diversification across uncorrelated risks also explains the rather low risk level in a diversified portfolio of hedge funds: The average fund of funds displays a volatility around 5–7%,[41] which compares to a volatility of 15–18% in an average equity mutual fund.

Although the future of hedge funds looks bright and a 'hedge fund bubble' scenario is unlikely to evolve,[42] four challenges could limit their continued acceptance and growth. First, hedge funds must now generate attractive returns in more challenging market conditions. Second, the industry must dispel misunderstandings about hedge funds' nature and legitimacy. Third, the industry must introduce reliable independent risk management. And, last but not least, the industry must find a fair compensation system that distinguishes between highly paid alpha returns and less costly beta performance. Let us look at each of these challenges in turn and explore ways to meet them.

Generate attractive returns in challenging market conditions

Paradoxically, the massive capital flows to hedge funds occurred in a period where hedge fund managers provided investors with rather disappointing absolute returns. The 7-year period beginning in spring 2000 provided the average hedge fund investor with significantly lower annualized returns than in almost any of the previous years, causing numerous skeptics to express their concern about future hedge fund returns or even to voice the likelihood of hedge funds being the next investment bubble.[43] The main reason for this hedge fund underperformance relative to historic returns was clearly the difficult situation in global equity markets in 2000–2003, when despite the claim of market-neutrality, many hedge fund strategies had not been able to escape the downward pull of falling stock markets. Furthermore, hedge funds did not fare quite as well in the period of sustained low volatility (and therefore low realized risk premia) in the subsequent years, 2003–2007.[44]

---

manager skill' by F. Edwards and M. Caglayan (2001); 'Portfolios of alternative assets: why not 100% hedge funds?' by R. McFall Lamm Jr. (1999).

[41] The HFR Fund of Funds index shows a standard deviation of around 6% over the period from 1990 to mid-2004.

[42] See also the discussion in the article by the author, 'The trouble with the bubble theory' (2002).

[43] See, for example, 'Hedge funds – the latest bubble?', *The Economist*, September 1 2001, 'The $500 billion hedge fund folly', *Forbes Magazine*, August 6 2001, 'The hedge fund bubble' (by Barton Biggs), *Financial Times*, July 9 2001.

[44] One important aspect which is often forgotten in the discussion is that the total level of hedge fund returns carries a direct dependency on the level of risk-free interest rates. Static returns as a result of short selling of stocks, the interest on margins for futures, or the coupon of a convertible bond, for example, are all a direct function of interest rate levels. Part of the lower absolute returns of hedge funds in the period 2000–2007 can therefore be attributed to the almost unprecedentedly low interest rate environment. This led most hedge funds to cite their performance target as excess return over Libor rather than as an absolute return number. With rising interest rates total hedge fund returns can reasonably be expected to be higher, correspondingly.

As more money enters the industry, hedge funds are becoming a more crowded place. This has implications for returns. More hedge funds chasing the same price discrepancies means that these discrepancies get eliminated faster, leading to smaller profits for the individual funds. Hence, additional money entering hedge funds in the future will typically not find average alpha returns of hedge funds to be as in the past. As a matter of fact, we can already observe today that the average hedge fund alpha has decreased in recent years.[45] Some strategies naturally have limited capacity, i.e. they are limited in the amount of money they can manage without deteriorating returns. This applies for example to Relative Value strategies (Convertible Arbitrage, Fixed Income Arbitrage, Capital Structure Arbitrage). In fact, capacity is one of the key challenges funds of funds face trying to put the increasing bulk of money they are receiving from their investors to work. In addition, the entry of many more hedge fund managers creates a second kind of crowding which can be expected to deteriorate the average performance of all hedge funds. A clear example of this problem is the performance of convertible arbitrage funds. The typical trade for a convertible arbitrage fund is to buy convertible bonds issued by a firm and to hedge the purchase with short sales of the stock of the firm. As more funds buy convertible bonds, the strategy becomes less profitable because the funds push the price up, so that the performance of this strategy falls.

Yet another development has started to jeopardize the attractiveness of hedge fund returns while at the same time opening up a door towards new opportunities: with the enormous success and unprecedented growth and the subsequent confrontation of difficulties in extracting sustainable returns in their traditional markets, hedge fund managers have started to search for return sources in new markets. And in this search they find themselves successful only beyond the familiar public security market. Consequently, hedge funds have started to invest in less liquid investments and private transactions, apply private equity techniques to public targets (activist investing), extend the investment horizon (longer lock-ups), and even hire private equity professionals. The strong flow of hedge fund assets into leveraged bank loans, mezzanine financings, insurance linked securities (ILS) or even direct leveraged buyout transactions reflects that development and requires hedge funds to compete against established private equity players. In summary, 'hedge funds have gone public to private'. The investment portfolios of today's large hedge fund managers (e.g. D.E. Shaw, Moore Capital, etc.) provide a first hand illustration of that new trend.

'But are hedge funds not just new wine in old wineskins?' some investors might ask. Fifteen years ago investing in emerging markets was marketed as a new way of decreasing overall portfolio risk. Experiences in the 1990s (Mexico, Thailand, Russia, Argentina, Brazil) have aligned the hype with reality. But the hype restarted nevertheless in recent years. The diversification benefits of hedge funds might be overestimated, as the hedge fund industry had a long equity bias in the equity bull markets of the 1990s and 2003–2007. It is not at all clear that hedge funds can isolate themselves from global economic trends in the future, as quite clearly they have not done so in the past. Further, given the strong inflows into hedge funds, one has to ask whether return expectations are decoupling from reality. Lower absolute hedge fund performance achieved in the years 2000–2007 may help to gradually align expectations with reality. It will be key for the industry to convince investors that hedge funds are not just

---

[45] W. Fung, D. Hsieh, N. Naik, T. Ramadorai, 'Hedge fund: performance, risk and capital formation', preprint (2007); see also Chapter 5 (Figure 5.14).

the new 'sales story' but have a legitimate status in the global asset management industry, even when their expected returns are no longer in the high teens.

Dispel myths about hedge funds

Many of the myths about hedge funds are of the industry's own making. The image of a 'star' trader who secretively employs proprietary trading techniques and is able to anticipate price movements and move fast from opportunity to opportunity has for long been a great marketing story. But falling returns, coupled with the influx of institutional investors, have led to closer scrutiny of return sources. It is one thing for wealthy individuals to put money in a black box when more money keeps coming out. But when that box is not putting out much return, institutional investors are more likely to want a look inside. When high returns cannot be taken for granted, hedge fund managers must disclose and help investors understand their return sources if the industry is to continue to grow in both credibility and asset value.

The trend in the hedge fund industry towards institutionalization has initiated a broader discussion in the financial community about how and under what conditions hedge fund managers generate returns. Investment professionals realize that in the past hedge funds have generated investment returns that were superior to typical equity and bond investments. Nevertheless, the new class of investors looks beyond historical return patterns and requires a better understanding of how hedge funds generate their returns. Investors continue to approach hedge funds with a certain degree of skepticism, and funds that are too secretive about how they make money will be seen as more risky. The industry needs to bridge the gap between hedge fund investors and managers and enable investors to look beyond historical data, the smoke screen of hedge fund marketers, and the commercial interests of the managers. It will only be when investors have a clearer understanding of the return-generation process and the economic rationales for these returns – in other words, after the 'black box' has been further opened – that hedge funds will in the future have their predicted profound impact on the global money management industry.

Introduce reliable independent risk management

Fifteen years ago, most of the money invested in hedge funds came from wealthy individuals who were willing to bear the disadvantages of illiquid and nontransparent investment strategies in exchange for the promise of attractive returns. But along with the asset growth has come a change in the investor base. In 2007, more than two-thirds of the money invested in hedge funds came from institutional investors. As a larger and larger fraction of the assets under management of the hedge fund industry comes from institutional investors – from pensions and endowments – the rules of the game have changed: institutional investors with fiduciary responsibility have different demands, and the 'black box' approach has today become harder to sell. Investors are more concerned about the diverse risks of hedge funds investments and want to understand what those risks are and how they are being managed. They see the low transparency, and limited liquidity which still characterize most hedge funds today as aggravating any risks inherent in the fund strategies as it limits their ability to control their exposure. Many potential investors continue to view hedge funds as too mysterious, secretive, and hard to get in and out of – a blind jump into a dark tunnel of indefinite length, with few exits. In other words, the institutionalization of hedge funds creates strong demand for independent risk management.[46]

Hedge fund managers are faced with new demands for disclosure, more clearly defined risk profiles, increased investment transparency, independent third-party risk management, and higher liquidity (i.e. shorter redemption periods). They must offer more insight into return sources, performance attributions, portfolio composition, and strategy details. Marketing efforts that provide to investors only a general pitch book, a blunt offering memorandum, delayed monthly estimates for net asset values, superficial monthly or quarterly letters, and lock-up periods of quarters to years are no longer sufficient. Institutional investors want disclosure of the details of hedge fund strategies. In addition, the widely publicized hedge fund failures of the past 10 years raised investor concerns about the 'extraordinary event risks' of their hedge fund investments.

Even as institutional investors have put risk management at the top of their priority list, rapid developments in risk analysis have made it possible. New techniques make risk analysis for even complex hedge fund portfolios feasible in near real-time. Financial risk technology has generally become computationally fast, efficient and considerably less expensive than a decade and a half ago. Similar to the current development towards 'institutionalization' of the investment process in the hedge fund industry, one can anticipate a trend towards standardization of hedge fund risk management tools. Naturally, when such analysis and risk management can be done, investors expect that it should be done. Even wealthy individuals, seeing the level of risk management now available to institutional investors, are not likely to settle for less.[47]

The request for transparency is not necessarily a request for increased hedge fund regulation. Rather, better transparency and disclosure to investors might actually diminish the push for regulation. An efficient risk management and control structure established within the industry itself is surely more preferable than a rigid set of regulations imposed by national or international regulatory authorities (which would probably come with much public credit but little real insights). Indeed, the hedge fund industry has surely played an important role in creating liquidity and making markets more efficient. The hedge fund industry could do so because it was generally not regulated, so that funds were free to take whatever positions they wanted and therefore to make full use of financial innovations. Regulation should leave alone financial innovators who create new strategies and find savvy and well-funded investors to bet on them. Without such financial innovators, capital markets will be less efficient.

The issue of fees

Let us have a closer look at fees for an investor in a hedge fund product managed by a fund of funds manager. The average fee to the hedge fund manager is today around 2% management fee plus 20% performance fee. The average fund of funds manager takes another 1% management fee plus 10% performance fee.[48] On top of that are administration costs which I conservatively

---

[46] See also the survey conducted by the Barra Strategic Consulting group as early as in 2001, published in 'Fund of hedge funds – rethinking resource requirements', September 2001.

[47] A more detailed description of hedge fund risks and risk management techniques is provided in the author's book, *Risk Management in Alternative Investment Strategies* (Financial Times/Prentice Hall, 2002).

[48] I leave the usual distribution fees to private and retail investors aside here. These would come out to another 1–2% fixed fee.

estimate to be around 0.5% altogether and extra performance fees paid by fund of funds of around 0.25%.[49] Given a return expectation before all fees of 20%, these fees would take out a total of 8.6% (43% of the pre-fee return) and leave the investor with 11.4%.[50] I claim that manager-skill-based alpha does by no means account for more than 44% of the average hedge fund manager's pre-fee return. And even if 40% of the average hedge fund return was alpha, the investor would not see anything of it. These fee levels are not sustainable, when returns broadly deteriorate. And I have not even listed countless intermediary parties structuring, packaging and selling hedge fund products. All this imposes several fee levels which lead to lower net returns for end investors. I refer to this phenomenon as the 'hedge fund fee trap'. But will this trap persist? That is one of the most asked and least answered questions in the industry. In the short run, it is silly to believe that strong demand will lead to lower fee levels. However, with the emergence of a larger supply base due to the continued attraction of talent into this investment class, supply will ultimately meet the demand, and fees are likely to fall.[51]

Hedge fund investors should not have to pay 'alpha fees' for beta returns. So separating beta from alpha and charging different fees for both can be a key element of an improved hedge fund investment proposal. Traditional asset index funds teach us that, net of fees, passive investment often offers the best returns. The emergence of 'hedge fund replication' and 'alternative beta strategies' products are a promising development in this direction. This is what this book is all about.

Hedge funds have only started to influence the thinking on how financial assets should be managed in the future. The continuation of this impact will not be steered by the 'absolute return' or 'alpha' paradigm which has dominated the public discussion so far. What is going to create the 'paradigm shift' will be rather the insight that hedge funds generate their returns largely through risk premia, i.e. in a similar fashion to traditional managers, albeit they cover a much broader spectrum of risk premia and employ less well-known investment instruments. In the future, the investment techniques of hedge funds are likely to be employed by the broad asset management industry, once the return-generation techniques of hedge funds are more broadly known, and investors realize that there are tools to analyze, quantify, and, last but not least, replicate hedge fund return sources systematically.

---

[49] A problem for fund of funds fees is that we might have to pay performance fees without performance: if six out of ten managers lose money, the four others will nevertheless be paid performance fees despite an overall negative performance in the entire hedge fund portfolio, see the 'option' argument for performance fees in the previous chapter.

[50] The reader is invited to perform this easy calculation with higher or lower levels of pre-fee hedge fund returns. Assuming 25%, the investor will end up with 15%, i.e. a 40% take out by fees.

[51] See also the discussion provided in the article by C. Asness, 'An alternative future, I & II' (2004).

3

The Individual Hedge Fund Strategies' Characteristics

This chapter elaborates in more detail the underlying characteristics of each strategy and thus serves as the basis for the discussion of replication in later chapters. In Figure 2.2, I presented a classification of the different hedge fund strategies discussed in this book. Different classifications are possible along the lines of the directional exposures of the various hedge fund strategies to equity and bond markets: 'directional long biased': net long equity markets; 'arbitrage strategies': no directional bias to equity markets but providing insurance against a large market turmoil; 'tactical trading': variable bias to equity markets. I will stick to the more broadly used classification given in Figure 2.2 and discuss the degree of directional exposure within the discussion of the individual hedge fund strategies.

The reader might find it not particularly difficult to comprehend the basic principles of each strategy. This reflects the fact that hedge fund strategies can be quite straightforward in principle and share similar general exposure profiles. Despite the apparent clarity of the strategies' principles, the implementation of a particular trading approach can be quite complex and difficult, however. Often execution of a particular strategy requires a unique skill-set and edge on the part of the manager. It is the experience and creativity of the single hedge fund manager in dealing with the complexity of the traded instruments, nuances of the hedging process, daily trade execution, and details of risk management that enable him to create value for investors. In other words, it is the complex details of the implementation of a particular trading strategy that make many individual hedge funds unique and difficult to copy.

3.1 EQUITY HEDGED – LONG/SHORT EQUITY

The Long/Short Equity strategy consists of creating an investment portfolio by buying a core set of stocks and partially or fully hedging this long equity position with short sales of other borrowed stocks. Sometimes options or stock index futures are also employed to create the same result.[1] In executing a Long/Short Equity strategy most managers have a long bias, i.e. their long market exposure is not completely offset by short positions.[2] This classifies the Long/Short Equity strategy as *directional long biased*. The focus of the strategy is stock selection with regional, sector-specific, or particular style emphasis (e.g. US equity, European equities, high tech focus, value versus growth), rather than market timing or prediction of

---

[1] Short positions have generally three different purposes. Firstly, the short positions are intended to generate returns as the stock price declines. Secondly, the short positions serve the purpose of hedging broad market risk. Thirdly, the manager earns interest on the short selling proceeds (the 'short rebate').

[2] Some categorize Long/Short Equity and Equity Market Neutral jointly as a 'Relative value strategy', e.g. J. Bernard and T. Schneeweis in 'Alternative investments: past, present and future', in *The Capital Guide to Alternative Investments*, ISI publications (2001). Here, I want to distinguish between market-neutral strategies and long and short equity strategies with a long bias.

the broad stock market direction. Typical examples of Long/Short Equity trades are long undervalued countries/sectors/stocks and short overvalued countries/sectors/stocks. A less common version of the strategy uses core long positions with a partial hedge overlay with short index futures positions, long out-of-the-money puts, or short covered call positions. The return profile of a Long/Short Equity strategy ideally resembles a call option. This ideal profile therefore includes full or partial participation of the broad market in bull markets (and possibly outperformance in absolute returns) and protection against losses (and ideally net gains from the short positions) in bear markets. However, the reality often looks different. As Long/Short Equity hedge funds have increased their equity exposure in the years of the bull market, the occasional market turmoils in recent years and the market crisis in 2007/2008 have led to rather significant temporary losses in this sector.

The amount of net exposure to the broad equity markets varies widely among different managers as does concentration level in specific industry sectors. Conservative managers mitigate market risk by maintaining net market exposure ranging from 0% to 100% while aggressive funds may magnify market risk by employing leverage exceeding 100%, market exposure, e.g. 160% long and 50% short. The net exposure is also adjusted dynamically and is a function of investment opportunities and the manager's top-down market or sector analysis. In very bearish markets managers can go so far as to have a net short exposure.

Long/Short Equity managers combine 'bottom-up' and 'top-down' approaches. The former entails following individual companies and picking trades on the basis of fundamental analysis. A 'bottom-up' fundamental analysis refers to the examination of the different factors that affect a company's stock price and determines which stocks are undervalued or overvalued, and are thus candidates for buying or selling. Managers analyze the individual company examining earnings, cash flow, balance sheet quality, assets and liabilities, earning and balance sheet ratios, etc., just as would a mutual fund manager trading in that stock. This goes along with an analysis of the industry sector with focus on the industry's competitive environment, the demand and supply situation, average industry sector profitability, and influences of foreign markets, again quite similar to a mutual fund manager's analysis. Qualitative analysis involves a detailed due diligence process and analysis of management. The manager thereby analyzes various sources of information: research reports from banks and brokers, journals and newspapers, trade shows and industry contacts, company visits and personal interviews with management, conference calls and press conferences, as well as discussions with competitors, suppliers, and distributors. Some managers have a particular focus on micro and small capitalization stocks, where inefficiencies are most prevalent. As most managers have limited capacity to conduct fundamental research, they focus on a limited universe of stocks, screened by some combination of market capitalization, industry sectors, value versus growth, or particular investment themes.[3]

A top-down approach tries to identify economic trends and upcoming 'investment themes' in certain industry sectors (e.g. technology, biotech, growth companies). Many Long/Short Equity managers have detailed knowledge and experience in particular industries and therefore focus their efforts on single sectors like technology, healthcare, energy, or financial companies. Others invest across various industries.

You might note from the above explanations that Long/Short Equity managers use much the same analysis techniques as their traditional colleagues; albeit with much greater freedom to

---

[3] See T. Demir, 'Managing risk of long/short equity strategies', in L. Jaeger (ed.), *The New Generation of Risk Management for Hedge Funds and Private Equity Investment* (2003).

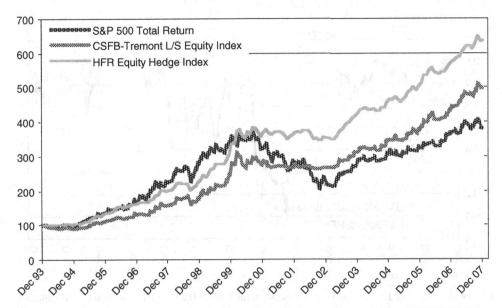

Figure 3.1   Cumulative return of the Long/Short Equity hedge funds compared to the S&P 500 index

trade derivatives, use leverage, and short sell stocks.[4] This casts doubt on the often-stated claim that Long/Short Equity hedge fund managers generate returns through some special 'manager skill' or unique trading. In fact, Long/Short Equity returns are to a large extent the result of risk premia available in the global equity markets. Long/Short Equity managers usually try to identify cheap stock, i.e. buy value stocks. Further, managers may find it easier to find opportunities in a rising market, and it may also be easier to short sell large cap stocks and find opportunities in small cap stocks. The stock picking styles of Long/Short Equity strategies come therefore with exposure to the broad equity market, firm size, and value stocks. In other words long/short equity strategies tend to be exposed to the broad equity risk premium as well as the small firm and value stocks risk premia.

A simple look at the performance of Long/Short Equity hedge funds in recent years illustrates how heavily Long/Short Equity returns depend on the equity risk premium. Figure 3.1 displays the cumulative return of the Long/Short Equity Hedge Fund Research Equity Hedge Index, the CSFB/Tremont Long/Short Equity Index, and the S&P 500 index. One can observe the strong returns of Long/Short Equity managers in the final years of the equity bull market (fall 1998 to spring 2000) and the subsequent decline return in subsequent years (2000–2003), followed by the continuation of strong gains coinciding with the strongly rising equity markets from 2002 to 2007. Further, Figure 3.2 shows the rolling 12-month correlation between the S&P 500 and the same two Long/Short Equity indices. The average correlation lies somewhere between 0.6 and 0.7, with values fluctuating between 0.1 and 0.9. The two figures clearly show that (equity) beta returns have been a major contributor to the overall returns for Long/Short Equity strategies.

---

[4] Many hedge fund managers coming from long only asset management have gone through painful learning experiences in handling the short side, in particular the risks of short squeezes, the different optics of short positions (possibility of unlimited losses, increase of exposure in losing positions), and the techniques of borrowing stocks.

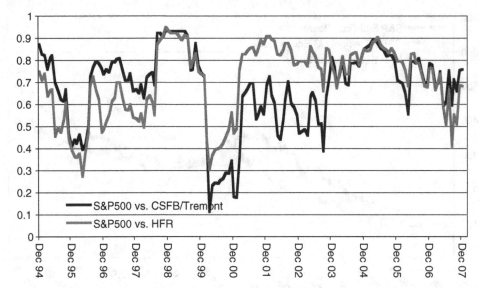

Figure 3.2   Rolling 12-month correlation between the S&P 500 and two Long/Short Equity indices

However, most Long/Short Equity managers claim to return significant alpha, too. They describe the investment process of Long/Short Equity as strongly experience- and skill-driven. Certainly, the manager's stock picking and trading skills are a meaningful source of generated returns. But the precise split between manager alpha and risk premiums is not always entirely clear, especially when looking at the marketing brochures of hedge fund managers! Market inefficiencies, and the chance to generate alpha by detecting and exploiting them, are most prevalent for small-cap companies which are often not well covered by analysts. One important feature of Long/Short Equity strategies is that managers are not limited in generating 'alpha' by the constraint of having to 'hug a benchmark'. They are not required to carry a portfolio position in which they have no insight or conviction simply to control the idiosyncratic risk of underperforming an index. In traditional index-benchmarked equity investment these positions are referred to as a portfolio's 'dead weight'. In a Long/Short Equity hedge fund, only positions about which the manager has insights and convictions are held. The art of the manager is to control nonmarket residual risk through other less capital-intensive techniques than holding 'dead weight' positions. Furthermore, hedge fund managers can use their freedom to sell short to create profit opportunities not available to traditional fund managers. Many investors face psychological or regulatory barriers to engaging in short selling. Regulatory authorities or internal compliance rules prohibit many financial institutions and asset managers from short selling. This creates market inefficiencies and price anomalies which Long/Short managers, who are under no such constraints, can exploit. When short selling is restricted, the pessimism of some investors is not fully represented in security prices, causing some stocks to be over-priced. Bankruptcy or restructuring can also create unique profit opportunities for short sellers.

More recently a certain variation of the Long/Short Equity hedge fund strategy has received increased attention: 'active 130–30 investing' or, to use a more general expression, '100X–X strategies'. These strategies are enhancements of active long only equity investment strategies that have started to integrate short positions in their investment approach. They simply expose a certain percentage of their assets (usually around 30%) to selected short positions and leverage by an equal amount their long positions. They constitute somewhat of a combination of long only investment techniques and hedge fund activities (but should rather be classified as an enhanced form of active equity management). These strategies are facilitated by modern prime brokerage structures which allow proceeds from short sales to be used to purchase extra stocks in excess of capital without the use of margin loans with the long only portfolio serving as collateral.[5] Most of today's 130–30 strategies are supported by quantitative stock picking models similar to those used in the Equity Market Neutral space (see below). We should therefore classify the 130–30 strategies as a combination of a long only investment with an Equity Market Neutral overlay.

3.2   EQUITY HEDGED – EQUITY MARKET NEUTRAL

Equity Market Neutral strategies involve having simultaneously long and short matched stock positions and thereby taking advantage of a relative outperformance of the long positions versus the short positions. In contrast with the Long/Short Equity strategy, Equity Market Neutral managers aim to generate returns, which are completely uncorrelated to the overall equity market and therefore usually insulate their portfolios from broad market risk factors. The total portfolio net exposure is kept to zero – in terms of size ($-neutral), beta (beta-neutral), country (country neutral), currency (currency neutral), industry (sector neutral), market capitalization (size neutral), style (e.g. value versus growth) neutral, or a combination thereof. Equity Market Neutral strategies can be roughly subclassified into Statistical Arbitrage trading and Market Neutral Long/Short Equity. Statistical Arbitrage usually involves model-based short-term trading, while Market Neutral Long/Short Equity strategies have longer holding periods, realizing profit when pricing disparities eventually capitalize.

Statistical Arbitrage strategies utilize quantitative and technical analysis to detect profit opportunities in undervalued and overvalued stocks of related companies, which in 'normal' periods should align themselves to fair value (a process called 'mean reversion' in statistics). One particular technique is 'pair trading', which takes a long and a short position that are closely related. For example, a manager might take paired long and short positions on two large cap bank stocks in the same country.[6] In the construction of the strategy, a particular type of profit opportunity is hypothesized, formalized into a set of trading rules and then back-tested with historical data. This way the manager expects to identify a persistent and statistically significant scheme to detect profit opportunities. Critics of the strategy refer to it as 'black box investing', as characteristics and details of the model are usually not disclosed to investors.

A pair trading example

The following example uses a simple pair trade to illustrate how these trades are used in an Equity Market Neutral strategy. The manager determines the company A to have a fair value of

---

[5] For a more detailed discussion on 130/30 strategies, see B. Jacobs, K. Levy, '20 myths about enhanced active 120–20 strategies' (2007).

[6] See also the paper by E. Gatev, W. Goetzmann, K. Rouwenhorst, 'Pairs trading: performance of a relative value arbitrage rule', NBER Working Paper, 1999.

$150 a share, while it is trading at $144 at the moment and is expected to pay a $3.0 dividend next quarter. Company B in the same sector with a similar business model, cost structure, distribution channels, suppliers, and financial performance is determined to have a fair value of $180 a share but trades at $189 and is expected to pay a $3.40 dividend within the next three months. The manager buys 13 125 shares of A for $144 and sells short 10 000 shares of company B for $180 (the short sale requires additional margin which is included under financing costs). Three months later she reverses the trade paying and receiving the fair values she determined (i.e. the market-adjusted prices to her valuation estimates).

Today:
Buy company A   (1 890 000) (13 125 * 144)
Sell company B   1 890 000 (10 000 * 189)
Transaction costs   (3 600)

Three months later:
Sell company A   1 968 750 (13 125 * 150)
Sell company B   (1 800 000) (10 000 * 180)
Bank A dividend (long)   39 375 (13 125 * 3.0)
Bank B dividend (short) (34 000) (10 000 * 3.4)
Financing costs   (14 175) (margin for short: 50% of 1 890 000 at 6% annualized rate)
Transaction costs   (3600)
                     $ 159 950

$$\text{The annualized return is} \frac{\$\,159\,950}{\$\,1\,890\,000} \times \frac{365}{90} = 34.32\%.$$

There are generally three steps in fundamental-focused Equity Market Neutral strategies: initial screening and ranking, specific stock selection, and portfolio construction. In the screening and stock selection part, hedge fund managers perform a rule-based decision making within a determined universe of stocks. They build portfolios of long positions in certain industries' strongest companies and short positions in those companies that show signs of weakness. The selection criteria are mostly related to various 'value factors' such as price-to-book, price-to-earnings, price-to-sales values, discounted cash flows, return on equity, operating margins, earnings growth, etc. or 'momentum' factors (e.g. price- or earnings-momentum, moving averages, relative strength and trading volumes). The precise definition and use of these factors varies among managers. Trading decisions flow from relative stock ranking systems based on the strengths of these indicators. The portfolio construction is finally performed with the help of computer algorithms using portfolio optimization algorithms. Powerful optimizers are commercially available from companies such as BARRA. However, most managers construct their own proprietary tool sets.

One part of Equity Market Neutral strategies is about detecting inefficiencies in the equity markets. Indeed, numerous studies show that the 'efficient market hypothesis' (EMH), at least in its semi-strong form, must be reconsidered.[7] A hedge fund manager detects inefficiency as the difference between market price and a theoretical 'fair value' price as determined by a (most often proprietary) valuation model. The basic assumption is that anomalies in relative

---

[7] See B. Rosenberg et al., 'Persuasive evidence on market inefficiencies' (1985). See also Chapter 5 for more details.

stock valuations may occur in the short term but, in the long term, these anomalies correct themselves as the market processes information. We will present in Chapter 5 a more detailed discussion on the EMH and possible deviations from it in the context of hedge fund performance. There we point out that excess returns can be due to both non-considered systematic risks and market inefficiencies extracted by Equity Market Neutral managers. Financial theory provides us with a variety of asset pricing models with more than one priced risk factor.[8] Broad market neutrality does not mean that the strategy bears no systematic risks. A portfolio with a zero net market exposure risk can still be susceptible to risks created by sector, industry, and geographical exposures as well as liquidity, leverage, and other factor risks. Equity Market Neutral managers have in practice various systematic biases in their strategies, such as a 'value bias', a 'small cap' bias or a 'momentum bias'. Specifically, 'value' and 'momentum' factors play a great role in Equity Market Neutral strategies. Various academic studies[9] have consistently identified that investing in 'value stocks' – companies considered to be priced cheaply as measured by indicators like book-to-price (B/P) or price-to-earnings (P/E) ratios – yields significant higher returns than what can be explained by the CAPM: companies with high B/P or low P/E ratios persistently outperform companies with low B/P or high P/E values. Analogously, other studies[10] indicate that momentum-based investing yields excess returns: a strategy of investing in companies which have recently outperformed ('winner stocks') and simultaneously selling stocks that have underperformed in the most recent time period ('loser stocks') displays significant positive returns. Thirdly, investing in stocks with small market capitalization yields excess return over large cap stocks. Figure 3.3 shows the cumulative returns to three simple strategies, expressed by the so-called Fama–French HML, SMB, and UMD factors.[11] The HML ('high minus low') indicator is the return to a strategy that buys high book-to-market stocks (i.e. value stocks) and short sells low book-to-market stock (also known as growth stocks). SMB ('small minus big') describes the returns of a strategy that buys stocks of small companies and short sells large cap stocks, and UMD ('up minus down') denotes the returns of a strategy that invests in recent winners and short sells recent losers.

The origin of these returns is the subject of intense academic discussion. E. Fama and K. French[12] argue on the one side that investors following investment strategies represented by HML, SMB, or UMD earn risk premia related to risks not covered by the CAPM such as recession risk (value stocks) or company leverage/bankruptcy risk (small cap stocks) rather than contradicting the EMH. They also tend to be followed by fewer analysts, which causes the reliability of information and thus price security to be lower. In addition the stock is also less liquid. High book to price stocks tend to be cyclical, so they are particularly hurt by a recession. The opposing argument is rooted in 'behavioral finance', which claims that these market inefficiencies derive from investor decisions that are not always rational.[13] Behavioral finance aims at accounting for market anomalies by considering psychological models of

---

[8] The APT model ('arbitrage pricing theory') is the model most frequently mentioned in text books; see also S. Ross, 'The arbitrage theory of capital asset pricing' (1976).

[9] See Chapter 5 for a more extensive discussion on returns from 'value' and 'momentum' strategies.

[10] See Chapter 5.

[11] See E. Fama, K. French, 'Multifactor explanations of asset pricing anomalies' (1996).

[12] See E. Fama, K. French, 'The cross section of expected stock returns' (1992).

[13] See H. Shefrin in *Beyond Greed and Fear: Understanding Behavioral Finance* (1999) and the article by M. Stratman, 'Behavioural finance: past battles and future engagements' (1999). See Chapter 5 for more references and a more extensive discussion on 'behavioral finance'.

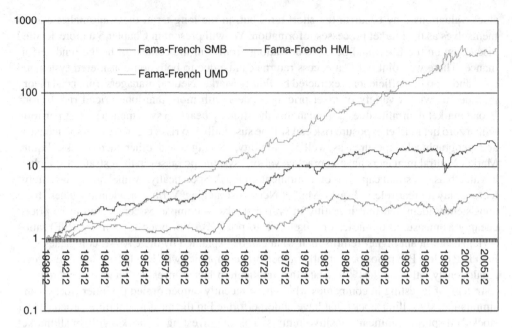

Figure 3.3   Cumulative returns of three Fama–French factors

human behavior. However, most hedge fund managers are indifferent to the discussion of which theory accounts for their premia as long as trading these strategies yields systematically attractive returns.

3.3   EQUITY HEDGED – SHORT SELLING

Short Selling strategies involve the selling of stocks not currently owned by the seller in order to take a directional bet on their anticipated price decline. To sell short, the seller borrows the securities from a third party in order to make the delivery to the buyer. Usually the seller borrows these shares from the lending department of a broker. The seller receives the proceeds as cash, on which she earns interest known as the 'short rebate interest'. At a later time, the seller returns the borrowed shares to the lender by buying replacement shares on the open market. If the short seller can buy the stock back at a lower price, she makes a profit. If the price of the stock has risen, she must still buy the replacement shares, and therefore takes a loss. Theoretically, the short sale, like the sale of a futures contract, does not require any initial capital. However, in practice, the stock-lending brokerage firm requires substantial collateral. On top of the cash received from the sale, a short seller usually must pledge cash or cash-like securities to the lender equal to 30–50% of the stock's market value.[14] Some managers use derivatives, including forwards, futures, and options on indices and stocks, to execute a Short Selling strategy. Others partially hedge the short sale with long positions or out-of-the-money call options, which makes the strategy a Long/Short Equity strategy with a short bias.

---

[14] A discussion about short selling in a portfolio context can be found in 'Efficient sets, short-selling, and estimation risk', by G. Alexander, *Journal of Portfolio Management* (Winter 1995).

The income on short positions has two components: profit from buying back stock at a lower price than it was sold at, and the short rebate interest. Similar to Long/Short Equity strategies or long only investing, the investment process requires a great deal of analysis. Many managers follow a bottom-up approach, in which they examine the individual company's financial standing and business prospects (earnings, cash flow, assets and liabilities, ratio analysis, products, costs, etc.), followed by an analysis of the industry sector (competitive environment, demand and supply, profitability, influences from foreign markets). But a pure fundamental approach to picking short candidates is much less appropriate than the equivalent strategy for long strategies. A common theme of Short Selling strategies is the identification of companies using aggressive accounting techniques. Most short sellers look for an additional catalyst that will expose the poor fundamentals of the company, e.g. an earnings revision.

Short Selling strategies face additional issues and potential problems, which managers on the long side do not.[15] Most of these problems are related to the process of borrowing stocks. These include: share availability, stability of the borrowing (a broker can always call back the stock), the level of short rebate interest earned, and protection against short squeezes, when a temporary sudden demand for the stock forces the short seller to cover his positions at an unfavorable price. Besides borrowing issues, another particularly tricky feature of Short Selling strategies is the inverse relationship between performance and exposure. A loss in a short position leads to a larger overall portfolio exposure to the losing position. Conversely the more successful a position, the less invested the manager becomes.

The unlimited risk of loss to which short sellers are exposed creates psychological barriers for many investors. Most investors never consider short selling. Analysts are hesitant to give a detailed analysis of a potential short selling candidate, and only a few of them give 'sell' recommendations. Additionally, many financial institutions and asset managers are prohibited by regulatory authorities or by internal compliance rules from short selling. The fact that so many investors either will not or cannot sell short leads to inefficiencies and opportunities for Short Selling managers. Without complete freedom to sell short, the pessimism of some investors will not be fully represented in security prices, and some stocks will be overpriced. Short sellers therefore contribute to the efficient capital allocation process within an economy, and are compensated in part for the risk they incur in doing so. However, the key performance driver of Short Selling strategies is security selection. As for the inverse strategy – active long equity investing – the manager's stock picking and portfolio management skills remain the most important sources of generated returns.

3.4 RELATIVE VALUE – GENERAL[16]

Relative Value strategies used to be referred to as 'arbitrage strategies'. This expression comes with a mixed blessing, as it disguises risk exposures these strategies do have. We should translate 'arbitrage' into 'non-equity-directional', which means these strategies come with no direct exposure to the global stock markets. However, that does not mean they bear no risk. Rather the opposite applies: these 'arbitrage strategies' often are the last insurer against market turbulences, i.e. they are short a put on the health of the global financial market.

---

[15] A good discussion about the issues involved is given in 'Short selling: a unique set of risks' by A. Arulpragasam and J. Chanos in *Managing Hedge Fund Risk* ed. by V. Parker.

[16] The following research paper elaborates on this section in much greater detail: R. Cagnati, M. Connors, 'PG hedge fund strategy paper – Relative Value', Partners Group Research (April 2007).

Table 3.1 The Relative Value universe and the primary and secondary market they are acting in

Primary asset class	Styles		
Government Bonds	Relative Value Fixed Income Arb	Macro Trading	Emerging Markets
MBS/ABS	Prime (e.g. Agency)	Sub-Prime	
Municipal Bonds	Insured	Credit	
Corporate Bonds	Long/Short Credit	High Yield	Long Bias (Bank Loans)
Convertible Bonds	Volatility Related	Credit Related	
Volatility	Index	Single Name	
Multi-Strategy/Diversified	Broad Multi-Strategy	Opportunistic	

Table 3.1 provides an overview of the Relative Value universe dividing it into six primary strategies (plus Multi-Strategy) with a varying number of sub-strategies. We categorized the strategies mainly according to the primary and secondary markets they are involved in (two columns in the table). The following discussion will elaborate on some of the main Relative Value strategies, 'Fixed Income Arbitrage', 'Convertible Arbitrage', 'Volatility Arbitrage', and 'Capital Structure Arbitrage'.

3.5   RELATIVE VALUE – FIXED INCOME ARBITRAGE

Fixed Income Arbitrage is a general description for a variety of trading strategies involving different fixed income instruments (first four categories above). Fixed Income Arbitrage managers operate in the most liquid government, municipal, securitized and corporate bond markets, trying to exploit second- and third-order effects (curvature, volatility, mispricing) of global yield curves with a resulting low to zero correlation to the overall direction of bond markets. Instruments traded include US government and agency debt, G7 government debt, sovereign emerging market debt, corporate debt, municipal debt, asset-backed securities, exchange-traded futures, interest rate swaps and options. The strategy generally seeks profits by trading the spread relationship (and possibly relative pricing inefficiencies) between related fixed income securities and their derivatives and aim to profit from relative movements or accrue positive carry over time. By investing in one or more securities and simultaneously taking an opposite position in another related instrument ('spread positions' (e.g. T-bill versus Eurodollar)), the Fixed Income Arbitrage manager neutralizes exposure to most systematic risk factors such as yield-curve changes.

Different types of Fixed Income Arbitrage strategies involve yield-curve trades (spread positions including bonds with different maturities), corporate versus treasury yield spreads, municipal versus treasury yield spreads, cash versus future, and on-the-run versus off-the-run treasury bonds. Managers differ quite substantially in terms of how and to what degree interest rate risks, credit risks, foreign exchange risks, and inter-market spread risks are hedged. Some managers even take 'directional bets' with respect to yield-curve or credit spread changes; others employ pure spread trades only.[17]

---

[17] See also M. Pintar's article 'Fixed income arbitrage' in L. Jaeger (ed.) *The New Generation of Risk Management for Hedge Funds and Private Equity Investment* (2003).

Sources of return for simpler Fixed Income Arbitrage strategies involving the yield curves of major developed markets (usually G7, with most of the trading taking place in G3 yield curves) are pure arbitrage opportunities (mispricings) as well as various small risk premia (TED spread, swap spread) which can largely be identified with liquidity risk premia. A high number of trades are indeed not based on 'arbitrage' opportunities but rather on small risk premia (alternative betas) like swap spreads/off-the-run versus on-the-run, etc.).[18]

The Fixed Income Arbitrage universe also includes a variety of strategies involving asset backed securities (ABS) and mortgage-backed securities (MBS). Managers and market participants seemed to use the term 'asset-backed' to denote almost anything that yielded cash flow and that was securitized. On the other side, as the sub-prime mortgage market stress hit the financial markets in early 2007, the term ABS seemed to become synonymous with sub-prime mortgage-backed securities.[19] Both views constitute somewhat of an extreme. We can break down the ABS market roughly into the following major buckets from largest to smallest: mortgage-backed securities, sub-prime mortgage-backed securities, home equity loans (include some 'sub-prime' exposure), 'other' – likely consisting of small business loan securitizations and other random buckets of mostly corporate asset securitizations, credit card receivables, CDO (cash) issuance, auto loans, and student loans. ABS/MBS hedge fund strategies have until about 2004 mostly been focused on holding long portfolios of fixed income and structured credit securities and earned a yield on that long portfolio (often highly leveraged).[20] Structured MBS securities, such as collateralized mortgage obligations (CMOs) and interest-only and principal-only 'STRIPs' (IOs and POs), allocate mortgage cash flows in a variety of ways to create securities with specific prepayment and maturity profiles. CMOs comprise a number of classes of bonds issued against specified mortgage collateral. The collateral can be agency pass-through pools, whole loans (typically nonconforming loans), or classes from other CMO deals (like CDO squared deals in the corporate space).[21] The vast majority of the underlying collateral for these securities are mortgages on residential housing and commercial buildings (mostly in the USA, but growing in other parts of the world), thus the dedicated name mortgage-backed securities (MBS). Securitization of mortgages, combined with US Government sponsored agencies has created a vast market (the largest fixed income market in the world) for trading in mortgage-backed securities in the primary and secondary markets.

---

[18] There is (virtually) no increased market 'efficiency' that causes opportunities to 'vanish' compared to the late 1990s because markets were fairly efficient at that time as well; apparently, free lunches in the fixed income markets have not been available since Meriwether and his team started the whole arbitrage concept in the 1980s while trading in the arbitrage group at Salomon Brothers. In addition to that, the 'convergence trade' in Europe (introduction of the euro) was a special tailwind for the strategy in the late 1990s that biased returns upwards.

[19] Possibly one of the most talked-about markets in finance in 2007, the sub-prime mortgage-backed security market does not differ all that much from its bigger brother the MBS market and certainly closely resembles the non-agency part of the MBS market with respect to basic structure (with the obvious distinction that the borrowers have lower credit ratings and the loans do not conform to more conservative agency standards).

[20] The mortgage-backed security and asset-backed security markets represent a veritable pillar of global fixed income markets. The market sizes are difficult to estimate as the number of issues as well as the sources of issuance are very diverse and fragmented as compared to government or even corporate bonds; however, we estimate that together the markets represent at least $8 trillion in debt and could be well over $10 trillion depending on sources (as of 2007).

[21] Just as in corporate markets, structured credit vehicles can take an infinite number of forms and properties. We will obviously not explore even a fraction of the different vehicles available other than to say that the financial markets have found ways to create mortgage securities to fit the needs and risk parameters of nearly any market participant and risk/reward profile.

Recently, the advent of credit derivatives has changed the landscape and opportunity set for market participants in MBS/ABS markets. The ability to effectively short securities in this market has suddenly become a reality, whereas prior to 2004 it was not even a viable option.

Municipal Bond Arbitrage hedge funds hold a long portfolio of municipal securities that is interest rate hedged via a short position in treasuries exploiting the different degrees of steepness of the municipal versus taxable curve. The complexity and heterogeneity of the fragmented municipal bond market allows the managers to benefit from inefficiencies through security selection as well as by participating in new issues. While the municipal market historically has been pretty insulated from other fixed income markets, due to its special appeal to US investors (tax exemption), the advent of derivatives and structured notes has changed the market considerably over the last few years, diminishing the arbitrage opportunity based on the steeper municipal versus taxable yield curve.

Strategies in corporate credit are as diverse as strategies in any asset category, including long only/long bias which relies on earning a positive carry from coupon income for most returns, market neutral which generally relies on fundamental credit analysis for security selection and returns from capital appreciation, and different arbitrage strategies such as capital structure arbitrage which take advantage of structural inefficiencies in the credit markets as well as relationships between different credit instruments and their counterparts in both the cash and derivative market. Credit default swaps as well as structured credit vehicles have virtually transformed credit markets over the last decade into a market where it is now possible, and relatively efficient, to take virtually any view and implement that view into a portfolio. Credit spreads have in 2005 to summer 2007 been at historically tight levels which has produced an extreme skew in the risk profile for traditional long portfolios in corporate credit. This has also led to a new phenomenon, perhaps never seen before: short bias credit funds. Credit portfolios, while positively correlated to equity markets if long bias, can add significant diversification to an alternative portfolio in their many forms.

Examples of market neutral (duration and credit neutral) Fixed Income Arbitrage trades include the following spread trades:

- Arbitrage between similar bonds (e.g. long underpriced 7-year duration US T-bond and short overpriced 7.2-year duration US T-bond). A common variation of this trade involves cheapest-to-deliver bonds underlying a futures contract on the bond or other forms of basis trades.
- Butterflies (e.g. long cheap 5-year and 7-year, short expensive 6-year). Relative mispricings along the yield curve often occur due to high institutional demand for certain benchmark bonds. The strategy is also referred to as 'yield-curve arbitrage'.
- Basis trades involve trading the spread between physical securities and their Futures (e.g. short overpriced US 10-year note Future, long underpriced US 10-year note). Bond Futures have a delivery option and a wild card option, which can lead to pricing inefficiencies and provides for arbitrage opportunities.
- Asset swap trades involve the purchase of fixed rate bonds versus pay fixed positions in interest rate swaps or vice versa (reverse asset swaps). The outright asset swap or reverse asset swap trades involve taking exposure to systematic risk while a combination of the two ('box trades') seek to hedge some of this risk.
- TED spread, i.e. spread between Treasury-bill Futures and Eurodollar Futures (this can be seen as a credit spread trade: government debt versus AA-rated inter-bank debt).

- Yield spread between on-the-run and off-the-run bonds (e.g. short the latest government issue of a 10-year note, and long the second most recent issue). The on-the-run issue trades at lower yields due to higher liquidity.

  Other, non-market-neutral, strategies include the following.

- Yield-curve spread trading based on a forecast of the directional change of the yield curve. Yield-curve trades often refer to very basic structures such as 'steepeners' or 'flatteners', which involve taking opposing positions in two maturities on the yield curve. An example could be going long the short end of the curve (up to 3-year maturities) and going short the long end (i.e. 10–15 years) anticipating a steeper yield curve in the future. Given that the slope of the yield curve is largely a function of the expectation of future short-term interest rates, these positions are directly related to anticipated central bank action. This obviously makes these trades resemble Global Macro trades.
- Credit spread trading capturing either credit pricing anomalies or more generally profiting from yield curve differentials for securities with different (but generally closely related) credit qualities (e.g. short a AAA-rated bond with a spread to T-bonds of 50 bp and long a AA-rated bond with a spread of 80 bp).
- Cross-currency government versus government spread trades.
- Asset-backed securities (ABS), e.g. credit card receivables, auto loans, or mortgage debt, offer enhanced returns for investors, which assume exposure to the embedded option features (prepayment, call option) and accept lower liquidity and possible credit risk on the ABS. Examples for ABS arbitrage strategies are:
  - Spread position ABS against T-bonds (e.g. long government-secured Fannie Mae or Freddie mortgage-backed securities (MBS), and short US Treasuries with similar duration).
  - Spread position of MBS against collateral mortgage obligations (CMO). An example is selling certain tranches of a CMO and buying a plain pass-through MBS.
  - Arbitraging between different CMO classes. Two examples are: (1) Going long interest-only tranches (IOs) and shorting principal-only tranches (POs); (2) Shorting a principal amortization class (PAC) tranche and going long a support tranche.

    The hedging of prepayment risk is rather complex but nevertheless commonly employed within ABS arbitrage strategies.

The spreads available for arbitrage strategies in fixed income markets tend to be small. In order to earn attractive returns, most Fixed Income Arbitrage strategies must employ a high level of leverage, which may range from 5 to 15 times the asset base (occasionally even more) and is created through borrowing, repo (repurchase) transactions, or the use of options, futures, or swaps. A creditworthy investor with good dealing relationships might be able to transact $100 million notional value while putting up less than $1 million collateral. The simpler strategies (e.g. basis trades) are generally more highly leveraged than trades that are systematically exposed to more risk and specific risk factors (e.g. ABS strategies).

Return opportunities in fixed income markets, both systematic risk premia and price inefficiencies, occur for a variety of reasons. These reasons include sudden market events, exogenous shocks to supply or demand, investors having maturity preferences or restrictions for fixed income investments, different credit ratings, recent downgrade in credit ratings, complex options/callable features connected to a bond, deliverable characteristics for futures contracts, and complex cash flow properties. Fixed Income markets display various pricing inefficiencies (particularly in less liquid sectors) for the following reasons: (1) agency biases: fiduciaries purchase securities, which displayed above average returns in the recent past; (2) structural reasons: tax, accounting or regulatory issues drive certain market participants to buy securities products for uneconomical reasons; (3) market segmentation: certain market participants are restricted from trading in particular products or markets or have particular liquidity preferences, which can lead to short-term flows large enough to create dislocations in the normal relationship between two securities.

However, returns are also due to systematic risk related to interest rate (term) risk,[22] credit risk, liquidity risk, or an (often complex) combination of these. Fixed Income Arbitrage managers are often long and short equal duration adjusted amounts of securities with unequal credit quality or liquidity. Thus the strategy earns risk premia for holding less liquid or lower credit quality instruments and hedges other risks (e.g. interest rates, term structure) by selling short securities with higher liquidity and credit ratings. One illustrative example is the abovementioned off-the-run versus on-the-run treasury bond spread. Even with identical coupon structure and maturity, they trade with a yield differential, which is uniquely due to liquidity differences. Aside from the assumed risks related to liquidity premium, there can be other systematic risks. These vary from implicit credit risks, as in government versus agency bond spreads, to monetary policy risks such as in cross-currency government versus government spread trades.

Fixed Income Arbitrage strategies are typically 'short volatility' strategies. In an abstract sense, Fixed Income Arbitrage managers sell economic disaster insurance and earn their spread as a risk (insurance) premium. They take positions that correspond to short put positions on financial market turmoil, exposing themselves to 'sudden event' risk when interest rates move rapidly, credit spreads widen, and liquidity dries up – the classic 'flight to quality' scenario. The risks of the Fixed Income Arbitrage strategies become apparent in market stress situations such as the summer of 1998 or the summer of 2007. These 'flight to quality' events usually happen when many market participants want to liquidate positions at the same time, everybody 'running for the door'. They occur relatively infrequently, but when they happen the value of Fixed Income Arbitrage portfolios can drop significantly on a mark-to-market basis. This can produce losses of several standard deviations ('tail risk'). Further, in volatile markets the strategy can easily become a captive of its extreme leverage. A single margin call on a position can destroy the entire portfolio. Prime brokers may withdraw financing at particularly difficult times, which might necessitate the liquidation of the portfolio. The failure of LTCM is an illustrative example of liquidity problems a Fixed Income Arbitrage strategy faces in times of market distress.

Excursion: LTCM[23]

LTCM (Long Term Capital Management) was founded in 1994 by John Meriwether and his team after they left Salomon Brothers (where they were known as the famous 'Arbitrage Group' since the early 1980s). The strategy started as fixed income arbitrage, mainly relying

---

[22] E. Dimson *et al.* describe the size and properties of the term premium in *Triumph of the Optimists: 101 Years of Global Investment Returns* (2002).

[23] See the classic book by R. Lowenstein, *When Genius Failed: The Rise and Fall of Long-Term Capital Management*, Random House (2000).

on convergence trades (e.g. among European sovereign bonds, 'off-the-run versus 'on-the-run' treasuries). With increasing assets, LTCM started to broaden its strategy universe: in addition to the fixed income relative value strategies, they started to focus on selling equity volatility, merger arbitrage/pair trades and long positions in emerging market debt (hedged with US treasuries and by selling Russian rubles). Great performance in early years caused assets to pour into the fund (over USD 4 billion at the peak); shrinking arbitrage opportunities combined with a bigger size forced the fund to increase its leverage to 30:1 in order to maintain return targets subsequently, though. The unexpected Russian default on its debt caused losses to the fund; the subsequent 'flight to quality' environment caused a dramatic increase in correlation of LTCM's trades and further increased its losses; falling equity and the inability to liquidate its huge positions led to a further increase in leverage to approximately 100:1. After LTCM took further dramatic losses in September 1998 due to Wall Street betting against the fund's positions, the equity of the fund dropped to a critical level (close to default). Subsequently the Federal Reserve Bank of New York organized a rescue package injecting USD 4 billion into the fund financed by major Wall Street banks in order to prevent a potential systemic meltdown of financial markets (if LTCM had defaulted on its USD 100 billion portfolio and its huge amount of USD 1.25 trillion of notional outstanding swap positions). Interestingly, although LTCM was terminated a few months later in 1999, Meriwether and most of his former colleagues were able to raise USD 2 billion which they still manage according to a similar strategy (with limited leverage of 15:1, though) as 'JWM Partners' since December 1999.

The successful implementation of a Fixed Income Arbitrage strategy requires a very high degree of sophistication, as prices of fixed income instruments depend on a large variety of factors with complex interactions between them. These factors include spot and forward yield curves, volatility curves, credit-spread curves, expected cash flows, prepayment features (for ABS), and option characteristics (e.g. call, put, and prepayments schedules). As in Convertible Arbitrage strategies, there is an inherent return component in Fixed Income Arbitrage strategies related to a 'complexity premium'. In the context of the overall market, the hedge fund manager is effectively paid to create liquidity and price transparency in complex pricing relationships which other market agents are unwilling or unable to be exposed to.

3.6 RELATIVE VALUE – CONVERTIBLE ARBITRAGE

Convertible securities are equivalent to holding a bond position plus an option on some underlying stock.[24] In its most basic and traditional form, convertible arbitrage involves the purchase of a security convertible into the issuer's stock and the simultaneous short sale of a certain percentage of that underlying stock. It is often stated that Convertible Arbitrage managers pursue arbitrage opportunities by identifying pricing disparities between the equity and the bond element of the convertible. The relative price movements are created when

- the credit profile of a name changes, the market changes its perception of said credit, or the market premium paid for a given level of credit risk changes;

---

[24] A description of the different components of a convertible security can be found in *Market Neutral and Hedged Strategies*, published by Hedge Fund Research, Inc. The authors also provide a discussion of Convertible Arbitrage strategies. Another helpful article is the one by B. Feingold 'Convertible Arbitrage strategy' in L. Jaeger (ed.), *The New Generation of Risk Management for Hedge Funds and Private Equity Investment* (2003).

- the volatility of the underlying equity changes or the market premium paid for a given level of volatility changes;
- interest rate movements change market yield requirements;
- relative richness/cheapness of the market value of the convertible versus its theoretical value changes.

However, even without any pricing anomalies in the convertible bond market, Convertible Arbitrage strategies can be profitable through what is called 'gamma trading' (positive convexity of the hedge ratio profile) and through the static exposure to credit risk (which earns higher coupons, or, depending on the sophistication of the calculation, imputed accretion in the case of a zero coupon bond). A good part of the strategy's return is thus based on the inherently positive static return profile of a hedged convertible position.

The typical Convertible Arbitrage hedge fund manager usually starts with a universe of convertible securities and screens candidates applying bottom-up valuation analysis. The goal is to take long positions in 'cheap' convertible securities and hedge the equity part of these positions by selling short the issuer's stock. 'Cheap' in this case can also refer to 'buying volatility' at little cost. Long positions in convertible securities include convertible bonds, convertible preferred stock and warrants. When the convertible ultimately achieves its 'fair value' relative to the stock price, the position is sold, and profits are realized. Besides equity risk, managers often hedge other risk factors such as credit and interest rate risk[25] using a variety of hedging techniques including credit derivatives for credit risk, and fixed income derivatives such as interest futures and options for duration risk.

In choosing suitable convertible bonds, managers take into account the convertible's market price, interest rate levels, the market price and volatility of the underlying stock, the bond floor, the credit quality of the issuer, the expected equity premium, the conversion price and ratio, the conversion premium, and other variables related to the issue (e.g. call/put schedule).[26] While most Convertible Arbitrage managers target a market (beta) neutral position, some take a fundamental view on the issuer and build this opinion into a net short or net long position. The equity hedge ratio or delta of the underlying option, which represents the price sensitivity of the bond with respect to the stock price, generally ranges from about 0.2 to about 0.8. Convertible Arbitrage managers employ leverage ranging from 1:1 to 5:1.

Different variations of Convertible Arbitrage strategies are:

- buying convertible bonds and selling short the underlying stock/stock option;
- buying convertible bonds and shorting index futures/index options;
- searching for price inefficiencies in complicated convertibles with numerous conversion characteristics and call and put schedules;
- focusing on low credit quality or distressed convertibles and their stock.

---

[25] With rising interest rates (or higher credit spreads), the straight debt value (the 'bond floor') decreases. Although stock returns tend to be negatively correlated to interest rates and positively correlated to credit deterioration, losses on the bond are usually only partly offset by the short equity position held against the bond. Another partial hedge is given by the positive rho of long convertible positions. The option value increases with rising interest rates. Many managers use interest rate derivatives such as interest rate futures and options on interest rate futures, swaps, and total return swaps to hedge against duration risk and credit risk. Option adjusted spread (OAS) is a concept widely used in valuing bonds with embedded options.

[26] For more details about the pricing and characteristics of convertible bonds the reader is referred to the book *Pricing Convertible Bonds* by K. Connolly.

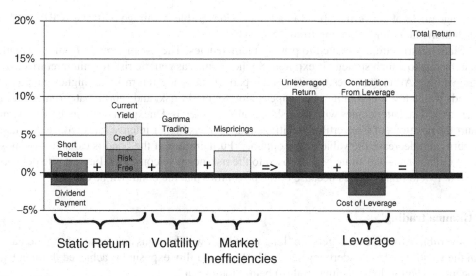

Figure 3.4   Systematic return sources of Convertible Arbitrage hedge funds

Managers pursuing Convertible Arbitrage strategies earn returns from three sources which I will explain in the following: (1) earning static returns in the form of coupon income and short stock rebates; (2) 'gamma trading' on stock volatility; (3) exploiting price inefficiencies. Figure 3.4 illustrates these different return elements.

Static returns

Static returns in Convertible Arbitrage strategies have two different sources:

 (i) convertible bonds pay interest or preferred dividends (current yield);
(ii) the short equity portion generates positive cash flow (interest income from short rebate minus dividends).

An important distinction between different Convertible Arbitrage managers is the 'moneyness' of the convertibles traded, i.e. how much the underlying option is in- or out-of-the-money. Some managers focus on deep-in-the-money convertibles, while others trade mainly out-of-the-money issues (or even 'busted convertibles', i.e. deeply out-of-the-money issues). The highest level of static return is earned with in-the-money convertibles. These come with a higher delta and thus more stocks sold short, which earns the manager higher short rebates.

Besides the moneyness of the option, credit quality, which represents the risk of downgrade, spread widening, or default of the convertible securities, is the other most important factor to consider. The level of dependency between the bond price and credit spreads is sometimes called 'omicron'. Together with prevailing interest rates, the credit quality determines the bond floor of the convertible security. Positions in issuers with lower credit quality earn higher static returns as the bond earns higher coupons compensating for the higher credit risk. The average grade of convertible bond in a typical Convertible Arbitrage portfolio is BB to BBB with individual ratings ranging from AAA to CCC.[27]

Static returns are not related to pricing inefficiencies. They stem directly from systematic risk factors to which strategy is exposed. So they comes as generic risk premium returns from Convertible Arbitrage investing. The main part of the static return is the higher coupon of bonds with a low credit rating, in compensation for credit risk, and short rebate from shorting the stock. The latter comes with the risk of higher dividends. Unexpected rise in dividends can hurt the positions of Convertible Arbitrage managers as higher interest rates reduce the static returns and decrease the value of the option.[28] Furthermore, if the bond is callable – as most convertibles are – the strategy is exposed to the risk-negative convexity. Interest rate declines will not yield higher prices because of the possibility that the bond will be called.

'Gamma trading'

Convertible Arbitrage managers are 'long volatility', which means they benefit from increases in the volatility of the underlying stock. The long volatility exposure is achieved through two means: (a) being 'long gamma' and (b) being 'long vega'.

'Long gamma'

The hedge fund manager initially delta hedges the convertible's equity exposure with a short position in the stock (example: with a delta of 0.5 the manager sells short 50 shares of stock for each 100 convertible bonds). With the price of the stock changing, she ensures that she remains 'delta neutral' through re-hedging. In other words, when a stock price increase raises the convertible bond's delta, she sells more stock. When a stock price decreases, lowering the bond's delta, she buys back the stock.

The re-hedging after larger moves in the stock price yields trading gains. When the stock price moves strongly up, the delta of the convertible bond's option itself increases, which implies that the overall convertible position increases in value more than the stock position. Inversely, a falling stock price lowers the delta of the convertible bond, which means that the convertible position will fall less than the stock. In other words, no matter in which direction the move occurs, the changing delta always works out in favor of the overall position of a long convertible bond with a hedged short position in the underlying stock. This is what Convertible Arbitrage managers call 'being long gamma' (gamma describes the rate of change in delta with changing stock prices).

Figure 3.5 shows the curvilinear profile of the theoretical option curve holding all variables constant and just moving the option price up and down the tangent to the curve whose slope is the first derivative – or instantaneous rate of change – at the point of tangency (theoretical

---

[27] However, as the default risk of the company is somewhat hedged by shorting the underlying common stock (degrading credit quality of the bonds usually comes along with a decrease in the market value of the stock), especially for high delta positions, i.e. in-the-money convertibles (less so for low delta positions), the overall risk of the combined position is considerably better than the agency rating of the non-hedged bond indicates. For low delta positions (e.g. 'busted convertibles') the bond might behave differently than the stock and can even fall faster than the stock in some scenarios, indicating the presence of negative gamma/vega.

[28] Investors learnt that lesson after US President Bush banned taxation on stock dividends in the summer of 2003, which led numerous companies to increase their dividend payout.

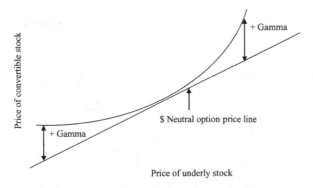

Figure 3.5 Gamma trading

delta). In this simple scenario we assume delta neutrality, and assume an instantaneous move from the point of tangency to two points, one up and one down. We observe a scenario gain from both moves equal to the difference between the dollar-neutral options price and the theoretical pricing curve (again this is holding assumed volatility and interest rates constant!).

The skillful manager adjusts his delta hedges at the optimal intervals. Too-frequent adjustments lead to giving up real profit opportunities from gap moves in the stock. On the other hand, traders who don't adjust often enough will miss chances to benefit from moves in the stock price. Striking the right balance between excessive and insufficient gamma trading is a key edge of an experienced Convertible Arbitrage hedge fund manager.

Figure 3.6 illustrates graphically how gains from gamma exposure can be created from taking advantage of the positive convexity described in the section above, and actively trading the hedge (dynamically delta hedging) in order to 'capture' profit from the volatility of the underlying instrument by buying and selling at predefined or opportunistic points in order to capture profit.

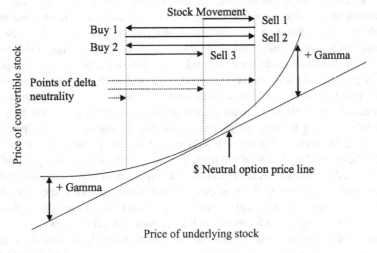

Figure 3.6 Delta hedging

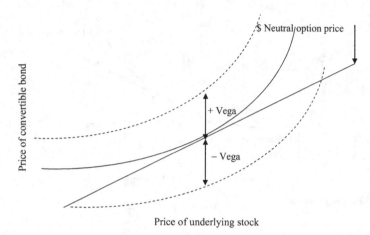

Figure 3.7 Exposure to volatility changes

'Long vega'

As the stock price volatility changes, the convertible's value will change due to the commensurate change in the inherent option value (conversion premium). The higher the volatility of the underlying stock, the more opportunity for the manager to realize trading profits.

As opposed to holding the volatility constant and moving the underlying, Figure 3.7 does the opposite and shows the theoretical gain on a higher implied volatility, effectively shifting the theoretical pricing curve up or down as assumed volatility goes up and down. Obviously a shift up in vega creates a scenario gain (again here it is important to note that an assumed constant is the discount/premium to theoretical value at which the option is trading) and a shift down creates a scenario loss.

Being long gamma and vega has little to do with exploiting pricing inefficiencies. Instead these characteristics relate to a generic return driver of the Convertible Arbitrage strategy. However, they do not come without risk. The risk in being 'long volatility' is an unexpected drop in implied stock price volatility. Lower implied volatility deteriorates the value of the option without a corresponding gain on the short equity positions. Further, lower realized volatility implies less pronounced moves in the stock price, which leads to less long gamma trading gains. With no such gains, the manager loses on his overall position as the option decays over time. She is not only long gamma and long vega (and neutral delta), but also short theta.

A further risk is related to liquidity. In periods of extreme stock market volatility, where investors embark on a 'flight to quality', the manager might not be able to perform the necessary delta hedging to keep his position neutral to moves in the stock price. This risk is highest for 'at-the-money' Convertible Arbitrage strategies, because they have the highest gamma. 'In-the-money' and 'out-of-the-money' convertibles have lower 'gamma' exposure, i.e. their delta hedges are less sensitive to changing equity prices. An incomplete delta hedge exposes the strategy to the risk of being over- or under-hedged with respect to future moves in the stock price. Those situations also give rise to convertible security prices falling rapidly and their liquidity drying up, as happened in the summer and fall of 1998.

The Convertible Arbitrage strategy consists of more than simply identifying 'cheap volatility'. The management of tail risk is a key component of a successful Convertible Arbitrage implementation. In addition to hedges for protection against movements in stock prices, most managers also seek to hedge interest rate and credit exposure. The analysis of credit risk has become one of the core edges of Convertible Arbitrage managers. Often their confidence in their own 'credit picking' skills determines the degree of credit risk hedging. Credit derivatives have become an important hedging tool for Convertible Arbitrage managers.[29] The level of sophistication in hedging techniques for Convertible Arbitrage strategies is developing rapidly. Figure 3.4 illustrates and summarizes the systematic return sources of Convertible Arbitrage hedge funds.

Although the strategy might appear conceptually rather simple, Convertible Arbitrage is actually quite complex to implement due to the wide variety of risk factors. Successful implementation requires experience and skill in managing these risks. Picking the right convertible bonds on which to take a long gamma position with the optimal static return expectations is a core skill of a good Convertible Arbitrage manager. The optimal trade also involves thorough analysis of the credit quality of the issuer ('credit picking' skills). The favorite position of a Convertible Arbitrage manager involves a company that is healthy from a credit perspective, with an overvalued stock. Convertible Arbitrage managers fared extremely well in the first 18 months of the 2000–2003 bear market, when all the overvalued growth companies moved back to reasonable price levels without the bond floor of their debt being affected as strongly.

Identifying pricing inefficiencies in the convertible bond market

Using quantitative models for determining the 'fair value' of a convertible bond, Convertible Arbitrage managers exploit mispricings in the complex equity–bond relationship of the convertible issue. They acquire 'cheap' positions and hedge their systematic risks. A particular 'mispricing' of convertible bonds occurs (or at least occurred in the past) at the time of issuance.[30] The issuer often sweetens the convertible bond with a discount from 'fair value'. When the position ultimately reaches fair value, the manager sells it and realizes profits. Identifying and trading on mispriced convertible bonds is therefore the main source of 'alpha' in Convertible Arbitrage.

Opportunities from market inefficiencies occur because the pricing relationship between the convertible bond and the stock is inherently quite complex. This complexity leads market prices to frequently deviate from 'fair values', particularly in volatile periods. The value of convertible securities depends on a number of different factors: the bond floor as determined by interest rates and credit quality, premium over conversion value (i.e. the 'moneyness' of the option component), stock price and stock price volatility, call and put schedules of the bond, and other factors including liquidity, open short interest of the stock, etc. To make matters worse, these dependencies are partly nonlinear. Therefore the Convertible Arbitrage manager is surely exposed to model risk, the risk that his valuation technique is inappropriate. Even a 'correct' model can lead to problems in the hands of a manager who blindly follows it, because models by their nature can only capture parts of the market dynamics. A subtler risk involving equity hedging is mark-to-market risk. While a position may in the long run prove successful

---

[29] For more about credit derivatives, see the book by J. Tavakoli, *Credit Derivatives: A Guide to Instruments and Applications*, 2nd edition (2001).

[30] Many convertible bonds are issued in the OTC market through private placements under Regulation S and can only be purchased by qualified investors under the provision of 144A.

it can bring about mark-to-market losses, especially when a stock moves sharply. Short and medium-term pricing will be determined in those instances by market agents willing to pay a premium from 'fair value' (e.g. other hedge funds readjusting their equity hedges). Thus Convertible Arbitrage managers must strike a balance between their own beliefs regarding a position and short-term market dynamics, to enable them to generate profits while controlling mark-to-market losses. I contend that model risk and mark-to-market risks themselves provide the convertible bond market with inherent returns. These returns are not necessarily related to pricing inefficiencies, but are actually risk premia. Complexity is often related to the perception of risk, which keeps agents out of these assets. Taking on the complexity risk means providing liquidity and fair valuations to other market agents, a service for which hedge funds expect compensation. As a result, issuers can float convertible debt into a more liquid and price-transparent market in recent years. This has given firms an additional option for raising capital and has thereby reduced their cost of capital.

An important factor in a manager's 'edge' is his competitive advantage in determining the appropriate value of the convertible bond. There are different possible focuses of the hedge fund manager. Often, pricing inefficiencies of convertibles are due to 'volatility mispricings', and Convertible Arbitrage means here the search for under-priced volatility and appropriately trading this volatility in the market, considering all the related price factors of the convertible bond (duration risk, credit risk, liquidity, call schedules). Another 'edge' lies on the credit side. More and more Convertible Arbitrage managers have developed into 'credit pickers', thus taking explicit credit exposure in what they determine to be undervalued issuers. If the manager's analysis determines that the issuer is substantially more creditworthy than the rest of the market believes (especially in situations of rapid decline of the equity value), she assigns a higher fixed-income value (also known as 'bond floor' value) to the convertible, thus leaving herself paying a relatively low price for the total security.

Returns of Convertible Arbitrage hedge funds have historically had very favorable correlation properties as the long volatility profile tends to lead to negative correlation to equity markets, even given a long credit exposure.

3.7   RELATIVE VALUE – VOLATILITY ARBITRAGE

Volatility Arbitrage strategies specialize in benefiting from the level and change of volatilities in particular instruments and asset classes through the sale or purchase of options and option-like instruments. Volatility arbitrage managers almost exclusively utilize options with a delta-neutral hedge to isolate implied volatility and neutralize sensitivity to directional movements in the underlying instruments. It is thus a strategy which uses options almost exclusively to construct positions which are sensitive to the volatility of the underlying instrument upon which the option is referenced. Generally, the Volatility Arbitrage manager takes a long position in what she perceives (statistically or fundamentally 'event-driven', or both) as 'cheap volatility', or a short position in 'expensive volatility'. The determination of what constitutes 'cheap' or 'expensive' volatilities is performed with the help of proprietary option valuation models. To go long on 'cheap volatility', the manager buys options on securities which display implied volatilities she judges to be too low compared to potential realized future actual volatility or compared to what her valuation tool tells her. To sell 'expensive volatility', she does the reverse by selling options on assets with implied volatility she judges to be too high. For example, when equity market volatility dropped dramatically in the later part of 2003, many

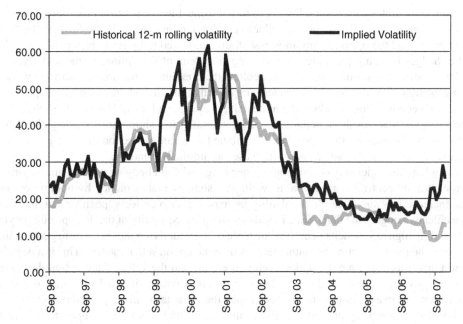

Figure 3.8 Implied versus the rolling 12-month actual volatility of the Nasdaq Index

Volatility Arbitrage managers bought straddles or strangles. These combinations of calls and puts on the same underlying take advantage of low implied volatilities, and thus cheap options. In the environment of the equity markets in the second half of 2003, these managers were betting on a strong stock market move up or down (which in 2003 did not occur). On the other hand, in periods of high and rising volatility that follow market shocks, implied volatility tends to be significantly higher than what can be expected to be realized in actual volatility. This is illustrated in Figure 3.8, where we show the implied versus the rolling 12-month actual volatility of the Nasdaq Index over the period from the summer of 1996 to 2007, a period rich in market shocks as well as an extended period of calmness. For example, the summer of 1998, the spring of 2000, or Q4/2002–Q1/2003 are such periods. Figure 3.8 shows significantly higher values of implied volatility than historical volatility, even compared to the future realized volatility. During these periods, Volatility Arbitrage managers would take advantage of these temporary 'mispricings' of volatility and sell the corresponding option or a combination thereof. It is debatable whether volatility is actually mispriced in this situation. It may well be that the market sets the risk premium to be paid to option sellers just that high, due to the strong sentiment of uncertainty or the risk of a more expressed market shake-out due, for example, to exogenous shocks. This exposes the option seller to significant tail risk.

There are many combinations of different trades managers can make to execute this strategy. Many involve more than just the purchase or selling of one option. Volatility Arbitrage managers can be long- or short-biased; however, given the collapse of the volatility in most financial assets in the years 2003–2007, the overwhelming majority of funds that have been successful in the space have been sellers of volatility, i.e. short-biased.

Short-bias strategies rely on selling options and collecting the premium for those options to make returns in general. The option seller is earning the time decay in the form of 'theta' as time passes and the option premium is essentially amortized to option expiration. The option seller hedges by using the underlying to hedge the delta of the options to the underlying in order to isolate the implied volatility and collect the premium of the option over time without being exposed to movement in the underlying directly (although shorting options exposes the seller to 'negative gamma' where dynamic delta hedging can lock in losses as the price of the underlying moves – in short, maintaining delta neutrality in a short option is a negative return driver). For the strategy to be profitable, combined premium collection must be greater than combined gamma losses and possible increases in (implied) volatility.

Long bias strategies rely on holding options long and delta hedging with the underlying to maintain delta neutrality in general as well. The strategy makes money by holding options that increase in value as implied volatility increases; it also collects 'positive gamma' from dynamically hedging the delta since it is always long the convexity of the delta profile (buying low, selling high to stay delta neutral as the price of the underlying moves). The negative return driver is the theta, or option premium decay which the option seller collects. This is a negative return driver as over time the option premium erodes and the value of the option decreases. For this strategy to be profitable, combined gains on increasing implied volatility, as well as gains from gamma trading, must be greater than the theta decay in the portfolio over time.

The decision-making process that drives the mix of trades is usually supported by quantitative models. Option valuation and volatility forecasting models are the key edge of most Volatility Arbitrage managers. Volatility forecasting has become an important discipline, which has quickly moved from academia to Wall Street in recent years. The literature offers a rich universe of methods.[31]

3.8   RELATIVE VALUE – CAPITAL STRUCTURE ARBITRAGE

Capital Structure Arbitrage involves taking long and short positions in different financial instruments within the capital structure of an individual company (thus the name), particularly between a company's debt, represented by credit spreads or its proxy credit default swap (CDS), and equity issues, sometimes also involving implied equity volatility skew. The idea behind the strategy is to benefit from relative discrepancies in movements of the equity and bond prices, in other words arbitraging pricing inefficiencies on the right-hand side of the issuer's balance sheet. The strategy allows the manager to rely somewhat on forecast relationships between bonds within the same capital structure given a fundamental view of the company and its credit quality to construct portfolio positions that will pay off if these relationships are forecasted correctly. The strategy constitutes a relatively new area within the hedge fund universe and offers an example of how quickly and dynamically new strategies emerge with the creation of new types of instruments and hedging techniques. Capital Structure Arbitrage was made possible by the development of a liquid credit derivatives market.

Investors have known for years of the axiomatic relationship between price movement in equities and bonds of non-credit-risk-free issuers. Debt investors effectively sell issuers a

---

[31] For a good overview, see J. Hull, *Options, Futures, and other Derivatives*, 4th edition, Prentice Hall (1999), Chapter 13. The ARCH/GARCH approach is well covered in the review paper: T. Bollerslev *et al.*, 'Arch modelling in finance,' *Journal of Econometrics* (1992).

put option on their own stock.[32] The Capital Structure Arbitrage strategy manager analyzes in depth the relationship between the price and volatility of a company's stock and the credit risk of its bonds. Alternatively, the Capital Structure Arbitrage manager analyzes the relationship between different tranches of the company's debt, such as senior versus junior. In some instances, Capital Structure Arbitrage managers also examine the relationship between credit spreads of the issuer's bonds (as they express themselves in credit default swap rates) and the implied volatility surface (also called the volatility skew) of the options on the issuer's stock.

Especially in times of high volatility and falling stock markets equity and bond prices do not always move in tandem as theory suggests. Shareholders are often slower than bondholders to assess the implications of a company's debt burden and widening credit spreads. So there can be time lags between the movement of companies bonds and the corresponding movement in the stock. Capital Structure Arbitrage hedge fund managers employ quantitative credit and equity option valuation models to detect these pricing anomalies.

The recent development of mature and liquid credit default markets, such as the market for credit derivatives, has enabled hedge fund managers and proprietary traders expert in managing credit risk to extend their trades across asset classes to create debt–equity trading. The pioneers of Capital Structure Arbitrage have been the Convertible Arbitrage managers – leveraging their expertise in convertible bonds, which are a debt–equity hybrid product. Since Convertible Arbitrage managers are interested in the equity volatility, they would aim to hedge out the debt component.

Since the late 1990s, credit derivatives have entered the mainstream of global structured finance as tools in asset securitization and credit risk management. As the Convertible Arbitrage managers moved deeper into credit analysis of the stock, they were better able to hedge credit risk with credit default swaps. The hedging allowed them to extend their focus into the relationship between the implied volatility surface of the stock and credit spreads. Many Capital Structure Arbitrage managers who have been or are still also Convertible Arbitrage managers execute a combination of both strategies. Today single name credit default swaps (CDS) are the most widely used instrument among Capital Structure Arbitrage hedge funds.

Here are five simple examples of Capital Structure Arbitrage trades:

(1) Buying the bond of the issuer and short selling the stock.
(2) Selling the bond of the issuer and buying the stock.
(3) Going short on a credit default swap by selling protection and buying a put on the stock.
(4) Going long on a credit default swap by buying protection and going short a put on the stock.
(5) Long one bond issue (e.g. a junior debt tranche) and short another bond tranche (e.g. a senior debt tranche).

---

[32] See the seminal paper by R. Merton, 'On the price of corporate debt: the risk structure of interest rates' (1974). For more recent work, see the paper by F. Longstaff and E. Schwartz, 'A simple approach to valuing risky fixed and floating rate debt' (1998). There are several credit risk analysis tools commercially available today, see also the description in L. Jaeger *Risk Management in Alternative Investment Strategies* (2002), Chapter 6. For one of the most widely used commercial credit analysis tools, see C. Finger (ed.) 'CreditGrades – technical document' (2002), available on the web page of RiskMetrics's CreditGrades (www.creditgrades.com).

In the third example the manager would buy low volatility in the credit market and sell high volatility in the equity markets. Conversely, if the manager judges the implied volatility in the equity market as too low compared to the credit risk, she would do the inverse trade.

The details of Capital Structure Arbitrage strategies can be quite complex. A wide variety of instruments, including equity options and default credit swaps, are available to the hedge fund manager in addition to the underlying bond and stock. But the general principle is simple. Capital Structure Arbitrage managers derive the theoretical relationship between the credit default swap rates of the issuer and the implied volatility smile curve from equity options on the company's stock from their detailed knowledge of the firm's leverage structure. Where they find discrepancies between the theoretical and actual relationships, they treat them as mispricings and trade to take advantage of them.

The returns of Capital Structure Arbitrage are a direct function of the manager's skill to detect mispricings in the credit or volatility characteristics of individual issuers. However, as with Convertible Arbitrage, I argue that the complexity of Capital Structure Arbitrage is itself a form of risk. This risk expresses itself to the hedge fund manager in the form of model risk and mark-to-market risks. Thus the Convertible Structure Arbitrage strategy has inherent returns, which are not always necessarily related to pricing inefficiencies, but are actually risk premia. By taking on the complexity risk, Convertible Structure Arbitrage managers provide liquidity and facilitate the price discovery process. This provides other market agents with access to fair valuations. Hedge funds expect a positive expected return for that. In fact, hedge funds have become an important stabilizing factor in the credit market.[33] The resulting benefits are obvious. Especially in times of increased equity volatility, price transparency and fair value prices are important to the market participants, including the issuer (it is mostly the hedge funds that bought the troubled assets off the investment banks' balance sheet during the credit crisis in 2007/208). Generally, issuing debt in a more liquid and price-transparent market provides companies with better options to raise capital and thereby reduces their cost of capital.

3.9 EVENT DRIVEN – GENERAL

There is admittedly some inconsistency in the hedge fund industry's classification of 'Event Driven' strategies. While this sector has in the past mostly consisted of Merger Arbitrage strategies, hedge fund managers have now engaged in a variety of investment strategies around 'events'. The strategy class 'Event Driven' therefore consists broadly of strategies in which hedge fund managers assemble a portfolio of mostly equity securities that are affected by (company-specific) events that materially impact their valuation. Due to the idiosyncratic nature of the event, the positions in the portfolio have little correlation with each other. Returns are generated by assessing (a) probabilities of the outcomes in an event (e.g. the likelihood of the closing of a merger transaction) and (b) by evaluating the impact on the value of the securities affected by the event. Based on this analysis, the Event Driven manager takes positions in securities she sees as undervalued or overvalued, either outright or relative to each other. Risks that are not related to the event, such as broad market risk, are hedged when appropriate.

---

[33] See N. Patel, 'Flow business booms: credit derivative survey' (2003).

The following provides a non-exhaustive list of investment strategies with Event Driven hedge funds:

- Cash takeovers and stock for stock mergers (Merger Arbitrage): This involves buying the stock of the acquisition target and, if the transaction is a stock deal, at the same time shorting the bidding company's stock.
- Divestments, spin-offs, special dividends, re-financings: These types of transactions often create temporary mispricings, e.g. because existing investors sell the shares spin-off (thereby temporarily depressing the price) or because the value released through a potential divestment is not adequately reflected in the share price of the selling company.
- Litigation plays: The uncertainty around the outcome and impact of a legal case (e.g. a bankruptcy under Chapter 11) and the unfamiliarity of most investors in assessing such a situation creates profit opportunities for the manager trading around such events.
- Post-bankruptcy: Companies emerging out of bankruptcy often offer interesting investment opportunities, as they come with a 'cleaner' balance sheet and a more clearly defined business plan. Further, many investors avoid buying post-bankruptcy stocks for reasons of reputation. Academic studies have shown that companies emerging out of Chapter 11 proceedings significantly outperform the broad market.[34]
- Index events: Changes in the index composition trigger buying or selling by passive money managers irrespective of the underlying asset, which often creates a temporary price shift of the affected securities, which the manager can profitably exploit.
- Holding company and share class arbitrage: This involves buying the shares of a holding company and simultaneously selling the shares of its assets (or vice versa). Similarly, share class arbitrage involves buying and selling different share classes of the same company. One particular example is listed holding companies whose main assets are exchange listed as well, which often trade at a discount to the value of their assets due to corporate governance, liquidity, and tax concerns.
- Activists: This more recently popularized class of hedge funds consist of managers that take significant positions in individual stocks with the aim to directly influence the management of the firm. The goal hereby is to unlock what the manager perceives to be hidden shareholder value. The influence the hedge fund manager is trying to take can cover a rather broad spectrum of measures ranging from 'open letters' to management urging for changes in the capital structure of the firm or requests for higher dividend payouts to gaining a majority in the shareholder assembly to direct the strategic focus or the composition of management in their favor. It has been the spectacular success of a few 'activist hedge funds' in blocking steps foreseen by management (such as the purchase of another company) or in directly ousting management that in the recent past have given activist managers a rather prominent stage in the popular press (such as 'TCI' or 'Atticus Capital' in Deutsche Börse's plans to buy the London Stock Exchange).

The main Event Driven strategies are discussed in the following sections. I would like to note that the Event Driven sector has changed considerably in recent years with hedge funds emerging into domains that traditionally have been the turf of private equity and private debt

---

[34] See the paper by A. Eberhardt, E. Altman and R. Aggarwal, 'The equity performance of firms emerging out of bankruptcy' (1999), and the paper by A. Davis and X. Huang, 'The stock performance of firms emerging from Chapter 11 and accidental bankruptcy' (2004).

players such as buyout transactions, senior bank loans, mezzanine transactions, etc. The 'hedge fund/private equity convergence' has thus been subject to some public debate.

3.10   EVENT DRIVEN – MERGER ARBITRAGE

The most prominent Event Driven strategy is Merger Arbitrage, also known as Risk Arbitrage. This strategy involves investing in securities of companies subject to some form of extraordinary corporate transaction. These transactions include acquisition or merger proposals, exchange offers, cash tender offers and leveraged buy-outs. A merger generally involves the exchange of securities for cash, other securities or a combination of cash and other securities.[35] The two basic types of merger offers are a 'cash tender offer', where a fixed amount of cash is offered for the acquired company's stock, and a 'stock swap', where stock of the acquiring company is being offered at a fixed ratio in exchange for the stock of the acquired company. More complex merger transactions may base the exchange ratio on the price of the acquiring company's stock when the deal is closed, or allow the target firm to call off the merger if the acquirer's stock falls below a certain value. Typically, Risk Arbitrage managers purchase the stock of a company being acquired or merging with another company. If the transaction is not a pure cash deal, Risk Arbitrage managers also sell short the stock of the acquiring company. The attractiveness of the Merger Arbitrage strategy comes from the fact that tender offers for a merger are usually made at a significant premium to the pre-announcement share price. During the negotiations of a merger the target company's stock typically trades at a discount to the announced value of the merger transaction, as there remains a residual 'deal risk' that the merger will fail and the stock price will drop back to the original pre-announcement level. Risk Arbitrage managers differ in the amount of deal risk they are willing to take as well as the level of leverage and diversification employed. Most managers only invest in announced transactions. Managers also often specialize in particular sectors or geographic locations.

Figure 3.9 exemplifies the evolution of the two company's relative stock prices in a successful merger situation. Hedge funds derive profits upon realizing the differential or 'spread' between the price paid upon entering the positions and the value ultimately received when the deal is consummated. In mergers, acquisitions and other corporate transactions the market is generally not completely information-efficient. As information is very specific and difficult to obtain, those situations offer opportunities to investors knowledgeable about the specific features of a deal. The experienced manager usually translates the spread into an annualized return, estimates the probability that the deal will be completed, and then gauges the risks of the particular deal against its return. She invests in deals that offer sufficient compensation for the estimated risk of the transaction failing.

However, despite the value of information in merger transactions the inherent return of Risk Arbitrage strategies is the risk premium for taking exposure in deals with uncertain closing. This is referred to as the 'deal risk premium'. The Merger Arbitrage manager assumes the risk that the deal fails in which case the manager assumes large losses. In other words, Risk Arbitrage positions are bets on the completion of merger transactions. The strategy's principal risk factor is 'deal risk', which includes everything that affects the deal's completion or the timing of its completion. These deal risk components include the risk of the acquirer getting

---

[35] In the book, *Deals, deals, and more deals*, by R. Pitaro, there are many examples of historical merger transactions. The book also offers an in-depth discussion of Risk Arbitrage strategies.

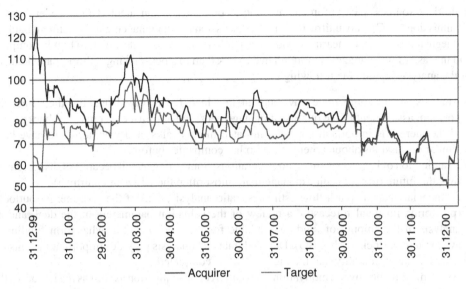

Figure 3.9 Illustration of the evolution of the two company's stock prices in a successful merger situation

out of the deal, the risk that shareholders will not approve the deal, the risk of federal or state regulators rejecting the deal. Translating the payoff profile of a typical merger arbitrage position reveals that the risk profile of a typical Risk Arbitrage position is comparable to a short position in a put option on the close of the deal. The manager receives a more or less predetermined risk premium for entering the position in return for accepting the risk of significant losses if the merger fails. The downside if the merger fails is large compared to the expected return if the merger succeeds. Although the premium paid by the acquirer in a merger deal may be quite large, the spread that remains between market price and offer price after the announcement of the deal is much smaller. While existing shareholders can expect a bonus in the difference between pre-announcement and offer prices, the spread available to Risk Arbitrage managers immediately narrows at the announcement to an amount that represents only the 'deal risk' premium.

Mitchel and Pulvino[36] provided interesting insights into the risk premium return sources of Merger Arbitrage hedge funds, when they constructed the historical performance of a rule-based merger arbitrage strategy. They back-tested a strategy that invests in all stock for stock and cash deals (long acquiree and short acquirer) with a prespecified entry and exit strategy. Their analysis was based on 4750 merger transactions from 1963 to 1998. The resulting simulated return for this strategy has similar characteristics to the returns of most Merger Arbitrage hedge funds. Their paper is the best quantification of the inherent return potential of the Merger Arbitrage strategy based on the deal risk premium available in merger transactions.

A successful Risk Arbitrage manager relies on solid fundamental research of the involved companies and the issues surrounding the deal. Information sources are stock market valuation,

---

[36] M. Mitchel, T., Pulvino, 'Characteristics of risk in risk arbitrage' (2001).

trade data sources, past enforcement policies of justice department (DOJ), Federal Trade Commission (FTC), and antitrust agencies, discussions with management, investment bankers and legal advisors, court hearings, and press publications. The deals are often highly complex, and the task of the manager is more related to risk than to stock-picking.[37] Important elements of the analysis include the following,

- Analysis of the competitive environment in which the involved operate, their financial position, assessment of the quality of management, and antitrust concerns. The background of the merger is important, e.g. who initiated merger talks, and whether there have been similar discussions about a merger with other companies before.
- Examination of key management considerations. Some mergers fail because of disagreement over the future roles of senior management (most often the CEOs or chairmen).
- A financial analysis (cash flow estimates, ratio analysis, etc.) of the post-merger outlooks (pro-forma financial forecasts), a review of the valuation parameters in the deal, and an analysis of the amount of funding available for the merger and in what form funding is available (e.g. stock, cash, LBO). Detailed financial analysis provides important insights for assessing the probability that the merger will be completed.
- Assessment of the buyer's motivation for the merger or acquisition as well as the impact of the contemplated transaction on his reputation, competitive position and financial performance. This includes the strategic rationale of the transaction. The merging companies should realize valuable strategic opportunities, such as geographic, product, or distribution expansion, new technological integration or applications, significant cost savings, or other synergies. A review of the buyer's past acquisition history might provide interesting insights.
- Evaluation of potential material adverse business developments at the target company which might undermine the proposed transaction. Most uncompleted mergers fail because the target company's situation deteriorates unexpectedly.
- Assessment of the efficiency of any anti-takeover devices available to the target company (poison pills, golden parachutes, etc.), if the takeover bid is hostile.
- Calculation of the spread on the deal. The spread is the difference between the price offered for the acquired company and the current market price. Based on the spread, the manager calculates the expected return upon closure of the deal.
- Examination of merger conditions. The terms of the transaction can contain conditions which may significantly impact the likelihood of the transaction completing and which therefore must be carefully assessed. Such conditions may include walk-away clauses, price provisions related to the acquirer's stock, financing contingencies, earnings tests, pending completion of due diligence, minimum shares to vote in favor of the merger, revenue or profit hurdles, or possible debt covenants.
- Estimation and constant monitoring of the likelihood of regulatory interference with the deal and the likely outcome of such. Different regulatory agencies have to be considered (from the perspective of a US merger): Federal Trade Commission (FTC)/Justice Department, SEC (must approve merger proxies), individual states, specific industry (banks: Federal Reserve; utilities: Federal Energy Regulatory Commission; communication: Federal Communications Commission), and foreign regulatory agencies (e.g. EU, specific countries).

---

[37] A thorough description of the different aspects of the Risk Arbitrage strategy is provided in *Risk Arbitrage: An Investor's Guide*, by K. M. Moore (1999).

- Time to completion. A time delay in the completion of the deal can significantly reduce the expected return.

A transaction can founder for a wide range of reasons, Some of the common deal-breakers are failure to achieve the required shareholder approval, lack of agreement between senior managers, negative earnings news from the target company, and a large decline in the stock price of the acquiring company. Along with an assessment of the probability of a transaction failing, the hedge fund manager must estimate the impact on the stock prices. The price of the target company's stock before the deal announcement can serve as a general guide as to where stock prices might go in case the deal does not go through. However, managers often find it appropriate to apply a discount to the pre-announcement stock price for the target company. Fundamental issues such as earning revisions of the target company can not only derail the deal, they can also drive the market value down below pre-merger-announcement level.

3.11   EVENT DRIVEN – DISTRESSED SECURITIES

Distressed Security strategies invest in or (on less frequent occasions) sell short securities of companies that have been, or are expected to be, in financial trouble. The uncertainty around the outcome and impact of the financial and legal issues surrounding a distress and the unfamiliarity of most investors in assessing such a situation creates opportunities for the knowledgeable investor to trade around such events. A company may fall into distress for any number of the following reasons: liquidity problems, operational or strategic shortcomings, changes in the competitive marketplace, legal or regulatory difficulties. Distressed Securities hedge fund managers invest in a number of different instruments, such as bank debt, bonds, subordinated debt, trade claims, letters of credit, common stock, preferred stock, or warrants. There may also be opportunities to buy specific assets being spun off by distressed companies who need to raise cash.

While the level of interest in distressed securities has increased over the years, the market remains relatively illiquid. Many private and institutional investors are unwilling to hold distressed securities in their books. For years distressed investing was seen as a 'dirty' business because investors attempt to profit from others' misfortune. However, Distressed Securities investors have begun to lose their 'vulture' image, as many institutions have come to see the benefits of an active secondary market for distressed debt. In particular, a more active secondary market for distressed debt significantly contributes to reintegrating troubled companies back into the economic cycle and thus reducing the financial 'cost of failure'. It has also facilitated the issuance of debt for companies with less strong balance sheets.

Investing in distressed securities requires specialist expertise and extensive pre-investment analysis in order to allow accurate assessment of the impact of restructuring negotiations and/or bankruptcy proceedings on the value of a company and its underlying securities. The investment process for Distressed Securities requires bottom-up fundamental research and analytical work. Managers generally take a core position in a distressed company's securities and hold it throughout the restructuring or bankruptcy process. The industry distinguishes between managers who participate actively in creditor committees and assist the recovery or reorganization process, and 'passive managers' who buy and hold distressed securities until they appreciate to the desired level. Some strategies are particularly focused on short-term trading in anticipation of specific events, such as the outcome of a court ruling or important negotiations. Managers may use some leverage, but generally the level of leverage is fairly low. Another form of Distressed Securities strategy is 'Capital Structure Arbitrage'-like, where the manager purchases the undervalued securities and sells the overpriced securities of the same firm, e.g. long mezzanine debt and short common stock. Fund managers may run a market hedge using S&P put options or put options spreads. Distressed Securities fund managers can benefit substantially from creative financial engineering.

Distressed Securities managers are confronted with a variety of legal questions, which become particularly important once insolvency procedures or litigation are initiated. Chapter 11 of the US bankruptcy law provides relief from creditor claims for companies in financial distress in order to allow for an orderly restructuring process. The objective is to save distressed companies from liquidation. In Europe and most other countries, though, bankruptcy laws are less debtor-friendly, so the chances of a company surviving as a going concern are reduced and sometimes eliminated. Important issues in the restructuring process are debt-restructuring practices and laws, ranking of creditor claims (particularly employee and tax claims), disclosure policies, voting rights of creditors, debt terms, and the treatment of secured claims. Distressed companies also often face lawsuits or legal threats that could significantly impact the company's financial position. The 'workout' process requires legal expertise and the navigation of legal pitfalls.

Examples of investment opportunities in distressed investments include the following.

- Anticipated restructuring. A corporate restructuring event caused by financial problems is pending. This can be the announcement of a restructuring plan, a change in management or the board, a refinancing, or even a merger/acquisition. Often the restructuring event will lead to a significant change in the management of assets and allocation of capital. Careful analysis may identify post-restructure value that is not yet reflected in the price of the company's securities.
- Chapter 11 reorganizations. The final stages of bankruptcy reorganizations may create attractive investment opportunities. The securities of companies undergoing Chapter 11 reorganizations are often under-followed by Wall Street analysts and may trade at depressed valuations versus the firm's fundamental value.
- Legal/regulatory overhang. Legal or regulatory issues which are not fully understood may depress the valuation of the securities to values below their fundamental fair value.
- Corporate restructurings/spin-offs/divestments/refinancings. These types of transactions often create temporary mispricings because existing investors often sell the shares of a spin-off (thereby temporarily depressing the price), or because the value released through a potential divestment is not adequately reflected in the share price of the selling company. Often the volatility created by such events creates additional return potential which can, for example, be exploited through selling options. An investor may provide buy-out capital in the form of equity or debt for privatizations (leveraged buy-outs from management), spin-offs, acquisitions or takeovers. Significant changes in the management of assets and allocation of capital tend to amplify and accelerate positive financial trends.

Returns of Distressed Securities strategies strongly depend on the skill and experience of the individual manager. There are many un- or under-researched and attractive investment opportunities, as there are generally only a limited number of analysts looking at such situations. The market for distressed securities is clearly not as efficient as the market for public equity, G10 government bonds, or the major currencies, and managers thus have the opportunity to

capitalize on restricted availability and flow of information. Due to the limited market efficiency the potential for generating excess return is high for Distressed Securities managers
compared to other hedge fund managers. Nevertheless, investing in distressed debt also comes
with exposure to systematic risk, specifically credit and bankruptcy risks, i.e. a part of Distressed Securities managers' return is also related to risk premia. It is therefore not surprising
that the strategy underperformed other hedge fund strategies in the period between 2000 and
2002 when conditions in the credit markets deteriorated, while it showed strong performance
in the period 2004–2007 when credit spreads narrowed significantly. In environments of falling
equity markets, rising interest rates, and widening credit spreads, the performance of distressed
securities investment is highly correlated to the broader market.

Another factor is that investments in Distressed Securities strategies are generally very
illiquid. The investor has to commit invested capital for a longer period of time and might
suffer significant losses if she redeems prematurely. The termination date of the investment is
not known in advance, as the length of bankruptcy proceedings is by nature very long. The
restructuring negotiations for moving out of bankruptcy and their outcome are very uncertain.
There is often no regular market for the security, and the positions are extremely difficult
to value. This lack of liquidity as well as the uncertainty about future cash flows leads the
investor to demand additional liquidity premia. In this respect Distressed Securities hedge
fund investments have similar characteristics to private equity, in particular to venture capital
investments.

3.12   EVENT DRIVEN – REGULATION D

Regulation D ('Reg D') strategies involve investing in publicly listed companies, mostly of
micro and small capitalization, in need of capital through privately negotiated structures. When
public companies need to raise capital, they basically have three alternatives: (1) debt issuance;
(2) secondary offerings; (3) private equity placements pursuant to Regulation D. Each of the
former two alternatives has certain requirements which make access to the capital a difficult and
time-consuming process. Encumbrances include limited borrowing capacity, high expenses
in the case of a secondary offering, and time constraints. These factors, along with other
more subjective issues, lead some companies to pursue the third option, which allows smaller
companies to raise equity capital more quickly, cheaply, and conveniently. The manager and
the company usually negotiate the investment, which can take the form of stocks, convertibles
or other derivatives (options, warrants) in return for an injection of capital. Most often the
investment is structured in the form of privately placed unregistered high-coupon convertible
security or debenture with maturities ranging anywhere from 18 to 60 months. These can, upon
registration with the SEC, partially or entirely be converted into ordinary shares of the issuer,
which usually happens at a predefined discounted price agreed between investor and issuer.
Investments are made pursuant to an exemption from registration as provided by Regulation
D of the US SEC Act of 1933. Normally after a few weeks or months, the SEC declares the
registration of the convertible securities effective. The Regulation D manager can then sell
the fully tradeable and registered shares in the public markets and realize the spread between
the market price and the discounted price of the stock she converts into (anywhere around
15–40%, depending on the riskiness of the deal) as a return. Unlike standard convertible bonds
or preferred equity, the exercise price can be floating at a predefined discount or subject to a
look-back provision. A floating price has the effect of insulating the investor from a decline

in the price of the underlying stock. Investments are therefore fully price-hedged. In some cases the manager also receives warrants on top of the debenture. The Convertible Debenture Arbitrage strategy can be seen as Convertible Arbitrage with privately structured debentures.

3.13   OPPORTUNISTIC – GLOBAL MACRO[38]

Another word for 'opportunistic strategies' is 'tactical trading'. Tactical trading refers in general to investment strategies with a variable exposure to the broad liquid asset classes (equity, bonds, currencies, commodities). The Global Macro strategy consists of trading interest rates securities, currencies, commodities, and equity based on the manager's anticipation of price movements in the global capital markets. Global Macro managers employ fundamental analysis (micro- and macroeconomic indicators) and/or technical indicators (such as trends and patterns in recent prices) to analyze conditions that shift global supply and demand in particular segments of the financial markets. They are often described as moving 'from opportunity to opportunity, from trend to trend, and from strategy to strategy'.[39]

Figure 3.10 shows the correlations of the Global Macro Index by Hedge Fund Research to a set of common risk factors in the form of a cobweb chart. The chart confirms a broad exposure to various risks/asset classes across the global capital markets and a general tendency to be long volatility.

The fundamental models managers use range from relative value to leading indicators, capital flow models, and scenario analysis, and more.[40] We note that the borderline between fixed income related Global Macro and Fixed Income Arbitrage is ambiguous, as many Global Macro managers employ a variety of fixed income instruments with varying degrees of hedging and eliminating directionality. Here are a few of the more common forms of analysis Global Macro managers perform in their trading:

- Bond carry analysis, using the yield difference between long duration bonds and shorter-dated instruments.
- Yield-curve relative value analysis, such as identifying undervalued and overvalued parts of the yield curves or evaluating the slope of one yield curve against the slope of another (e.g. the swap curve against the treasury yield curve).
- Analysis of interest rate differentials on currency (carries). Using the potential profits from a carry trade to predict future exchange rates.
- Purchasing power parity. For example, analyzing currencies based on the domestic purchasing power.
- Equity valuations models, such as the dividend discount model for trading relative equity market valuations.
- Leading indicators analysis, using indicators such as changes in unemployment or growth forecasts to analyze, for example, fixed income instruments.

---

[38] The following research paper elaborates on this section in much greater detail: R. Cagnati, 'PG hedge fund strategy paper – Global Macro', Partners Group Research (May 2006).

[39] M. Strome in *Evaluating and Implementing Hedge Fund Strategies*, R. Lake (ed.), Euromoney Books, 1996; J, Mauldin, *Analysing Global Macro Funds*, Millennium Wave Investments (2005).

[40] See P. Säfvenblad, 'Global Macro and Managed Futures strategies' in L. Jaeger (ed.), *The New Generation of Risk Management for Hedge Funds and Private Equity Investment* (2003).

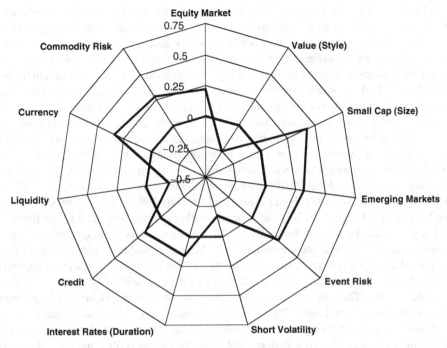

Figure 3.10   Cobweb of risk exposures for Global Macro hedge fund strategies

Equally, the transition from Global Macro to Global Equity Long/Short is continuous, as some Global Macro managers seek out opportunities in the global equity markets.

Traditionally, Global Macro strategies were associated with large multi-billion-dollar hedge funds of the like of George Soros's Quantum fund and Julian Robertson's Tiger fund, which made highly leveraged bets with assets large enough to have an impact on the outcome of their trades. The most prominent example of such a bet was Soros's run against the British pound in 1992.[41] However, many of these 'old school' Global Macro funds suffered a series of losses during the Russia crisis, the sudden end of the yen carry trade in 1998, and the burst of the TMT bubble in 2000.[42] The reasons are manifold but can be related to rather commonsense reasoning: the big-name macro managers simply grew too big; the influx capital forced managers to focus on highly liquid (and efficient) markets, where their edge was smaller. Today there is increased competition for the returns from such simple approaches as currency carry trades or trend following. Further, the introduction of the euro currency reduced the number of liquid bond and currency markets drastically; it further meant the end of the 'easy' and profitable convergence trades based on the introduction of the common currency

---

[41] In the paper 'Measuring the market impact of hedge funds', W. Fung and D. Hsieh examined the role of hedge funds during market turbulences of the 1990s.

[42] Ironically, in the case of J. Robertson's 'Tiger' fund, after he had incurred losses due to a 'long value, short growth' approach and having to close his fund in the final phase of the Nasdaq bubble, the markets turned strongly in Robertson's favor almost at the same time as he made the announcement proving his prediction correct that 'a Ponzi pyramid is destined for collapse'.

(1993–1999). And finally due to spectacular returns on the equity markets, managers were under pressure to deliver stellar returns in each and every calendar year. Managers tried to compensate for this and the smaller opportunity set by taking bigger risks. This, combined with virtually no risk management/control, for most managers can easily spell disaster. Risk management was covered by the manager having invested all his personal net worth in the funds ('I feel the pain in the stomach' approach). Managers had a '007 license' to opportunistically invest across global markets ('cowboy mentality'). These reasons, combined with the lower risk tolerance of a changing investor base, have changed the characteristics of Global Macro trading in the last few years towards tighter risk control and more stable return patterns. Global Macro managers today prefer to have a 'bought option' profile (see the cobweb chart of Figure 3.10). A number of managers reacted to the shrunken opportunities in FX and sovereigns by moving into credit and ABS/MBS markets or increasing their focus on sectors/industries rather than countries. The assets held by huge multi-billion-dollar discretionary Global Macro funds have been outstripped by those of a larger number of relatively small hedge funds.

A key distinction between different Global Macro managers is the degree of discretionary versus systematic trading techniques employed.[43] Managers trading in a discretionary framework typically employ a large number of different trading strategies or analytical approaches and shift flexibly between them. Style drift can therefore be said to be 'built in' to Global Macro hedge funds. They often borrow techniques from other strategies, such as Fixed Income Arbitrage and Long-Short Equity. The large discretionary Global Macro hedge funds are actually often set up as umbrella organizations with independent trading desks, each pursuing their own trading within an overall risk budget. Global Macro managers often have a background as traders at the proprietary trading desks of investment banks or as macro investment strategists of the same. Systematic managers on the other hand use well-defined trading models and focus their efforts on optimizing those. Examples of these models include trend following and counter-trend models, currency carry models, and global tactical asset allocation programs ('GTAA'). Systematic Global Macro strategies strongly overlap with Managed Futures program to the point where the distinction becomes quite blurry. Therefore they are now often discussed in the same framework.

Compared to fund managers who pick from a large universe of individual securities, Global Macro managers are actually restricted to a quite limited number of markets. They trade in the yield curve, currency, and equity markets of around a dozen countries, but have a great deal of freedom in selecting instruments for a particular trade. These are today relatively efficient markets with few arbitrage opportunities. However, even these markets may not be completely efficient all the time. Arbitrage opportunities can arise from slow information flow, behavioral biases of investors, or regulatory constraints. Successful Global Macro managers earn returns for having access to better information or by their ability to analyze existing information more accurately than others. They aim to benefit from short-run price deviations from true economic equilibrium, before all available information is correctly discounted. These deviations occur because information is not a free good. Investors must spend time and resources to acquire and properly interpret new data. New information is incorporated gradually rather than instantaneously into market prices. Most market participants tend to focus on headline reports, which reduce the market's collective ability to analyze data correctly. A lot of these headline

---

[43] This distinction is further elaborated in 'The case for hedge funds', Tremont, Partners, Inc. and TASS Investment Research, Inc., 1999.

reports are survey-based (ISM Purchasing Managers Index, Tankan Report) which are being revised afterwards; hard economic data are usually released only with a time lag. Further, increased price volatility may cause investors to react emotionally in ways not consistent with a dispassionate analysis of economic factors. This leads to a herd mentality: investors tend to over-generalize in certain situations, which creates opportunities for Global Macro strategies. For example: the Russian default in 1998 led to a 'flight to quality' and withdrawal of capital from emerging markets, regardless of the specific situation of a country (Brazil was a very vulnerable economy at the time compared to Chile, which had rock solid fundamentals). Further, non-profit-maximizing market participants such as central banks knowledgeably deviate from an optimal investment strategy (e.g. interest rate convergence before the introduction of the euro or opportunities after Argentinian peso devaluation). Finally, trade restrictions (e.g. currency regimes) can prohibit prices from moving to their real economic value. One goal of Global Macro strategies assumes that prices will sooner or later converge to levels consistent with investor rationality as determined by economic fundamental factors. Global Macro managers work to identify long-term macro-economic trends that determine that fair value, and trade when prices deviate substantially from what the manager judges that value to be.

However Global Macro strategies show significant correlations to the global capital markets' systematic risk factors, in particular the bond and currency markets. Strong bond markets provide Global Macro managers of all types with strong returns, and, vice versa, sudden reversals in bond prices lead Global Macro managers to incur losses. The term 'structure risk premium' can therefore be easily identified as a main part of Global Macro managers' return source. Another systematic source of returns is the foreign exchange risk premium, which is exploited in 'carry trades': investing in high-yield currencies financed by borrowing in a low-yield currency yields a static return in the form of the interest rate differential, which is nothing but a risk premium for assuming exposure to unexpected exchange rate movements. Unlike many other hedge fund strategies, Global Macro strategies bear little exposure to liquidity and credit risk.

Criteria for classifying Global Macro hedge fund managers into categories can be manifold due to the heterogeneity of the strategy sector. A few of them are listed below:

- investment process (discretionary vs. systematic);
- primary asset class focus;
- investment approach (top-down vs. bottom-up);
- amount of directionality (hedged vs. directional);
- degree of diversification (concentrated/theme based/diversified);
- time horizon (short-term vs. long-term oriented);
- liquidity.

Acknowledging the difficulty in bringing an order into the opaque and heterogeneous spectrum of Global Macro hedge fund managers we can break the sector down into 10 sub-strategy buckets. Table 3.2 classifies the sub-strategies according to investment process and primary asset class focus. Note that the blank strategy areas in the table virtually do not exist (although there are a small number of niche players that pursue such strategies).

The managers falling into the 'Discretionary Global Macro' bucket follow an opportunistic strategy and are the historical successors of the 'old school' Global Macro hedge fund (the kind of managers that used to be referred to as the 'cowboys' in the hedge fund industry). They compete for the 'best favorite trade' on annual industry conferences. Investment decisions

Table 3.2 The Global Macro universe and the primary and secondary market they are acting in

Primary asset class	Investment process	
	Discretionary	Systematic
Equities	Global Long/Short	
Fixed Income	Fixed Income/Trading	
Currencies		FX Strategies
Commodities	Commodities	
Emerging Markets	Emerging Markets/Asia	
Volatility	Volatility	
All	Discretionary Global Macro	Systematic Global Macro/CTAs
	Multi-Strategy	

are taken based on the concept of economic equilibrium (return to the anticipated fair value of asset prices) and not necessarily directly model-based (models/frameworks are used for investment analysis, though). Portfolios are usually concentrated and centered on a small number of investment ideas.

Managers of the category Systematic Global Macro take a model-driven, quantitative investment approach. The investment universe usually covers the most liquid (e.g. G10) currency, bond, and equity index markets. Models are mostly factor-based, using value (in the case of currencies and bonds usually yield), momentum (or flows) or macro-data. From a time frame perspective, the models are designed to capture mid- to long-term trends (e.g. >6 months). Due to their systematic nature, these strategies are sometimes referred to as 'feedback approaches'. The strategy has its roots in the mid-1990s, when big asset managers started to implement the first purely quantitative asset allocation strategies/overlays at Goldman Sachs and like-minded firms.

The FX strategies typically have their roots in currency overlay management or as specialized programs offered by CTAs. Currency Trading strategies are quite similar to Managed Futures strategies (see below) in that they apply similar underlying strategy and trading approaches using currency instruments. Currency strategies include technical trend-following, discretionary trading based on fundamentals, information-based short-term trading, complex option arbitrage, interest rate carry, and cross rate arbitrage. The investment approach is usually implemented via systematic trading models; discretionary currency managers are rather the exception. Generally, systematic currency strategies revolve around three risk premia in the currency space: momentum (trend), carry (yield), and volatility (options).

Commodity managers can be split into two categories: pure commodity players invest only in commodities themselves (futures and forwards); these strategies tend to be systematic (trend-following, mean reversion, fundamental factors), but there are also discretionary players. Commodity-related managers also cover other asset classes than commodities; these are mostly commodity-related stocks, but also currencies (especially AUD, CAD and ZAR) may be part of the strategy. These strategies usually are discretionary/opportunistic.

Managers from the Fixed Income/Trading arena are located somewhere at the borderline between Global Macro and Fixed Income Arbitrage. In contrast to Discretionary Global Macro, these managers focus mostly on bonds/money markets (often currencies are included) and adopt a trading approach (short- to mid-term oriented). The approach usually is not limited to strict 'arbitrage' but typically takes relative value views within and across curves.

Emerging Markets Global Macro managers almost entirely follow a discretionary approach. While the strategy centers around emerging markets, trades may be set up in a way that developed market securities (e.g., bonds, equities) are used as a hedge. Most managers cover multiple asset classes: equities, local and external debt, and currencies. Although there is no explicit commodity exposure, the commodity industry sector plays a big role in the equity markets.

The strategy Global Long/Short has similarities with Equity L/S, but usually has a broader investment universe (not only in terms of regions, but also in terms of investment instruments). In addition to that, managers tend to be more variable with regards to their net exposure to the equity markets. Due to their primarily top-down focus, most managers tend to have less of a 'value' bias than the average Equity L/S fund. Investments are usually centered on themes; the difference from many other Discretionary Global Macro managers is that they drill down one level further, rather than implementing thematic views via sector swaps or equity index futures.

Multi-Strategy managers cover a wide range of strategies and are essentially competitors to funds of hedge funds. While the investment universe is usually not limited, these managers distinguish themselves from others in that strategies are run internally in a segregated way, rather than funds being managed in an integrated framework. In addition to that, the different sub-strategies are often managed by pretty independent persons/teams, rather than a key person having substantial influence over each single strategy.

Although volatility indirectly plays a role for most Global Macro managers, the ones categorized in this sub-strategy are specifically focused on volatility as an asset class. Approaches vary significantly in terms of volatility long/short/no bias and range from arbitrage to directional trading (based on cheap versus expensive volatility).

Even with risk premia determining a large part of their return profile, Global Macro strategies rely heavily on the individual manager's skill. A large part of that skill lies in finding the right 'expression' of a particular trade idea. Based on their market view, Global Macro managers try to select the set of instruments with the best risk–reward ratio for the trade. They specifically aim to reduce the downside risk of a particular trading idea while keeping its full upside intact. For example, managers try to create positions with a strong long option profile using options and stop losses.

3.14 MANAGED FUTURES

Managed Futures strategies, also known as 'CTA' strategies seek returns through taking long and short positions in the global futures markets. Futures and currencies provide cheap and efficient trading opportunities, as usually only a fraction of the margin exposure must be covered by cash. Margin to equity ratios, the relationship between margin and total notional exposure, range from 5% to about 25%. Managers may trade futures in commodities (metals, grains, energy, etc.) or financial securities (fixed income, foreign exchange, and equity indices). The managers are in most cases registered with the National Futures Association (NFA) and the Commodity Futures Trading Commission (CFTC) as 'commodity trading advisors' (CTAs) and 'commodity pool operators' (CPOs). Within the set of Managed Futures strategies, we distinguish between discretionary and systematic strategies. Discretionary Managed

Futures strategies trade on long-term fundamentals and short-term information. They are more or less indistinguishable from Global Macro managers but limit themselves to the global futures markets. Systematic Managed Futures strategies are based on proprietary models with particular trading techniques such as trend following, countertrend trading, or spread trading. Discretionary managers are typically more knowledgeable and éfficient in trading an individual market than systematic managers. But systematic managers make up for their lower efficiency by better diversification across markets and consequently more efficient use of risk capital. A systematic manager can identify a larger number of profitable trading opportunities, although the value of each trade will be lower. This is because systematic analysis allows him to follow and trade in more individual markets, and handle portfolios with more individual positions.

I emphasis that the distinction between Managed Futures and Systematic Global Macro managers has become increasingly blurry, because both evaluate broad macroeconomic information and bet on particular asset moves. Often the distinction disappears entirely (which is why I included CTAs in the Global Macro Table 3.2 above).

3.15 MANAGED FUTURES – SYSTEMATIC

Systematic Managed Futures strategies generate buy and sell decisions from computer models combining various technical factors and indicators. Trading is largely or entirely systematic and is usually executed in highly liquid markets with low transaction costs. Trend following is the dominant trading style within Systematic Managed Futures strategies. The basic trend following trading techniques are quite easy to implement, and a rich literature covers trend-following trading systems.[44] Essentially the manager takes positions corresponding with the current trend, as measured using technical indicators such as momentum, the relative size of moving averages, or breakout indicators. Positions are usually sized inversely to their volatility. The various trend-following programs vary in the dimensions followed; the markets traded, average trade length, and entry/exit rules. Trend followers select markets for liquidity. The time frame, or average time a trend follower stays in a particular position, ranges from a few days to several months. The time frame is built into the model through correspondingly constructed indicators, such as moving averages. There are numerous entry and exit rules, but managers usually take positions according to an identified trend. The manager exits a position typically when a trailing stop-loss or a profit target is hit, or a reversing signal is generated by the model.

Many of the trades executed in a trend-following strategy are unprofitable. Nevertheless, the strategy can generate positive returns because it closes losing positions quickly and stays in profitable positions to let profits run. And although technical strategies may be inefficient in an individual market, they can be efficient overall by trading in many markets. The improved diversification will make up for the inefficiency of trading individual markets. The payoff profile of trend following essentially looks like a 'long straddle' position.[45] The trend-following

---

[44] See, for example, the website www.turtletrader.com, which provides rich information on a particular trend-following technique, so-called 'turtle trading'.

[45] The straddle property of trend following is described by W. Fung and D. Hsieh in 'The risk of hedge fund strategies: theory and evidence from trend followers' (2001).

strategy is now referred to more as 'Systematic Global Macro' because CTAs tend to capture the same successful trades by waiting for price confirmation first.

Excursion: the turtles

In 1984, Richard Dennis and William Eckhardt made a bet whether trading skills could be taught or were based on talent. To settle the dispute, they placed ads in the *New York Times*, hiring a group of 14 inexperienced people with different backgrounds (e.g. actors), whom Dennis taught a basic trend-following trading methodology. Dennis won the bet, as the group of traders earned an average annual compound rate of return of 80% in the 1.5 years afterwards. The turtle trading style is basically long-term trend following, with a significant amount of risk tolerance over the short to mid-term. Many of the 'turtles' became successful investment managers afterwards, among the most prominent today are Jerry Parker (Chesapeake) and Paul Rabar (Rabar Research).

Most systematic trading models have been optimized and back-tested for a number of years on past data. The managers thereby choose the parameters of the model (e.g. the time horizon or the stop-loss limit) such that the model shows optimal performance for certain time periods in the past. This is a dangerous undertaking and bears the risk of over-fitting, also referred to as 'curve fitting'. The real test of a trading model is the 'out-of-sample test', measuring performance on data that the model has never seen before. The more complicated the model and the more parameters are involved, the higher the risk of over-fitting. Simple trend-following models bear less risk of over-fitting than complicated 'nonlinear' modeling approaches that have many different parameters.

The reader can easily verify that trend following is profitable by looking at the out-of-sample performance of simple technical trading rules. Figure 3.11 displays the cumulative performance of the sGFII index, a simple trend-following strategy on 25 different liquid futures markets,[46] which has been calculated since 1990 and has returned approximately 12.7% per annum in the period between 1990 and March 2008.

At first glance, it seems surprising that such a simple trading approach as trend following is profitable at all, given the efficiency of the underlying markets. Managers often claim that the returns of trend-following models are a result of mob psychology. Yet academic research provides no clear support for claims of trend persistence in futures prices.[47] Likewise, managers claim that currency exchange rates exhibit serial correlation. But again, this is not convincingly supported by empirical studies.[48]

Why then do trend-following strategies earn positive returns? The simple answer is that trend following is a way to identify risk premia that are revealed in the time series pattern of market prices. In futures markets, commercial hedgers are in effect offering a risk premium based on their desire to minimize price risk inherent in their business. The hedge fund manager willing to assume the natural price risks of the commercial hedgers earns in return this risk

---

[46] See L. Jaeger *et al.*, 'Case study: the sGFI Futures Index' (Summer 2002), for more details of the underlying trading systems, and on the Bloomberg information system (ticker: sgfii <Index>) for performance updates.

[47] See Chapter 7 of *Investment Analysis and Portfolio Management* by F. Reilly and K. Brown and references therein.

[48] One way of reasoning as to why currency markets should trend is that central banks attempt to smooth foreign exchange rate movements through intervention; see, for example R. Arnott and T. Pham, 'Tactical currency allocation'.

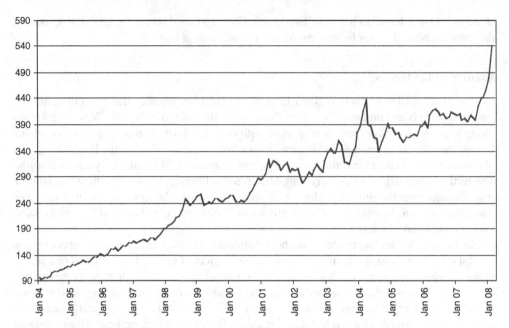

Figure 3.11   Cumulative performance of the sGFII index (see text for details)

premium.[49] It is the speculative agency of the hedge funds that provides the futures markets with the liquidity needed to fulfill their risk transfer function.[50] Evidently, a risk premium implies that trend-following strategies do have a risk. They are especially exposed to losses in nontrending, directionless market environments, which exhibit numerous price reversals ('whip-saw markets').

For most of the 1990s, CTAs had great returns and the predominant philosophy was 'never change a successful system'; adaptive systems were blamed as 'curve-fitting'. As a reaction to mediocre performance and increased competition in the 2000s, most CTAs started to hire big research teams, actively trying to enhance their strategies. CTAs have been taking two main roads of development:

- Enhance trend-following systems by incorporating non-price (fundamental, macro) data (e.g. inventory data for commodity models).
- Diversify the business by adding other strategies outside the futures space into a more multi-strategy type of approach.

---

[49] For historical and regulatory reasons most trend-following traders are limiting themselves to futures markets. There is, however, no reason to believe that trend following would not work in other markets with clear risk premia such as interest rate swaps or options.

[50] Originally, it was J. M. Keynes who articulated the theoretical argument for a risk transfer premium in the futures market. In addition to specifying the theory, however, he also declared that he expected the premium to manifest itself as a consistent downward price bias in the futures relative to spot prices. He termed this postulated price bias 'normal backwardation', see J. M. Keynes, *A Treatise on Money*, Vol. II. New York: Macmillan & Co. (1930).

It seems that the industry motto is more like 'adapt or die' nowadays. Very few managers are merely sticking to their guns and waiting for a better environment.

Other examples of Systematic Managed Futures strategies are:

- Short-term models using counter-trend signals (usually with tight stop losses). Here, the basic setup is the identification of short-term patterns that make price reversals or price continuations more likely. Short-term trading is often related to a market making strategy. As a result, managers in this category often have a 'sold option' return profile, with long periods of relatively stable returns, followed by occasional large losses.
- Trading based on technical pattern recognition (e.g. Elliot waves, Fibonacci numbers). More exotic approaches are based on nonlinear models, neural networks, genetic algorithms, network or other applications of 'artificial intelligence'.
- Taking positions according to the degree to which the asset is trading in contango or backwardation (backwardation means that a contract with a later expiry date trades at a lower price than the one nearest to expiry). This gives an alternative indication of the net direction of commercial hedging activities. A well known argument going back to J. M. Keynes (see footnote 51) is that because of storage costs for commodities, they naturally tend to trade in backwardation and returns should be generated through rolling contracts over time.[51]

Short-term trading is the Managed Futures manager's equivalent to Statistical Arbitrage. Managers with this focus seek to exploit brief price inefficiencies or forecast trend reversals. Short-term Managed Futures is a very trading-intensive strategy with trade lengths from a few hours to a few days. For liquidity reasons, short-term trading strategies can only be meaningfully implemented in the most liquid futures and currency markets.

Since most trend-following managers are fully systematic, manager skill does not manifest itself in daily decisions. Instead manager skill is linked to the building and testing of trading systems: choosing the right markets, time frames, and entry and exit rules. The other major component of manager skill lies in the nearly frictionless execution of the strategy. Each trade in this strategy has a very low expected value. So transaction costs can grind away the returns of a manager who is poor at controlling them, while a more cost-conscious manager executing a very similar model skates frictionlessly to prosperity.

3.16 MANAGED FUTURES – DISCRETIONARY

Most Discretionary Managed Futures managers have a long experience investing in commodity or currency markets. Many were formerly commodity or currency traders, or hedged commercially for banks, oil companies, etc. The discretionary manager's competitive advantage is knowledge of the fundamentals (e.g. worldwide inventory level of a commodity) and ability to anticipate changes in supply and demand affecting commodity prices. By monitoring relevant supply and demand factors, the manager works to identify a state of disequilibrium that has yet to be reflected in the price of the underlying commodity. Factors such as weather, the economics of a particular commodity, government policies, domestic and foreign political and economic events, and changing trade patterns all come into play. Most discretionary managers have and capitalize on fast access to relevant information.

---

[51] A good summary of the arguments for this strategy is provided in the paper by C. Erb and C. Harvey, 'The tactical and strategic value of commodity futures' (2005).

Commodity investing was heavily influenced by the history of Princeton-based Commodities Corporation. The firm was founded in 1969 by Helmut Weymar and Amos Hofstetter. It adopted a combination of a fundamental (a group of traders) and a technical (trend-following) approach. Many successful traders/hedge fund managers (mostly trend-following/commodities related) started their careers at Commodities Corp.: Mike Marcus, Paul Tudor Jones, Bruce Kovner (Caxton), Grenville Craig, Willem Kookyer (Blenheim), Ed Seykota, and Louis Bacon are among the most prominent ones. Commodities Corp. was bought out by Goldman Sachs in 1997.

Examples of Discretionary Managed Futures trades are:

- Directional long-term positions based on fundamental analysis, e.g. in one currency against another, in a particular commodity, in one country or firm's debt, or in a particular equity market sector or country.
- Short-term positions based on particular information flow, e.g. corporate currency-hedging activity, a country's central bank policy, or the inventory management of particularly influential global corporations.
- Cross rate arbitrage, interest rate carry arbitrage, investing in high yield currencies.
- Inter-product spread trade between futures of related commodities, currencies, or fixed income products, e.g. soybean versus soybean oil, euro versus Swiss franc, German Bund versus British gilts.
- Directional volatility positions and other option strategies such as calendar spreads of derivatives with different maturity times.
- Equity sector arbitrage, such as long undervalued sector futures and short overvalued sector futures.
- Convexity trades, for example long Eurodollar futures and short Eurodollar forward.

Similar to Global Macro hedge fund strategies, Discretionary Managed Futures strategies exploit temporary mispricings through faster and better access to information. The specific skills and experience possessed by managers are the most important source of returns generated. For example, they might have knowledge about the inventory levels of oil or corn producers and can interpret new information accordingly. Their activities generate liquidity in the futures and underlying cash markets.

The reason for returns of discretionary trading in the major global currency markets – the most liquid in the world – is related to the economic function currency speculators perform. They generate liquidity and price continuity. The activity of speculators adjusts the FX rates to create the necessary liquidity in anticipation of the deal flow created by a large transaction. This deal flow and need for liquidity can be created by a major commercial market participant's transaction that finds no direct commercial counterparty. The following serves as an idealized example. Germany-based Siemens needs to exchange USD 1 billion into EUR. The market anticipates this deal flow, and the price shifts accordingly in advance of the transaction. As a result the company pays a higher price for the EUR. However, both Siemens and other market participants wishing to buy euros will find a sufficient number of willing sellers to satisfy their needs. The market remains liquid. Further, when major shifts in the supply–demand balance occur due to a macroeconomic event, such as the Mexico crisis of 1995, FX traders continue to provide liquidity and price continuity in a fundamentally overvalued or undervalued market.

3.17   CONCLUSION OF THE CHAPTER

The distinction between risk premia and true alpha, i.e. exploiting market inefficiencies, is not easy within individual hedge fund strategies and managers. The industry's almost hysterical search for alpha gives investors a false impression of how returns are generated. This chapter has aimed to clarify the technical mechanisms of how hedge funds of the various kinds operate. The reader will have already noticed that hedge funds are by no means mysterious or incomprehensible for outsiders, but operate on the basis of some core principles and return sources, which directly relate to the associated risks they bear. Armed with this understanding, we can now tackle the discussion of the returns, their sources, and how to replicate them in the following chapters.

4

Empirical Return and Risk Properties of Hedge Funds

There exists today a solid body of research on the empirical risk and return properties of hedge funds as well as the overall benefits investors receive by including them in their overall portfolios.[1] The various studies have applied a range of statistical measures: expected return, volatility, higher moments (skew and kurtosis), maximal draw-downs and various correlation attributes. This chapter restates and summarizes the results of these studies on the basis of given different hedge fund performance indices.[2] However, the financial industry has not yet found a clear consensus on what performance measures are most suitable to account for the complexity of hedge fund returns. Therefore I will begin the discussion with the issues involved in measuring that complexity.

4.1 WHEN THE SHARPE RATIO IS NOT SHARP ENOUGH

Hedge fund proponents often make their case by pointing out – besides their low correlations to traditional assets – hedge funds' attractive reward-to-risk characteristics. The most often mentioned measure of risk-adjusted performance is the 'Sharpe ratio', the ratio of annualized monthly returns (minus the benchmark risk-free return) and the annualized monthly volatility. Hedge funds' high Sharpe ratios support the claim that hedge funds have much lower risk than equity investments, while yielding similar levels of returns. However – more than equities – some hedge fund strategies show negative outbreaks exceeding the range of three and more standard deviations much more frequently than expected by a normal distribution. That is, these strategies show 'kurtosis' – a fatness of the tails of the distribution[3] – and negative skew – an asymmetry in the size of negative returns versus the size of positive returns. This tail risk is of major concern to investors and remains unrecorded, if only standard deviations are used

---

[1] Past studies include the following: *The Benefits of Alternative Investment Strategies in the Global Investment Portfolio*, by L. Jaeger, Partners Group Research Paper (2003); *The Benefits of Hedge Funds* by T. Schneeweiss and G. Martin (2000); *Understanding Hedge Fund Performance: Research Results and Rules of Thumb for the Institutional Investor* by T. Schneeweiss *et al.* (2001); A. Ineichen, *Absolute Returns* (2002); 'Benefits and risks of alternative investment strategies', by N. Amenc *et al.*; 'The performance of hedge funds: risk return, and incentives' by C. Ackermann *et al.* (1999); 'On taking the "alternative" route: the risks, rewards, and performance persistence of hedge funds' by V. Agarwal and N. Naik (2000); 'On the performance of hedge funds' by L. Bing (1999); 'Hedge fund performance: 1990–1999' by L. Bing (2001); 'Hedge fund performance and manager skill' by F. Edwards and M. Caglayan (2001); 'Portfolios of alternative assets: why not 100% hedge funds?' by R. McFall Lamm Jr. (1999).

[2] The reader can find a more elaborated discussion on the analytical properties of hedge funds in S. Lhabitant, *Hedge Funds: Quantitative Insights* (2004).

[3] An excess kurtosis value larger than zero indicates fatter tails than the normal distribution, i.e. higher probability of extreme moves. Kurtosis is defined as $\int [(x - m)/\sigma]^4 \, dx$ (where m is the mean and σ the standard deviation). The kurtosis of the standard distribution is 3. In our discussion, we refer to excess kurtosis which is defined as $\int [(x - m)/\sigma]^4 \, dx - 3$.

for hedge fund risk quantification. The Sharpe ratio does not account for these distributional properties of hedge funds.[4]

4.2 CHALLENGES OF HEDGE FUND PERFORMANCE MEASUREMENT – THE ISSUE WITH HEDGE FUND INDICES

Efforts on indexation and benchmarking of hedge fund performance go back to times way before hedge funds entered the stage of mainstream finance. Unfortunately, publicly available data on historical individual hedge fund performance is limited, so industry analysis relies on aggregated returns as provided by a dozen different consultants and database vendors. These differentiate hedge fund performance across categories based either on managers' self-disclosed strategy characteristics or certain statistical methods. We refer to this as the 'peer-group-based approach to hedge fund index construction'. Correspondingly, the performance characteristics of hedge funds presented in this chapter rely on a set of hedge fund return indices developed by commercial data providers. Although the resulting indices constitute an important tool for comparison and possibly benchmarking within and outside the hedge fund industry, measuring manager performance, classifying investment styles, and generally creating a higher degree of transparency in this still rather opaque industry, the qualitative nature of the approach is not fully reliable and can lead to curious performance differences between similar-sounding strategy groups. These hedge fund indices may be the best performance measurements currently available, but they should still be viewed with caution due to several significant problems.[5]

The standard way to construct a hedge fund index is to use the median performance of a set of managers.[6] But, unlike for traditional asset classes, where performance data is readily available and fairly reliable such as the S&P or MSCI indices for equities, the reporting infrastructure for hedge funds is still insufficiently developed. Data availability and quality does not yet compare to traditional asset classes. Indices constructed from averaging single hedge funds thus inherit the errors and problems of the underlying databases of data providers, more than a dozen of which have emerged in recent years. As a result, the performance of hedge funds shown by different index providers can vary significantly and depend more on 'committee decisions' regarding index construction criteria – such as asset weighting, fund selection, and chosen statistical adjustments – than on objectively determined rules. Furthermore, the request for privacy by most hedge fund managers and the unregulated nature of the industry results in a lack of a standard format for performance reporting. As a result, although at the aggregated level, broad-based indices of hedge fund performance have more recently exhibited smaller variations among different index providers, on the level of the sub-indices significant

---

[4] See also the article by W. Goetzmann *et al.* 'Portfolio performance manipulation and manipulation-proof performance measures' (2007).

[5] Most of these issues are well known to practitioners. A good overview of the problems can be found in A. Kohler, 'Hedge fund indexing: a square peg in a round hole', State Street Global Advisors (2003). See also 'Hedge Fund Indices' by G. Crowder and L. Hennessee, *Journal of Alternative Investments* (2001); 'A review of alternative hedge fund indices' by Schneeweis Partners (2001); 'Welcome to the dark side: hedge fund attrition and survivorship bias over the period 1994–2001' by G. Amin and H. Kat (2003); W. Géhin, M. Vaissié, 'Lighthouses or tricks of light? An in-depth look at creating a quality hedge fund benchmark', *The Journal of Indexes*, May/June 2005.

[6] Median manager indices already have generally well known pitfalls in traditional asset classes. See the article by Jeffrey Bailey, 'Are manager universes acceptable performance benchmarks', *The Journal of Portfolio Management* (Spring 1992).

discrepancies among index providers continue to be wide. As the most widely used hedge fund indices are defined by the available manager universe and not actual risk factors and market opportunities, they are well suited neither for constructing passive investment strategies nor for objective performance evaluation.

Although this is also somewhat of a problem in traditional asset class indices, it is severely exacerbated in hedge funds by the diverse, dynamic, and opaque nature of the hedge fund universe. In particular, the variability of manager performance within strategy sectors is significantly larger for the hedge funds universe than for traditional equity and fixed income investments. This makes performance analysis based on indices and averages of manager sets less representative. Second, while the construction of traditional asset class indices rests on the assumptions that the underlying assets are reasonably homogeneous, and that the investor follows a 'buy and hold' strategy, hedge funds are diverse and subject to dynamic change. Thirdly, hedge fund data and indices come with a set of nasty biases. Some of these are well known in the world of traditional investments, but they are magnified by the still rather nontransparent nature of the hedge fund industry. The most important of these biases are the survivorship, the backfilling, the asset weighting, the selection, and the autocorrelation bias.

Survivorship

Survivorship bias is a result of unsuccessful managers leaving the industry, thus removing unsuccessful funds from the representative index. Only their successful counterparts remain, creating a positive bias. Indeed, many hedge fund databases only provide information on operating funds, i.e. funds that have ceased operation are considered uninteresting for the investor and are purged from the database. This leads to an upwards bias in the index performance, since the performance of the disappearing funds is usually worse than the performance of the surviving funds.[7] In the most extreme case this is like lining up a number of monkeys, letting them trade in the markets, taking out all those that lost money, and then checking the performance of the rest. The survivors may all be in good shape, but they hardly represent the performance of the entire original group! Consensus estimates about the size of the survivorship bias in hedge fund indices vary from 2% to 4% (it is possibly higher for the monkeys).

Backfilling

A variation of the survivorship bias can occur when a new fund is included into the index and his past performance is 'backfilled' into the database. This induces another upward bias: new managers usually are included into a database after a period of good performance, when entry seems most attractive or when they receive some attention. Since fewer managers enter during periods of bad performance, bad performance is rarely backfilled into the averages.[8] A related bias is induced by a fact that affects the global hedge fund industry as well as individual

---

[7] The survivorship bias is also well known in the world of mutual funds; see, for example, the paper by S. Brown *et al.*, 'Survivorship bias in performance studies' (1992).

[8] R. Ibbotson estimates this bias to account for a total of up to 4% of reported hedge fund performance (presentation at GAIM Conference, 2004). See also S. Brown, W. Goetzmann, R. Ibbotson, 'Offshore hedge funds: survival and performance 1989–1995' (1999). A recent estimate of the backfilling bias is given by B. Malkiel and A. Saha in their paper 'Hedge funds: risk and return' (2004) where the backfilling bias is estimated to be in the same region as Ibbotson's.

strategy sectors: managers report most of their past performance on a significantly smaller asset base compared to what they are currently managing. We all know it is harder to make money on an existing big pot of money than it is on a small pot. So we cannot and should not translate the past per cent performance of a hedge fund manager, a strategy or the global hedge fund industry as a whole into actual dollar performance.

Asset weighting

Indices that are asset-weighted give large funds a bigger impact on the index returns, while equal-weighted others give the same impact to large and small funds alike. The rebalancing rules defined by the index provider implicitly assume particular portfolio strategies, which may not necessarily match the reality of how hedge fund investors act. Neither approach is innately wrong, but each comes with its own built-in bias. Asset weighting can lead to a few large managers dominating the index, while equal weighting might be less representative for the average investor. An equally weighted index implicitly assumes a contrarian approach where the best performers are sold in favor of the underperformers. Asset-weighting schemes on the other hand contain an implicit momentum bias, where past winners are given increasing influence on the index's total return characteristics. Asset weighting further tends to overemphasize the performance of 'asset gatherers' at the expense of successful managers who might decide to close their funds at a certain level of assets under management to protect performance. There is no single unique way to weight an index that will be suitable for all investors. The investor must consider how the different index weighting methods fit with his portfolio objectives.

Selection

Unlike public information used to compose equity and bond indices, hedge fund index providers often rely on hedge fund managers to voluntarily and correctly submit return data on their funds. Hedge fund managers are not required to make public disclosure of their activities, and some bluntly refuse to submit data to index providers. Further, hedge funds often have discretion over how they get classified into a database. This 'self-selection bias' causes significant distortions in the construction of the index and often skews the index towards a certain set of managers and strategies. Sampling differences produce most of the performance deviation between the different fund indices. Hedge fund indices draw their data from different providers, the largest of which are the TASS, Hedge Fund Research (HFR) and CISDM (formerly MAR) databases. These databases have surprisingly few funds in common, as most hedge funds report their data – if at all – only to one database. Counting studies have shown that less than one out of three hedge funds in any one database contributes to the reported returns of all major hedge fund indices.[9]

Autocorrelation

Time lags in the valuation of securities held by hedge funds induce a smoothing of monthly returns which leads to volatility and correlation properties being significantly

---

[9] See the study by W. Fung, *et al.*, 'Hedge fund: performance, risk and capital formation' (2007); W. Fung and D. Hsieh, 'Hedge fund benchmarks: a risk based approach' (2004); and V. Agarwal *et al.* in 'Flows, performance, and managerial incentives in hedge funds' (2004).

underestimated. Statistically this effect expresses itself by significant autocorrelation in hedge fund returns.

Understanding that all hedge fund indices have limitations and biases, let us look at the attributes of a good index:[10]

(1) *Clear and unambiguous definition.* The construction of the index should follow clear and objective guidelines, and be based on transparent methods revealed publicly in advance. The index should be easily replicable by a third party.
(2) *Representativeness.* Complete coverage of the asset class is essential for a high-quality index. All available managers and strategies should be directly or approximately represented.
(3) *Accuracy.* The index should be accurately measured through a price discovery process that is regular, accurate, and verifiable by an independent third party. The underlying data should be reliable and readily available.
(4) *Investability.* Investors should be able to achieve exposure easily. The index should therefore represent a well-defined risk premium available to investors through passive investing.

None of these requirements are entirely fulfilled by currently available hedge fund indices. The variety of different methods and the opaque nature of most existing indices violate the 'clear definition' criterion. Instead of clear, rule-based decision-making, the decision to include or exclude a fund is often subjective. Clear definition is also violated with the underlying strategies not being unambiguously classified and indices often not being replicable because the index construction method is not fully disclosed. Most indices also violate 'representativeness', due in varying degrees to survivorship, asset weighting, selection, and classification biases. To make matters worse, many indices lack a clear price discovery process, and so are unable to make up for inconsistent, and often unaudited reporting by fund managers. And most hedge fund indices are not investable (see below for some more discussion on this point).

The built-in flaws of existing indices have as much to do with the built-in complexities of hedge funds as with any fault of the index developers. It is simply more difficult to create unambiguous index construction guidelines for the heterogeneous hedge fund universe. The reader will note that in traditional asset classes, the average return of the index has a strong theoretical basis. It is based on the index-determining 'market portfolio', which is the asset-weighted combination of all investable assets in that class (or a representative proxy thereof). According to asset pricing theory – e.g. Sharpe's Capital Asset Pricing Models (CAPM) – this market portfolio represents exactly the combination of assets with the optimal risk–return trade-off in market equilibrium.[11] It is therefore not surprising that traditional equity indices became vehicles for passive investment only after the development of a clear theoretical foundation in the form of the CAPM.[12] Traditional indices are designed to capture directly a clearly defined

---

[10] See J. Bailey, T. Richards, D. Tierney, 'Benchmark portfolios and the manager/plan sponsor relationship', *Journal of Corporate Finance* (Winter 1988).

[11] It is worth noting that equity indices remained almost solely performance analysis tools rather than investment vehicles for many years.

[12] The first index tracker fund (on the S&P index) was started in 1973 by Wells Fargo Bank, only about five years after the CAPM became broadly accepted.

risk premium available to investors willing to expose themselves to the systematic risk of the asset class. So an investor in the S&P 500 index knows exactly what he is getting; broad exposure to the risks and premia of the US large cap equities market. It is exactly this theoretical framework which is missing for today's hedge fund indices. There is no clear rationale to assure us that a portfolio which aggregates the median performance of a basket of hedge fund managers is an optimal portfolio. Nor is it clear which particular risk premium is represented by such a portfolio. No matter how those constructing a hedge fund index arrive at 'average' performance of the hedge fund universe, the result does not represent a market-determined optimal equilibrium solution or a representation of a well-defined premium. Rather, it is an arbitrary result of a more or less subjectively chosen selection and weighting scheme. This is evidenced by the strong deviations between the results of differently constructed indices.

Ironically, the theoretical and practical problems described above do not disappear when the index is designed to be investable. As a matter of fact, the problems are actually exacerbated. A prerequisite for creating an investment vehicle is that the underlying managers provide sufficient capacity for new investments. This creates a severe selection bias, as closed hedge funds are *a priori* not considered in the index. In traditional assets, an investor in the S&P 500 index need not worry that Microsoft is closed for further investment.[13] But for an investable hedge fund index, capacity with top managers, i.e. availability of specific funds, is indeed an issue. The selection of the index participants is biased towards the access the index providers have to various hedge funds. The investment capacity of most hedge fund managers is a scarce resource, for which investable index providers must compete with other investors such as funds of funds. This 'access bias' can lead to a severe distortion in the resulting index. In nonpublic markets, access is not determined by market price, but by the investors' ability to get and keep direct access to the individual fund manager. Often this is influenced by relationships and other 'soft factors'. Thus, the distinction between indices and regular funds of funds disappears upon a closer look. The indices struggle for capacity, must perform due diligence on hedge fund managers, and have similar subjective means to select and assign weights to hedge funds. It is therefore not surprising that they often charge similar levels of fees as funds of funds and in almost all cases actually also operate as such. They are essentially disguised funds of funds that have discovered the marketing value of the 'index' label.[14] They currently offer neither lower fee structures nor the clearly defined risk profiles comparable to a passive index fund in traditional asset classes. The performance deviation between investable hedge fund indices and their noninvestable counterparts created by the same providers is eye-catching: the average monthly underperformance of the investable index universe ranges somewhere from 30 bps to 65 bps, which translates into an average annual underperformance of about 4–8%! For these reasons investable hedge fund indices have lost a lot of their appeal to investors who had originally been attracted to the label 'index'.

---

[13] To be more precise, Microsoft stocks are in fact 'closed for further investments' as there are only a finite number around. In this way they actually resemble closed hedge funds. However, any investor who wants can freely purchase Microsoft shares due to its high degree of liquidity in the 'secondary market'. That is what stock markets are all about. In this sense the comparison serves us well here.

[14] One important difference between the index provider and a fund of hedge funds remains, though: the fund of funds manager is actively searching for alpha and trading talent, which justifies the comparably high fee level charged. He is not in the business of 'averaging the alpha', an undertaking which almost by construction will lead to lower results in the case of hedge funds. Note that alpha extraction is on a global scale a 'zero sum game'.

The true test of whether a hedge fund index is a valid investment vehicle is whether one can construct derivatives from it and whether it can be sold short. The possibility of short selling and constructing synthetic positions based on derivatives creates the prospect of arbitrage opportunities in hedge fund indices. Ironically such arbitrage opportunities would most likely be exercised by hedge funds, in a sort of Klein bottle of investments that contain themselves. Whether or not such trades emerge will eventually prove whether hedge fund indices can sustain market forces, which ultimately enforce an arbitrage-free market equilibrium.

Can we even hope to ever have appropriate indices for benchmarking hedge funds? And if so, what would be the guidelines for constructing those indices? The answer begins with our understanding that hedge fund performance is not all about alpha, but is largely about beta. By isolating and subtracting out beta, I believe indexing is possible. This is the important message of this book and it touches directly on the core subject of hedge fund replication. A proper hedge fund index has to be based on a decomposition of returns into systematic risks and idiosyncratic components – a separation of beta from alpha. An index should project the various risk premia hedge funds earn and should thereby not include the 'alpha' component of their performance. In other words, hedge fund indices should be exclusively governed by the systematic risk factors of the hedge fund strategies. The idiosyncratic, i.e. manager-specific components of returns – be it real alpha returns or return-free unsystematic risks – must not be part of the index. The reader will recognize that indices defined by the median performance within a set of managers cannot fulfill this criterion. But alpha and beta in hedge funds do not reveal themselves too easily as they do not come separately in hedge funds. A complete theory of hedge fund return sources, which links the systematic risk factors in the global capital markets directly to the hedge fund returns remains to be developed; however, significant progress in this direction has been made in recent years as this book shows. Further, the performance characteristics of a single hedge fund manager as well as an entire strategy sector often correspond to a combination of various risk premia. Future efforts in the construction of hedge fund indices will possibly be oriented in the direction of 'beta benchmarking' of hedge funds rather than manager sampling.[15]

While the currently available investable hedge fund indices come with many pitfalls and are flawed by the commercial interest of their designers, hedge fund indices in general have certainly validated a key request and addressed a main challenge of the hedge fund industry: the search for better transparency, in terms both of investment performance and of risk management. Despite their failure to define unambiguous strategy representations and pure styles, hedge fund indices nevertheless provide the industry with – even if far from perfect – performance measures and investment style classification. Without them investors would feel even more clueless about how to judge hedge fund managers' performances.

4.3 SOURCES OF EMPIRICAL DATA

For all their flaws, the current hedge fund indices still provide the best empirical basis for the analysis of performance of the various hedge fund strategy sectors. In this survey, I try to offset some of the shortcomings of each individual index by using three different indices:

---

[15] See also Chapter 9 in the author's book, *Through the Alpha Smoke Screens: A Guide to Hedge Fund Return Sources* for an early discussion.

(1) The Credit Suisse First Boston (CSFB) Tremont indices. This series of asset-weighted indices has been adjusted for survivorship bias since its inception in January 1994.
(2) The Hedge Fund Research (HFR) indices. This series of indices is equally weighted among managers and adjusted for survivorship bias since 1995. Some indices began in 1987, but we will mostly work only from the set beginning in January 1994. The HFR Index does not include Managed Futures strategies.
(3) The CISDM (formerly Zurich and MAR) indices for Managed Futures strategies. These indices date back to the early 1980s, we will again mostly examine only data beginning with January 1994.

4.4   RISK AND RETURN PROPERTIES OF HEDGE FUND STRATEGIES

Table 4.1 presents the results of a risk–return analysis for the different hedge fund strategy sectors from January 1994 to December 2007 (this period shall apply to all statistics in this chapter). The chart compares performance of the HFR, CSFB-Tremont, and CISDM indices to that of representative traditional indices. Returns are calculated on annualized monthly data as geometric averages (cumulative returns) of the log-differences of consecutive (monthly) prices. The volatility calculation is based on the standard deviation of returns.

As the reader can see, the average annual returns for the aggregate of all hedge funds stand at 11.6% and 11.1% according to the HFR Composite Index and the Tremont Composite Index. These returns come with a volatility of 6.7% and 7.5%, respectively. The average investor in a fund of hedge funds saw his investment rise 7.9% per year with a volatility of 5.7% according to the HFR Fund of Funds index (HFR is the only index provider considered here that reports fund of funds performance data).

The risk–return properties of the different hedge fund strategy sectors are very heterogeneous. For example, in Global Macro and Long/Short Equity strategies, high returns come with high risk. Just how high the risks and returns appear, however, varies between indices. CSFB Tremont shows an average annual return for Global Macro funds of 13.8% per annum over the period. But with 10.3% standard deviation, Global Macro ranks among the most volatile strategies. CSFB-Tremont assigns the strategy a Sharpe ratio of 0.86. In contrast, the HFR index gives Global Macro an average annual return of 10.1%, a volatility of 6.9%, and a Sharpe ratio of 0.76. Long/Short Equity also displays high returns and high risk. HFR reports a 14.0% annualized return, 8.5% volatility, and a Sharpe ratio of 1.08, while Tremont reports 12.2% return, 9.7% volatility, and a 0.75 Sharpe ratio. The kurtosis numbers for Long/Short Equity strategies are slightly higher than those for Global Macro. Neither Long/Short Equity nor Global Macro display significant skew in their historical return distribution.

Providing similar or slightly lower average returns, but better stability on the risk side are Event Driven, Equity Market Neutral, Convertible Arbitrage, and Distressed Securities strategies. Equity Market Neutral Strategies demonstrated particularly impressive risk-adjusted performance in both the HFR and Tremont databases. With returns of 8–10% and a volatility of less than 3%, this strategy shows an impressive Sharpe ratio. Event Driven displays attractive double-digit returns with volatilities around 6%, but has a significant skew (negative) and kurtosis.

Drawdown statistics help the investor to further differentiate between the strategies in terms of risk beyond volatility. Please note the large deviation in the drawdown figures between

Table 4.1 Risk and return of the various hedge fund strategies and traditional asset class returns as measured by different index families

	Return	Volatility	Skewness	Kurtosis	Max. drawdown	Sharpe ratio
Distressed Securities						
HFRI	11.96%	5.21%	−1.75	10.38	−12.78%	1.36
Long/Short Equity						
HFRI	14.00%	8.46%	0.16	1.99	−10.30%	1.08
Tremont	12.20%	9.71%	−0.06	4.33	−15.04%	0.75
Equity Market Neutral						
HFRI	7.76%	2.95%	0.25	0.95	−2.72%	0.97
Tremont	9.96%	2.80%	0.31	0.48	−3.54%	1.81
Event Driven						
HFRI	13.02%	6.23%	−1.35	6.13	−10.78%	1.31
Tremont	11.87%	5.62%	−3.66	27.69	−16.05%	1.24
Macro						
HFRI	10.12%	6.88%	−0.02	1.21	−10.70%	0.76
Tremont	13.80%	10.33%	−0.22	3.72	−26.79%	0.86
Regulation D						
HFRI	14.92%	6.95%	0.60	1.55	−12.42%	1.44
Relative Value						
HFRI Relative Value	9.78%	3.08%	−2.58	18.82	−6.55%	1.59
Convertible Arbitrage (HFRI)	9.01%	3.59%	−0.99	1.88	−7.34%	1.15
Convertible Arbitrage (Tremont)	8.76%	4.60%	−1.37	3.34	−12.03%	0.84
Fixed Income Arbitrage (HFRI)	5.83%	3.72%	−3.34	19.92	−14.42%	0.25
Fixed Income Arbitrage (Tremont)	6.27%	3.69%	−3.10	17.31	−12.48%	0.37
Short Selling						
HFRI	0.94%	19.95%	−0.08	2.64	−53.36%	−0.20
Tremont	−1.81%	16.54%	0.63	1.26	−46.57%	−0.41
Fund of Funds						
HFRI	7.85%	5.66%	−0.43	4.50	−13.08%	0.52
Composite						
HFRI	11.56%	6.74%	−0.65	3.83	−11.42%	0.99
Tremont	11.05%	7.43%	−0.06	2.64	−13.81%	0.83
Managed Futures						
Tremont	6.46%	11.87%	−0.11	0.27	−17.74%	0.13
CISDM CTA Universe	7.98%	8.37%	0.16	−0.21	−8.25%	0.37
CISDM Systematic Active	6.84%	9.03%	0.16	0.33	−8.32%	0.22
CISDM Discretionary Active	9.36%	5.75%	0.91	1.63	−5.60%	0.78
CISDM Trend-Following	5.30%	13.60%	0.25	0.01	−26.90%	0.03
Passive (sGFII)	11.45%	11.43%	−0.57	1.56	−22.57%	0.57
Currency Trading						
Barcley Currency Index	4.24%	6.34%	1.06	1.60	−14.83%	−0.10
Equity						
S&P 500 TR	10.46%	14.01%	−0.76	1.32	−44.73%	0.40
MSCI World TR USD	9.37%	13.52%	−0.85	1.46	−46.26%	0.33
MSCI EU TR USD	12.01%	14.61%	−0.67	1.51	−45.50%	0.49
Bonds						
Citigroup World Gov. Bond USD	6.24%	6.36%	0.26	0.23	−96.86%	0.21
Citigroup World Gov. Bond 3–7 yr	5.78%	6.64%	0.28	0.34	−9.68%	0.13
MSCI US Treasury Bond Index	5.71%	4.51%	−0.48	1.11	−5.34%	0.18
Commodities						
Goldman Sachs Commodity Index	9.49%	19.92%	−0.12	−0.01	−48.26%	0.23

Calculation: Author; Data: 01.94–12.07.

the HFR and Tremont databases for Global Macro, Long Short Equity, Convertible Arbitrage and Event Driven strategies. While the equal weighted HFR Global Macro Index shows the most severe drawdown of −10.7% the asset weighted Tremont index shows a substantially worse −26.8% in an overall shorter time period. The deviations for Long/Short Equity and Event Driven strategies are less remarkable, but still significant, at −10.3% HFR versus −15.0% Tremont for Long/Short Equity and −10.8% HFR versus −16.1% Tremont for Event Driven. For Convertible Arbitrage, HFR displays a quite low drawdown of −7.34 compared with −12.0% for the CSFB/Tremont index. The wide differences between the two databases underline the value of understanding both the way data is collected, and what that data truly represents.

The Equity Market Neutral strategy shows the lowest drawdown in the hedge fund strategy universe.[16] According to HFR data, Convertible Arbitrage strategies experienced their single worst drawdowns in the single digits, significantly lower than Fixed Income Arbitrage. In contrast, Event Driven, Regulation D and Distressed Securities strategies exhibited drawdowns of about double these amounts.

Looking further at kurtosis provides an even more complete picture:

- Fixed Income Arbitrage: 20.0 (HFR) and 17.3 (Tremont);
- Convertible Arbitrage: 1.9 (HFR) and 3.4 (Tremont);
- Distressed Securities (HFR): 10.4;
- Event Driven: 6.1 (HFR) and 27.7 (CSFB/Tremont);
- Equity Market Neutral: 1.0 (HFR) and 0.5 (CSFB/Tremont).

The large kurtosis for Fixed Income Arbitrage was largely caused by the events of fall 1998.

Table 4.1 further shows that most hedge fund strategies come with a significant amount of negative skew in their return distribution, especially the Event Driven (Merger Arbitrage, Distressed Securities) and the Relative Value strategies (Convertible Arbitrage, Fixed Income Arbitrage). The negative skew and the excess kurtosis put the low-volatility characteristics of these strategies into a new light. In exchange for lower risk in the second moment (the middle − normal − part of the return distribution) investors incur higher tail risks on the negative side of the distribution.[17] This is an important caution for when evaluating mean–variance optimized portfolios, which do not take the higher moments into account. Equity Market Neutral strategies in contrast display in our study no significant skew and only a small excess kurtosis in their historical return distribution.

Short selling is clearly the worst-performing strategy during the studied period. Suffering through a combined decade and a half of bullish equity markets, short sellers returned an average of 0.9% with a volatility of 20.0% according to HFR, while CSFB-Tremont reports negative return averages. The rather frightening maximum drawdown figure of −53.4% sheds further light on the difficulties faced by these managers during the bull market of the 1990s. However, Short Selling strategies were not surprisingly among the best performers

---

[16] However, the low average number hides the fact that many so-called Equity Market Neutral 'quant-funds' suffered extensive losses in the summer of 2007 when a liquidity crisis forced many multi-billion-dollar funds to cut their positions simultaneously. Most of the drawdown occurred intra-month.

[17] See the article 'The difficulties of measuring the benefits of hedge funds' by A. Signer and L. Favre (Summer 2002).

during the two years from 2001 to 2002; although the exact results differed between the two indices.

Regulation D strategies showed average annual returns of 14.9% and volatility 7.0%, yielding a Sharpe ratio of 1.44. The maximum drawdown was −12.4%. However, true volatility in this strategy, as well as the one for Distressed Securities strategies, is less accurately reported due to the strategy's lack of liquidity. In the absence of mark-to-market pricing, value appears to change infrequently. In fact, the true market value of such an investment may well change every day as the companies' fortunes shift. However these frequent changes are not marked by public market transactions. These changes are trees that fall in the woods when no one is there to hear them. Absent frequent *and recorded* changes in pricing, volatility appears artificially low. The returns of this strategy partly represent a liquidity premium the investor receives for accepting a relatively long lock-up period, and perhaps an additional premium for the lack of mark-to-market valuations, i.e. for holding an investment whose volatility cannot be easily calculated.

The stand-alone return-to-risk ratios of Managed Futures strategies are not quite as impressive as those of other hedge fund strategies. Their main value lies in their correlation attributes, which provide useful diversification within an overall portfolio. The average Managed Futures strategies yielded 7–10% with volatilities even higher. The resulting Sharpe ratios are well below 0.5 on average. Quite impressively stands out the performance of the saisGroup Futures Index (sGFII), a systematic trend following approach mimicking the generic trading rules of CTA managers.[18]

4.5   COMPARISON WITH EQUITIES AND BONDS

The returns of hedge funds vary by strategy, but compare favorably, both individually and collectively, with the returns of traditional investments. In the equity markets – represented here by the S&P 500, the MSCI Europe and the MSCI World – return to risk ratios are generally lower than their hedge fund counterparts. The 10.5% total return and 14.0% volatility of the S&P 500 does not meet the standard of high return paired with low volatility set by a diversified hedge fund portfolio. Further, from 2000 to 2003 the S&P 500 experienced a 44.7% drawdown. The MSCI Europe Index's (including dividends) average annual return of 12.0% and volatility of 14.6% shows similar results, while the MSCI World displayed 9.4% returns (again including dividends) and 13.5% volatility. The maximum drawdowns for the MSCI World Index stand at the very intimidating figure of −46.3%.

On the bond side of the equation, the news is hardly different. The Salomon Smith Barney World Government Bond Ten Market Index (in US dollar terms) and the MSCI US Treasury Bond Index represent fixed income as the traditional complement to stocks. Although these indices' volatilities (6.4% and 4.5%) are comparable to hedge funds, their returns of 6.2% and 5.7% are significantly lower than those of the average hedge fund.

---

[18] sGFII stands for 'saisGroup Futures Index', a systematic Passive Futures strategy index developed by the author and his partners at saisGroup (now Partners Group). Please refer to the following article for further details about this index: 'Case study: The sGFI Futures Index', by L. Jaeger, M. Jacquemai, and P. Cittadini (2002). The outperformance of this index is mostly due to the lack of fees for this systematically constructed 'CTA index'.

4.6   DEVIATION FROM NORMAL DISTRIBUTION

The kurtosis values in Table 4.1 have already provided some indications that the return distributions of some hedge fund strategies are not normally distributed. I would like to provide some further empirical details on this observation with the help of two statistical tools available to examine the distributional properties of hedge fund returns in the extremes.[19] The so called 'quantile–quantile plot' or, in short, 'QQ plot' is another graphical means of determining whether two datasets come from populations with a common distribution. It plots all quantiles of one set against the other. If the distributions are similar, the points should line up on the diagonal axis. Large differences, e.g. in the tails, indicate that the distributions are different. Figure 4.1 provides such a QQ plot for seven different strategies against the normal distributions. As we can clearly observe, deviations in the tails are especially expressed for the arbitrage strategies as well as for Event Driven strategies, a result which confirms our results in Table 4.1.

4.7   UNCONDITIONAL CORRELATION PROPERTIES

In addition to attractive risk-adjusted returns, hedge funds also attract investors through their low correlation to traditional asset classes. The HFR Composite shows a correlation of 70% to the S&P 500 and 0% to the bond markets, compared to 44% and 0% for the HFR Fund of Funds index. Thus, including hedge funds in traditional portfolios provides asset managers the opportunity to diversify their overall portfolio risk and produce more consistent returns. Table 4.2 provides a correlation matrix with the different strategy sectors and traditional assets. In order to keep the matrix readable, I only report on the HFR indices and the CISDSM index for Managed Futures.

Short Selling strategies obviously have the lowest correlation to the equity markets with a −0.70 correlation to the S&P 500 and −0.67 to the MSCI World equity index, as well as zero correlation to the world bond index. Fixed Income Arbitrage strategies have a zero correlation to equity markets and a slightly negative correlation to bonds.

Equity Market Neutral, Convertible Arbitrage, Regulation D, Distressed Securities, and Global Macro also have relatively low correlations to the S&P 500 and other stock indices. Their correlations to the equity markets are low enough to act as an effective diversifier, with figures ranging from 0.1 to 0.4. Although not negatively correlated to the equity markets, all display zero or low positive correlation to the bond markets. This makes them a further valuable tool for a diversification portfolio, as bonds are normally an integral part of the traditional portfolio.

Some hedge fund strategies, however, do have rather high correlations to the S&P 500. The figures that follow are drawn from the HFR, with the corresponding Tremont figures (not shown in Table 4.2) in parentheses. Event Driven shows a correlation of 0.62 (0.55). Long/Short Equity shows 0.64 (0.58). The low correlations of these two strategy sectors to fixed income securities provide some diversification value. But overall, these strategies do not, strictly speaking, provide a good hedge. In particular, they should not be used to hedge a traditional portfolio that otherwise consists largely of equities.

---

[19] For more details on statistical tools, see the book by P. Embrechts, C. Klüppelberg, and T. Mikosch, *Modelling Extremal Events*, Springer (1999).

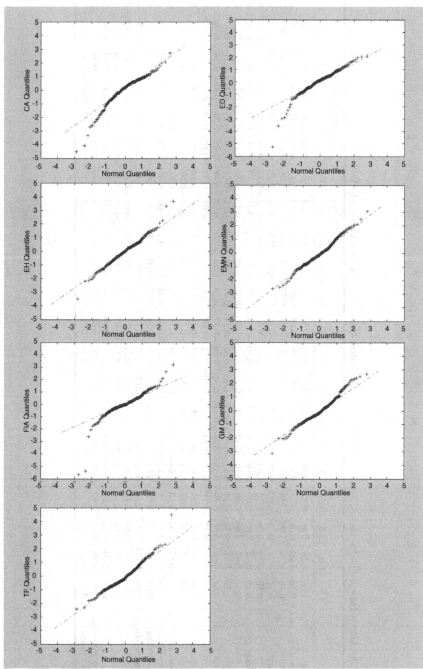

Data: HFR, CISDM; Jan. 1994–Dec. 2007. CA: Convertible Arbitrage, ED: Event-Driven,
EH: Equity Hedge, EMN: Equity Market Neutral, FIA: Fixed Income Arbitrage, GM: Global Macro,
TF:CISDM Trend Follower Index.

Figure 4.1 QQ plots of standardized hedge fund strategy return quantiles versus standard normal
quantiles.

Table 4.2 Correlations between hedge fund strategies and traditional investment classes (sources and dates as in Table 4.1)

	CA	DS	LSE	EMN	ED	FIA	GM	RD	RV	SS	FoF	Comp	Sys	Dis	TF	sGFII	MSCI EU	MSCI World	S&P	CWGB	GCI
Convertible Arbitrage	1.00	0.56	0.46	0.22	0.58	0.15	0.41	0.30	0.61	-0.31	0.49	0.54	0.01	0.18	-0.01	0.06	0.24	0.28	0.29	0.03	0.04
Distressed Securities	0.56	1.00	0.59	0.21	0.79	0.36	0.47	0.37	0.68	-0.48	0.60	0.73	-0.14	0.09	-0.13	-0.11	0.39	0.40	0.40	-0.09	0.02
Long Short Equity	0.46	0.59	1.00	0.38	0.78	0.09	0.60	0.54	0.55	-0.77	0.77	0.93	-0.00	0.20	-0.05	-0.05	0.56	0.64	0.66	0.00	0.16
Equity Market Neutral	0.22	0.21	0.38	1.00	0.25	0.09	0.28	0.22	0.29	-0.11	0.37	0.32	0.10	0.16	0.12	0.11	0.14	0.11	0.14	0.09	0.13
Event Driven	0.58	0.79	0.78	0.25	1.00	0.19	0.56	0.45	0.65	-0.63	0.67	0.88	-0.04	0.12	-0.13	-0.09	0.56	0.62	0.64	-0.05	0.03
Fixed Income Arbitrage	0.15	0.36	0.09	0.09	0.19	1.00	0.15	0.08	0.30	-0.04	0.26	0.19	-0.09	-0.01	-0.10	-0.04	0.07	0.02	-0.04	-0.16	0.07
Global Macro	0.41	0.47	0.60	0.28	0.56	0.15	1.00	0.33	0.41	-0.39	0.72	0.69	0.35	0.43	0.32	0.17	0.39	0.43	0.38	0.13	0.11
Regulation D	0.30	0.37	0.54	0.22	0.45	0.08	0.33	1.00	0.32	-0.37	0.47	0.50	0.07	0.15	-0.01	0.05	0.28	0.31	0.31	-0.13	0.13
Relative Value	0.61	0.68	0.55	0.29	0.65	0.30	0.41	0.32	1.00	-0.39	0.53	0.63	-0.08	0.08	-0.18	-0.07	0.34	0.37	0.36	-0.06	0.10
Short Selling	-0.31	-0.48	-0.77	-0.11	-0.63	-0.04	-0.39	-0.39	-0.37	1.00	-0.50	-0.77	0.16	-0.03	0.21	0.17	-0.55	-0.67	-0.70	0.01	-0.03
Fund of Funds	0.49	0.60	0.77	0.37	0.67	0.26	0.72	0.47	0.53	-0.50	1.00	0.83	0.17	0.44	0.16	0.08	0.44	0.48	0.44	-0.05	0.20
HF Composite	0.54	0.73	0.93	0.32	0.88	0.19	0.69	0.50	0.63	-0.77	0.83	1.00	0.01	0.21	-0.07	-0.08	0.61	0.70	0.70	-0.02	0.10
CISDM Futures Systematic	0.01	-0.14	-0.00	0.10	-0.04	-0.09	0.35	0.07	-0.08	0.16	0.17	0.01	1.00	0.45	0.84	0.49	0.01	0.04	-0.02	0.28	0.12
CISDM Futures Discretionary	0.18	0.09	0.20	0.16	0.12	-0.01	0.43	0.15	0.08	-0.03	0.44	0.21	0.45	1.00	0.44	0.38	0.01	0.09	-0.00	0.13	0.19
CISDM Futures Trendfollowers	-0.01	-0.13	-0.05	0.12	-0.13	-0.10	0.32	-0.01	-0.18	0.21	0.16	-0.07	0.84	0.44	1.00	0.46	-0.15	-0.15	-0.13	0.26	0.10
saisGroup Futures Index (sGFII)	0.06	-0.11	-0.11	0.11	-0.09	-0.04	0.17	0.05	-0.07	0.17	0.08	-0.08	0.49	0.38	0.46	1.00	-0.09	-0.13	-0.17	0.22	0.09
MSCI Europe TR USD	0.24	0.39	0.56	0.14	0.56	0.07	0.39	0.28	0.34	-0.55	0.44	0.61	0.01	0.01	-0.15	-0.09	1.00	0.89	0.74	0.23	-0.04
MSCI World TR USD	0.28	0.40	0.64	0.11	0.62	0.02	0.43	0.31	0.37	-0.67	0.48	0.70	0.04	0.09	-0.15	-0.13	0.89	1.00	0.86	0.17	-0.02
S&P 500 TR	0.29	0.40	0.66	0.14	0.64	-0.04	0.38	0.31	0.36	-0.70	0.44	0.70	-0.02	-0.00	-0.13	-0.17	0.74	0.86	1.00	0.04	-0.08
Citigroup World Gov. Bond Index	0.03	-0.09	0.00	0.09	-0.05	-0.16	0.13	-0.13	-0.06	0.01	-0.05	-0.02	0.28	0.13	0.26	0.22	0.23	0.17	0.04	1.00	0.10
Goldman Commodity Index	0.04	0.02	0.16	0.13	0.03	0.07	0.11	0.13	0.10	-0.03	0.20	0.10	0.12	0.19	0.10	0.09	-0.04	-0.02	-0.08	0.10	1.00

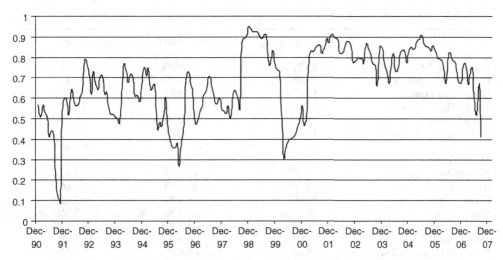

Figure 4.2   Rolling 12-month correlation between the S&P 500 and the HFR Composite Index.

Managed Futures strategies have usefully low correlation with traditional assets. All Managed Futures strategies show either negative or zero correlation to the S&P 500. The Trend Following sector represented by the sGFII has a statistically (marginally) significant negative correlation of −0.17 to the S&P 500. Managed Futures strategies also demonstrate low correlations to bond markets with figures ranging between 13% and 28%. With these correlation properties to equity and fixed income investments, Managed Futures generally serve as an excellent hedge within the globally diversified portfolios.

One problem in using these unconditional correlations in quantitative portfolio optimization is that the correlation characteristics of hedge funds vary significantly over time. For example, Figure 4.2 displays the rolling 12-month correlation between the S&P 500 index and the HFR Composite. Clearly there are large fluctuations in the correlation figures, which range from about 0.1 to more than 0.9. The correlation fluctuates depending on the equity market environment (the end of 2007/beginning 2008 provides the most recent example of such dynamical adjustments of hedge fund exposure in a changing market environment).

Another (maybe less widely recognized) pitfall of correlations is that they measure only the relative co-movement between past average returns. The mean returns and the variances of the individual return time series are not considered in calculating correlations. For example, a positive correlation to the S&P 500 in down months does not necessarily mean the strategy had negative returns in those months. It only means that it is underperforming its own historical return average.[20]

A last well-documented aspect of hedge fund returns is that they display significant autocorrelation properties, which indicates a valuation problem: the price discovery process of hedge funds is often exposed to time-lag processes. This is a problem if one considers the simultaneous correlations of hedge funds to other asset classes which are not exposed to

---

[20] In order to take mean return and variance of two return series into account the concept of 'co-integration' was developed (for which the Nobel Prize Committee awarded a Nobel Prize in 2003). See R. Engle and C. Granger, 'Co-integration and error correction: representation, estimation, and testing' (1987).

Table 4.3   Autocorrelation of different hedge fund strategies as measured using HFR data

	Autocorrelation (lag 1)	Autocorrelation (lag 2)	Autocorrelation (lag 3)
Convertible Arbitrage	52.21%	19.49%	4.66%
Distressed Securities	41.68%	10.49%	0.42%
Long/Short Equity	17.95%	4.98%	3.65%
Equity Market Neutral	7.86%	8.97%	11.45%
Event Driven	27.31%	2.22%	−1.41%
Fixed Income Arbitrage	33.30%	5.93%	13.12%
Macro	12.72%	−11.09%	−4.46%
Market Timing	1.84%	−2.25%	−4.12%
Merger Arbitrage	22.59%	12.49%	13.82%
Regulation D	38.00%	28.01%	14.86%
Relative Value	31.40%	16.49%	3.52%
Short Selling	9.50%	−11.23%	−3.56%
Fund of Funds	31.13%	4.82%	−3.84%
Hedge Fund Composite	20.95%	0.04%	−5.18%
Managed Futures (CISDM)	5.83%	−7.94%	−4.22%

lagged valuation, as pointed out by several studies.[21] Table 4.3 shows a result of a study on autocorrelations of the various hedge fund strategies up to lag 3.

4.8   CONDITIONAL RETURNS AND CORRELATIONS

We now want to look at the performance behavior of hedge funds in different market environments, in other words their *conditional properties*. Conditional returns provide a more direct look at the general return drivers of the different hedge fund strategies. Figures 4.3(a), 4.3(b), and 4.3(c), show the average returns of the HFR and CISDM (plus the sGFII) indices, conditional on the return of the S&P 500, MSCI US Treasury Bond Index, and the change of equity market volatility as measured by the VIX index[22] (we refer to these indices as 'benchmarks' in the following). For the averaging procedure, the months in the time period from January 1994 to September 2007 were categorized into six sets depending on the return of the respective benchmark index:

(1) Months with benchmark returns lower than minus 1.5 standard deviations below the geometric mean.
(2) Months with benchmark returns lower than minus one standard deviation but above minus 1.5 standard deviations relative to the geometric mean.
(3) Months with negative benchmark returns between zero and one standard deviation relative to the geometric mean.
(4) Months with positive benchmark returns between zero and one standard deviation relative to the geometric mean.

---

[21] See the paper by C. Asness *et al.*, 'Do hedge funds hedge?', *Journal of Portfolio Management*, 28, 1 (Fall 2001), also available on http://www.aqrcapital.com

[22] The VIX is an index provided by the CBOE (Chicago Board Options Exchange) which measures the implied volatility of the S&P 100 index as given by the options market.

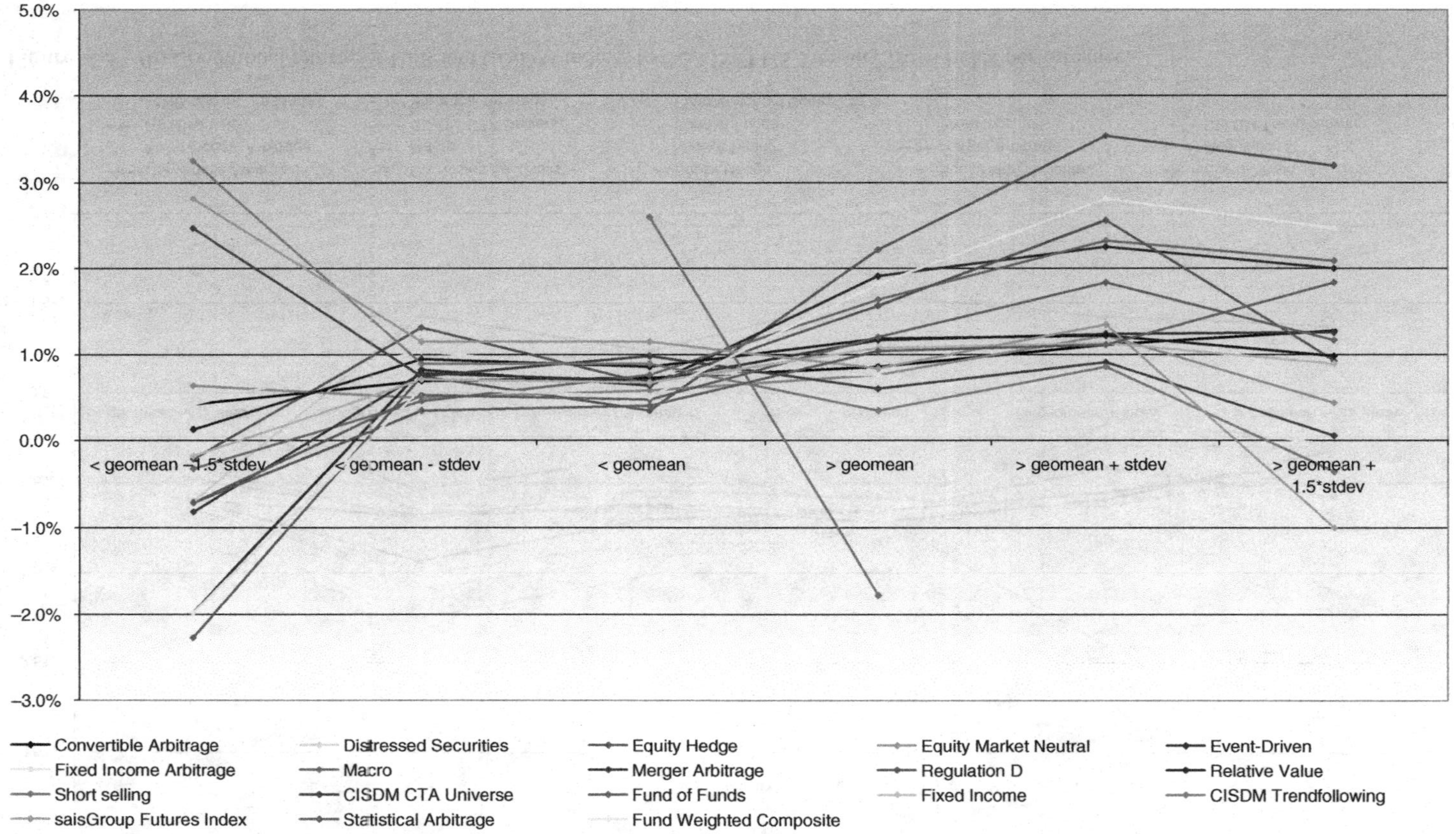

5.0%
4.0%
3.0%
2.0%
1.0%
0.0%
–1.0%
–2.0%
–3.0%
< geomean –1.5*stdev
< geomean - stdev
< geomean
> geomean
> geomean + stdev
> geomean + 1.5*stdev
Convertible Arbitrage
Distressed Securities
Equity Hedge
Equity Market Neutral
Event-Driven
Fixed Income Arbitrage
Macro
Merger Arbitrage
Regulation D
Relative Value
Short selling
CISDM CTA Universe
Fund of Funds
Fixed Income
CISDM Trendfollowing
saisGroup Futures Index
Statistical Arbitrage
Fund Weighted Composite

Figure 4.3 (a) Conditional returns of HFR and CTA indices to S&P 500 performance.

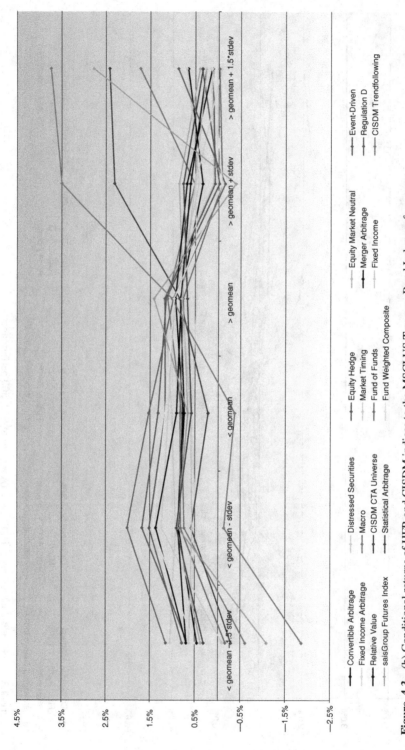

Figure 4.3 (b) Conditional returns of HFR and CISDM indices to the MSCI US Treasury Bond Index performance.

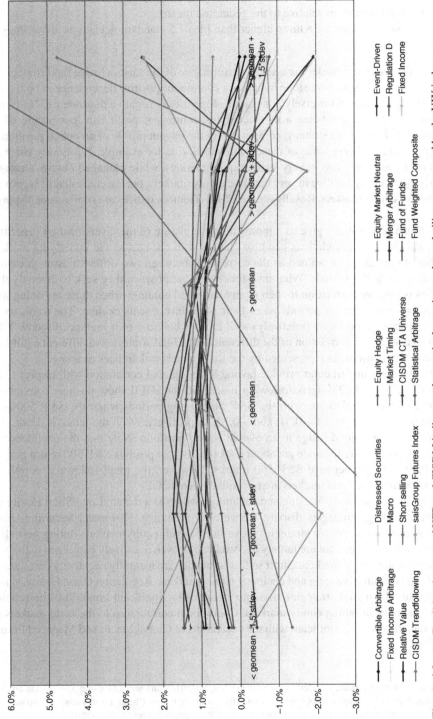

Figure 4.3 (c) Conditional returns of HFR and CISDM indices to changes in the equity market volatility as measured by the VIX index.

Convertible Arbitrage
Fixed Income Arbitrage
Relative Value
CISDM Trendfollowing

Distressed Securities
Macro
Short selling
saisGroup Futures Index

Equity Hedge
Market Timing
CISDM CTA Universe
Statistical Arbitrage

Event-Driven
Regulation D
Fixed Income

Equity Market Neutral
Merger Arbitrage
Fund of Funds
Fund Weighted Composite

(5) Months with benchmark returns higher than plus one standard deviation but below plus 1.5 standard deviations relative to the geometric mean.
(6) Months with benchmark returns higher than plus 1.5 standard deviations above the geometric mean.

In each of the sets, we consider the average performance of the various hedge fund strategies in the same months.[23] A positive slope indicates a continuous positive dependence in both rising and declining markets. Conversely, a negative slope means negative dependence. Nonlinear, i.e. nonconstant slopes indicate a more complex contingent profit and loss profile of the corresponding hedge fund strategy, comparable to the payout profile of an option position.

The reader can observe some of these nonlinearities, as for example, L/S Equity strategies tend to return relatively less in very strong equity markets, while Managed Futures strategies tend to be particularly positive in very negative equity markets, but not equivalently negative in very positive equity markets. Results for the CSFB-Tremont indices are similar (not displayed here).

Conditional correlations give us a more complete picture of the diversification benefits of hedge funds because correlations can also change with changes in the underlying markets. Conditional correlation is defined as the correlation between two different assets measured only during particular periods. What investors ideally want when they seek to diversify their portfolios is positive correlation to their equity and bond holdings when those are doing well, and negative correlation in periods when their other investments decline. The result would be that the strategy performs (relatively) well in both bull and bear markets. Figures 4.4(a) and 4.4(b) display the correlation of the different hedge fund strategies in different equity and bond market conditions, as represented by the same benchmark indices as above.

CTAs strategies in particular provide favorable conditional correlation with respect to equity markets. The CISDM Trendfollowing index and the sGFII show positive correlations, respectively zero correlations, with the S&P 500 during periods when the S&P 500 is up and a negative correlation of −0.31, and −0.12, respectively, when the index is down. This property serves as a good hedge in an overall equity portfolio. Note that the confidence intervals for statistical significance are about [−0.14:0.14] for positive S&P 500 return periods, and [−0.19:0.19] for negative S&P 500 returns. However, the trend followers' correlation properties against the bond markets are not equally beneficial.

Positive correlation in both rising and declining markets is a feature Long/Short Equity and Statistical Arbitrage strategies display. Convertible Arbitrage, Distressed Securities, Fixed Income Arbitrage and Macro strategies move in line with equity markets during periods of declining equity markets, but are largely uncorrelated or even negatively correlated to the S&P 500 in advancing equity markets. Short selling strategies are naturally negatively correlated to the S&P 500 in both advancing and declining equity markets. Regulation D and Equity Market Neutral (thus the name) strategies show no statistically significant conditional correlation, either in rising or in falling equity markets. Conditional correlations to the bond markets are overall statistically less significant with the exceptions of Global Macro and Managed Futures strategies.

---

[23] The mathematically trained reader will realize that we are performing something like a regression analysis, and that the slope of our graphs bears resemblance to the sensitivity factors ('betas') well-known in statistics. The difference is that we average over certain returns intervals before regressing over all observations.

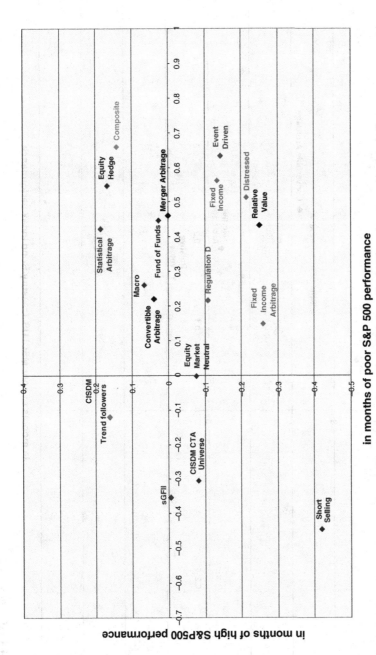

Figure 4.4 (a) Conditional correlation properties of HFR and CISDM indices to stocks. (b) Conditional correlation properties of HFR and CISDM indices to bonds.

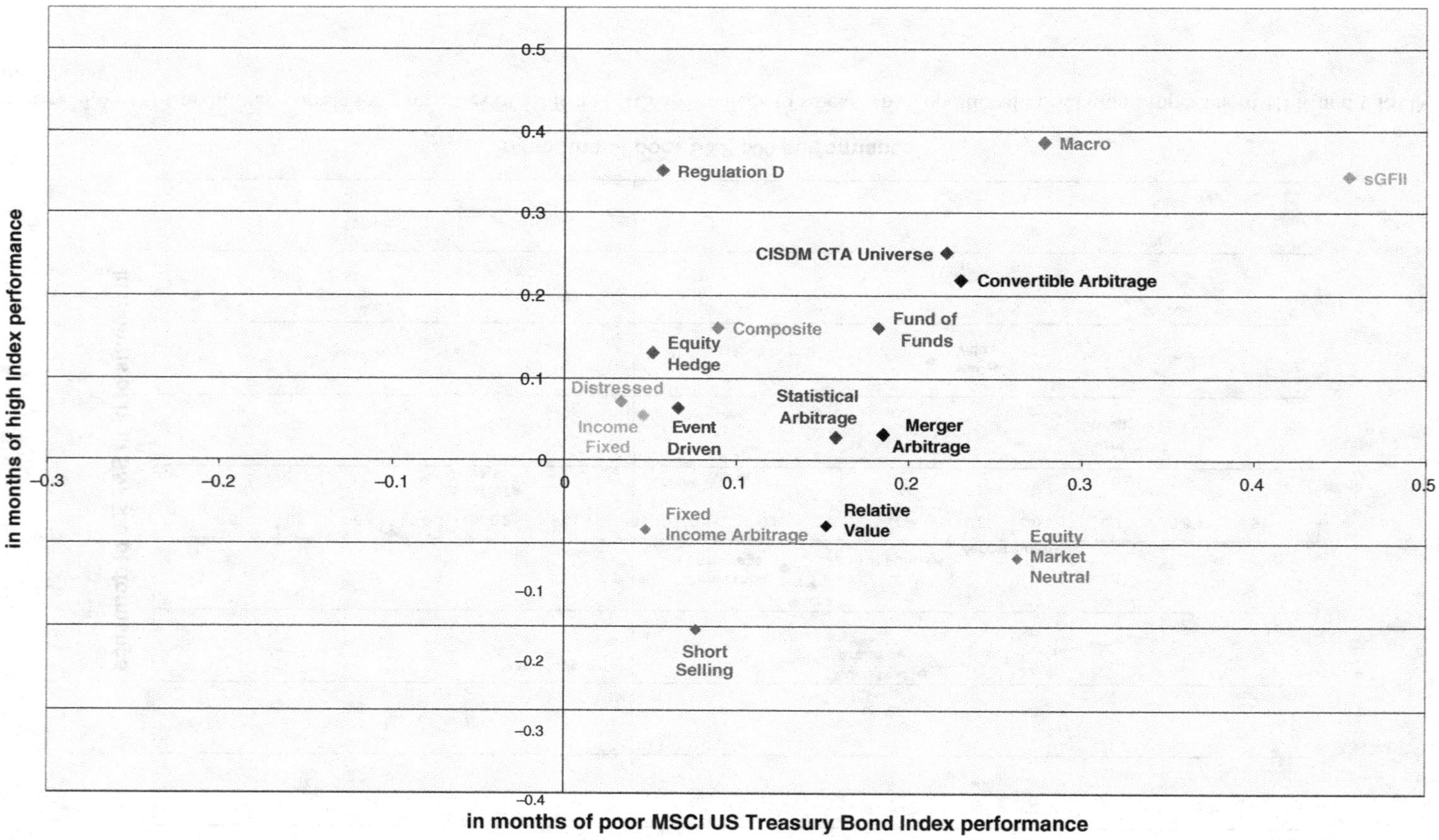

in months of poor MSCI US Treasury Bond Index performance

in months of high Index performance

Figure 4.4 (Continued).

4.9   HEDGE FUND BEHAVIOR IN EXTREME MARKET SITUATIONS

Having looked at how hedge funds respond to changes in the markets, let's look at how they have responded to some specific extreme events. For the following discussion, I have selected seven such periods to illustrate the behavior of hedge funds during market turmoil:

(1) rising interest rates (bond crash) in early 1994;
(2) the Asian crisis in 1997;
(3) the Russian default crisis in 1998;
(4) the 'TMT crash' in 2000/2001;
(5) the terrorist attacks in September 2001;
(6) the period of significant equity market downturn during the summer of 2002;
(7) the credit crisis in the summer of 2007.

The performance of each strategy sector during these periods is displayed in Table 4.4. I have also included the performance of the average hedge fund of funds to indicate the return of multi-manager hedge fund portfolios. Equity and bond performance during the same periods is included for comparison. Let's walk through the results for each of these events.

(1) From February to April 1994 an unexpected hike in Fed interest rates quickly drove the US and European yield curves up by about 150 basis points. This rate hike caused major losses in traditional bond portfolios. Within the hedge fund universe, Global Macro and Convertible Arbitrage managers suffered most. Long/Short Equity hedge funds lost around 3%. Conversely, Fixed Income Arbitrage and Short Sellers made significant gains of +3.6% and +16.2%, respectively. The average fund of funds lost −5.6%, because most were highly exposed to Global Macro strategies at the time.

(2) During the Asian crisis following the devaluation of many Asian currencies in the second half of 1997, all hedge funds earned significant positive returns. Futures strategies led, followed closely by Long/Short Equity, Regulation D and Event Driven. Fixed Income Arbitrage with +1.7% displayed the lowest returns of all strategies. Fund of funds returned 6.2% on average.

(3) The market crisis following the Russian bond default in August 1998 is also referred to as the 'hedge fund crisis'. The average fund of funds lost −11.6% in the three-month period from August to October! This was largely due to heavy allocations to Fixed Income Arbitrage strategies which lost −13.2% in these few months. Distressed Security strategies also lost significantly. However, the period also had some clear winners. Managed Futures proved themselves as great diversifiers during this period.

(4) The equity market downturn and the Nasdaq crash marked the burst of the technology bubble in March 2000 led to a decline of 23% in the S&P 500 during the following 19 months. This downturn is one reason for the tremendous increase of investors' interest in hedge funds. Interestingly, the performance of an average fund of funds during this period was actually negative! Again, this was caused by the over-exposure in many funds of funds to a strategy that lost significantly. In this case, it was Long/Short Equity that lost most in the 19-month period. Conversely, several other strategies were

Table 4.4 Hedge fund returns in extreme market environments

	Bond crash 02/94–04/94	Asian crisis 07/97–12/97	Russian default 08/98–10/98	TMF crash 04/00–09/01	Terrorist attack September-01	Equity Market slide June–Sept 2002	Sub-prime crisis July 2007–Jan 2008
Convertible Arbitrage	-4.62%	5.67%	-4.69%	20.74%	0.64%	-0.19%	0.43%
Fixed Income Arbitrage	3.58%	1.70%	-13.18%	7.57%	-1.54%	4.05%	1.14%
Equity Market Neutral	1.94%	7.31%	-1.48%	21.43%	1.31%[d]	0.34%	-0.76%
Risk Arbitrage	0.70%	9.91%	-2.00%	13.78%	-2.72%	-2.87%	0.29%
Distressed Securities	-1.38%	6.98%	-12.43%	8.32%	-0.37%	-2.07%	-3.40%
Regulation D	NA	13.83%	2.08%	-7.42%	-2.09%	-3.15%	2.37%
Global Macro	-10.70%	6.88%	-5.93%	3.98%[b]	0.63%	3.39%	7.36%
Long/Short Equity	-2.85%	13.50%	-2.38%[a]	-7.89%	-3.73%	-6.19%	-1.91%
Short Selling	16.15%	1.97%	4.15%	95.56%[c]	8.52%	17.77%	15.57%
Futures CISDM CTA Universe	-1.03%	6.40%	8.12%	11.40%	1.47%	13.22%	6.62%
Futures CISDM Trendfollowing	0.96%	10.48%	18.19%	23.40%	6.03%	27.94%	0.58%
saisGroup Futures Index	0.71%	14.00%	4.81%	28.65%	2.87%	9.79%	17.56%
Fund of Funds	-5.59%	6.23%	-11.60%	-2.62%	-1.58%	-4.20%	-0.81%
S&P 500 (Incl. dividends)	-5.76%	10.58%	-1.57%	-23.05%	-8.17%	-23.17%	-9.17%
MSCI US Treasury Bond Index	-5.04%	6.91%	5.24%	15.85%	-0.35%	8.89%	8.59%

[a] -7.65% in 08/98.
[b] 28.76% for the Tremont index.
[c] 43.72% for the Tremont index.
[d] for Stat Arbitrage: -2.00%

very successful in this climate. Relative Value provided very high returns (more than +20% for Convertible Arbitrage and Equity Market Neutral, and +7.6% for Fixed Income Arbitrage). Futures strategies also did well. However, the stars of the industry were Short Sellers with +95.6% returns. Note that the performance numbers for Short Selling strategies deviate significantly between different data providers. CSFB/Tremont shows a still-impressive return of about +43.7%. This deviation comes from the small number of Short Selling managers. The information reported by each index depends strongly on the inclusion and weighting of managers. Global Macro strategies also made a comeback. Again the CSFB/Tremont numbers are significantly different from those of the HFR; possibly due to different weighting schemes. The Tremont indices are asset-weighted, which puts most emphasis on a relatively small number of large hedge funds.

(5) The month of September 2001 proved to be another real stress test for hedge funds. Generally speaking, the industry held up well. The average fund of funds lost less than −2% compared to −8.2% for the S&P 500 and −0.4% for bonds. Long/Short Equity, Fixed Income Arbitrage and Event Driven lost the most, while Trendfollowers again served as an excellent hedge in the hedge fund portfolio.

(6) Global equity markets fell sharply in the summer of 2002. The S&P 500 lost almost 25% in the four months of June to September, while bonds rallied during the same period. In addition to Short Sellers, the big winners were again Managed Futures strategies, and to a lesser degree Global Macro and Fixed Income Arbitrage. The latter two benefited from the falling interest rates. Long/Short Equity once again experienced the most extended losses of more than −6%, followed by Event Driven managers ranging around −3% each. The average fund of hedge funds had to take losses of about −4.2%.

(7) After an extended period of almost no major market shock the summer of 2007 brought back almost forgotten memories of how volatile the global capital markets can be: the crisis in the US sub-prime market, which sent its shock waves around the world, drove the credit and the inter-bank lending market into paralysis and led to subsequent losses in the global equity markets which continued into the year 2008. As of January 2008 most global equity markets fell back into bear market territory. The hedge fund fared quite well during this crisis with losses occurring only by Distressed Securities and some CTA managers. However, the performance dispersion of managers was large; they can largely be classified into two categories: those who had been short sub-prime and made a killing and those who were not and who encountered more difficulties in showing strong performance. We should further note that the months following January 2008 brought more trouble to hedge funds with less frequently valued portfolios.

4.10 BENEFITS OF HEDGE FUNDS IN A TRADITIONAL PORTFOLIO

In order to demonstrate the effects of including hedge funds in a traditional portfolio of bonds and equities, Figure 4.5 presents the results of a mean–variance optimization in the form of efficient frontiers of a traditional portfolio with and without investment in hedge funds. I used the S&P 500, the MSCI World, the MSCI Europe, the Salomon Smith Barney World Government Bond Index, and the Lehman Brothers US Bond Indices to represent a traditional investor's portfolio. To represent hedge funds, I chose the HFR strategy sector sub-indices,

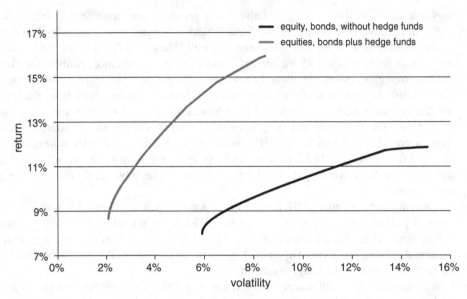

Figure 4.5 Mean–variance optimized portfolios (efficient frontier analysis) in an allocation framework with and without hedge funds (data: S&P 500, MSCI World, MSCI Europe, Salomon Smith Barney World Government Bond Index, Lehman Brothers US Bond Index, HFR strategy sector indices, CISDM Managed Futures Indices, and the sGFII Futures Index).

the CISDM Managed Futures Indices, and the sGFII Futures Index. Graphs like the one in Figure 4.5 are among the most popular elements in every hedge fund marketing or conference presentation.

Before getting out the party hats, potential hedge fund investors need to absorb a few cautions about these figures. Quantitative portfolio optimization techniques, such as the one applied here, are subject to certain assumptions about the risk and return inputs, which are not completely fulfilled for many hedge fund strategies. There is not yet a clear consensus whether mean–variance optimization techniques are applicable to hedge funds. The tail properties – kurtosis and skew – in the return distributions of some hedge fund strategies violate the underlying assumption of normal distribution of returns. Some critics argue that quantitative analysis based on past performance and correlation data is of little value in the hedge fund industry,[24] as statistical analysis and Markowitz-type portfolio optimizations are very sensitive to the return and risk input used for the calculation. The statistical significance and predictive power of historical hedge fund performance data is generally low due to suboptimal quality of past performance data. Indeed, all suggestions of how to measure and monitor hedge fund performance inherit this problem.

As a result of these statistical problems, the effect of including hedge funds in a balanced global portfolio on portfolio efficiency is surely overestimated, if one only considers their impact on mean–variance optimization. The true benefits of hedge funds are surely large enough that they do not need to be exaggerated by spurious claims.

---

[24] The author actually belongs to this group of skeptics.

4.11   QUANTITATIVE PORTFOLIO OPTIMIZATION FOR HEDGE FUNDS REVISITED

There have been several suggestions made in the literature how to cope with the shortcomings of traditional mean–variance optimization in the application to hedge fund portfolios. One of the most prominent is taking estimates of higher moments (and cross-moments) into account by using the Cornish–Fisher expansion. This entails substituting the standard deviation sigma as a risk measure with a measure for 'value at risk' (VaR) defined by rescaling sigma with the z-factor defined by the confidence interval. In this particular approach the z-factor is defined through using the first three cumulants of the Cornish–Fisher expansion.[25] This explicitly considers estimators for the third moment (skew) and fourth moment (kurtosis) of the distribution.[26] However, this extension tends to be unstable in the presence of higher values for the third moment, such as, for example, for Event Driven strategies. Another possibly more useful risk measure for hedge funds is the expected shortfall (also called 'conditional VaR'[27]), which describes the mean portfolio value conditional on the portfolio loss exceeding a certain threshold (which is usually chosen to be the 95% or 99% confidence limit VaR). Expected shortfall supplements volatility or VaR-based risk measures by providing more insight into the tail properties of the return distribution.

At the end of this chapter I would therefore like to demonstrate how the result for the optimal portfolio depends on the chosen risk measure in the optimization. As an example, I have selected two different risk measures for a portfolio optimization: VaR at a 95% confidence interval based on a normal portfolio return distribution, and conditional VaR on a 95% confidence interval calculated based on a Monte Carlo simulation of the historical return distribution of a portfolio.[28] The optimization was performed on the same set of seven individual hedge fund strategies. Figure 4.6 displays the resulting two efficient frontiers, and Figures 4.7(a) and 4.7(b) show the corresponding portfolio compositions of the optimal portfolio at different levels of required (monthly) return. The differences are clear to see: the weights for Event Driven, Convertible Arbitrage and Global Macro are consistently lower in the conditional VaR-based optimization. In other words, if we choose a risk measure, which accounts for higher tails in the distribution such as conditional VaR, these strategies obtain less weight in an optimal portfolio. On the other hand, Managed Futures strategies get assigned a significantly higher weight in the conditional VaR-optimized portfolio. This should not come as a surprise: in periods of market stress where many hedge fund strategies display their worst losses, Managed Futures often show their best performance and thus act as a good balance in the overall portfolio.

---

[25] See E. Cornish, R. Fisher, 'Moments and cumulants in the specifications of distributions', (1937), reprinted in R. Fisher, *Contributions to Mathematical Statistics*, John Wiley & Sons, Inc. (1950).

[26] See A. Signer, L. Favre, 'Mean-modified value-at-risk optimization with hedge funds' (2002).

[27] For more details on conditional VaR see the publication by S. Uryasev and T. Rockafellar, 'Optimization of conditional value-at-risk', *The Journal of Risk*, 2, 3, 2000, pp. 21–41; also available on http://www.ise.ufl.edu/uryasev/roc.pdf. Specifically in the context of hedge funds, see also: P. Blum, M. Dacorogna and L. Jaeger, 'Risk management techniques for hedge funds', in *The New Generation of Risk Management for Hedge Funds and Private Equity Investment*, ed. by L. Jaeger (2003).

[28] For more details, see A. Eibl, 'Risk and return properties of hedge funds' (2004).

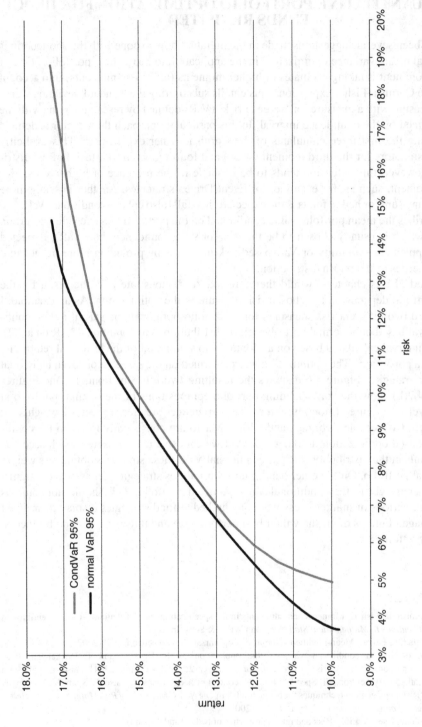

Figure 4.6 The efficient frontiers for an optimization based on normal VaR and conditional (Monte Carlo based) VaR: the underlying portfolios consist of seven hedge fund strategy sectors as measured by the HFR indices for Convertible Arbitrage, Equity Hedge, Equity Market Neutral, Fixed Income Arbitrage, Global Macro, and the CISDM Trendfollowing Index

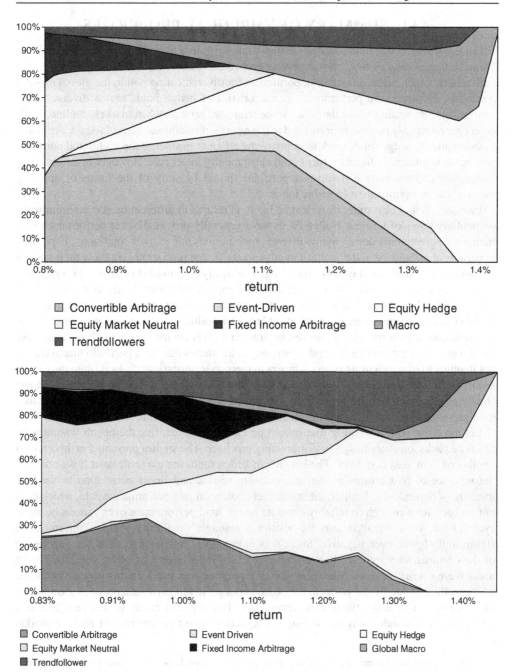

Figure 4.7 (a) The composition of the optimal portfolio at different points on the efficient frontier (specified by the values of the maximum monthly returns) of the normal VaR-based optimization in Figure 4.6. (b) The composition of the optimal portfolio at different points on the efficient frontier (specified by the values of the maximum monthly returns) of the conditional VaR-based Monte Carlo optimization in Figure 4.6

4.12   SUMMARY OF EMPIRICAL PROPERTIES

Taken as a whole, hedge fund strategies demonstrate very attractive risk–reward characteristics. Some strategies display low, zero, or even negative correlations to traditional assets (and to each other), which offers attractive opportunities for diversification within the global investor portfolios. However, the performance characteristics of hedge funds are as diverse as the instruments and trading styles they use. Some strategies do well when markets decline, while others are constantly positively correlated to the returns of traditional asset classes. Considered in their entirety, hedge funds work to improve the efficient frontier of the traditional portfolio, producing significantly higher returns with substantially lower risk. However investors using hedge funds to diversify a traditional portfolio should be wary of the limits of applying mean–variance optimization to hedge funds.

Investors should also study historical hedge fund returns in different market environments, particularly times of turmoil. Hedge funds have generally provided better performance than traditional investments during many different time periods and market conditions. Especially in periods of turbulence in the global capital markets, hedge fund strategies show their relative strength against traditional types of investing. The equity bear market of 2000–2003 provides the best example. But also the most recent performance of hedge funds in the year 2007 supports that observation. While (developed) equity markets experienced a rough second half of the year, hedge funds were in aggregate able to show (albeit small) gains and ended the year in low double-digit territory.[29] However, in stressed market environments funds of funds have fared worse than the average individual strategy. This shows that fund portfolio managers are not immune to overweighting recent winners in their style allocations.[30] As is often the case in traditional assets, yesterday's winners are often tomorrow's losers. Finally, Managed Futures strategies stand out as having generally performed well during market crises. This justifies their presence as a 'hedge' in a multi-manager, multi-strategy portfolio.

Let me close with a warning that should perhaps be printed, like the health warnings on cigarette packs, on every hedge fund marketing brochure. The studies presented in this chapter are flawed in at least two ways. The benefits of hedge funds are overestimated if we consider the variance of past returns as the sole measure of risk and linear correlation as the sole measure of dependence. Further, the studies rely solely on past performance data, which does not go back long enough to reliably estimate hedge fund performance over various business cycles. Even when overall returns are positive, a manager's real excess 'alpha' return can be significantly lower, even negative. Since it is in managers' interests to show the superiority of their returns, they may tend to characterize all of their returns as alpha while forgetting about these alternative risks. Managers who 'believe their own press' in this way are in danger of overselling hedge funds' performance based on a period of favorable prevailing economic circumstances that make them look very smart. But this can result in a severe backlash when investors wonder why the manager's IQ has dropped so severely in adverse market

---

[29] The dispersion in performance across managers was very high, though. While big funds like Goldman Sachs' 'Global Alpha' lost 39% in 2007, other funds were up several hundred per cent. One major reason of this and the fact that hedge funds in aggregate did well was the tremendous return opportunity of the 'short US sub-prime' position. Whether a portfolio manager had that trade in his or her portfolio or not determined whether he or she had a good or a bad year. This applies to funds of funds equally (whether the fund of funds manager had a manager in his portfolio that had this trade on).

[30] The 'short sub-prime' observation from the previous footnote applies here as well.

environments. Equally a manager that might otherwise have been average or below average could suddenly hit the jackpot with one single (often lucky) trade. The short sub-prime trade of several hedge fund managers in 2007 made them look extremely smart. Whether they have really become smart overnight, or just lucky, remains to be seen.[31] When managers oversell the alpha portion of their returns while underselling beta, investor disappointment is inevitable.[32] Finally, the hedge fund universe continues to be subject to change, as new strategies emerge and others vanish. In fact, most hedge fund marketing brochures are obliged to come with such a disclaimer: 'Past performance is not indicative of future performance'.

4.13   APPENDIX: DATA PROVIDERS FOR PAST HEDGE FUND PERFORMANCE

Altvest, New York (www.altvest.com, www.investorforce.com) tracks 13 strategies from a database that allows managers to input their own data. Each fund is assigned to the category in which the largest percentage of its assets is invested. There are no performance criteria for inclusion in the index. Index results are based on reports from more than 1400 hedge funds in a database of 1800 funds. Data goes back to 1993. Altvest is owned by InvestorForce and the website requires registration in order to gain access to the indices.

EDHEC Alternative Indices (www.edhec.com) differ from other indices in that they are constructed from other indices by using the statistical technique of 'principal component analysis' on the historical data of selected other indices.[33]

Evaluation Associates Capital Markets, EACM (www.eacmalternative.com) is based on 100 funds selected to be representative of 13 strategies, arranged in five clusters. The Index is an equally weighted composite of unaudited performance information provided by the funds. EACM bases its results on the same funds from month to month, allowing no manager who had a bad month to avoid inclusion. Funds are assigned categories on the basis of how closely they match the strategy definitions. Names of the funds are not disclosed. The index is rebalanced annually. It was launched in 1996 with data going back to 1990. Capital Markets is owned by Evaluation Associates.

CISDM (formerly 'MAR' and 'Zurich') (www.marhedge.com, www.cisdm.org) reports in each of 15 categories, 10 of which are combined into four sub-medians. CISDM also reports separately on the performance of Managed Futures strategies. The variety of the CISDM databases contains 1300 funds. Managers usually select their own categories. The firm's website identifies the number of funds and assets in each category. MAR, the former publisher of the index, sold its database business to Zurich Financial Services in spring 2001, which subsequently turned over the database to the CISDM (Centre of International Securities

---

[31] Surely they have become very rich: the biggest fee payout to a single hedge fund manager in history went to the hedge fund Paulson Capital amounting to 2.7 billion USD.

[32] Maybe, this is what Warren Buffet refers to when he predicts investors' disappointment over hedge fund returns in the future.

[33] For more details see the paper by the EDHEC Risk and Asset Management Research Center, 'EDHEC Alternative Indices' (2003).

and Derivative Markets) research centre. Dow Jones has launched an investable version of the CISDM index consulted by Schneeweiss Partners.

Credit Suisse First Boston/Tremont (www.hedgeindex.com) covers nine strategies and is based on 340 funds, representing $100 billion in invested capital, selected from a database of 2600 funds. It is the only asset (capitalization) weighted hedge fund index. The CSFB/Tremont Index discloses its construction methods and identifies all the funds within it. CSFB/Tremont accepts only funds (not separate accounts) with a minimum of $10 million under management and an audited financial statement. If a fund liquidates, its performance remains in the Index for the period during which the fund was active in order to minimize survivorship bias. The index was launched in 1999, with data going back to 1994. It incorporates the TASS+ database. Credit Suisse also launched an investable version of this index in 2003.

Hedge Fund Research (www.hfr.com) includes 29 categories plus subtotals. The index is equally weighted and based on 1100 funds, drawn from a database of 1700 funds. Funds of funds are not included in the composite index. Funds in the database represent $260 billion in assets. The index was launched in 1994 with data back to 1990. Funds are assigned to categories based on the descriptions in their offering memorandums. The indices aim at eliminating the survivor bias problem by incorporating funds that have ceased to exist. Hedge Fund Research also launched an investable version of this index in 2003.

Hedgefund.net (www.hedgefund.net), also referred to as 'Tuna Indices', covers 31 strategies arranged into three subtotals. They are updated from a database of 1800 hedge funds and funds of funds. The data goes back to 1979 and managers select their own categories. HedgeFund.Net is operated by Links Securities LLC, an NASD-registered broker-dealer, and owned by Links Holdings and Capital Z Investments.

Hennessee Group (www.hedgefnd.com) reports 22 investment style categories. The indices were created in 1987 and first published in 1992. Results are based on 450 funds, including 150 in which Hennessee clients are invested, from a database of 3000 funds. Assets of $160 billion are represented in the index. Each reporting fund is placed in the category that reflects the manager's core competency.

LJH Global Investments (www.ljh.com) tracks 16 different equally weighted indices, each composed of approximately 50 managers. It is the only index that presents performance exclusively in graph form. To be included, funds must have an audited statement and have passed some level of LJH due diligence. Funds are assigned to categories based on LJH's screenings. The index is rebalanced quarterly or semi-annually, depending upon the strategy. For a fee, LJH provides data on index components.

Morgan Stanley Hedge Fund Indices is a more recently (09/02) launched index platform with about 1500 hedge fund managers. Selection and classification criteria are investment process, asset classes of the traded instruments, and geographical region. MSCI also provides an investable version of its index, which is based on the platform of Lyxor (subsidiary of Société Generale). MSCI provides three composite indices based on fund size, four levels of aggregation, and in total over 140 indices. The indices are equally weighted at the four levels of aggregation and asset-weighted at the composite levels. MSCI also launched an investable version of this index in 2003.

FTSE Hedge Fund Indices is a more recently launched set of purely investable indices containing about 40 managers. The index aims to provide both a daily indicative measure and monthly official performance of the universe of open, investable hedge funds appropriately diversified by 'trading strategy' and 'management style'. The objective of the FTSE Hedge is to produce a series of indices that represent the risk and return of investable hedge fund investment across a number of recognized hedge fund strategies. Unlike other index providers, FTSE has no non-investable counterpart.

Van Hedge Fund Advisors International (www.vanhedge.com) is derived from the performance of an average of more than 750 funds separated into US and offshore funds covering 14 strategies and combined into a separate global index. There are no performance or size criteria and funds are assigned to categories based on their offering memorandums and interviews with the individual managers.

Zurich Capital Markets (www.zcmgroup.com) provides the Zurich Hedge Fund indices in partnership with TRS Associates to track the performance of various hedge fund strategies. They differ from existing hedge fund indices by focusing only on those funds/managers most likely to be considered for investment by institutional and other sophisticated investors. Focusing is on those funds/managers that: (1) are strategy pure in their style; (2) have a two-year minimum performance track record; and (3) have sufficient assets under management to demonstrate organizational and managerial infrastructure, scalable strategies, and the ability to raise funds from sophisticated investors. Highly leveraged strategies and strategies involving complex derivatives are excluded. There is no requirement that these funds be open to new investments, because the indices themselves are not designed to be directly investable and are constructed only to reflect the returns of a particular hedge fund strategy. The indices are equally weighted.

5

The Drivers of Hedge Fund Returns

In this final chapter on hedge fund return sources, I try to bridge the gap between the promises made to investors by hedge fund marketers and the reality of hedge fund managers' performance. For this purpose I will take the reader towards a closer look into the general sources of returns common to hedge fund strategies. This will help us to see through the 'alpha smoke-screen' of hedge fund marketers, understand and appreciate hedge funds' real return sources and finally guide us to the replication thereof. I intend to open up the 'hedge fund black box' by separating the two main elements of its returns, their 'alpha', which is nothing but the result of the hedge fund manager's capability to exploit market inefficiencies, and the 'beta', which is the fair compensation for systematic risk assumed. This lays the groundwork for the ultimate goal of this book – to illustrate how we can systematically analyze, quantify, and at last replicate hedge fund returns.

5.1 ALPHA VERSUS BETA

The discussion on alpha and beta is as old as the Capital Asset Pricing Model which defined these terms some 40 years ago. The discussion has finally reached the hedge fund industry; and the debate on the sources of hedge fund returns is creating one of the most heated discussions within the industry. Hedge fund marketers claim their funds deliver skill-based absolute returns – but do they really? And if the often quite attractive returns of hedge funds do not come purely from alpha, where do they come from? The industry is split into two camps. Following results of substantial research, the proponents on the one side claim that hedge fund returns come from the funds' exposure to systematic risks, i.e. come from their betas. Conversely, the 'alpha protagonists' argue that hedge fund returns depend mostly on the specific skill of the hedge fund managers, a claim that they express in characterizing the hedge fund industry as an 'absolute return' or 'alpha generation' industry. As usual, the truth is likely to fall within the two extremes, but where precisely? We can identify hedge fund returns as a (time-varying) mixture of both systematic risk exposures (beta) and skill-based absolute returns (alpha).

Hedge fund return = Manager's alpha + Market beta(s) + Random fluctuations/luck

The final element of the equation represents random noise in performance which by definition has a zero average. However, with the survivorship bias in empirical returns this term actually carries a positive mean in available past performance data, which vanishes, however, when it comes to future returns. The fundamental question from this equation is: How much is beta, and how much is alpha?

The separation between alpha and beta is further also essential for the risk manager. Beta is free of idiosyncratic, i.e. manager-related, risk, but gives exposure to systematic risks and thereby provides market-driven returns. Alpha, in contrast, is free of systematic risks (a more popular term is 'market neutral') but comes with idiosyncratic risks (for example, of the hedge fund manager blowing up), while its return is driven by manager skill rather than market moves.

There is no consensus definition of 'alpha', and correspondingly there is no consensus model in the hedge fund industry for directly describing the alpha part of hedge fund returns. We define alpha as the part of the return that cannot be explained by the exposure to systematic risk factors in the global capital markets and is thus the return part that stems from the unique ability and skill-set of the hedge fund manager. There is some more agreement in modeling the beta returns, i.e. the systematic risk exposures of hedge funds, which will give us a starting point for decomposition of hedge fund returns into 'alpha' and 'beta' components. I begin with stating the obvious: it is generally not easy to isolate the alpha from the beta in any active investment strategy. But for hedge funds it is not just difficult to separate the two, it is already quite troublesome to distinguish them. We are simply not in a position to give the precise breakdown yet. In other words, the ongoing excitement about hedge funds has only started to be subject to the necessary amount and depth of academic scrutiny. We argue that the better part of the confusion around hedge fund returns arises from the inability of conventional risk measures and theories to properly measure the diverse risk factors of hedge funds. Measures of alpha inextricably depend on the definition of benchmarks or beta components. The ways in which techniques for measuring alpha in a traditional asset management environment are inappropriate or otherwise undermined by the specific characteristics of hedge fund exposures. Moreover, most techniques for measuring hedge fund alpha tend to reward fund managers for model and benchmark mis-specification, as imperfect specification of benchmark or beta exposure tends to inflate alpha. This is why only recently progress in academic research has started to provide us with a better idea about the different systematic risk exposures of hedge funds and thus give us more precise insights into their return sources. Academic research and investors alike begin to realize that the 'search for alpha' must begin with the 'understanding of beta', the latter constituting an important – if not the most important – source of hedge fund returns.

However, at the same time we are starting to realize that 'hedge fund beta' is different from traditional beta. While both are the result of exposures to systematic risks in the global capital markets hedge fund beta is more complex than traditional beta. Some investors can live with a rather simple but illustrative scheme suggested by C. Asness:[1] if the specific return is available only to a handful of investors and the scheme of extracting it cannot be simply specified by a systematic process, then it is most likely real alpha. If it can be specified in a systematic way, but it involves nonconventional techniques such as short selling, leverage and the use of derivatives (techniques which are often used to specifically characterize hedge funds), then it is possibly beta, but in an alternative form, which we will refer to as 'alternative beta'. In the hedge fund industry 'alternative beta' is often sold as alpha, but is not real alpha as defined here. If finally extracting the returns does not require any of these special 'hedge fund techniques' but rather 'long only investing', then it is 'traditional beta'.

The discussion on hedge fund returns relates directly to the academic dispute about the rationality of investors and market efficiency, two cornerstones of modern financial theory. The current state of hedge fund research bears analogies to atomic physics at the beginning of the twentieth century. We want to understand the 'atoms' of investment returns in the global capital markets, i.e. their breakdown into individual components. And what we currently observe is the emergence of an underlying fundamental theory, or in analogy to physics, the theory of 'quantum mechanics of global investment'.

---

[1] C. Asness in 'An alternative future, I & II', *Journal of Portfolio Management* (2004).

5.2 THE ENIGMA OF HEDGE FUND RETURNS

One of hedge funds' central selling points has been the claim of providing investors with 'absolute returns'; performance uncorrelated to the direction of the global capital markets. This claim rests on the notion that hedge funds derive their returns from special manager skill rather than from systematic risk. However, the actual fund performance numbers discussed in Chapter 4 call into question the broad claims of both market neutrality and 'absolute returns'. Hedge funds have in recent years converged with conventional asset classes in showing poor total performance during stressful market conditions (the most recent example we experienced during the market turbulences from the summer of 2007 to spring 2008 following the US sub-prime crisis). Figure 5.1 shows the 3-year rolling performance of various hedge fund strategy sectors as calculated by Hedge Fund Research (HFR) from the mid-1990s to the beginning of 2008. Performance fluctuates widely, rather than showing the steadiness that purely alpha-based performance would predict. More telling still is the significant downtrend of many strategies during the bear equity market of 2000 through 2003 followed by the uptrend in the subsequent years of equity rallies. Finally, the last little dip on the very right clearly indicates that hedge funds were not immune to the market turbulences in the summer of 2007 and subsequent months.

Conceptually, we need to separate hedge fund returns into two separate components. The first part consists of premia for exposure to systematic risk factors, i.e. beta. The second part is what asset pricing theory language refers to as 'alpha'.[2] These returns are the real 'excess return' over the fair compensation for exposure to systematic risk and are uniquely based on manager skill. Or, as Alexander Ineichen puts it simply: 'Alpha is honest pay for a hard day's work'.[3] At core, it means skill in finding and exploiting pricing inefficiencies across the global capital markets.

Generally, active asset managers across all asset classes endeavor to generate returns above the benchmark they are measured by. In other words, they focus on achieving 'above market' returns, i.e. 'alpha',[4] on the basis of their skill. The three sources of alpha commonly referred to are:

- Security (e.g. stocks) picking: Appropriate selection of individual securities.
- Market timing: Choosing the right entry or exit points for an investment into the market.
- Best execution: Executing trade ideas at best prices.

It is well known that the large majority of traditional active asset managers do not create excess returns for investors; in fact, most do not even cover their own fees.[5] This result came as a huge surprise to active asset managers when academics like W. Sharpe published their pioneering studies in the late 1960s.[6] Hedge fund managers are largely trading in the same markets as their traditional counterparts, using similar investment techniques, albeit with more

[2] I am leaving out the 'luck component' of hedge fund returns which also has its Greek symbol: 'epsilon'.

[3] A. Ineichen, *Absolute Returns* (2002).

[4] In its original meaning, 'alpha' refers to the y-intercept (minus the risk-free rate) in a linear factor model, i.e. the part of the return that cannot be explained by systematic risk factors included in the model (the sensitivity to which is referred to as 'beta').

[5] See the seminal paper by W. Sharpe, 'Mutual fund performance' (1966). For a more recent discussion see: 'Another puzzle: the growth in actively managed mutual funds' by M. Gruber (1996) and references therein.

[6] See P. Bernstein's fabulous description of the development of modern Wall Street in *Capital Ideas* (1993) for more details.

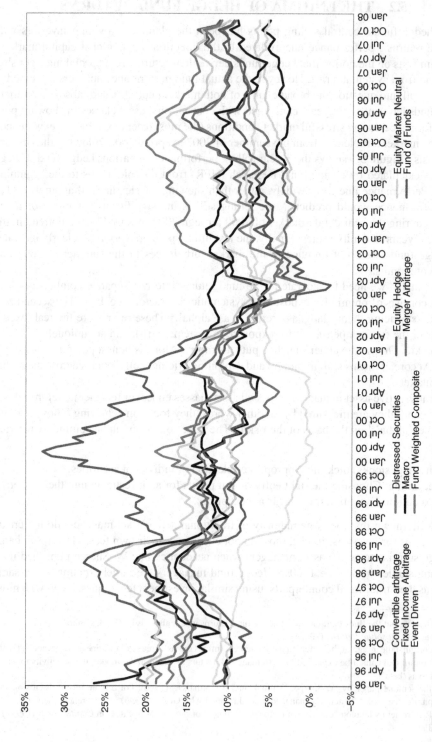

Figure 5.1 The rolling 3-year return of various hedge fund strategies as given by Hedge Fund Research

flexibility to sell short, leverage, and use derivatives. Yet they seem to beat benchmarks defined for traditional fund managers, especially when those benchmarks are risk-adjusted.

We have seen in the previous chapter that over their whole history hedge funds have generated higher average returns with lower risk than traditional investments. This outperformance props up the widely held belief that hedge funds earn their returns by identifying market 'inefficiencies' not recognized by other participants. But skeptical investors familiar with the modern theory of finance must ask themselves some critical questions. Are hedge fund managers really so much smarter than traditional managers? Can the trading flexibility enjoyed by hedge fund managers to leverage and short sell be a sufficient explanation for alpha? Even if one answers 'yes' to all of these questions, what about the future? If hedge fund performance is largely based on market inefficiencies, how sustainable are these returns in light of increasing money flow into the industry? Can there possibly be enough remaining inefficiencies in the liquid global capital markets to provide a steady stream of alpha to the growing USD 2+ trillion hedge fund industry?

Some hedge fund marketers claim that greater trading flexibility generates excess returns compared to traditional investments. Hedge fund managers do indeed enjoy greater freedom to short sell, take concentrated positions in single securities, leverage, or engage in derivatives trading. Yet, these techniques alone do not generate alpha. Leverage is simply a way to scale risk and return. Like the height and width of an enlarged photograph, scaling up the return dimension proportionately scales up the risk dimension as well. Furthermore, short selling and derivatives are central assumptions of all equilibrium-based asset-pricing models. Since these types of trades are already in all models of efficient markets, no excess return can be expected from them beyond normal compensation for taking risk. As for concentrated positions, all asset pricing theories indicate that concentrated bets in individual securities increase (idiosyncratic) risk but not expected returns.

There is a surface logic to the idea that excess hedge fund returns must be due to special manager skill. Investors' logic is simple: if hedge fund managers produce absolute returns while most traditional fund managers do not outperform their benchmark indices, the excess returns must be due to the skill of the hedge fund managers. Seeing returns as due to personal manager alpha, some hedge fund investors try desperately to invest with perceived star managers. Finance magazine features testify to this manager personality cult. Investors' 'search for Alpha' has therefore also produced a 'quest for capacity' with perceived star managers in the past. Yes, hedge fund managers are among the smartest actors on Wall Street. But are we to believe that they are so much smarter that they can consistently and indefinitely exploit inefficiencies in the world's most efficient markets? We should go into some details of the hedge fund return generation process, an undertaking that I also want to refer to as the 'critique of pure alpha'.[7]

5.3 HEDGE FUND RETURNS: HOW MUCH IS ALPHA?

If we believe neither trading flexibility nor manager skill at exploiting market inefficiencies fully accounts for the excess returns of hedge funds, where do these returns actually come from? I assert that the major source of hedge fund returns is not manager alpha, but rather

---

[7] In analogy to Immanuel Kant's *The Critique of Pure Reason*, which he published in 1781, and which caused the 'Copernican revolution' in philosophical metaphysics.

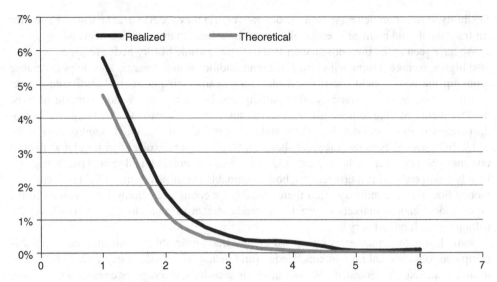

Figure 5.2 Persistence of top quartile performance as measured by the Sharpe ratio for hedge funds (data source: Tass database (about 4000 managers))

market beta, i.e. various types of risk premia. The main reason for the persistent confusion between the two is that standard finance models do not adequately describe the diverse risks for which hedge funds earn these premia. In order to characterize hedge returns as 'excess' (i.e. alpha), and therefore due solely to manager skill, we must first properly assess the systematic risk factors to which hedge managers expose their funds. In other words, to repeat my pledge: the 'search for alpha' has to start with the understanding and identification of beta.

If alpha was the dominant element of hedge fund returns, we would expect strong persistence in individual manager performance on an absolute scale, as well as relative to other managers. It is indeed persistence which distinguishes alpha from luck (the third hedge fund return source, I should add). Performance persistence is particularly important in hedge funds, because they suffer a much higher failure rate than traditional mutual funds.[8] While we would expect the most skillful managers to show their skill year after year, a low degree of persistence in hedge fund managers' performance makes it difficult to say that a good year's performance is due to alpha rather than luck. Few of us become enormously smarter or dumber on an annual basis. It is reasonable to assume the same holds for hedge fund managers.[9]

There are several studies on hedge fund persistence in the literature,[10] most of which report surprisingly low persistence in performance. In Figure 5.2 I report some results of my own studies. The figure shows two graphs. One represents the evolution of the first quartile of hedge fund managers over the years. The upper graph shows how many of the original best 25%

---

[8] See S. Brown, W. Goetzmann, R. Ibbotson, 'Offshore hedge funds: survival and performance 1989–1995', *Journal of Business*, 92 (1999).

[9] I mentioned the '2007 short subprime trade' as an example in footnote 29 of Chapter 4: whether a manager had that trade in his or her portfolio or not determined whether he or she had a good or a bad 2007. Such a trade could be the result of great forecasting skills (in this case foreseeing the US housing trouble) or just a lucky trade.

[10] See, for example, V. Agarwal, N. Naik, 'Multi-period performance persistence analysis of hedge funds' (2000).

managers continue to be in the top quartile after the subsequent two, three, four, etc. years and thus measures the actual outperformance persistence measured within a set of around 4000 hedge fund managers in the well known TASS database. For reasons of comparison I made a crude assumption for the second graph: outperformance is simply a matter of chance, i.e. the actual performance of each single hedge fund manager corresponds to a random walk around some common mean. In other words, there is no real persistence in outperformance by any hedge fund manager. The mathematics behind the second graph is simple: 25% of the original 25% remain top quartile in year two by pure chance, 25% of 25% of 25% in the third year, etc. The graph represents a simple exponential function. The difference between these two graphs is thus a measure of real outperformance persistence in the hedge fund industry. We see that this measure does not yield impressive results. It is rather small (albeit larger than the persistence in outperformance we can observe in mutual funds).

If manager performance is not persistent, are perhaps some strategies more alpha-laden than others? That is, are some strategies simply more adept at exploiting market inefficiencies? In a simple study, summarized in Figure 5.3, I ranked performance of the different hedge fund strategy sectors in different years. Each sector has one tint across all years. The reader can clearly observe the wild fluctuations of relative and absolute performance of the different strategies across the years. Again, if alpha were the main driver of hedge fund returns, there would be more consistency in relative strategy sector performance from year to year. These first rather straightforward observations merit a more detailed examination of the question of how much alpha is actually in hedge fund returns.

5.4 THE EFFICIENT MARKET HYPOTHESIS

More than a century ago, Louis Bachelier broke ground for the entire structure of modern finance theory when he wrote: 'Past, present, and even discounted future events are (all) reflected in market prices.'[11] The modern expression of Bachelier's seminal idea is the theory known as the 'efficient market hypothesis' (EMH).[12] EMH states that consistent alpha generation, i.e. performance exceeding the return from systematic risk and the risk-free interest rate, should not be possible in the global capital markets. In other words, there is no 'free lunch' in financial markets.

The EMH comes in three different forms: the strong, the semi-strong, and the weak version. These are distinguished by just how efficient they claim the markets to be and the amount of information they consider to be accounted for in security prices. The weak form asserts that historical data (on prices, volumes, etc.) are fully reflected in the pricing of securities at any time, so technical analysis cannot be persistently profitable. The semi-strong hypothesis states that prices fully reflect all publicly available information, so on top of chart analysis fundamental analysis cannot be persistently profitable. The strong version states that there is no price relevant information available to *any* investor that is not yet reflected in market prices, including nonpublic information. This version of the EMH implies that there is simply no way to earn any alpha in financial markets. Any excess return is the result of pure luck and coincidence. In other words, active investment professionals should all just go home.

---

[11] L. Bachelier, *Theory of Speculation* (1900).

[12] See the seminal paper by E. Fama: 'Efficient capital markets: II', published in the *Journal of Finance*, December 1991, and the book by B. Malkiel, *A Random Walk down Wall Street* (1973).

	1994	1995	1996	1997	1998	1999	2000	2001	2002	2003	2004	2005	2006	2007
1	Short Bias 14.9%	Global Macro 30.7%	Emerg Markets 34.5%	Global Macro 37.1%	Futures/CTA 20.6%	Long Short 47.2%	Conv Arbitrage 25.6%	Global Macro 18.4%	Futures/CTA 18.3%	Emerg Markets 28.8%	Event Driven 14.5%	Emerg Markets 17.4%	Emerg Markets 20.5%	Emerg Markets 20.3%
2	Emerg Markets 12.5%	Long Short 23.0%	Global Macro 25.6%	Emerg Markets 26.6%	Long Short 17.2%	Emerg Markets 44.8%	Short Bias 15.8%	Conv Arbitrage 14.6%	Short Bias 18.1%	Event Driven 20.0%	Emerg Markets 12.5%	Short Bias 17.0%	Event Driven 15.7%	Global Macro 17.4%
3	Futures/CTA 12.0%	Event Driven 18.3%	Event Driven 23.1%	Long Short 21.5%	Eq Market Neut 13.3%	Event Driven 22.3%	Eq Market Neut 15.0%	Event Driven 11.5%	Global Macro 14.7%	Global Macro 18.0%	Long Short 11.6%	Long Short 9.7%	Long Short 14.4%	Long Short 13.7%
4	Risk Arb 5.3%	Conv Arbitrage 16.6%	Conv Arbitrage 17.9%	Event Driven 20.0%	Risk Arb 5.6%	Conv Arbitrage 16.0%	Risk Arb 14.7%	Eq Market Neut 9.3%	Eq Market Neut 7.4%	Long Short 17.3%	Global Macro 8.5%	Global Macro 9.2%	Conv Arbitrage 14.3%	Event Driven 13.2%
5	Event Driven 0.7%	Fixed Inc Arb 12.5%	Long Short 17.1%	Eq Market Neut 14.8%	Global Macro -3.6%	Eq Market Neut 15.3%	Global Macro 11.7%	Fixed Inc Arb 8.0%	Emerg Markets 7.4%	Futures/CTA 14.1%	Fixed Inc Arb 6.9%	Event Driven 9.0%	Global Macro 13.5%	Eq Market Neut 9.3%
6	Fixed Inc Arb 0.3%	Risk Arb 11.9%	Eq Market Neut 16.6%	Conv Arbitrage 14.5%	Conv Arbitrage -4.4%	Risk Arb 13.2%	Event Driven 7.3%	Emerg Markets 5.8%	Fixed Inc Arb 5.8%	Conv Arbitrage 12.9%	Eq Market Neut 6.5%	Eq Market Neut 6.1%	Eq Market Neut 11.2%	Risk Arb 8.8%
7	Eq Market Neut -2.0%	Eq Market Neut 11.0%	Fixed Inc Arb 15.9%	Risk Arb 9.8%	Event Driven -4.9%	Fixed Inc Arb 12.1%	Fixed Inc Arb 6.3%	Risk Arb 5.7%	Conv Arbitrage 4.0%	Risk Arb 9.0%	Futures/CTA 6.0%	Risk Arb 3.1%	Fixed Inc Arb 8.7%	Short Bias 6.0%
8	Global Macro -5.7%	Futures/CTA -7.1%	Risk Arb 13.8%	Fixed Inc Arb 9.3%	Short Bias -6.0%	Global Macro 5.8%	Futures/CTA 4.2%	Futures/CTA 1.9%	Event Driven 0.2%	Fixed Inc Arb 8.0%	Risk Arb 5.5%	Fixed Inc Arb 0.6%	Risk Arb 8.1%	Futures/CTA 6.0%
9	Conv Arbitrage -8.1%	Short Bias -7.4%	Futures/CTA 12.0%	Futures/CTA 3.1%	Fixed Inc Arb -8.2%	Futures/CTA -4.7%	Long Short 2.1%	Short Bias -3.6%	Long Short -1.6%	Eq Market Neut 7.1%	Conv Arbitrage 2.0%	Futures/CTA -0.1%	Futures/CTA 8.1%	Conv Arbitrage 5.1%
10	Long Short -8.1%	Emerg Markets -16.9%	Short Bias -5.5%	Short Bias 0.4%	Emerg Markets -37.7%	Short Bias -14.2%	Emerg Markets -5.5%	Long Short -3.7%	Risk Arb -3.5%	Short Bias -32.6%	Short Bias -7.7%	Conv Arbitrage -2.5%	Short Bias -6.6%	Fixed Inc Arb 3.8%

Figure 5.3 Ranking for performance of the different hedge fund strategy sectors in different years. Each sector has one tint across all years. Data source: CSFB/Tremont

Although it is a foundation stone of modern finance, the EMH remains one of the most hotly debated topics in the financial community. Most investment professionals and academics do not adhere fully to the EMH, at least in its strong or semi-strong form (the weak version is more broadly accepted by academics and experienced investors alike). Over the years the EMH has been argued over and even refuted, but it remains the null hypothesis of any asset pricing model, the theory to beat.[13] Market efficiency advocates such as E. Fama[14] base their arguments on the rationality of investors: investors always act in their objectively and rationally determined best interest. Yet a counter-movement has developed and been supported by research based on a branch in psychology referred to as 'behavioral theory' that shows that human investment decisions are not always rational. However, academics and investors alike recognize that efficiency varies across different capital markets. The foreign exchange markets for the major currencies, G7 government bond, and the large capitalization segment of major international equity markets are regarded as quite 'efficient'. Therefore 'alpha' returns are most difficult to obtain in these markets. Less liquid markets like the small cap segments of the equity markets, securities of distressed firms, collateralized debt securities, convertible bonds, or the markets for exotic options and other complex instruments are seen as less efficient.

5.5 QUESTIONING THE EFFICIENT MARKET HYPOTHESIS: BEHAVIORAL FINANCE

Behavioral finance claims that most investors are not acting rationally and as a result the global financial markets are not fully efficient. This enables some more rational investors to extract excess returns from market inefficiencies produced by the irrational behavior of the majority. Behavioral finance advocates have formulated a variety of different deviations from rationality in investors' behavior to explain pricing anomalies. Much of the current research in the field of behavioral finance stems from the work of two psychologists, Daniel Kahneman and Amos Tversky.[15] Starting from their previous research into psychological biases, Kahneman and Tversky studied how people fall short of the standard paradigm of investor rationality. This formed the basis of their 'Prospect Theory'.

The classical analysis of decision making under risk is based on three assumptions regarding investors' behavior: asset integration, risk aversion, and rational expectations. Asset integration means that investors always base their preferences for holding a security on their overall portfolio, P, i.e. they prefer a security x over y, if they prefer $P + x$ over $P + y$. Risk aversion means that investors prefer the less risky investment among choices with a given expected return. One would rather hold a Treasury bill than a junk bond if both are expected to yield 5%. Rational expectation is the notion that investors are coherent and unbiased forecasters, who

---

[13] Standard finance proponents argue that market efficiency is not testable because such tests must be jointly accompanied by a test of an asset pricing model.

[14] See E. Fama, 'Market efficiency, long term returns and behavioral finance' (1998).

[15] See their seminal works 'Prospect theory: an analysis of decision making under risk' (1979) and *Judgment under Uncertainty: Heuristics and Biases* (1982). Kahneman was awarded with the Nobel Prize in economics in 2002 (unfortunately, Amos Tversky died in 1996 and did not get his share of the fame). For references on more recent work in the field of behavioral finance, see: H. Shefrin, *Beyond Greed and Fear: Behavioral Finance and the Psychology of Investing* (1999), revised version: Oxford University Press (2002); Stratman, M., 'Behavioral finance: past battles and future engagements' (1999).

incorporate all available information. This implies that, in the absence of insider information, investors would all agree on a single price for a security.

Behavioral finance proponents cast serious doubts on these assumptions. They claim that investors are often subject to what they call 'cognitive illusions' that keep them from making fully rational decisions. What are some of these illusions?

(1) Loss aversion: Classical economic theory expects the rational investor to respond in exactly the same way to a choice, whether it is formulated in terms of gain or loss. Behavioral finance predicts instead that investors will choose differently when a choice is formulated in terms of loss rather than gain. This is because investors' attitudes toward risks concerning gains are often different from their attitudes toward risks concerning losses. For example, when given a choice between getting $100 000 with certainty or having a 50% chance of getting $250 000 they most often choose the certain $100 000 over the uncertain chance of getting $250 000 even though the mathematical expectation of the second, uncertain option is $125 000. This is considered a perfectly rational attitude in standard finance, which is referred to as risk-aversion. But when investors are confronted with a certain loss of $100 000 versus a 50% chance of no loss or a $200 000 loss they often choose the risky alternative. They seek risk rather than avoiding it. There is a clear asymmetry of choices investors make with respect to prospective losses or gains. There is considerable evidence that investors' risk aversion holds for the domain of gains but risk seeking holds in the domain of losses.[16] While standard theory maps investor behavior to the standard logarithmically shaped utility function, behavioral finance formulates a new 'value function' defined in terms of differences in wealth levels.[17] Investors frame their decision in terms of gains and losses, not in terms of terminal wealth. This leads many investors to hold on to their losses in a certain security although it would be rational to sell the security and realize the loss. Investors generally hold on to losers too long in order to avoid the embarrassment of realizing a loss, even as they sell winners too early to be certain of a gain.[18]

(2) Reference framing (generalized version of loss aversion): One of the major claims of behavioral finance is that the reference point of the investor becomes a critical factor in his evaluation of possible choices and his ultimate decision. This reference point is based on where he stands with the P&L of his investments, his wealth, and other factors. Behavioral finance theory claims that alternatives are not evaluated in terms of financial outcome but of gains and losses relative to the reference point. In other words, investors' preferences depend on how decisions are framed, not just on the objective probabilities of outcomes.

(3) Asset segregation: Investors tend to evaluate investment options one at a time and not in the context of an aggregated portfolio. A house and stock portfolio are evaluated separately,

---

[16] Kahneman and Tversky define the necessary multiple of offered return for the positive outcome coin flip to the possible loss after a negative outcome, as the 'coefficient of loss aversion'.

[17] See A. Tversky, 'The psychology of decision making', in *Behavioral Finance and Decision Theory in Investment Management* (1995).

[18] See also the research by T. Odean and B. Barber, 'The courage of misguided convictions: the trading behavior of individual investors' (1999). Based on the analysis of data from a discount brokerage house in the US and 10 000 randomly selected accounts, the authors state that the average underperformance of stocks that investors bought was more than 3% compared to the stocks that were sold on a time frame of one year.

even though a perfectly rational investor would treat them as elements of a single overall portfolio.

(4) Mental accounting: Investors tend to organize their investments in terms of mental accounts. A security that posts a loss in one account is treated differently from a loss in another account. This notion of mental accounting offers an explanation for why investors prefer stocks that offer dividends.[19] According to standard finance theory, an investor (ignoring the effect of a possible different tax treatment) should be indifferent to whether gains are paid out as dividends or show up as appreciation of the stock price ('Miller and Modigliani principle'). There should be only one mental 'bucket'. However, behavioral finance claims that many investors treat a dollar earned on capital gains differently than a dollar earned in dividends, even after factoring out tax and transaction costs. They put the dividend into the 'for consumption' account, while the former remains in the 'savings account' and cannot be spent. Rational investors would not separate these two accounts and would simply sell shares when they wanted to spend their gains.

(5) Overconfidence: A major claim of behavioral finance is the phenomenon of investor overconfidence. Simply put, the average investor (or driver, or tennis player) believes their skills are above average! Therefore there is a clear tendency for investors to be overconfident in their forecasts. If analysts are 80% confident that a stock will go up, they are right in about 50% of the cases. Investors are often too sure about a future outcome or a future security price. So it is hard for them to accept that the outcome they believe to be a near certainty is actually quite uncertain. Since overconfidence is as prevalent in finance as in every other human endeavor investors are consistently more confident of their conclusions than their hit rate would justify. They are 'often wrong but never in doubt'. Overconfidence produces the illusion of control, a lack of critical self-assessment, insensitivity to evidence on predictive accuracy, and misperception of the role of chance. Judgments are consistently biased. Overconfidence also leads investors to trade too much which leads to significant underperformance.[20] This helps to explain why investors often trade to excess on new information, extrapolate current trends, and mistake randomness for predictable patterns. Overconfidence also explains investors' love affair with recent winners. They are confident that performance repeats itself, or they simply extrapolate most recent trends (again this is not limited to investors only). This same notion also leads many investors to believe that a one-year track record is proof that a particular manager has skill. So investors chase mutual funds (as well as hedge funds) with the best recent performance, despite clear empirical proof that their performance is not persistent.

(6) Representation bias: Standard finance models do not account for behavioral bias driven by the incentive schemes and career considerations of professional money managers. Managers whose accounts are reviewed frequently are motivated to buy securities that have recently done well, as this makes them look better to their clients in the review. The tendency to select 'good companies' rather than 'good stocks' in an effort to make the

---

[19] See also: M. Miller, 'Behavioral rationality in finance: the case of dividends' (1986).

[20] T. Odean in 'Do investors trade too much?' (1999) and (with B. Barber) 'Trading is hazardous to your wealth: the common stock performance of individual investors' (2000). Odean uses data from over 60 000 households from a large discount brokerage firm and analyses the performance of individual investors from February 1991 to December 1996 and finds a poor performance of those households that trade the most – lagging the gross of fee performance of the average household by about 8–9%.

portfolio look attractive to clients is clearly driven by concerns of reputation rather than rational portfolio management.

Behavioral finance has carved out a respectable niche in academic economics, although it stills lacks a unified theory. Researchers as well as practitioners have found the behavioral finance paradigm is well-suited to explaining at least some of the excess returns in hedge funds. An interesting extension of behavioral finance was suggested by George Soros, one of the godfathers of hedge funds. In his book *The Alchemy of Finance: Reading the Mind of the Market* he agrees that market participants are biased and subject to cognitive errors. Further, he states that no market agent has perfect information. He then extends the argument and claims that these biases can have a significant impact on the fundamentals themselves. In other words, there is a recursive relationship between prices as determined by biased economic agents and the real fundamentals in the economy. Soros believes that financial markets cannot correctly discount for the expected future outcome, as standard finance assumes, because the markets themselves help to shape the future. He calls this recursive effect 'reflexivity'. One implication of his reflexivity theory is that the market equilibrium, the holy grail of standard finance, is never reached.[21] However, the jury is still out on the key practical question: do these deviations from rationality lead to predictable errors and systematic mispricings upon which more rational investors can consistently capitalize? Answering this question is key for those interested in hedge fund returns, since the claim for alpha flies in the face of the efficient market hypothesis.

5.6 THE THEORETICAL FRAMEWORK OF MODERN FINANCE: ASSET PRICING MODELS AND THE INTERPRETATIONS OF ALPHA

In order to drill down into the distinction between alpha and beta, we must first have a clear grasp of the basic assumptions and implications of common financial asset pricing models. Let's take a moment to review those and discuss how hedge funds fit into these models.[22] The Capital Asset Pricing Model or CAPM assumes the following:

(1) Normal return distribution: Mean and variance, i.e. return and volatility, explain the return characteristics of the investment completely. Evaluation of risk and return can therefore occur in a mean–variance framework, in which utility is a linear function of expected return and a quadratic function of risk.
(2) A single source of systematic risk: There is only one priced risk for which investors are rewarded, which is the broad market risk. Strictly speaking this is not an assumption but an implication of the CAPM.
(3) Frictionless trading: There are no transaction costs, taxes, etc. Investors can sell short securities without any restrictions.

---

[21] Soros's thoughts are strongly influenced by the philosopher Karl Popper and his ideas about the evolution of thoughts and scientific ideas. See: K. Popper, *The Logic of Scientific Discovery* (1933), original German title: *Die Logik der Forschung*.

[22] Most finance books cover the CAPM, including its fundamental assumptions, in great detail, e.g. F. Reilly, K. Brown, *Investment Analysis and Portfolio Management*, The Dryden Press (1997).

(4) Homogeneity of investor behavior: Investors act on identical and constant investment time horizons, and they have homogeneous expectations about returns, volatilities, and correlations of securities and asset classes.

While none of these assumptions strictly apply to traditional investments' returns, they apply even less to the positions and instruments applied by hedge funds.

Normal return distribution

If returns are normally distributed, then mean and the standard deviation (volatility) are the only two factors one needs to know. As a result, analyzing risk versus return is easy. Therefore, traditional asset pricing models tend to assume a normal distribution. But this assumption contrasts with reality when the probability distribution of investment outcomes is skewed (i.e. nonsymmetric) or leptokurtic (i.e. possesses fat tails). Numerous hedge fund strategies have negatively skewed return distributions. Furthermore statisticians commonly agree that the return distributions of most financial instruments themselves are actually leptokurtic. Hedge funds are no exception: some strategies actually display rather expressed fat tails. Table 5.1, for example, shows the first four moments[23] of different Event Driven and Relative Value strategies taken from Table 4.1. Risk-averse investors usually have a preference for positively skewed outcomes and an aversion to negatively skewed and fat-tailed performances. This investor bias is not captured by a risk measure like the standard deviation that weighs each part of the distribution identically and does not sufficiently consider the probability of extreme events (fat tails). Therefore, standard mean–variance optimization is not universally appropriate when hedge funds are part of the investment portfolio.[24]

A good example of fat-tail risk combined with negative skews is the short option exposure of certain hedge fund strategies. Selling naked options generates attractive premium income with comparably rare occasions of larger losses. The resulting return profile can create impressive Sharpe ratios, and quantitative mean–variance-based portfolio optimization tends to recommend inappropriately large allocations to these strategies.[25] Often the risk inherent in these strategies has not yet manifested itself during the manager's relatively brief performance history. How can we account for these extra risks, which express themselves in the higher moments of the return distribution? One way to do so is by simply subtracting the price of a far-out-of-the-money option from the returns of these strategies. These options would constitute a fictive hedge against these rare but, if they occur, heavy losses. They therefore represent the premium required by a rational investor for bearing these extra tail risks.

---

[23] See also the discussion in Chapter 4. The third and the fourth moment of a probability distribution describe the skew and kurtosis, respectively. The author notes for the purpose of mathematical correctness that the estimates provide no indication that these higher moments actually exist, i.e. the corresponding integral that defines their converges.

[24] See also the discussion in Chapter 4. Some research on the difficulties of measuring the effects of hedge funds in a portfolio and a consideration of higher moments in the optimization is presented by A. Signer and L. Favre, 'The difficulties of measuring the benefits of hedge funds' (Summer 2002) and reference therein. However, their research so far lacks convincing applicability in an optimization framework beyond mean–variance optimization.

[25] Further, the use of historical data for the purpose of hedge fund strategy and manager selection in combination with conventional portfolio optimization techniques usually results in portfolios with inappropriately high nonconsidered risks and low liquidity (e.g. large allocations to Regulation D and Distressed Debt securities).

Table 5.1 The first four moments (mean return, standard deviation, skew, excess kurtosis) of the return distribution of Event Driven, Convertible Arbitrage and Fixed Income Arbitrage strategy sector indices of Tremont and HFR. Additionally, the maximal drawdown and the Sharpe ratio (calculated with 5% risk-free interest rate) are shown. Data is taken from January 1994 to December 2007

	Return	Volatility	Skewness	Kurtosis	Max. drawdown	Sharpe ratio
Event Driven						
HFRI	13.02%	6.23%	−1.35	6.13	−10.78%	1.31
Tremont	11.87%	5.62%	−3.66	27.69	−16.05%	1.24
Relative Value						
HFRI Relative Value	9.78%	3.08%	−2.58	18.82	−6.55%	1.59
Convertible Arbitrage (HFRI)	9.01%	3.59%	−0.99	1.88	−7.34%	1.15
Convertible Arbitrage (Tremont)	8.76%	4.60%	−1.37	3.34	−12.03%	0.84
Fixed Income Arbitrage (HFRI)	5.83%	3.72%	−3.34	19.92	−14.42%	0.25
Fixed Income Arbitrage (Tremont)	6.27%	3.69%	−3.10	17.31	−12.48%	0.37

A single source of systematic risk

The notion of a single source of systematic risk in a portfolio is plainly false if applied to hedge funds. Indeed, it is the very nature of hedge funds to be long in other types of systematic risk. In general, any nondiversifiable risk such as low liquidity, credit risk, or sector risk will carry a risk premium, usually in the form of a positive expected return. The use of historical data for the purpose of hedge fund strategy and manager selection in combination with conventional portfolio optimization techniques and methods usually results in portfolios with inappropriately high nonconsidered risks and low liquidity, e.g. large allocations to Distressed Debt securities.

But hedge funds are not only exposed to an entire additional set of underlying systematic risk factors, to make matters worse their exposure to these risk factors evolves dynamically over time. This constant shift in the mix of risk exposure is itself a sort of meta-risk factor. The standard asset pricing models – even in multi-factor forms – do not allow the dynamics of this exposure to be taken into account. They only measure average exposure, and not exposure variability.[26]

Hedge fund managers reinterpret the assumption of a single source of risk when they call themselves 'absolute return' oriented. In effect some are claiming to have a zero equity market beta. While this may be true of a few strategies, such as Equity Market Neutral and some Relative Value strategies, most strategies certainly do have positive market beta. But most importantly, besides a positive market beta, hedge funds can have a nonzero exposure to a variety of other betas.

Frictionless trading

Frictionless trading is of course never the case in the real world. Transaction costs are a factor of consideration for any investor. Hedge fund managers often have an edge in controlling

---

[26] The use of conditional beta models has been suggested in Chapter 4 by looking at conditional correlations and return. Another study is the one by T. Schneeweis and H. Kazemi in 'Conditional performance of hedge funds' (2003).

transaction costs. On the beta side, managers can use derivatives and leverage to scale up returns from low-risk/low-reward trades that would otherwise be consumed by the cost of the trade. On the alpha side, hedge fund managers' specific market knowledge helps them know when and how to trade to minimize transaction costs. Of course, the purchase and sale of hedge funds has its own friction. Investors pay transaction costs in the form of extended redemption periods or exit penalties (not to mention possible fees paid to intermediaries).

Homogeneity of investor behavior

Hedge fund strategies are not 'buy and hold' strategies. Managers change positions frequently and use leverage, short selling, and derivative instruments. So the payoff profiles of hedge funds are often highly nonlinear. Since hedge fund managers do not behave like other market participants, the fit of standard asset pricing models to hedge fund returns is further undermined.

Looking at the poor match of all of these common CAPM assumptions to hedge fund returns, it is not so surprising that standard models do not fully capture the sources of hedge fund returns. Much recent academic research has highlighted the inadequacy of the CAPM and related multi-factor models and highlighted the (often nonlinear) exposure of hedge funds to alternative factors such as credit, liquidity, and volatility risk.[27]

5.7 SYSTEMATIC RISK PREMIA: THE PREVALENCE OF BETA IN THE GLOBAL CAPITAL MARKETS

In capital markets, risk premia are the result of imperfect risk sharing: some investors do not want to hold certain risks while others do (and ask a premium for it). As most readers will remember from standard finance textbooks, the Capital Asset Pricing Model (CAPM) states that the expected returns of an individual security are proportional to its exposure to the market – expressed by its specific 'beta' – and are independent of the security-specific (idiosyncratic) risk. This is because the security-specific risk can be perfectly diversified away, and therefore securities with high idiosyncratic risk do not enjoy higher expected returns. Only the risk of the 'market portfolio' is a 'priced risk factor', so all expected returns above the risk-free rate will be related to the market portfolio.

Many investors assume that this simple result from the CAPM must be true in an efficient market. They argue that excess returns must be due to temporary deviations from the CAPM, and that these market inefficiencies can be extracted using some vaguely defined manager skill. However, this argument reveals a serious misunderstanding of asset-pricing models. In fact, there are many asset-pricing models with more than one priced risk factor.[28] Generally, any risk that is incompletely shared will carry a risk premium and be classified as a *systematic risk*. This includes risks with no relationship to equity markets. Incomplete risk sharing means that the underlying risk cannot be fully diversified away by *all agents*. Depending on the overall structure of investors' risk aversion, risk premia may be positive or negative. Assets

---

[27] Research by several groups: W. Fung/D. Hsieh, T. Schneeweis, N. Amenc/L. Martellini, N. Naik, and others, cited throughout the book.

[28] The APT model ('Arbitrage Pricing Theory') is the model most frequently mentioned in text books. See S. Ross, 'The arbitrage theory of capital asset pricing' (1976). A good text book for the introduction to CAPM and further asset pricing models is F. Reilly, K. Brown, *Investment Analysis and Portfolio Management*, 5th edition (1997).

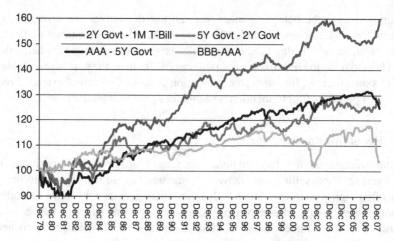

Figure 5.4   Returns to the various term structure risk premia; 2-year Government bonds versus one-month T-bill, 5-year Government bonds vs. 2-year Government bonds, AAA corporate bond vs. 5-year Government bonds; and BBB corporate bonds vs. AAA corporate bonds. Source: Salomon Smith Barney, Lehman Brothers

that hedge other risks can have a negative risk premium, as in the case of long positions in put options. (The return expectations of a long put (or all) position remain a subject of academic dispute, but most would assign a negative return expectation to a long option position.) It is important to understand that a risk premium is the equilibrium outcome of the various choices of economic agents. This means that, unlike market inefficiencies, risk premia can persist and be different across assets without being competed away.

Several risk premia relate to the large macro markets. Both the equity and the fixed income markets are so large that they will be a part of all agents' risk exposure. Similarly credit risk is so pervasive that it cannot be fully diversified away.[29] The corresponding risk premia are called the 'equity risk premium', the 'term structure premium' and the 'credit risk premium'. Because these risks cannot be fully diversified away, asset classes exposed to them offer substantial returns over short-term risk-free interest rates. Figure 5.4 shows how treasury bonds have performed better than cash and corporate bonds better than treasury bonds over the last 20 years. Figure 5.5 provides the returns of the US equity markets in the last 130 years.

Because of large international capital flows, it is natural that currency markets also exhibit risk premia. For example, financing the current account deficit of the United States or the cost of German reunification requires investors to accept significant exchange rate exposure. An exchange rate risk premium is necessary to provide incentives to foreign investors to hold assets exposed to exchange rate risk. FX risk premia express themselves as the positive interest rate carry between two currencies. The 'carry trades' were among the most popular trades in the classical 'Global Macro' funds in the 1980s and 1990s. In these trades the hedge fund buys a high-yield currency and finances the buy by short selling a lower-yield one. For example, traders in the mid- to late 1990s shorted the US dollar to buy emerging market currencies such as the Thai baht, or shorted the JPY to buy the USD, or in 2002–2005 shorted the USD and

---

[29] Historical evidence on the size and character of risk premia can be found in the book *Triumph of the Optimists: 101 Years of Global Investment Returns* by Elroy Dimson, Paul Marsh and Mike Staunton (2002).

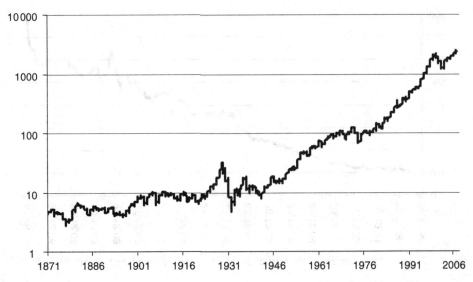

Figure 5.5 Long-term returns of the broad equity market (data updated from R. Shiller, *Irrational Exuberance* and Bloomberg – S&P 500)

bought the GBP (currently at the time of writing of this book the most promising carry trade involves shorting the JPY and buying the New Zealand or Australian dollar, AUD and NZD). Figure 5.6 provides the return streams of a combination of simple carry strategies in different currencies as provided by the Deutsche Bank Carry Index.

Mergers and acquisitions are another case where a risk premium is awarded. After the merger has been announced there is significant event risk that most investors find difficult to diversify away. And because the risk is specific to the company, large investors such as

Figure 5.6 Cumulative returns from 'Carry Trades' in currency markets (source: Bloomberg)

Figure 5.7   Cumulative returns of the saisGroup Futures Index (Bloomberg ticker sGFII Index)

the controlling shareholders cannot diversify it away. There is thus a risk premium related to Merger Arbitrage investment, which corresponds to the spread between offer price and market price. By systematically assuming this event risk, Merger Arbitrage managers are earning an event risk premium.[30] The risk profile of this trade is actually similar to a short position in a put option on the merger: A predefined premium is the possible gain in the more likely case that the merger is exercised, while rather large losses occur in the less likely occurrence of the merger falling through. Merger Arbitrage positions are no free lunches, but rather compensation for taking on the risk that the transaction may go sour.

The basic economic function of futures markets is to act as a risk transfer vehicle. In these markets commercial hedgers effectively offer a risk premium to speculators, driven by their desire to hedge their natural price risk. Speculators willing to assume the price risks of the commercial hedgers provide liquidity to futures and derivatives markets. Thus it is the speculators who ensure the marginal price stability that allows commercial hedgers to transfer their undesired price risks. Based on the demand for commercial hedging, speculators earn a corresponding risk premium, which we call the 'commodity hedging demand' premium.[31] By taking the opposite position of hedgers, speculators provide a form of 'price insurance' to hedgers. A simple way to earn these risk premia is momentum-based investing, in other words trend-following. This is by far the most prominent strategy of Managed Futures (CTA) strategies.[32] Figure 5.7 shows the return stream of the sGFII index, a simple trend-following strategy, which can be interpreted as the inherent return from commercial hedging demand in the futures markets.

---

[30] M. Mitchel and T. Pulvino give an interesting discussion of the available risk premium in merger transactions in 'Characteristics of risk in risk arbitrage' (2001).

[31] An early description of the risk premium for hedging demand was given by J. M. Keynes in his work *A Treatise on Money*, p. 127ff (1930).

[32] See also L. Jaeger., M. Jacquemai, P. Cittadini, 'Case study: the sGFI Futures Index' (2002). An early advocate of trend following strategies was R. Donchian, see Chapter 3 for historical details.

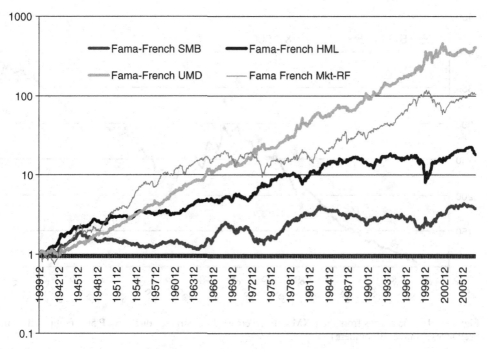

Figure 5.8 Returns from the book-to-market effect, the small firm effect, and the momentum effect, as well as the broad equity risk premium. Source: Ken French's website http://mba.tuck.dartmouth.edu/pages/faculty/ken.french/

Even in equity markets we can distinguish risk premia beyond the broad equity risk premium. The small cap, value premia, and momentum premia are described by the Fama–French HML, SMB, and UMD factors.[33] 'HML' (high minus low) is the return to a strategy that buys high book-to-market (i.e. value) stocks and sells low book-to-market (growth) stocks short. SMB (small minus big) describes the returns of a strategy that buys stocks of small companies and short sells large company stocks. Finally, UMD (up minus down) describes a strategy that buys stocks, which have recently performed strongly above average (high momentum) and sells those stocks short which have recently performed most poorly (weak momentum). Figure 5.8 shows the cumulative returns from these strategies together with the (excess) returns of the broad equity markets (above the risk-free rate of return). Whether returns from the HML and UMD strategy are systematic risk premia or the result of market inefficiencies due to irrational investor behavior remains a major academic dispute.[34] However, advocates of both sides of that dispute agree that these effects have persisted over time in the past and there is good reason to believe that they will persist in the future, and thus constitute a systematic return available to investors pursuing these strategies.

---

[33] See E. Fama, K. French, 'Size and book-to-market factors in earnings and returns' (1995) and M. Carhart, 'On persistence in mutual fund performance' (1997); the small cap effect was first described by R. Banz in 'The relationship between returns and market value of common stocks' (1981).

[34] See the discussion in the previous section.

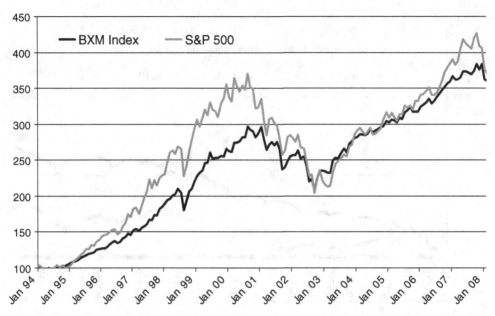

Figure 5.9   The returns from the BXM Index, a covered call strategy on the S&P 500, compared to the S&P index (source: Bloomberg)

Investing in emerging markets comes with additional risks, which require an extra expected return to provide incentives for the investor. These include credit and counterparty risks, as well as the risks from less secure legal, regulatory, settlement, and fiscal infrastructure. Emerging market securities often come with significantly lower liquidity, which of course imposes liquidity risk. Therefore investors obviously should demand a higher return when investing in these markets.

Another risk premium is available to those who write options and effectively insure other market agents against prices moving against them. Figure 5.9 displays the returns of a simple strategy that involves buying equity and selling simultaneously covered call options. This strategy is economically identical to selling put options plus earning interest rates on cash (in option theory this relationship is called 'put-call parity') and yields similar to more attractive returns to the S&P 500 with significantly lower volatility.

Investors who are willing to accept lower liquidity on their investments ask for a liquidity premium. This compensates them for extended time periods in which they cannot access their capital or the risk of being forced to liquidate the investment early and, perhaps, at an unfavorable price. A good example is private equity. In contrast to investors in public equity markets, a private equity investor has no direct access to his capital for several years. He is further exposed to uncertainty about the size and timing of future cash flows, which places him at significant reinvestment risk. Figure 5.10 shows how much private equity investments have outperformed the large cap segment of US public stocks (data for the last quarters of 2007 and the first quarters of 2008 were not yet available at time of the writing of this book, but I suspect that the market turbulence in 2007/2008 will eventually have its impact – albeit time-delayed – on private equity returns). In the case of hedge funds liquidity risk is often strongly correlated with other risk factors, specifically credit and counterparty risk. In some

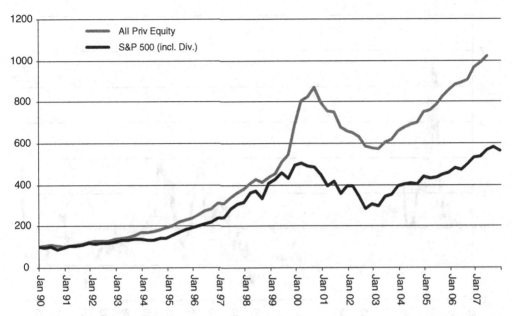

Figure 5.10 The returns of private equity investments compared to the S&P 500 (data source: Bloomberg, Thompson Venture Economics)

cases liquidity premia can be interpreted as 'complexity premia'. This is the case for securities which are hard to value, such as CDO debt tranches, private equity sponsored senior bank loans, callable convertible bonds, or exotic option contracts. For these investments there is thus not only price and liquidity risk, but also a so-called model risk. This is the risk that the valuation models employed may not be fully applicable for valuation and hedging. The returns here can be viewed as a premium for the risk of mis-modelling the underlying financial instrument and its complexity, and thus suffering an unexpected loss as a consequence. In other words, the manager is short an option on the correctness of his model.[35] The more recent developments during the credit turmoil in 2007/2008 actually led to more and more investor voices expressing concerns about the increased complexity of hedge fund activities.

It is important to understand that risk premia can change over time. The changes over time are easy to understand in stock and bond market investments. When the risk premium drops, the price increases. As the risk premium increases prices fall again. Figure 5.11 shows the development of the yield spread (or credit risk premium) between Treasury and BBB US corporate bonds going back to the end of World War I. The chart shows large fluctuations in the 1930s, 1970s and 1980s, and most recently the sudden increase in spreads in the credit crisis that started in the summer of 2007. Investors are surely warned that there is no guarantee of excess returns in the short run when investing in risky assets, i.e. assets with an attached risk premium. Most investors, though, expect returns from taking systematic risks such as the equity risk premium or the excess returns (over the short-term risk-free rate) of bonds to be positive in the long term.

---

[35] See N. Talib, 'Bleed or blowup. On the preference for negative skewness' (2004).

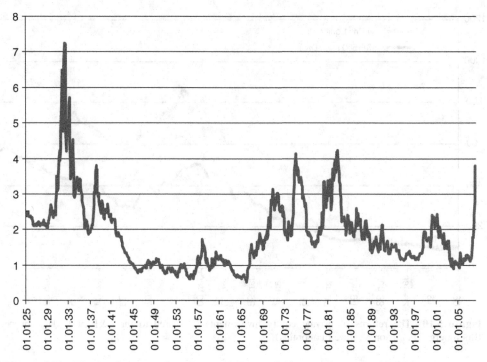

Figure 5.11 The development of credit spreads between 10-year Treasury and BBB-rated corporate bonds in the US.

Certain risk premia may disappear (temporarily or even permanently) as the market allows better risk sharing through new forms of diversification. Both HML and SMB returns were consistently positive until the mid-1980s. Why exactly the risk premia on value stocks or small capitalization stocks seemed to have disappeared over the period from 1985 to 2000 just to reappear again seven years ago is beyond the scope of this discussion. But it is clear that risk premia cannot be expected to stay constant over time in an evolving global capital market.

Awareness of the erosion of risk factor returns is important when evaluating hedge fund strategies. For example, Long/Short Equity strategies tend to be exposed to both small firm and value stocks. If the inherent return from these simple strategies had been reduced or competed away, the expected returns to the strategy in the future would be lower. Further, the fact that Long/Short managers also have positive net exposure to the equity market leads us easily to understand their poor performance from spring 2000 to spring 2003 (and their subsequent strength in the equity bull market from 2003 to 2007, again followed by expressed losses in the summer of 2007 and the winter of 2008).

Figure 5.12 gives a perhaps incomplete but illustrative overview of the various risk premia in financial markets.

5.8   RISK PREMIA AND ECONOMIC FUNCTIONS

Risk premia are related to various functions financial markets have in the global economy. Hedge fund strategies that capture risk premia must therefore also have economic functions.

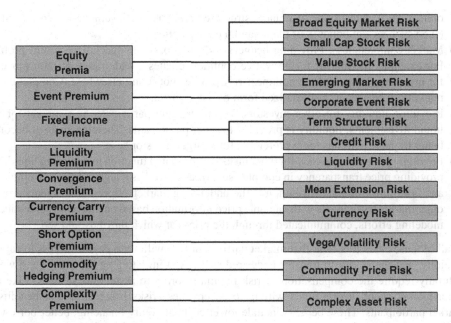

Figure 5.12   The universe of risk premia in capital markets

Understanding these functions allows hedge fund investors to make strategic allocations that explicitly diversify across economic functions and their corresponding risk premia. The most common economic functions for the capital markets in which hedge funds participate are:

(1) Providing capital for investments: Companies, governments or individuals plan to use the proceeds of equity or debt issues in order to invest in physical or intangible capital. The issuers plan to repay the debt or equity using the returns on their investment. In the case of equity, the investors are invited to share in the returns of the investment, while debt is expected to be repaid with interest. This function serves in the private as well as the public (listed) markets.

(2) Providing capital for consumption: The borrower knows that she will be able to pay back the money later based on future income. In many cases borrowers are prepared to pay more to borrow long-term.

(3) Risk transfer for commercial hedgers: Companies and individuals use financial markets to hedge unwanted risk. If the hedging demand is sufficiently large, exploitable risk premia can emerge in the major markets for commodities, currencies, fixed income, and (albeit to a lesser degree) equities. The primary place for commercial hedgers to offload their unwanted price risks are the global futures markets. Speculators willing to assume the natural price risks of commercial hedgers enable the hedgers to transfer their undesired risks. In exchange the speculators capture the hedging demand premium.

(4) Risk transfer for financial intermediaries: Financial intermediaries such as banks and insurance companies have a need to design their overall risk exposure flexibly at their discretion and transfer undesired risks to other agents. Examples include mortgage or other bank loans related to things like car or credit card purchases (structured and sold as asset-backed securities such as MBS (mortgage-backed securities) or CLOs (collateralized loan

obligations)), catastrophe insurance (structured and sold as 'insurance-linked securities' (ILS) such as 'cat bonds'), or plain vanilla equity options.

(5) Market completeness: Providing hedgers and investors with specialized return profiles. For example, the market for derivative contracts creates a wide range of return profiles for investors. These include nonlinear risk profiles not found elsewhere. Completing the market can be seen as a specialized form of risk transfer.

(6) Providing liquidity for other investors: When an agent participates in a market for less liquid investments, liquidity is provided to other participants. Thereby, an asset becomes better tradable and thus more preferable for a larger investor base.

(7) Providing price transparency for other investors: A related function to providing liquidity is providing price transparency in complex securities as well as a higher degree of efficiency and faster information distribution to the underlying markets. Speculative agents provide other market participants with valuable price information based on their own sophisticated modeling efforts, communicated through the prices at which they buy and sell.

In all of these cases it is clear that market participants are willing to pay for access to capital, liquidity, and the ability to transfer undesired risks. And investors on the other hand would naturally require the compensation of risk premia in order to assume these risks. Like any other market agent, hedge funds willing to accept these risks bring important benefits to market participants. These benefits include lower costs of equity financing, better borrowing conditions, and higher liquidity for large groups of investors. For example, as mentioned in Chapter 3 hedge funds buy a large fraction of issued convertibles and distressed companies' debt. The spread of convertible securities 15 to 20 years ago provided companies with an additional option for raising capital and has thereby reduced the cost of capital for many firms. Lately, hedge funds have become participants in leveraged buy-out transactions providing financing to these deals. Hedge funds that invest in distressed securities similarly help to reduce the economic cost of bankruptcy by ensuring a smoother bankruptcy workout process. Hedge funds help to evaluate various claims correctly, making the market for distressed securities more efficient and liquid. This contributes significantly towards reintegrating troubled companies back into the economic cycle and thereby reducing the financial and economic (and maybe also political) cost of failure.

5.9 MARKET INEFFICIENCIES: THE 'SEARCH FOR ALPHA'

Next to efficiently extracting nontraditional and noncorrelating risk premia, the direct exploitation of market inefficiencies is the other main reason why hedge funds can earn attractive returns. Proponents of EMH and behavioral finance alike do agree that it is very difficult to design profitable trading strategies that persistently exploit market inefficiencies. This statement appears to reach a broad acceptance across believers and nonbelievers in the EMH. We could therefore redefine the EMH towards saying 'Investors cannot systematically beat the markets', rather than orthodoxly stating that market prices are rational at all times.[36] Markets have many participants, which helps make them efficient as participants chase the excess return related to any inefficiency.[37] They also develop and change, often faster than participants can grasp.

[36] See, for example, M. Stratman, 'Behavioural finance: past battles and future engagements' (1999).

[37] The statement that those who exploit market inefficiencies effectively put themselves and their colleagues undertaking the same endeavors out of a job by making markets overall more efficient is referred to as the

Opportunities disappear as quickly as they emerge, and the new types of risk are difficult to understand and to control. Peter Bernstein says that the current understanding of capital markets is 'suspected of suffering from kurtosis, skewness, and other less familiar malignancies' and is 'frequently made irrelevant by exotic new financial instruments that come in unfamiliar shapes and hedge unfamiliar risks'.[38] In other words, new sources of inefficiencies constantly appear in the dynamic developments of the global capital markets. One example is the emergence of 'Capital Structure Arbitrage' (see Chapter 3 for details), which did not develop until liquid and mature credit derivatives markets had emerged.

The only way an investment manager can generate persistent 'alpha' performance is to constantly adapt himself and his trading technology to adjust to changing market conditions. Generating alpha means hedging the beta risks. A solid risk management process is a prerequisite of successfully generating alpha returns. Hedge fund managers are surely among the best skilled and fastest participants as well as most sophisticated risk managers in the global capital markets, prepared as best possible to undertake this challenge.

The claim for alpha refers to market inefficiencies of either a fundamental or a statistical nature. These correspond to violations of the semi-strong version and the weak version of the EMH, respectively. In claiming alpha, that is referring to their ability to exploit market inefficiencies based on fundamental information, hedge fund managers usually claim the following analytical edges:

- Superior research and analysis skills and proprietary valuation models. This is the 'star analyst' edge claimed by most fundamentally oriented hedge funds.
- Faster and better access to relevant information. This claim rests on personal contacts, industry network, knowledge of world supply and demand, etc. In other words, the manager claims to be able to carry out fundamental analysis faster and more deeply than others.
- Superior ability to anticipate mass behavior patterns of investors.
- Better and faster interpretation of relevant macroeconomic information.

The greatest potential for 'pure skill' based strategies is where information is not freely and broadly available, as in inefficient and less liquid markets. Typical cases would be strategies in distressed securities, private markets, or complex instruments such as asset-backed securities or convertible bonds, where the manager's experience to pick the right security out of many prospects is crucial. I also note that manager skill will be most visible on the downside, finding securities that respond favorably in good times with less downside risk. However, inefficient markets often come with an asymmetric profile, in which opportunities generally come at higher transaction costs, and failed trades come at higher costs, in the form of lower liquidity, that is higher selling costs. The reader will by now grasp the idea that this asymmetric 'alpha payout profile' itself can be seen as a systematic risk derived from the liquidity or complexity of the underlying market.

Managers who focus on statistical methods to locate market inefficiencies claim a different set of edges:

'Grossmann–Stiglitz paradoxon', see S. Grossman and J. Stiglitz in their seminal work, 'On the impossibility of informationally efficient markets' (1980).

[38] In 'Risk as a history of ideas' (1995).

- Superior prediction of market behavior through better statistical models, including the use of trends, seasonalities, autocorrelation through investor behavior patterns, and mean reversions.
- Identifying underpricing/overpricing of volatilities. For example, implied volatility in regime shifts and prepayment patterns in mortgage-backed securities.
- Technical analysis of patterns, such as triangles, head–shoulder–head formations, etc.

However, the different types of inefficiencies emerge and disappear with time, making it difficult for a hedge fund manager who has had an edge in the past to maintain this advantage persistently over time. Even the best proprietary valuation models and analysts often fail to adapt when markets change rapidly. So it is no surprise that many trading styles work only for a limited time. Furthermore, what looks like a pricing anomaly may actually be a hidden risk factor which itself is subject to rapid change. In other words, what the investor, or even worse the hedge fund manager himself, takes to be alpha may actually be hidden and highly variable beta. In that case the market price is likely to be right, and it is probably the manager's estimate of the 'true' value that is wrong.

There exists another, third, way to extract alpha besides exploiting informational and statistical inefficiencies, which is possibly more persistent than the former two: it is based on the hedge fund manager's more efficient use of trading techniques and technologies, exploitation of better financing opportunities, more cash-efficient collateral and exposure management, and superior short selling capabilities. When a hedge fund manager has access to financing or short selling conditions that the average investor does not have, she earns an excess return over the average investor, in other words she extracts alpha. For example, a hedge fund manager who builds up exposure to various risk factors in a very cash-efficient way and who manages margins and collateral optimally obtains an advantage in that she can obtain better (i.e. lower cost) leverage financing conditions or superior short selling opportunities. This will enable her to extract above-average returns.

As difficult as it is to generate alpha in the first place, it is perhaps even harder to independently verify it. The investor or fund of funds manager needs her own special expertise to verify manager skill and separate true alpha from hidden beta to which the individual fund manager is unknowingly exposed, or – even more tricky – from pure luck. How can one know if the manager's edge is still there, or if his model still works? The central question for the assessment of a manager's alpha is: How persistent is the perceived 'alpha'? After all, as I said elsewhere, it is persistence that distinguishes alpha from luck. Persistence also provides a measure of either the durability of the inefficiencies the manager is exploiting, or his ability to change his analysis or models to find new inefficiencies as the markets change. In Chapter 9, I will provide more details on the challenging task of properly assessing hedge fund managers' skills, separating the skills from luck, and understanding the underlying return sources of particular hedge fund managers. The techniques of hedge fund replication introduced in the following chapters will prove to be quite helpful in this context.

Across all agents in the global capital markets, 'alpha' is a zero-sum game. Whatever one investor is able to receive as an excess return above the fair value of the risk he or she is taking, another agent loses. If hedge funds benefit from market inefficiencies and generate alpha, then who are the losing parties? Behavioral finance would say the losers are all the agents who are acting with imperfect rationality. That is to say, the people lose when they act on cognitive biases such as loss aversion, extrapolation of trends, and mental accounting (see above). Other losing parties would be central banks that act in the currency and bond markets with motivations other than generating profit. The list of potential losers is necessarily incomplete, because broadly speaking a loser is anyone who is paying too much or earning too little and thus stands at the origin of a market inefficiency. For example, structural overpricing of volatilities in the mortgage-backed securities market comes broadly at the expense of US house-owners.

Actually, when transaction costs are factored in, alpha creation becomes a negative-sum game. The entire crowd of investors must fall short of the fair market return by the amount of cost they occur. At the same time the alpha-generating manager incurs transaction costs and charges management fees to capture other investors' loss as his investors gain. This means that even where managers do generate alpha, they must also tightly control costs for any of that alpha to flow through to their investors. Costs occur at numerous places: first, and most prominently, management and performance fees to the hedge fund manager and perhaps to a fund of funds manager, marketing expenditures, distribution fees, brokerage commissions, transaction costs, short selling margins, and custody, legal and security processing expenses. Taking costs into account should make the reader even more skeptical when evaluating the alpha-generation potential of hedge funds. The less efficient the traded market and the higher the perceived margin from exploiting inefficiencies, the higher the cost incurred by the managers and their investors to exploit them. But while inefficient markets may create opportunities to earn alpha returns by a larger margin, they inevitably also create the chance to lose by an even larger margin. Higher fees reduce the overall sum of possible alpha across all agents in these markets.[39] The overall fee load faced by a hedge fund investor can easily wipe out any alpha which the skill of the hedge fund manager was originally able to generate.[40]

5.10   AN ILLUSTRATION OF THE NATURE OF HEDGE FUND RETURNS

I contend that what appear to be market inefficiencies, price anomalies, and arbitrage opportunities are often actually less visible systematic risks, carrying corresponding risk premia. In other words, they are beta in alpha's clothing. Despite the difficulty of separating true alpha from beta, distinguishing risk premia from pure manager skill provides the clearest framework in which to analyze how hedge funds earn their money.

Figure 5.13 shows a simplified illustration of the problem. Long-only managers (represented by the left bar) have two sources of return: the market exposure and the manager excess return, his 'alpha'.[41] As research and the empirical intuition of many experienced investors show, this alpha is negative for the average long-only manager (after their fees). The difference between long-only investing and hedge funds is largely that the hedge fund will hedge away all or part of the broad market exposure. In order to achieve this risk reduction, the hedge fund manager employs a variety of techniques and instruments not used by the long-only fund manager such

---

[39] Following along the lines of standard financial theory this asymmetric 'alpha payout profile' itself should make investors ask for a higher return.

[40] Many discussed 'market inefficiencies' published in academic journals and the corresponding systematic trading approaches designed to capture alpha return fall short of working in the real markets, simply because of the incurred cost.

[41] However, for many managers (in the hedge fund as well as the mutual fund space) this proclaimed 'alpha' still contains elements of systematic risks. This is why we put alpha in quotation marks here.

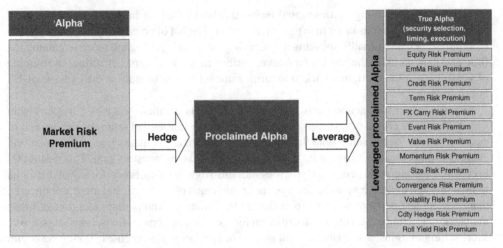

Figure 5.13 A simplified model for hedge fund and traditional funds' return sources

as short selling and the use of derivatives. These result in an apparently 'pure alpha' product with low expected returns and low expected risk.[42] But in order to be attractive as a stand-alone investment, the hedge fund manager has to conform to the market standard for return. This leads him to scale the risk by using leverage (the third common characteristic of hedge fund investment techniques), which provides the desired magnification of return and risk. In this magnified configuration, systematic elements of risk and return that before were hidden in the 'alpha' are suddenly large enough to be analyzed separately. In other words, we now have the necessary magnifying glass to separate out the 'beta in alpha's clothing'. In analogy to the biologist in the seventeenth century who for the first time in history used a microscope to investigate the detailed structures of an insect's body, we now see ourselves in a position to examine hedge fund returns more directly.

One of investors' most frequent mistakes is not to look deeper into the hedge funds' proclaimed 'alpha'. As is illustrated in Figure 5.13, many different sources of returns can contribute to the observed 'alpha', for example, systematic credit risk, liquidity risk, exchange rate risk, or commodity risk. Furthermore, contingent and complex-looking trading strategies may replicate the simple risk profile of a 'short option' position. These risk premia are rewarded by an expected positive return in a market in equilibrium. This means that even when overall returns are positive, a manager's real excess 'alpha' return can be lower, often even negative, after we account properly for the beta component of these returns. Since it is in the manager's interest to show the superiority of their returns, they may tend to characterize all of their returns as alpha while forgetting about these alternative risks. Managers who 'believe their own press' in this way are in danger of overselling hedge funds' performance based on a period of favorable prevailing economic circumstances that make them look like geniuses. But this can result in severe backlash when investors wonder why the manager's IQ has dropped so

---

[42] As both the bond and equity market have positive expected returns, it is not optimal to fully hedge away the market risk. This is one of the reasons why many hedge funds maintain a net long bias in equity and/or bonds.

severely in adverse market environments. When managers oversell the alpha portion of their returns while underselling beta, investor disappointment is inevitable.

Although a hedge fund strategy may be focused on earning a particular risk premium, it may still be implicitly exposed to other risks as well. Investors, and occasionally hedge fund managers, may not be fully aware of this second-order exposure. Merger Arbitrage provides a simple example, as it is indirectly exposed to the risk of the broad market. When the stock market falls sharply, merger deals are more likely to break (the most recent example is the period of Q4 2007/Q1 2008).[43] The strategy has a positive stock market beta, not from the individual positions but from the correlation between the exposure to the particular event risks and the market.

The illustration above suggests that hedge funds returns are primarily not the result of market inefficiencies. Instead hedge funds take on various systematic risks and are compensated for the risk in the form of realized risk premia. In the words of Bill Gross: 'The modern invention of hedge funds depends on similar structures [as the bank industry]: they are unregulated banks in disguise, borrowing short/risk-free and investing in riskier long-term investments, which offer much higher returns'.[44] This is not to say that alpha is nonexistent or negative in hedge fund returns as in mutual funds. As a matter of fact, the average hedge fund does produce alpha, but in lower quantity than is largely assumed.

While hedge funds vary widely, the general pattern becomes clear and thus provides the key to the hedge fund 'black box'. Hedge funds take exposure to several well-known risk factors and thus possess well-understood sources of return. They generate returns primarily through risk premia and only secondarily by exploiting inefficiencies in imperfect markets. Conceptually hedge funds are therefore nothing really new in that, just as an equity mutual fund extracts the equity risk premium, a hedge fund may try to extract various other risk premia awarded for, say, credit risk, interest rate risk, or liquidity risk. The important difference, however, is that the underlying risk premia are more diverse than those in traditional asset classes. For this reason we refer to them as 'alternative betas'. This insight has now spread among the most sophisticated circles in the hedge fund industry. The underlying systematic risks can be readily analyzed and understood by investors, while the remaining parts of returns from inefficiencies are more difficult to describe in an unambiguous way. But beyond being analyzed and understood, these returns can also be replicated, which is what this book is finally about.

5.11 THE DECREASE OF ALPHA

There is good reason to believe that generally the average alpha extracted by hedge fund managers is destined to decline with the further attraction of capital and talent into the hedge fund space. As a matter of fact, we can already today observe that alpha has grown smaller in size over time, as Figure 5.14 indicates for some particular strategies: Long/Short Equity, Convertible Arbitrage, Merger Arbitrage, and Event Driven. I display the obtained alpha of a rolling regression over a 60-month time window. Independently of our research, the attenuation of alpha has been observed elsewhere. Fung *et al.* in a recent paper report on the

---

[43] Authors tend to be captured by the most recent events at the time when their book is written. This happens to be the unfolding of the credit crisis in late 2007/early 2008 in my case here.

[44] Pimco Investment Outlook, April 2003.

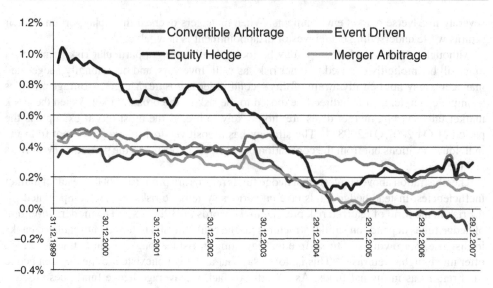

Figure 5.14 The decline of alpha in various hedge fund strategies (author's own calculation; data from Hedge Fund Research)

same phenomenon.[45] One possible explanation for this development comes quickly to mind (and is confirmed by anecdotal evidence in the financial industry): as more money chases a limited supply of market inefficiencies, the average available amount of inefficiency decreases ('capacity argument'). In other words, the global capacity for alpha is limited and with the growth of the hedge fund industry is now distributed across a larger number of participants. Furthermore, there is some economic reason to believe that the global 'capacity for alpha', which is ultimately a function of how many market inefficiencies the average global investor (and the corresponding regulatory agencies) will tolerate, did not increase as rapidly as the hedge fund industry, and parts may have actually decreased in their total size. And this is not necessarily a result of the activities of hedge funds. While hedge funds grow strongly and possibly have to compete harder with other 'alpha chasers' they remain a rather small portion of the global investment activity. In the last 10 years we have been able to observe a gradual withdrawal by government agencies and central banks from politically inspired policies such as exchange rate convergence which used to hand nice opportunities to hedge fund managers. The interventionist forces have become less pivotal as the 'free-market paradigm' found more and more its way in the global system of financial markets.[46] As a result inefficiencies from these 'non-rational agents' can be safely assumed to have grown smaller and to be continuing to do so.

Another explanation for the discernible decrease in alpha is the decline in quality of the average hedge fund manager. The number of managers has multiplied in recent years, and it is reasonable to assume that today's low entry barriers to starting a hedge fund have attracted

---

[45] W. Fung, D. Hsieh, N. Naik, T. Ramadorai, 'Hedge fund: performance, risk and capital formation' (2007).

[46] Ironically it is the moment of crisis when many of the 'free-market voices' scream the loudest for government and central bank help. The 2007/2008 crisis provided another great example of that phenomenon of hypocrisy.

numerous managers with a comparatively lower level of skills. These tend to dilute the average performance and thus the average alpha of the hedge fund industry as a whole ('hedge fund bubble argument'). An interesting research topic which we leave for future efforts is to test for the average alpha in the top percentile of managers. Some new research examining the tails of the distribution across single managers' performance (an increase of the left tail hints at the 'hedge fund bubble' argument while the decrease of the right tails hints at the 'capacity argument') indicates, however, that the alpha decrease stems from the decrease in the top alpha quartile rather than the bottom quartile.[47] In other words, the 'capacity argument' seems to hold better than the 'bubble argument'. The question remains open at this point. Will the 'alpha' in hedge funds disappear entirely? Probably not, but it will certainly become harder to identify and isolate in the growing jungle of hedge funds.

However, we see that alpha remains a significant variable in most regression models (albeit having over time grown significantly smaller in size) as I will demonstrate in more detail in the next chapter. We may be missing explanatory variables in our models, and future modeling effort will hopefully lead us to better models to answer this question. Another approach is to model the behavior of the alpha output of our models in changing market conditions as well as over time. Alpha may depend on market-related variables other than prices which are not so easily captured in our risk-based linear factor models, such as trading volume, open short interest on stocks, insider activity, leverage financing policies of prime brokers, etc. A direct dependency of the hedge fund managers' alpha creation from these variables will lead us to a better understanding of their time variability that we empirically observe in our models. This will ultimately lead us to an understanding of the very alpha creation process of hedge funds, the part of hedge fund returns which remains still in the dark for most investors. However, little research effort has been put into this task so far.

Although modeling techniques continue to improve, for the moment investors must combine modeling with common sense in evaluating manager alpha. Comparing individual fund performance with alpha-free rule-based trading strategies (see Chapter 8), as well as with other funds in the same strategy sector, will provide the investor with an improved rough-and-ready guide to making informed choices. This will lead us directly into the core of this book: hedge fund replication.

5.12 THE BEAUTY OF ALTERNATIVE BETA

The attraction of alpha, if we can find it, is obvious. Who would not want to take advantage of uncorrelated returns free of any systematic risks? But with alpha come less obvious and less transparent manager-specific risks. In the end it is up to the manager to extract the alpha in whatever way he deems necessary, including the flexible employment of leverage, the use of less liquid instruments, and other things investors are easily scared by. The charms of beta are more mundane, but also more abundant, and the risks are more obvious, but also more transparent. The particular charm of alternative beta is that it provides us with a new way of extracting systematic sources of return which are not highly correlated to traditional risk premia, as Figure 5.15 illustrates. Alternative beta can therefore provide significant efficiency

---

[47] See Z. Zhong, 'Why does hedge fund alpha decrease over time? Evidence from individual hedge funds', (January 2008).

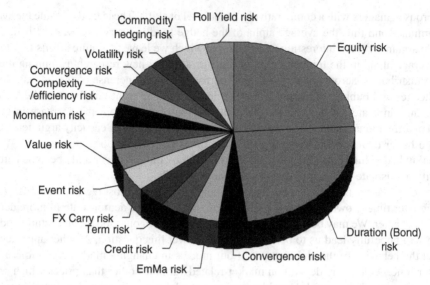

Figure 5.15 Traditional investors benefit only from a few risk premia (grey on the right) available in the market place and miss multiple other return sources (on the left)

enhancement to investors' global portfolios. This makes them 'valuable pearls' in the vast ocean of the global capital markets waiting to be found by investors.

A simple numbers game should illustrate our case here. It is safe to assume that alternative betas on a stand-alone basis do not yield more attractive risk–return profiles than traditional risk premia which give Sharpe ratios – or whatever more sophisticated risk-adjusted performance measure we want to choose – of around 0.2 to 0.3, for example, returns of 6% with a volatility of 8%, anything but impressive (the flexible use of leverage can scale the returns up or down without changing the Sharpe ratio). But that is what beta provides: not more, not less. But now let us take say 15 of these not highly correlated alternative beta factors into a combined portfolio. What happens? The return of the resulting portfolio remains at 6%. However, volatility can drop to as low as 2%. Here is our Sharpe ratio of one! The ugly beta duckling has grown up into a very powerful 'alternative beta' swan, equally or even more attractive to investors than pure alpha alone.

Investors should realize both the scarcity and idiosyncratic risks of true alpha and the power of alternative beta. It is the power of diversification into orthogonal risk factors which will ensure that hedge funds remain broadly attractive for investors. While the search for alpha surely remains compelling, I believe it is investment in alternative betas which may become more and more the key to successful hedge fund investing in the future. The real benefits from hedge funds do not necessarily come from accessing today's star trader, but from the persistent benefits of alternative risk premia. And when it comes to the hedge funds' beta there is surely a great deal larger capacity available to investors than is the case for alpha. In fact, the future growth prospects of the hedge fund industry become quite compelling, considering that we are far from any limit with respect to 'beta capacity' in the hedge fund industry. While the search for alpha surely remains compelling, I believe it is investment in alternative betas which will be more and more the key to successful hedge fund investing in the future.

5.13   THE FUTURE OF HEDGE FUND CAPACITY

The discussion on return sources and the separation between alpha and beta has some important implications for the global capacity of the hedge fund industry, a question that touches the heart of future hedge fund growth. As the number of available free lunches is limited, the capacity for alpha must be equally limited. Nobody is willing to give out a free lunch. Rather, the free lunch is extracted by taking a grain of rice from many unknowing contributors. But with more and more money chasing after alpha, the number of available rice corns will be smaller.

Let me perform a set of rather simple but illustrative calculations in the context of the capacity discussion.[48] We know that the global market capitalization of all public stocks and debt is around 100 000 billion USD (about 55 000 USD in bonds, 45 000 USD in equity) – give or take 10 000 billion.[49] At the same time we realize that generating alpha in the global capital markets is an overall zero-sum game, i.e. if hedge fund managers win this game, i.e. generate positive alpha, there must be other market participants on the losing end. We must thus assume an average tolerance level for inefficiencies, i.e. negative alpha, by equity and bond investors world-wide before competitive (or regulatory) forces step in to keep this number from getting larger. We estimate this number to be in the range of 0.25% p.a. on average across all equity and bonds investors.[50] With this number we can calculate the overall alpha available in the global equity and bond market to be USD 250 billion. We must further assume that hedge funds can participate from this 'alpha pie' only to a certain extent next to other professional players who are likely also to be 'positive alpha players' and thus compete with hedge funds for alpha (proprietary trading operations, large institutions, mutual funds – before their fees, etc.). It seems realistic to assume that hedge funds can take no more than one-fourth of that pie[51] (a proportion which might grow larger over time, however, as more players from the other 'alpha parties' move into the hedge fund space). This implies that there are USD 63 billion pure alpha available to hedge funds each year. Further, we must assume that hedge fund investors require at least a 15% p.a. return *gross of fees* (before management, performance, trading fees, etc.), which amounts to a net return of around 8–10% and constitutes probably the minimum investors would require from hedge funds. This implies an overall capacity of hedge funds *based on alpha only* of

$$USD\,63\,billion/0.15 = 420\,billion\,USD$$

This number is about one-fifth of the actual size of assets in the hedge fund industry. Even with different, more beneficial assumptions on the overall investor tolerance for inefficiencies and on how much hedge funds can participate in the total 'alpha pie', we would by no means come up with a capacity significantly higher than the current size of the industry, and in most scenarios it would be one that is significantly lower. As a result, based on the assumption of

---

[48] Note that this calculation is very similar in spirit to, and takes some of its concepts from, the work of H. Till, 'The capacity implications of the search of alpha' (2004).

[49] Source: www.fibv.com/publications/Focus0605.pdf and http://www.imf.org/external/pubs/ft/GFSR/2005/01/index.htm

[50] H. Till uses another number but aggregates the overall size of the market only over the holdings of HNWI, mutual funds and institutional funds. Considering our base number of 100 000 billion USD our resulting assumptions are rather similar.

[51] The reader is invited to perform his own calculation with different numbers.

inefficiencies in the global capital markets alone, we are not just lacking a satisfying economic explanation of hedge fund return sources, we also find ourselves in a position of not being able to explain the current size of the industry!

But by now we understand that a large portion of hedge fund returns is not related to pure alpha, but rather to 'alternative beta'. The analysis in our research suggests that a large part of the average hedge fund return stems from alternative beta rather than alpha. I now consider our estimate for that part to be as high as 80%, based on our calculation above as well as my own research that I will present in the following chapters.[52] Well, this raises the bar for hedge fund capacity significantly higher. Going along with our conclusion and estimating that only 20% of the industry returns is related to pure alpha, we can calculate the capacity of the industry to be

$$420 \, \text{billion USD}/0.2 = 2100 \, \text{billion USD}$$

which is just about where the industry currently stands. However, as large as this number seems, it is greatly exceeded by some of the estimates given by industry protagonists as to what level the industry will grow within the following years. How can this growth be managed considering our numbers? The answer is obvious: only by including a larger and larger share of alternative beta in the overall return scheme of hedge funds. Assuming that the ratio of alpha versus alternative beta becomes 10%, the capacity reaches the number of 4200 billion USD (assuming that the capacity of alternative beta is not limited at these levels, a fair assumption in my opinion).

Summarizing, there is indeed plenty of room for the hedge fund industry to grow, albeit only at the expense of becoming more and more beta-driven. This development will inevitably occur with the future growth of hedge funds. Recent performance suggests that this process is well on its way.

5.14 MOMENTUM AND VALUE

Two particular investment strategies inspire roiling disputes over market efficiency, even as they form the basis of many successful hedge funds. These are the value strategy and the momentum strategy. Researchers, as well as such illustrious investors as Warren Buffet, have convincingly demonstrated that value strategies, choosing stocks by using such indicators as book-to-market value or the cash flow-to-price ratio, work quite well in predicting relative stock returns and outperform the average return of equity markets.[53] Equally, there exists ample evidence that momentum strategies based on buying past winners and selling past losers can also generate excess returns.[54]

The academic work on value and momentum strategies has had a strong impact on professional investment management, including hedge funds. Value-versus-growth and momentum

---

[52] The reader is referred to L. Jaeger, C. Wagner, 'Factor modelling and benchmarking of hedge funds: Can passive investments in hedge fund strategies deliver?', *Journal of Alternative Investments* (Winter 2005).

[53] See E. Fama, K. French, 'Size and book-to-market factors in earnings and returns' (1995), and 'The cross section of expected stock returns' (1992); see also J. Lakonishok *et al.*, 'Contrarian investment, extrapolation, and risk' (1994).

[54] See N. Jegadesh, S. Titman, 'Returns to buying winners and selling losers: implication for stock market efficiency' (1993) and 'Profitability of momentum strategies: an evaluation of alternative explanation' (2001); M. Carhart, 'On persistence in mutual fund performance' (1997).

strategies are now widely recognized specialities for money managers. The explanation why these strategies work is incomplete at best. Conflicting explanations have been offered for their success by proponents of EMH and behavioral finance. EMH proponents attribute the higher returns of value and momentum strategies to their increased risk, or different risk profile respectively. Those in the behavioral finance camp suggest that cognitive biases underlying investor behavior and inefficiencies from the agency friction of professional investment managers are at the roots of these returns.

Fama and French[55] argue that stocks with high book-to-market value are more likely subject to financial distress and more correlated to the business cycle. They are therefore inherently riskier than growth stocks to most investors as they correlate with their income generation, and thus earn a higher expected return. Lakonishok, Shleifer, and Vishny offered a competing explanation for the outperformance of value stocks drawing on behavioral considerations and agency costs.[56] They claim investors choose stocks on the basis of simple heuristics, such as extrapolating the past into the future, or the representation bias of money managers. These heuristics lead them to invest in glamorous stocks which are easier to explain in analyst reports or media coverage. That in turn can make value stocks underpriced and growth stocks overpriced. Investors have exaggerated hopes of growth stocks and overly pessimistic outlooks on value stocks. This leaves them under-allocated to future outperformers and disappointed when past stars fall short.

Behavioral finance advocates offer ready explanations for excess returns from momentum strategies as well. They suggest that the nonrational patterns of investor behavior generate abnormal inertia in the prices of certain securities, creating arbitrage opportunities for the more rational investors. The behavior patterns cited include expectation extrapolation, under- or overreaction in updating expectations,[57] overconfidence, and selective information conditioning. Some argue that momentum profits are due to industry sector autocorrelations,[58] others argue that they are mostly due to cross-sectional correlations among stocks.[59] EMH proponents are hardly ready to concede the debate, however. Some argue that the momentum strategies' apparent excess return may simply be a compensation for extra risk, and results from cross-sectional variation in unconditional mean returns rather than a predictable time series variation of stock returns.[60] In this interpretation, momentum-based excess returns are related to the business cycles and mainly reflect the persistence in time-varying expected returns, or risk premia. In other words, business cycles or external shocks may play a significant role in a firm's changing systematic risk and expected returns.[61] This implies that 'excess' returns are really just a premium for assuming that type of varying risk. Regardless of the precise origin of momentum strategy profits, they remain an anomaly that cannot be easily explained by the

---

[55] In their paper 'Multifactor explanations of asset pricing anomalies' (1996).

[56] In their paper, 'Contrarian investment, extrapolation, and risk' (1994); see also L. Chan and J. Lakonishok, 'Value and growth investing: review and update' (2004).

[57] There are indeed explanations which refer to investors under-reacting to information in the short run (H. Hong and J. Stein, 'A unified theory of underreaction, momentum trading, and overreaction in asset markets' (1999)), while others argue that excess returns are due to investors overreacting (K. Daniel, D., Hirshleifer, A. Subrahmanyam, 'Investor psychology and security market under and overreactions' (1998)). Both are presented in a coherent explanatory framework.

[58] See T. Moskowitz, M. Grinblatt, 'Do industries explain momentum?' (1999).

[59] See A. Lo, A. MacKinlay, 'When are contrarian profits due to stock market overreaction?' (1990).

[60] See J. Conrad, G. Kaul, 'An anatomy of trading strategies', Review of Financial Studies, 11 (1998).

[61] See also T. Chordia, L. Shivakumar, 'Momentum, business cycle, and time-varying expected returns' (2002).

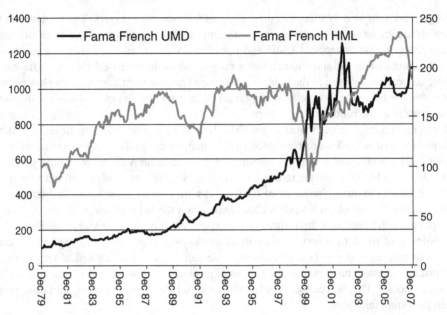

Figure 5.16 The returns of a pure value versus growth and a momentum strategy according to the Fama–French factors (right scale refers to value versus growth). The value versus growth strategy buys the stocks with the lowest price-to-book ratio and sells the stocks with the highest price-to-book ratio, while the momentum strategy buys the stocks with the best performance in recent months and sells the stocks with the worst performance in recent months. (Source: Ken French's website http://mba.tuck.dartmouth.edu/pages/faculty/ken.french/)

otherwise very successful Fama–French three-factor model. Thus they remain very puzzling for advocates of the EMH.

Can you create a successful hedge fund strategy that purely follows a text book momentum strategy or a value strategy as described in the academic literature? The answer is 'probably not'. A hedge fund that buys only the recent winners and sells or shorts the recent losers, or purely buys those stocks with low price-to-book value and sells those with high valuations, will generate positive returns but will exceed the risk tolerance of most hedge fund investors. The performance of a pure value versus growth and a momentum strategy according to the Fama–French factors is displayed in Figure 5.16. However, many hedge funds do use momentum or value signals as one of several indicators and combine these with possible other factors using the 'magic of diversification' to construct acceptable rates of return.

5.15   ACTIVE STRATEGIES AND OPTION-LIKE RETURNS

In the previous sections, I established that hedge funds earn returns through exposure to broad-based market risks and well-known risk factors. However, since most hedge fund strategies involve actively trading in response to opportunities, there is an additional factor to take into account: the dynamic change of exposure to risk factors. A manager can take more or less of different types of risks depending on the market environment. This dynamism in hedge funds' trading style and risk taking can be interpreted with the help of instruments displaying contingent payout profiles, that is options.[62] The reader is by now surely aware that hedge funds employ enhanced investment techniques beyond the traditional 'long-only buy and hold' investment strategies, such as short selling, the use of derivatives, and leverage. The combination of such techniques generates returns profiles which are more complex, less linear, contingent, and dynamic in their nature.

First, certain strategies contain significant 'sold option' characteristics, that is, their risk–reward structure is similar to selling naked options. The investor receives a fixed premium for being exposed to the possibility of large losses if the market moves sharply and the options end up deeply in the money. From the discussion in Chapter 3 we realize that styles with pronounced 'sold option' exposure include:

(1) Merger Arbitrage/Event Driven: short put option on equity.
(2) Distressed Securities: short put option on equity and/or company's assets.
(3) Fixed Income Arbitrage: short put and call option (short straddles/strangles) on bonds.

The 'sold option' exposure helps to create high Sharpe ratios in normal periods, but can ultimately lead to large losses following a 'stress event', i.e. when the sold option ends up deep in the money. For most of these strategies, quoted risk-adjusted returns are overestimated, because their proponents cite solely standard deviation based on historical data for the measurement of risk.

This holds true for most 'arbitrage styles' (also referred to as 'Relative Value' strategies), including Fixed Income, Merger, Convertible Bond, and Statistical Arbitrage. In these styles the manager generally seeks to 'buy value'. When shocks hit the market the spread between bought and sold securities may increase sharply.

Other hedge fund strategies replicate 'bought option' exposures. In most cases the manager implements these through strict stop-loss limits and flexible profit targets ('cut your losses, let your profits run'). Strategies with a 'bought option' profile are:

(1) Global Macro and Managed Futures: long call option, long put option (long straddles or strangles) on bonds, foreign exchange rates, and commodities.
(2) Long/Short Equity, Equity Market Neutral: long call option, short put option on equity.

The option-like exposure of many hedge fund strategies compels hedge fund investors to understand their funds' return sources and the related risks. Figure 5.17 shows a striking example relating to the credit crisis of 1998. Before 1998, Fixed Income Arbitrage had fantastic performance with a Sharpe ratio of 1.9 from 1990 to 1997. As the market shock of the summer and fall of 1998 unfolded, hedge funds with credit risk exposure faced very large losses. When we use data that includes this event we get a very different perspective on risk-adjusted returns. During the 17-year period 1990–2007 the Sharpe ratio is a mere 0.5, lower than many directional strategies. Since these events are rare, we cannot say that either of the two estimates is the correct one. But before putting money into such a strategy, the investor must judge the probability of a second 1998 event (the 6-month period following the summer of 2007 might turn out to come close to such as we can observe on the far right of the chart).

---

[62] In an early work, R. Merton ('On market timing and investment performance' (1981)) showed that a manager pursuing a strategy of changing market exposures between several risk factors and risk-free assets generates similar return patterns to a position in options.

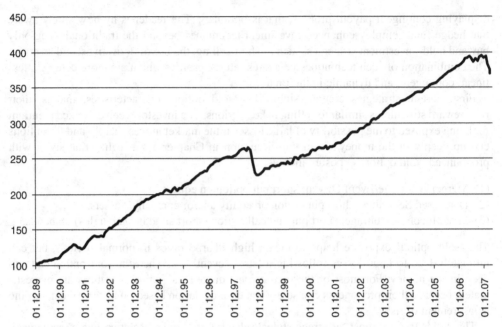

Figure 5.17 The performance of Fixed Income Arbitrage hedge funds. (Data source: Hedge Fund Research)

John Meriwether of LTCM characterized the move as a '10 sigma event', that is, something that could be expected to happen every one million years or so.[63]

The option profile of many hedge fund strategies requires a corresponding contingent approach in the simulation and modeling of their returns. It is insufficient to model hedge fund risk and return characteristics with standard asset class factors or factors displaying only linear exposure profiles to standard asset classes. As hedge fund managers change their exposure to standard risk factors with the prevailing market conditions, contingent and nonlinear factors have to enter the model. In other words, option type of exposure requires that option factors come into play. This will be discussed in the context of hedge fund replication in more detail in the following three chapters.

5.16 WHY MANAGER SKILL MATTERS

Although hedge fund returns are certainly not entirely driven by alpha, manager skill is still crucial. Manager skill manifests itself not only in the search for alpha, but also in the management of (alternative) beta. Even if risk premia are a dominant source of hedge fund returns, it requires that the skillful manager is expert at extracting and controlling them. His returns are based on sophisticated bets that take systematic risk with limited downside risk and high upside potential to achieve a positive expected return. He correctly values and manages

---

[63] 'Riding for a fall', *Newsweek* (October 5, 1998).

risks and properly executes trades. Therefore, manager skill remains the key foundation of hedge fund returns, whether those returns stem from alpha or (alternative) beta.

The risk premia available to hedge fund managers are the same as those available to other investors. However, extracting those premia in markets unfamiliar to many investors requires special expertise. The prevalence of beta in hedge fund returns does not imply that every market participant is equally in a position to trade on it. Many investors are, for example, restrained from short selling or using derivatives. This inhibits them from extracting beta in a way a hedge fund manager does. Like the mining engineer who can profitably extract gold from low-grade ore that would previously have been left in the ground, skilled fund managers are simply more efficient in identifying existing risk premia and trade with minimal extra risk exposure and transaction costs to extract them. Even if hedge fund managers do not create alpha, they can still add value for investors by providing access to relatively pure risk premia and well-defined return profiles. So the hedge fund industry has at least one argument to justify its high fees: in a certain sense, alpha is simply what most investors cannot get access to. This automatically includes a large part of the 'alternative beta' discussed in this chapter.

On the other hand, when hedge fund managers are truly exploiting market inefficiencies, this can obviously produce attractive returns. There are hedge funds that do derive most of their returns from an individual manager's skill in detecting underpriced securities, exploiting market inefficiencies and acting quickly upon particular market moves. However, market inefficiencies come and go very quickly. As discussed above, a manager's edge can disappear over time, either through markets changing or when other market participants copy a proven strategy.

5.17   BUYER BEWARE: SOME FINAL WORDS OF CAUTION ABOUT HEDGE FUND RETURNS

It should by now be clear that it is inherently difficult to separate alpha and beta. Returns are often a combination of the two, or one disguised as the other. Many hedge funds come with 'phantom alphas', which are beta returns sold as alpha. The industry's almost hysterical search for alpha gives investors a false impression of how the majority of hedge fund returns are generated. This has some malignant consequences: although phantom alphas yield positive returns, misattributing those returns to alpha means investors are exposed to systematic beta risks of which they are not aware. Unwanted systematic risks can easily lead to the opposite of the desired diversification in the global portfolio of the investor: DI-WORSE-IFICATION. This happens especially when hedge fund managers, trying to leverage what they perceive as their skill, magnify the systematic risk exposure. Even worse is when the manager himself is not aware of this magnification.

History and common sense tell us that the real danger for hedge fund investors comes from two sources:

(1) unwanted, unknown and uncontrolled leveraged systematic risk;
(2) uncontrolled manager-related risk (style drifts, faulty operations, fraud, etc.).

To be successful, the hedge fund investor needs to ensure that these two sources of danger are well addressed. It is perfectly desirable that hedge fund managers take risks. However, risk that is unintended, misunderstood, mismanaged, mispriced, or unintentionally leveraged is not acceptable and can lead to investment disaster. Only after fully accounting for all systematic risk factors in the portfolio and controlling the manager-specific risk can a hedge fund investment provide its expected and desired steady long-term performance.

Despite the ambiguities that come with the classification scheme, distinguishing beta 'risk premia' from true alpha 'market inefficiencies' is the most useful framework for analyzing hedge fund returns. This distinction also forms the starting point for all endeavors to replicate hedge fund returns to which we will now finally turn. It equally guides the investor in the construction of most efficient portfolios, the selection of the best hedge fund managers, and finally optimal risk management, all topics I will discuss in the context of hedge fund replication in Chapter 9.

6

A First Approach to Hedge Fund Replication – Linear Factor Models and Time Series Replication Models

Academic research in recent years has provided insight into hedge funds' systematic risk exposures and return sources. The current method of choice for analyzing and modeling hedge fund returns is broadly known as 'linear factor-based analysis'. In this chapter I will present the merits and pitfalls of applying linear factor models to hedge fund returns. The question of how successful is not just academic; investment companies have stepped in to deliver these models in investable format. Linear factor analysis is the approach employed in the 'first generation' of hedge fund replication products.

This chapter also provides a practical understanding of the risk factor exposure of single hedge fund strategies. First-hand examples of actual models will clearly illustrate the merits and limitations of this approach and show that the explanatory power of available linear factor models is much greater for some hedge fund strategies than for others.

6.1 REVISITING SHARPE'S APPROACH

Multi-factor models are the simplest method for modeling the linear dependencies of a variable from other variables – in our case modeling the returns of a hedge fund from its systematic risk factors. These models are based on the statistical method of multilinear regression analysis.[1]

W. Sharpe introduced a unifying framework for such style models in 1992, in an effort to describe active management strategies in equity mutual funds.[2] His model describes a given active investment style as a linear combination of a set of asset class indices. In other words, it models an active investment strategy as a linear combination of passive, i.e. long-only, buy-and-hold, 'strategies', i.e. a linear combination of given asset classes. The models Sharpe introduced have been impressively successful at explaining the lion's share of the mutual fund performance. In doing so, Sharpe's breakthrough at the very least opened the door for others to recognize that it might be possible to model hedge funds as well. This insight itself is a key building block of hedge fund replications.

Let us examine how well Sharpe's specific approach applies to the task of replicating hedge fund returns by assuming the hedge fund strategy we are modeling invests long and short in certain asset classes. We then construct our model by selecting the basket of asset classes

---

[1] See the text book *Quantitative Methods for Investment Analysis* by R. DeFusco *et al.* (2001) or any other text book on statistical methods for more details on this broadly used method.

[2] See 'Asset allocation: management style and performance measurement' (1992) by William Sharpe and the articles by Eugene Fama and Kenneth French 'Multifactor explanations of asset pricing anomalies' (1996) and 'Common risk factors in the return of stocks and bonds' (1993). More information can also be found at the websites of William Sharpe, www.wsharpe.com, and Ken French, http://mba.tuck.dartmouth.edu/pages/faculty/ken.french/

that correctly approximates that individual hedge fund strategy. The resulting factor equation would then account for all hedge fund return variation that derives from risk exposure to the selected asset classes, but not those from manager alpha. If we add alpha to the equation, we can decompose the return of the hedge fund in a very simple equation:

$$\text{Hedge fund return} = \text{Manager's alpha} + \sum (\beta_i * \text{factor}_i) + \text{Random fluctuations}$$

The systematic part of a hedge fund's return depends on the manager's choice of exposure to the beta risk factors and the prevailing market conditions. The alpha part of a hedge fund's return can be attributed to the manager's skill relative to the appropriate compensation the capital markets provide for the risk he has chosen to take.

6.2 UNDERSTANDING LINEAR FACTOR ANALYSIS: CRITERIA FOR THE FACTOR MODEL APPROACH

Linear factor analysis starts from a general equilibrium model. This model relates investment returns to their systematic risk exposures, represented by directly observable prices in the capital markets. The simplest version of this is the well-known Capital Asset Pricing Model (CAPM) for equity markets.[3]

There is now a vast and growing body of academic literature both on these systematic risk factors, and on hedge funds' (linear) exposure to them – known as the funds' 'factor loadings'. Since the goal of this approach is to replicate some statistical properties of a given past hedge fund return time series, let's refer to it as the 'time series replication approach'.

Two criteria must be met for linear factor models to successfully replicate the properties of a time series of investment returns:

(1) A large portion of the time series' behavior must be explained by linear dependence on the chosen factors. In other words the return time series must be heavily correlated to those factors. This is an obvious requirement, since linear correlation with the factors is the only predictive lever available to us in this approach. Clearly a model in which the factors collectively explain 80% of the time series' behavior will be more predictive than one in which the factors explain only 40%.
(2) The measured exposures to the chosen factors must not vary, or must vary only very slowly over time. Even if the factors are linearly correlated with a time series of returns, varying exposure to factors over time will throw the model off. The mathematical term for the property of stable exposure is 'stationarity' – a fancy way of saying that the level of exposure to the modeled factors essentially stays put. The exposures must remain stationary so that the exposures suggested by the linear factor models – based on past exposures – still resemble the *current* exposures of the investment. Since the linear factor model reflects the *average* exposure over the history of the model, variations in exposure will make the model's profile lag behind that of the hedge fund strategy.

We will revisit these criteria later in the chapter, since individual hedge fund strategies vary considerably in how much they 'cooperate' with these requirements.

---

[3] While the CAPM is considered 'dead' by most academics, there are extensions of it in various forms that continue to be the subject of research. Further the CAPM is still in extensive use by practitioners.

6.3   THE MODEL SPECIFICATION PROBLEM

Of course, if modeling hedge funds were that simple, this book could end here! But as you can see there are a good few pages left to go, because replicating hedge funds presents special challenges that strain the multi-factor approach. Simple extension of Sharpe's model is not enough. Unlike equity mutual funds – with their clear and transparent asset class exposures – hedge funds' exposures to the main asset classes are less obvious. To add further complication, those exposures vary widely across different hedge funds.

This makes model specification for multi-factor analysis of most hedge fund strategies quite difficult, as it is much less obvious which factors to choose. And without the correct factor selection, the model has little value: it will not correctly replicate the time series returns of the underlying hedge fund. Poor or arbitrary factor selection risks both under-specifying the model by omitting true factors, and over-specifying it by including spurious ones.

Even if the chosen factors are correct, a time-varying or market-state-contingent exposure to the asset class factors can still degrade the explanatory power of the model. Some researchers, therefore, suggest introducing option factors into the models to account for the contingent payout profiles of most hedge fund strategies,[4] an extension I will discuss in more detail in Chapter 8.

The model specification problem places us in immediate danger of seeing more alpha than is actually present. As our earlier formula describes, we infer a hedge fund's alphas by measuring and subtracting out the betas, times the beta factors. We can look at alpha as the 'dark matter' of the hedge fund universe. It can only be measured by separating out everything we can otherwise account for, and calculating what is left. In other words, alpha is never directly observable, but is measured jointly with beta by subtracting beta out. The inferred value for alpha therefore depends on the risk factors chosen to represent beta. If we leave a relevant factor out of the model, the alpha will come out as fictively high. If dark matter seems too high-flown a metaphor, we can get more down to earth and say that what we call alpha is the garbage bin of the regression. After we separate out as many of the recycleable bottles and cans of beta that we can through our factors, we are forced to toss whatever is left over into alpha. We simply have nowhere else to put it.

As a consequence, some of the returns not accounted for by multi-factor models are almost certainly unaccounted for beta rather than alpha. Just because our model of systematic risk factors is incomplete it does not mean additional risk factors do not exist – only that we do not yet know how to model them. To draw another image from astronomy, the outer planets of our solar system existed and exerted their gravitational pull long before we had telescopes sensitive enough to see them.

So if we are honest, the previously cited simple formula for hedge fund returns should actually be a bit less simple. It must include the un-modeled risk factors as follows:

$$\text{Hedge fund return} = \text{Manager's alpha} + \sum (\beta_i * \text{factor}_{i(\text{modeled})})$$

$$+ \sum (\beta_i * \text{factor}_{i(\text{unmodeled})}) + \text{random fluctuations}$$

---

[4] The idea of option factors for the purpose of hedge fund modeling was actually introduced in the earliest work on hedge fund models by W. Fung and D. Hsieh, 'Empirical characteristics of dynamic trading strategies: the case of hedge funds' (1997), and has since then been discussed in many academic studies.

If the model designer is humble enough to admit that his model is imperfect, then he should acknowledge that apparent alpha values in factor models are just that: apparent. Measured alpha can derive from any combination of two elements. One element is true alpha, manager skill in generating return without systematic risk. The other is un-modeled beta, beta that is not captured because of a mis-specified or incomplete model. This could occur either because an important risk factor has been left out of the model entirely, or because a hedge fund has a type of exposure, such as state-contingent or nonlinear, that a linear multi-factor model cannot correctly account for. These two rather gaping loopholes should make us look at alpha statistics, even from the best available regression models, with a healthy degree of skepticism.

We can illustrate the problem with a simple example of a strategy in which the model gives one answer and common sense gives quite another. Consider a put writing strategy on the S&P 500, or equivalently a covered call writing strategy, as represented by the Chicago Board of Trade's BXM index. In this strategy, monthly at-the-money call options on existing equity positions are written with one-month maturities. If we regress the BXM index against the S&P 500 over a period of 11 years from 1994 to 2007, we obtain a statistically significant alpha (the y-intercept of that regression) of around 3.9% p.a. Yet common sense tells us that there is surely not much true skill-driven alpha in writing put options on equities.[5] So all or most of the 4% must be spurious or 'phantom' alpha. The phantom alpha results from the imperfect specification of the chosen model (regression against the S&P 500) instead of the appropriate factor (the covered call strategy). So we should not confuse pure manager skill with an imperfect model. This is a common problem of multi-factor models in the literature which claim to prove high alphas. So we must take any statistics of alpha with a grain, if not a large shaker-full, of salt.

6.4   THE DATA QUALITY PROBLEM

The low quality of available hedge fund data also raises another barrier to correctly modeling returns. Empirical data about hedge funds contains several biases that make returns – and therefore alpha values – look bigger than they actually are (see Chapter 4). A study by B. Malkiel and A. Saha shows consistent upward biases in hedge fund indices.[6] And the broader consensus of studies on data quality is that these biases account for at least 2–3% of reported hedge fund outperformance. Even more concerning, the short measurement periods available may not include the risk event for which the strategies earn their premia. This is like measuring the financial performance of a company writing hurricane insurance for only the 10 years prior to hurricane Katrina. The picture in year 11 would obviously look quite different! Underestimating the real risk type and magnitude of a strategy make that strategy appear less risky – and therefore more lucrative and more alpha-driven – than it really is.

In the following sections I will outline the results of a my own modeling efforts of hedge fund strategies based on various regressions on systematic risk factors, most of which has been published in a research paper in 2005.[7] Although this paper has been frequently cited, I

---

[5] Writing put options and investing the collateral in cash is identical to writing covered calls, a property that is known as 'put call parity' in option theory.

[6] B. Malkiel, A. Saha, 'Hedge funds: risk and return' (2004).

[7] L. Jaeger, C. Wagner, 'Factor modeling and benchmarking of hedge funds: Can passive investments in hedge fund strategies deliver?', *Journal of Alternative Investments* (Winter 2005) awarded 'paper of the year' by the publishers.

want to be clear that these regressions – based on publicly available hedge fund indices – also inevitably suffer the above data-quality problems. The only other possible dataset would have been the investable indices, which do not contain these upward biases. However, as discussed in Chapter 4, investable indices contain selection biases that make them less representative. Furthermore, their history is even shorter than the non-investable hedge fund indices. Therefore, I chose the non-investable indices as the best, or 'least bad', basis for regression.

6.5   THE DEVELOPMENT OF HEDGE FUND FACTOR MODELS

Fung and Hsieh, in 1997,[8] were the first to extend Sharpe's model to hedge funds. Starting from techniques similar to those Sharpe had applied to mutual funds, they added short selling, leverage, and derivatives into their model. Fung and Hsieh performed multilinear regressions of hedge fund returns against eight different asset class indices: US equities, non-US equities, emerging market equities, US government bonds, non-US government bonds, one-month Eurodollar deposit rate, gold, and the trade-weighted value of the US dollar. They identified five style factors (in statistical language, principal components), which they defined as modeling the following hedge fund strategies: Global Macro, Systematic Trend-Following, Systematic Opportunistic, Value, Distressed Securities.

Fung and Hsieh further argued that hedge fund strategies are highly dynamic and create option-like, nonlinear, contingent return profiles. These nonlinear profiles, they said, cannot be modeled in simple asset class factor models. In later research they explicitly incorporate assets with contingent payout profiles, such as options.[9]

Most of the studies that followed show results consistent with Fung and Hsieh.[10] Recent literature offers an increasing number of studies around the question of common style factor exposure and contingency in payoff profile for hedge funds.[11] These studies show good, though incomplete, progress in creating accurate models. The newer ones have good explanatory power for some hedge fund strategies, although explanatory power of cross-sectional variation is still lower than for most traditional investment styles.

6.6   BASIC AND ADVANCED FACTOR MODELS FOR HEDGE FUND STRATEGIES

Let's examine and compare the results of two different sets of asset class factor models for hedge funds. The first set of models is a simpler one based on six conventional main asset class

---

[8] W. Fung, D. Hsieh, 'Empirical characteristics of dynamic trading strategies: the case of hedge funds' (1997).

[9] See their recent work: W. Fung, D. Hsieh, 'Asset based style factors for hedge funds', *Financial Analyst Journal* (September/October 2002).

[10] See, for example, the article by S. Brown and W. Goetzmann, 'Hedge funds with style' (2003). The authors identify eight style factors, i.e. three more than Fung and Hsieh in their research.

[11] See W. Fung, D. Hsieh, 'The risk in hedge fund strategies: alternative alphas and alternative betas' in L. Jaeger (ed.), *The New Generation of Risk Management for Hedge Funds and Private Equity Investment* (2003); 'Benchmarks of hedge fund performance: information content and measurement biases' (2004); 'The risk in hedge fund strategies: theory and evidence from trend followers' (2001); 'Asset based style factors for hedge funds' (2002); T. Schneeweis and R. Spurgin, 'Multifactor analysis of hedge funds, managed futures, and mutual fund returns and risk characteristics' (1998); V. Agarwal, N. Naik, 'Performance evaluation of hedge funds with option-based and buy-and-hold strategies' (2001); D. Capocci, G. Hübner, 'Analysis of hedge fund performance' (2004); J. Hasanhodzic, A. Lo, 'Can hedge fund returns be replicated? The linear case', (2007).

factors, similar to those used in much of the earlier literature. The second model set includes a variety of other more suitable factors, chosen specifically for the given hedge fund strategy. The difference between the explanatory powers of the two illustrates how oversimplified regression models understate the true nature of the hedge fund risk exposure.

Table 6.1 provides the results of a first and simpler set of regressions against different hedge fund strategy sector indices. The indices studied are from the data provider Hedge Fund Research (HFR). Returns are calculated on monthly data as geometric averages (cumulative returns) of the log-differences of consecutive (monthly) prices. Further, the risk-free rate of return was explicitly subtracted from all independent as well as dependent variables, with the apparent exception of spread factors. As a risk-free rate I chose the US 3-month Libor. The independent variables chosen are the equity markets (large cap stocks: S&P 500; small cap stocks: Russell 2000, emerging markets: MSCI Emerging Markets Index), government bonds (MSCI US Treasury Index), the high-yield bonds (Credit Suisse High Yield Bond Index), and equity volatility (VIX index).[12] These represent the main asset classes outside of currency and commodity markets. Currency and commodities are not significant to the exposure characteristics of any hedge fund strategies except Managed Futures.

The values for alpha (the intercept of the regression) are positive with strong statistical significance for all strategies except Managed Futures. Short Selling strategies display the highest alpha value at about 12% p.a. Long/Short Equity strategies come in second at 8.8% p.a., followed by Event Driven strategies at around 8%. Relative Value strategies display alpha values around 6% p.a. and Global Macro strategies show alpha values around 5% p.a. In contrast, Managed Futures strategies do not display any statistically significant alpha. The quality of the model differs strongly between strategies. The R^2 values are quite high for Long/Short Equity, Short Selling and Event Driven strategies. However the model's explanatory power dips as low as 20% for Managed Futures and Equity Market Neutral strategies.

Rather than simply concluding that some strategies must have a 12% p.a. alpha, let us try to improve our model. We can do this by considering more elaborate and more specific sets of risk factors in our regression. Table 6.2 summarizes the results of a multilinear regression of such sets of factors that incorporate among others the autoregressive factor AR(1) – which is a one-period lagged time series of the dependent variable itself. The AR(1) factors are included, if statistically significant, to account for the fact that some hedge fund prices do not adjust instantly to changing market conditions. Instead their adjustment is delayed, either because the underlying markets they trade in are less liquid or because they smooth their reported returns over time.[13]

The new models capture a much larger percentage of hedge fund return variability, which expresses itself in higher R^2 values. The average alpha value drops by almost 4% p.a., shedding about half of the value given by the simpler model. About half of this alpha decline is caused by the autoregressive term AR(1), which is significant in the regression in five out of ten strategies. We can interpret this autocorrelation as a sign of persistent price lags in hedge

---

[12] All data available is used for the regression up to December 2007. The minimum number of months for such a regression is 182, and the maximum number is 204 months. All reported asset class factors are highly significant (higher than 99%). Insignificant factor exposure was omitted.

[13] A thorough discussion of the autoregressive factor can be found in M. Getmansky, A. W. Lo, I. Makarov, 'An econometric model of serial correlation and illiquidity in hedge fund returns' (2004). See also the paper by C. Asness et al., 'Do hedge funds hedge?' (2001).

Table 6.1 Results of linear asset class factor modeling for the different hedge fund strategies with a restricted set of asset-class-based risk factors (based on monthly data: HFR from January 1994 to December 2007; for Managed Futures: CISDM Qualified Universe and Trend Following from January 1994 to December 2007)

Alternative factors
HFR Index

01/94–12/07	Asset class factor		Beta (Alpha)	t-value (absolute)	Adj. R^2
Equity Hedge	Russell 2000		0.35	11.72	76.22%
(Long/Short Equity)	MSCI Emerging Markets		0.06	2.65	
		Alpha	0.0073	6.88	
Equity Market Neutral	Russell 2000		0.08	3.96	18.79%
	MSCI US Treasuries		0.18	3.65	
	MSCI Emerging Markets		−0.04	2.55	
		Alpha	0.0053	7.77	
Short Selling	Russell 2000		−0.78	−10.42	71.13%
	S&P 500		−0.28	3.56	
		Alpha	0.0098	3.56	
Event Driven	Russell 2000		0.18	8.05	75.39%
	CSFB High Yield		0.28	5.15	
	MSCI Emerging		0.04	2.58	
	Markets VIX		−0.02	2.14	
		Alpha	0.0067	8.56	
Distressed	CSFB High Yield		0.37	6.36	57.88%
	Russell 2000		0.09	3.71	
	MSCI Emerging		0.04	2.02	
	Markets VIX		−0.04	3.62	
		Alpha	0.0067	7.80	
Merger Arbitrage	Russell 2000		0.08	4.02	40.24%
	CSFB High Yield		0.09	1.95	
		Alpha	0.0063	8.82	
Fixed Income Arbitrage	CSFB High Yield		0.21	3.61	19.05%
	VIX		−0.04	3.41	
		Alpha	0.0045	5.36	
Convertible Arbitrage	CSFB High Yield		0.26	4.89	27.56%
	VIX		0.02	1.81	
		Alpha	0.0051	6.49	
Macro	MSCI US Treasuries		0.59	6.28	43.83%
	MSCI Emerging Markets		0.13	4.63	
	Russell 2000		0.12	3.28	
		Alpha	0.0038	2.90	
Managed Futures	MSCI US Treasuries		0.73	5.31	17.55%
	MSCI Emerging Markets		0.09	2.35	
		Alpha	0.0032	1.65	

Table 6.2   Results of linear asset class factor modeling for the different hedge fund strategies with a broader set of risk factors (based on monthly data: HFR from January 1994 to December 2007; for Managed Futures: CISDM Managed Futures Qualified Universe and Trend Following Indices from January 1994 to September 2004)

Alternative factors HFR Index 01/94–12/07	Asset class factor		Beta (Alpha)	t-value (absolute)	Adj. R^2
Equity Hedge	Citigroup Convertible		0.59	24.28	86.43%
(Long/Short Equity)	Small-Cap Spread (Wilshire)		0.14	6.21	
	CPPI S&P 12M		0.25	4.09	
	AR(1)		0.08	2.50	
		Alpha	0.0037	4.86	
Equity Market Neutral	Fama–French UMD		0.09	8.24	34.51%
	S&P 500		0.06	3.74	
	Value Spread (MSCI)		0.00	2.34	
	Small-Cap Spread (Wilshire)		0.03	2.10	
		Alpha	0.0019	3.46	
Short Selling	Citigroup Convertible		−1.30	10.42	77.57%
	S&P 600 Small Cap		−0.20	2.56	
		Alpha	0.0050	2.24	
Event Driven	S&P 500		0.25	12.77	78.06%
	Small-Cap Spread (Wilshire)		0.21	10.39	
	CSFB High Yield		0.26	5.40	
	AR(1)		0.21	5.82	
		Alpha	0.0036	5.21	
Distressed	AR(1)		0.42	9.63	70.04%
	S&P 500		0.13	6.52	
	Small-Cap Spread (Wilshire)		0.12	6.13	
	CSFB High Yield		0.34	7.06	
		Alpha	0.0020	2.94	
Merger Arbitrage	S&P 600 Small Cap		0.10	5.75	49.43%
	Russel 3000 Value		0.01	0.27	
	BXM Covered Call Writing Index		0.07	1.86	
	Merger Fund		0.09	3.60	
		Alpha	0.0035	5.82	
Fixed Income Arbitrage	CSFB High Yield		0.16	4.32	45.11%
	Citigroup Convertible		0.08	0.55	
	AR(1)		0.28	4.61	
	JPMorgan EM Global Bonds		0.03	2.52	
		Alpha	0.0008	1.06	
Convertible Arbitrage	AR(1)		0.47	9.19	57.55%
	Citigroup Convertible Inv. Grade		0.24	5.41	
	CSFB High Yield		0.22	6.13	
	S&P 500		−0.10	3.79	
		Alpha	0.0010	1.89	

Table 6.2 (*Continued*)

Alternative factors

HFR Index 01/94–12/07	Asset class factor		Beta (Alpha)	t-value (absolute)	Adj. R^2
Macro	MSCI US Treasuries		0.31	5.76	51.67%
	Citigroup Convertible		0.25	4.97	
	sGFI		0.28	3.69	
	MSCI EM Global Equity		0.08	2.90	
		Alpha	0.0024	1.91	
Managed Futures	sGFI		0.67	4.47	18.33%
	Citigroup WGBI		0.35	2.79	
	Goldman Commodity Index		0.10	2.44	
		Alpha	−0.0012	−0.49	
Managed Futures Trend Followers	sGFI		1.40	12.22	48.42%
	Citigroup WGBI		0.11	1.19	
	Goldman Commodity Index		0.05	1.49	
		Alpha	0.0007	0.39	

fund valuation. This implies that such simple measures of risk as Sharpe ratio, volatility, and correlation with market indices significantly underestimate the true market risk of hedge fund strategies. Autocorrelation both drives down estimated volatility and distributes the effects of changing market conditions and shocks – as measured by the risk factors – over several periods. The AR(1) factor thus measures some lagged beta that would otherwise be missing from the model. Excluding this autocorrelation factor causes some unaccounted beta to be misinterpreted as alpha. The other half of the alpha decline is due to a wider coverage of risk factors in the models underlying Table 6.2.

6.7   HOW GOOD ARE OUR MODELS?

However encouraging the results of these extended models, we should ask how far one can get with linear specification of asset class factor models. To answer this question, I undertook an (otherwise undesired) exercise in data mining. I started with 60 potential asset class factors – including various stock market and bond market indices, commodity indices, spreads, and option strategies. For each index, I applied a stepwise forward regression, including additional explanatory asset classes until the increase in the incremental F-value was below 2. In other words, I kept adding asset classes until adding another one did not significantly improve the model. Table 6.3 summarizes the results of this stepwise regression for the HFR indices considered above.

Notice first that the factor models in Table 6.2 are not bad compared to the results in Table 6.3. The stepwise regression increases the average adjusted R^2 by little more than 20% by using an additional 12 asset class factors. In particular, the models in Table 6.2 for Equity Hedge, Event Driven and Short Selling strategies already capture a good part of what can be explained with any linear model.

The second key result of this exercise concerns the overall value R^2. It is 52% on average for the factor models in Table 6.2, and around 71% for the stepwise regression. This means that,

Table 6.3 Results for a regression with 60 potential asset class factors including various stock market and bond market indices, commodity indices, spreads, and option strategies (see text for a detailed description). (Data as in Table 6.1)

HFR Index	Number of asset class factors	Adj. R^2
Equity Hedge (L/S Equity)	22	91.2%
Equity Market Neutral	12	45.2%
Short Selling	11	83.4%
Event Driven	10	82.1%
Distressed	18	78.1%
Merger Arbitrage	19	57.2%
Convertible Arbitrage	16	65.1%
Global Macro	13	58.3%

although much of the variation of hedge fund returns is captured by these factor models, another substantial part is still missing. Furthermore, the factor models are much more successful at explaining some hedge fund strategies than others. While they do well at explaining Long/Short Equity, Short Selling, and Event Driven strategies, they are much less successful with Equity Market Neutral, Merger Arbitrage, and Managed Futures.

Despite these shortcomings, the obtained R^2 values imply that we can model at least some of hedge fund variation with linear factors, validating the hypothesis that hedge funds earn a substantial part of their returns by taking on systematic risk. However, the nature of these risks often differs from the standard notion of systematic (market) risk. In the case of stock market risk, it is often small cap risk (Russell 2000), nonlinear risk (convertible bonds, BXM), or default risk (high yield, emerging markets), rather than the risk of the overall stock market. In the case of bond market risk, it is often credit risk that is assumed by hedge funds.

6.8 VARIABILITY OF RISK EXPOSURES AND PERSISTENCE OF FACTOR LOADINGS

Investors in hedge funds should realize that both the factor loadings and the underlying risk factors themselves can change. Figure 6.1 provides an example. It shows the time variation of the credit spreads between AAA and BBB (Baa) US corporate bonds. The sudden increases in credit spread – both in the summer of 1998 and, more recently and more dramatically in the summer of 2007 – led to severe losses of Fixed Income (in 2007 specifically mortgage-backed) hedge funds. These losses caught by surprise those investors who placed their faith in manager alpha, without realizing the systematic risks inherent in this strategy.

Even as levels of the various systematic risk factors change, the exposures of hedge fund managers to those risks are also shifting. For example, both the collection of strong market stresses in the last decade and the equity bear market at the beginning of this one have caused many fund managers to change their risk exposures over time. Figure 6.2 provides an example. We plotted the sensitivity of Convertible Arbitrage managers to the Credit Suisse High Yield Bond Index based on a rolling regression over 60 months. Fung and Hsieh have further documented the claim that managers adjust their bets over time.[14]

The regression results above also merit a more detailed look at the stability of our models, a subject that has received surprisingly little coverage in the literature. For this purpose I cited

---

[14] For example, see the paper by W. Fung, D. Hsieh, 'Hedge fund benchmarks: a risk based approach' (2004).

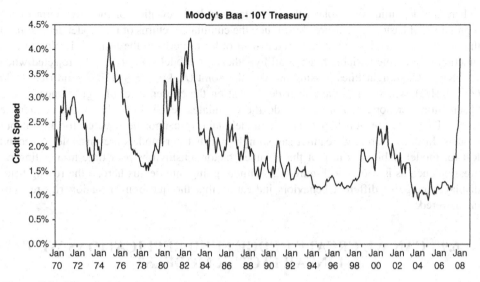

Figure 6.1 Historical development of credit spreads

some results of the performed CUSUM tests in my research paper which are designed to test whether the obtained regression models are stable to any statistically significant degree. The CUSUM test considers the cumulated sum of the (normalized) recursive residuals w_r:

$$W_t = \sum_{r-K+1}^{r-t} \frac{w_r}{\hat{\sigma}}$$

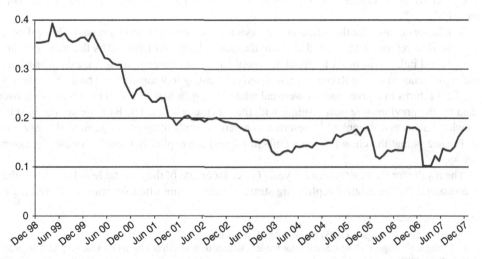

Figure 6.2 The development of high-yield beta (sensitivity to the Credit Suisse High Yield Bond Index) for Convertible Arbitrage managers based on a rolling regression over a 60-month time window. The risk factors were chosen as in Table 6.2

(where the denominator displays the predicted standard deviation of the error term of the regression). It basically measures how much the cumulated returns of the model deviate from the original time series' cumulated returns. In order to perform the test, W_t is plotted as a function of the time variable t. The null hypothesis of model stability can be rejected when W_t breaks the straight lines passing through the point $(K,+/-a(T-K)1/2)$ and $(K,+/-3a(T-K)1/2)$, where a is a parameter dependent on the chosen level of significance. In our observation, for none of our models do the cumulated residuals W_t break the confidence levels. Therefore the null hypothesis of model stability cannot be rejected for any of our models. In other words, we cannot say straight out that our models are unstable. A second test for model stability is to plot the obtained factor sensitivities over time in a rolling regression such as is shown in Figure 6.2. Without going into details here,[15] the rolling betas display a range of different behaviors indicating that the question of stationarity remains unanswered.

6.9   CAN WE CREATE HEDGE FUND REPLICATIONS WITH LINEAR FACTOR MODELS?

The idea of using a linear factor model setting to replicate hedge fund returns precedes the more recently commercialized versions by investment banks. The first systematic study on using linear factor models as trading tools to replicate hedge funds appeared in my above-mentioned 2005 paper.[16] Most of the results that follow are taken (and updated) from that paper.

In concept, the scheme of hedge fund replication by using linear factor models is rather simple: one calculates the factor loadings and subsequently invests directly into the factor exposures taken from the regression. We can calculate the obtained performance as the cumulative returns of the factor variables multiplied by the obtained beta values:

$$\text{Return}(t) = \sum (\beta_i * \text{Factor}_i(t))$$

We refer to these models as 'replicating factor strategies' (in the following abbreviated to 'RFS').

The factors chosen for the following analysis are the same as in the regression above. I compare the RFS returns as calculated above to the realized returns displayed by the corresponding hedge fund indices. In order to avoid the problem of data mining and in-sample over-fitting, the factors chosen for the RFS were calculated on a rolling looking-forward basis. Specifically, the RFS returns in a given month were calculated using factors obtained by a regression over data for the previous five years ending with the previous month. The RFS are similar in spirit to what Jensen and Rotenberg[17] describe as a generic replication of hedge fund strategy. The difference is that the chosen factors (sub-strategies) are explicitly modeled in the regression set up.

The results for the most recent six years (since inception of the investable indices) are rather astonishing: the cumulative replicating strategy's returns are often superior to the returns of

---

[15] See L. Jaeger, C. Wagner, (2005) for more details on such analysis.

[16] l. Jaeger, C. Wagner, (2005). Some prior but less systematic research has been undertaken by G. Jensen and J. Rotenberg (2003).

[17] G. Jensen and J. Rotenberg, 'Hedge funds selling beta as alpha' (2003), updated in 2004 and 2005.

Table 6.4 Cumulated performance of the RFS and the HFRX (investable) and HFRI (non-investable) from March 2003 to December 2007 (CISDM data for Managed Futures)

Strategy	RFS	HFRX	HFRI
Equity Hedge	156.2%	34.6%	79.0%
Market Neutral	4.2%	5.5%	28.3%
Short Selling	−48.4%	N/A	−20.4%
Event Driven	54.3%	54.1%	91.6%
Distressed	63.5%	44.8%	95.4%
Merger Arbitrage	19.8%	28.7%	45.3%
Fixed Income	51.1%	N/A	43.4%
Convertible Arbitrage	23.4%	4.8%	23.1%
Global Macro	52.8%	29.5%	60.6%
Managed Futures	57.2%	N/A	39.1%

the hedge fund indices, especially in their investable versions. For the latter, performance of the RFS is better or equal for almost every single strategy sector.

Let's examine our results for each individual hedge fund strategy compared to the investable and noninvestable indices from Hedge Fund Research, summarized by a comparison in Table 6.4.[18]

Long/Short Equity

Most Long/Short Equity managers have significant exposure to the broad equity market, particularly small cap stocks. The reasons for this are easy to spot: managers may find it easier to find opportunities in a rising market, and also find it easier to short sell large cap and buy small cap stocks. Our factor models in Tables 6.1 and 6.2 confirm these results. The most significant factors are related to broad equity and small cap equity markets. The explanatory power of the linear factor models is relatively high with an R-squared value of more than 85%, by far the highest among all models. Fung and Hsieh obtain similar results in a specific study on the Long/Short Equity strategy.[19] They chose as independent variables the S&P 500 index and the difference between the Wilshire 1750 index and the Wilshire 750 index (as a proxy for small cap risk). I obtained very similar results (having chosen the Russell 2000 and Russell 1000 for the calculation of the small cap spread).

With the rise in popularity of investing in emerging markets, hedge funds number among the crowd of investors that deploy capital in these regions. It is therefore not surprising that the emerging markets factor has become statistically significant for Long/Short Equity hedge funds. Further, for the most recent time period international equities need to be added to the factor set. I summarize that linear factor models with equity factors do a good job in explaining and modeling Long/Short Equity hedge fund returns.

Figure 6.3 presents the performance of the Long/Short Equity RFS next to the HFR non-investable (HFRI) and the investable versions of HFR (HFRX). The chart confirms what

---

[18] The reader may also note the large performance deviation between the investable and noninvestable versions which we discussed in detail in Chapter 4.

[19] See W. Fung, D. Hsieh, 'The risk in Long/Short Equity hedge funds' (2004).

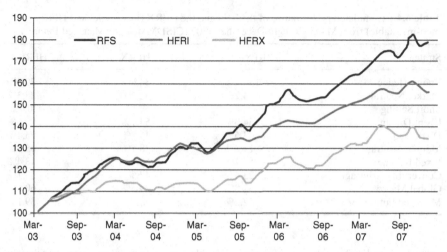

Figure 6.3 Performance of the Long/Short Equity RFS next to the HFR non-investable (HFRI) and the investable versions of HFR (HFRX)

the numbers already indicated: one can replicate very well the performance of the average Long/Short Equity manager in the index by using an RFS model with similar performance and volatility. The RFS performs along the HFRI index despite some alpha displayed in Tables 6.1 and 6.2. Figure 6.4, which shows the rolling alpha of the Equity Hedge and Event Driven hedge funds, sheds some light on this discrepancy. Table 6.2 displayed the *average* alpha over the regression period. However, Figure 6.4 indicates that this alpha has declined quite rapidly over time. Figure 6.3 in contrast only matches the most recent performance since 2003. There is much less alpha shown by Long/Short Equity managers in that most recent period. Further, the RFS outperforms the investable version of the index (HFRX) significantly.

Equity Market Neutral

Equity Market Neutral strategies aim for zero exposure to specific equity market factors. Correspondingly, the model in Table 6.2 shows only a small, although statistically significant, exposure to broad equity markets. However, the results indicate that the Equity Market Neutral style is sensitive to the Fama–French momentum factor UMD and the value factor (the spread of the MSCI value and growth indices). The R^2 value of the regression for Equity Market Neutral is the third lowest of all the strategies, beating out only Managed Futures and Fixed Income Arbitrage. This indicates that simple linear models fail to explain a significant chunk of the variation of returns for this hedge fund style. However, to mix the right combination of systematic risk exposures of Equity Market Neutral strategies, we must distinguish two distinctly different sub-styles of this strategy. One (often system-based) approach buys undervalued stocks and sells short overvalued stocks according to a value- and momentum-based analysis. A more short-term approach, also referred to as 'Statistical Arbitrage', trades in pairs based on a statistical analysis of relative performance deviation of similar stocks. Each of these sub-styles naturally has a different exposure to the factors examined here.

Figure 6.5 shows that the RFS underperforms the HFRI index by a large margin reflecting the positive alpha in Table 6.2. However, it performs in line with the HFRX investable index and outperforms it significantly on a risk-adjusted basis.

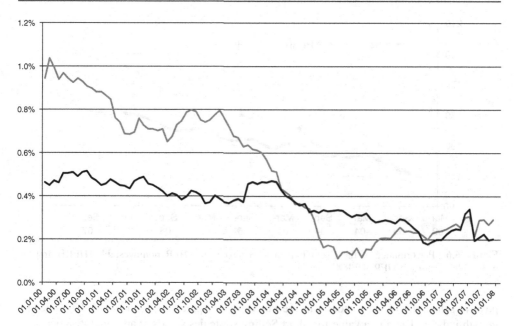

Figure 6.4 The development of alpha for Long/Short Equity and Event Driven hedge funds (HFR sub-indices) based on a rolling regression over a 60-month time window. The risk factors were chosen as in Table 6.2

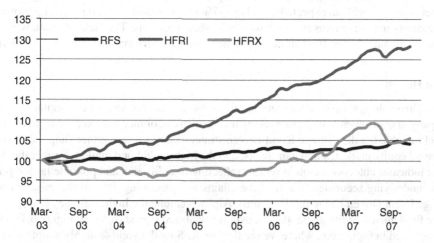

Figure 6.5 Performance of the Equity Market Neutral RFS next to the HFR noninvestable (HFRI) and the investable versions of HFR (HFRX)

Short Selling

The main exposure of the Short Selling strategy is, quite obviously, being short the equity market. Interestingly, the exposure to the broad equity markets can best be modeled with the same factor as for Long/Short Equity. This indicates the same type of linear exposure profile as for the Long/Short Equity strategy, with the signs inverted. Short Selling displays

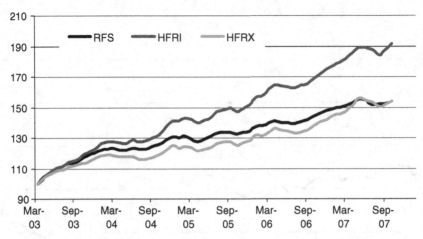

Figure 6.6 Performance of the Event Driven RFS next to the HFR noninvestable (HFRI) and the investable versions of HFR (HFRX)

positive sensitivity to value stocks, as measured by the spread between the MSCI value and growth indices. The alpha value for Short Selling strategies stands at around 4–5% p.a. This indicates that the short side does offer some profit opportunities, perhaps explained in part by most investors being restricted from selling short. However, the alpha of this strategy must be high in order for the strategy to generate any profits at all. That's because shorting the equity markets starts off with an expected negative 4–7% return, based on the long-term performance of the equity markets minus short rebate for the short positions. This helps explain why Short Selling is the only hedge fund strategy with negative past performance over the last 15 years.

Event Driven

Event Driven hedge funds constitute an ensemble of various investment strategies around company-specific events, including restructuring, distress, or mergers. According to our factor model in Table 6.2 the average Event Driven strategy comes with a rather simple exposure to the broad equity market, small cap stocks, and the high-yield bond market. Further the AR(1) factor indicates autocorrelation in returns reflecting liquidity risk and possible lagged pricing of the underlying securities. The model explains an astonishing 78% of the variation of the average Event Driven hedge fund's returns. Alpha is among the highest for any strategy in the hedge fund universe with about 4% p.a. over the analyzed period (but note Figure 6.4). This is also reflected in Figure 6.6, where we see that the RFS model yields roughly about two-thirds of the return of the Event Driven managers in the HFRI index. However, the RFS performs in line with the HFRX investable index version.

Merger Arbitrage

Linear regressions on Merger Arbitrage hedge funds yield very low explanatory value. A conditional correlation analysis sheds light on why that is the case: Merger Arbitrage strategies display rather high correlations to the equity market when the latter declines and conversely low correlations when stocks trade up or sideways. This corresponds to a profile similar to that of a sold put on equities. As a matter of fact, the payout profile of Merger Arbitrage strategies corresponds directly to a sold put option on announced merger deals. This short put profile is reflected in the significance of the (nonlinear) BXM factor in Table 6.2. Shorting put options provides limited upside but full participation in the downside (less the option premium). This argument extends beyond the immediate exposure to merger deals breaking up: when the stock market falls sharply, merger deals are more likely to break. In addition, a sharp stock market decline will reduce the likelihood of revised (higher) bids and/or bidding competition for merger targets. Falling stock markets also tend to reduce the overall number of mergers, which increases the competition for investment opportunities and thereby reduces the expected risk premium. The strategy therefore has a slightly positive stock market beta, but strongly nonlinear. This overall exposure profile to equity markets comes more from the correlation between the event risk and the market than from the individual positions.

Our regression shows, as expected, some small exposure to the equity markets, in particular to the small cap segment (furthermore the value sector), and the BXM index. However, the explanatory strength of the model is not particularly high. As with other Event Driven strategies, the alpha value is above average for this strategy at around 4% p.a.

Distressed Securities

Distressed Securities strategies come with a simple set of systematic exposures to credit, equity (particularly small cap), and liquidity risks. These are exactly the factors which show up in Table 6.2. The AR(1) factor bears the largest sensitivity, reflecting the low degree of liquidity offered in Distressed Securities investing. The lack of regular pricing and valuation induces autocorrelation in the return streams. The explanatory power of the linear factor models, however, is 70% (R^2). The level of alpha for Distressed Securities hedge funds is around 3–4% p.a., which is, along with its peers in other Event Driven sectors, among the highest in the hedge fund industry. We see in Figure 6.7 that the RFS model yields roughly about

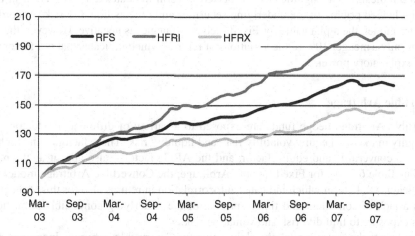

Figure 6.7 Performance of the Distressed RFS next to the HFR noninvestable (HFRI) and the investable versions of HFR (HFRX)

two-thirds of the return of the Distressed Securities funds in the HFRI index, but outperforms the HFRX investable index.

General Relative Value

Relative Value strategies – represented here by Fixed Income Arbitrage and Convertible Arbitrage – have three types of systematic exposures. They first capitalize on price spreads between two or more related financial instruments, which often represent a compensation for particular risks such as credit or interest rate term structure risk, liquidity risk, or exchange rate risk. Secondly, they provide liquidity and price transparency in complex instruments by employing proprietary valuation models to value complex financial instruments. Related returns can be referred to as liquidity and 'complexity' premia. The latter is related to the risk of mis-modeling the complexity of the underlying financial instrument. The hedge fund manager is short an option which turns strongly into the money when his valuation model is inaccurate. Finally, Relative Value hedge fund managers prefer negatively skewed return distribution, where steady but small gains are countered with rare but large losses. In other words, the managers are short some sort of volatility, which makes the return profile resemble the payout profile of a short option position. It is therefore not surprising that linear factor models on asset class returns fail to provide satisfactory results for most Relative Value strategies. Clearly, more sophisticated models, such as those discussed in Chapter 8, are needed.

Fixed Income Arbitrage

Fixed Income Arbitrage strategies expose themselves to a combination of liquidity, credit, and term structure risks. For example, they might employ credit barbell strategies that take long positions in lower-quality short-term debt and short positions in long-term government bonds, yield curve spread trades, or on-the-run versus off-the-run treasury bond positions. Exposure to credit risk, convertible bonds, and emerging market bonds securities are most prevalent, as Table 6.2 indicates. The significance of the AR(1) term indicates autocorrelation in returns signaling lagged pricing of the underlying securities and reflects liquidity risk. According to our factor model, the alpha value for Fixed Income strategies is negative. However, the model explains only a meager 10% of the variations of returns, which indicates that our factor model has no explanatory power.

Convertible Arbitrage

Convertible Arbitrage hedge funds are exposed to a variety of different risk factors: credit risk, equity market and equity volatility risk, and liquidity risk. These factors – the high yield factor, the convertible and equity factor, and the AR(1) factor – also appear as the relevant factors in Table 6.2. As for Fixed Income Arbitrage, the Convertible Arbitrage model shows a significant AR(1) term which indicates autocorrelation in returns also for this strategy. This signals a lack of consistent and timely pricing of the underlying convertible securities and reflects exposure to liquidity risk and valuation risk.

According to the factor model, the alpha value for Convertible Arbitrage Income strategies is about 1% p.a. The model explains a low 58% of the variations of returns. This indicates that

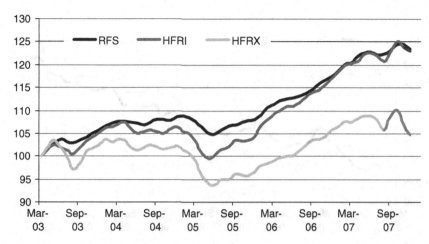

Figure 6.8 Performance of the Convertible Arbitrage RFS next to the HFR noninvestable (HFRI) and the investable versions of HFR (HFRX)

the linear approach is missing some important characteristics of this strategy. After reading the section on Convertible Arbitrage in Chapter 3, you may not be too surprised by this. The complexity of the strategy produces some features that escape the linear modeling framework. Chapter 8 will explore this in more detail.

However, we can see that for the more recent period an RFS model performs in line with the HFRI Convertible Arbitrage strategy with significantly less volatility, as shown in Figure 6.8. The outperformance becomes striking when considering the investable HFRX index in Figure 6.7.

Global Macro

Global Macro managers of all types do better in strong bond and emerging markets, as indicated by the sensitivity to the bond markets shown in Table 6.2. Other direct exposures are less obvious: the R^2 value for the regression of Global Macro comes out low (40%). One reason lies in the heterogeneity of the strategy itself. Global Macro trading includes a wide range of different trading approaches, and a broad index does not reflect this diversity. A manager-based analysis would probably be more appropriate here. Furthermore, the particular markets traded by the individual manager and his particular investment techniques define the available risk premia and inefficiencies targeted far more than a broad asset-class-based index. Global Macro managers employ dynamic trading strategies that escape a linear approach.

Our model RFS gives an alpha value of around 3% p.a. for the average Global Macro manager. Figure 6.9 shows an underperformance of RFS to the HFRI index. But again, the noninvestable HFRX version underperforms the RFS by a wide margin.

Managed Futures

The RFS models provide very little explanatory power for general Managed Futures (CTA) strategies, but do a little better for trend followers. The R^2 values of linear factor models are

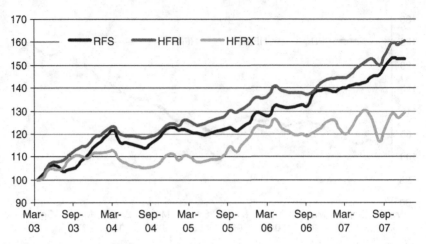

Figure 6.9 Performance of the Global Macro RFS next to the HFR noninvestable (HFRI) and the investable versions of HFR (HFRX)

among the lowest for any hedge fund strategy (18% and 48% respectively). This should not surprise us, as we saw in Chapter 5 that the trend-following characteristics of this strategy create a highly nonlinear type of exposure, namely a 'long straddle' exposure profile and V-shaped payout function. This profile, by its very design, cannot be captured by linear models.[20] I will discuss the appropriate approaches to model Managed Futures hedge fund strategies in Chapter 8.

Note that the Managed Futures strategy is one of only two hedge fund sectors that display no significant alpha. We can observe the corresponding performance pattern of CTAs compared to the RFS in Figure 6.10: the performance of the RFS actually beats the average CTA in the CISDM Managed Futures Qualified Universe Futures Index as well.

6.10   THE LIMITATIONS OF LINEAR FACTOR MODELS

The results described above look quite promising for some selected strategy sectors, such as Long/Short Equity and Event Driven. These strategies can be modeled with simple directional equity factors. However, results are less satisfying for most other strategies. Results fall especially short for strategies with less well defined nondirectional exposure profiles such as, Equity Market Neutral, Relative Value, and Global Macro strategies. These strategies do not lend themselves to replication via a linear factor model approach. In-sample R^2 are not sufficiently high to indicate satisfactory model quality (in-sample fit), while out-of-sample results suggest that hedge fund return replication is mediocre at best. While the factor-based approach is the simplest and most obvious way to tackle hedge fund replication, it has mostly failed in thorough empirical tests to produce satisfactory out-of-sample results across the entire spectrum of hedge fund strategies.

---

[20] Unless we include this nonlinear factor itself into the equation as I did for Table 6.2. This is in fact in the spirit of the 'bottom-up approach' which I will discuss in Chapter 8.

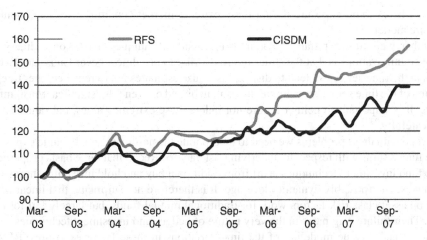

Figure 6.10   Performance of the Managed Futures RFS next to the HFR noninvestable (HFRI) and the investable versions of HFR (HFRX)

Let's return to the two underlying assumptions of this method – linear dependence and stationarity – to shed some light on the unsatisfactory real-world results. It quickly becomes apparent that hedge fund returns do not fulfill either of these assumptions:

(1) Hedge funds contain contingent payout profiles, imposed either explicitly through the inclusion of options into a typical hedge fund portfolio, or implicitly through managers employing conditional rule-based trading strategies.
(2) The beta exposure of hedge funds is not stationary. Most hedge fund strategies involve active trading in response to opportunities and changing market environments. In other words, hedge fund managers react dynamically to changing market conditions with shifts in their exposure profile.

A related issue is that RFS relies on past data only. In contrast to hedge fund managers who base their decisions on current data, RFS adjusts exposures with a significant time lag. This can be problematic in a fast-changing environment! Consequently, linear factor models lag significantly in adjusting their risk exposures. So replicating hedge funds based on estimating the parameters of the linear regression factors relying on past data is like steering a car only by looking into the rearview mirror.[21] There is good reason to believe, and some research to support,[22] that there occur sudden and structural breaks in the systematic risk exposures of hedge funds that cannot be captured in a linear mode. Market shocks often bring to light these nonlinear exposures of hedge funds. Examples are easy to find: the blow-up of LTCM in the summer of 1998, the burst of the stock market bubble in the spring of 2000, the turn in the equity market in March 2003, and most recently the credit crisis of 2007/2008. In order

---

[21] There is nothing bad about a rearview mirror, actually. As a matter of fact it is illegal to drive without one. And in some sense all investors use some past data or experience to make investment decisions. It is just dangerous to blindly follow the rearview exclusively.

[22] W. Fung, D. Hsieh, N. Naik, T. Ramadorai, 'Hedge fund: performance, risk and capital formation', Preprint (2005).

to model hedge fund exposure during these extreme market conditions, we need nonlinear exposure models.

Another well-known pitfall of common regression techniques (based on ordinary least squares minimization) is that the 'true' return distribution is almost never Gaussian. Extreme values in the time series can lead to distortions, cause estimates not to represent the 'true' distribution of the time series, and ultimately result in biased or even false significant/insignificant factors. It is important to neither ignore nor delete these extreme values, but rather analyze them carefully.[23]

To cope with these problems we need to incorporate the nonlinear and dynamic exposure of hedge fund returns with respect to underlying risk factors. Recall that three basic properties set hedge fund investment techniques apart from traditional buy and hold investing: short selling, derivatives, and (possibly dynamic) leverage. It is therefore not surprising that linear models based on asset class risk factors work for traditional mutual funds, but largely fail for hedge funds. Their failure originates in the very nature of hedge fund investment techniques.

Since it lacks a true modeling of the time-variations in these factor exposures, RFS will be limited in its scope to directional strategies such as Long/Short Equity, and then only in nonchanging market environments. To model and then replicate the entire range of hedge funds, we must consider more than just their static linear exposures. The attentive reader has probably already noticed that some of the factors chosen in the models discussed in this chapter in Table 6.2 already bear some of these 'dynamic' and nonlinear properties (such as the sGFII factor used to model CTAs).

An interesting indication for the pitfall of the linear regression approach became evident in the latter part of 2007, when most regressions on Event Driven hedge funds showed a negative exposure to the high-yield credit factors. With some insight into the average positioning of hedge funds in this sector, it became quickly evident that hedge funds in aggregate were not positioned in a credit protection position. Those few that were made a windfall profit. The reason why regressions gave a negative exposure to this factor was simply that many long credit positions (like senior loans or mezzanine deals) were not marked to market. With stale prices (also indicated by a significant AR(1) term) a combination of a nonpriced long exposure with a partial hedge in liquid short positions in credit default swaps would result in a virtual overall negative factor loading. Ironically, a replicating factor strategy profited from such an erroneous factor estimate when credit markets deteriorated further in late 2007 and early 2008.

6.11 CURRENTLY AVAILABLE HEDGE FUND REPLICATION PRODUCTS BASED ON RFS

With RFS for hedge fund return replication unable to generate fully satisfactory results in the academic realm, it is surprising that a number of hedge fund replication products based on RFS type of models have recently been popularized by several investment banks. What is even more surprising is that these initiatives do not undertake the effort to replicate hedge fund strategy by strategy sector but rather on aggregate broad hedge fund industry indices. The heterogeneity of strategies within the universe of hedge funds sharply contrasts with the homogeneous approaches offered by these providers, which do not distinguish between

---

[23] The analysis of extreme events is a mathematical discipline of its own. See P. Embrechts *et al. Modelling Extremal Events* (1999) for more details.

strategies as different as Convertible Arbitrage and Managed Futures and use rather simple factors to replicate overall hedge fund returns. The index most used for factor-based replication is the global *Hedge Fund Research Index* – either in the equally weighted form or in its version for fund of funds. The results discussed in this chapter and elsewhere strongly indicate that a distinction between the various strategy sectors is essential, as the quality and thus practicability of RFS varies strongly across hedge fund strategies. To overlook these differences and ignore the lack of explanatory power for many hedge fund strategies is to ignore the pitfalls of using linear factor models for replication.

Failing to distinguish between strategy sectors and limiting the RFS approach to a broad hedge fund index has some rather unpleasant consequences: instead of modeling the rich diversity of alternative beta within hedge fund strategies (see Chapter 5) the resulting models are only able to incorporate the most straightforward of hedge fund exposures: plain vanilla equity.

Let us have a closer look at a well-publicized product offered by the investment bank Merrill Lynch, a provider that chose to make its model component publicly available.[24] This product is based on a regression of the global (equally weighted) hedge fund index by Hedge Fund Research (the HFRI Composite) on the following risk factors: the S&P 500 index, the MSCI EAFE (World equity ex-US) index, the MSCI Emerging Markets Index, the Russell 2000 (small cap) Index, the FX USD trade-weighted index, and US Libor.[25] The FX factor does not enter into the regression with any sustainable statistical significance and serves solely as a currency hedge for the international equity factors. The US Libor index is not a risk factor but merely the risk-free rate of return. Consequently, this model uses equity factors exclusively to model hedge fund returns. And it actually performs a decent job in extracting the equity portion of hedge fund returns. Unfortunately investors are not particularly interested in that portion. In other words, this type of hedge fund replication works only where investors need it least: the extraction of the equity exposure of hedge funds. This model captures traditional but not alternative beta. And it is alternative beta, beta that is less correlated to equity markets, that investors in hedge funds and therefore also hedge fund replication products are seeking.

This approach then is not an acceptable method to 'replicate hedge funds'.[26] This method can claim some success in absolute return numbers from 2003 to mid-2007, when equity markets soared.[27] However, it would have failed miserably in the bear market from March 2000 to March 2003 – a period when hedge funds in aggregate made money, despite heavy losses in the equity markets.

A further point worth noting is that model quality and obtained weights of the factors depend highly on which hedge fund return time series one is trying to replicate. A simple but revealing study[28] makes a comparison of the linear factor replication using the 'Merrill Lynch factors' introduced above on various different hedge fund indices: the HFRI Composite, the

---

[24] In contrast to their competing peers from other investment banks that do not allow such public disclosure of their factors and decide to keep their factor model to themselves despite their claims for the high transparency their product can be characterized by. Merrill has to be given credit here.

[25] S. Umlauf, B. Bowler, 'Merrill Lynch Factor Index: a new approach to diversified hedge fund investing', presented at the Hedge Fund Replication and Alternative Beta Conference, London (February 2007).

[26] The term 'hedge fund replication' has somehow become a synonym for using linear regression techniques and factor models to mimic hedge fund returns. I will comment on this in Chapter 8 in more detail.

[27] Which is exactly the period most providers choose to display when they show their back-tested performance to attract investors.

[28] Northwater Capital Management Inc., 'Northwater Capital Management's thoughts on hedge fund replication' (May 2007).

CSFB-Tremont index, the CSFB-Tremont Long/Short Equity index, and the CSFB-Tremont Market Neutral index. While in-sample replication of the HFRI Composite yields highest rolling R^2 values (never below 90%) results for the global CSFB-Tremont index show much lower R^2 (between 0.5 and 0.9). The lowest R-squared the authors obtained, not surprisingly given our results in this chapter, was for the Equity Market Neutral index.

The same study indicates that for the period 2003 to 2007 linear replication is capable of providing Sharpe ratios similar to the original indices for all cases with the exception of the CSFB Equity Market Neutral Index. However, if we consider a longer time horizon, the situation changes dramatically: the linear replicas of all indices, and in particular the HFRI Global Index, perform poorly relative to its original over the 10-year time horizon from 1997 to 2007. And although replication of the CSFB-Tremont Index results in a lower correlation to the original index than the replication model of the HFRI Composite index, the CSFB-Tremont replica provides better performance. This indicates that the expected out-of-sample performance of the replication model is not necessarily related to its R^2. So, a significant historical R^2 is a necessary requirement of linear factor replication, but it is not a sufficient indication that out-of-sample replica performance will match the original index performance in the future.

What is the lesson of these studies? Many hedge fund replication providers have tried to attract investors with the help of back-tested performance numbers of their linear factor models. However, based on the discussion in this section we must convey a clear warning to investors: as attractive as back-tested performance numbers may be, they must by no means be taken at their full face value. It is quite likely that they are a result of the provider's selection bias in terms of chosen index, chosen factors, and chosen back-testing time series. Good models (i.e. high and stable R^2 values) do not necessarily mean satisfactory out-of-sample performance. An older wisdom holds true: we have seen in history a number of investment strategies which looked great on paper but failed in reality.

6.12   SUMMARY AND CONCLUSION OF THE CHAPTER

Replication factor strategies (RFS) are the trading model (out-of-sample) application of linear factor decomposition of hedge fund returns. It is largely this method that has been applied by hedge fund replication product providers to broad-based hedge fund indices. These models yield satisfactory results for only a few hedge fund strategies, namely the ones with directional equity exposure. But for these, we are left with the average equity exposure hedge funds hold which is not necessarily what we want in the first place.[29] In other words, hedge fund replication of this kind works when investors need it least. Further, the problem of factor stability depends very much on the speed of and extent to which the index betas change over time. Current research is not entirely conclusive about whether this is a prohibitive issue in any real application.

We noted further that the replication technique of linear factor models works better if one tries to replicate the features of a diversified index over the individual hedge fund strategies. The resulting factors tend to be more uniform as some of the smaller alternative beta factors simply diversify away in a broad hedge fund index. Linear factor models are not satisfactorily

---

[29] This being said, investors should still be very cautious about putting too much confidence into back-tested performance, though, and consider products that have proven their validity in a real trading environment.

successful when applied to most hedge fund strategy sectors, specifically nondirectional and Relative Value hedge funds or indices. In order to cope with these strategies we have to employ more complex market factors and/or dynamically adjusting factors which include nonlinear profiles. These factors are likely to represent dynamic trading strategies that capture alternative risk premia with their contingent and nonlinear payout profiles. To put it in other words, the alternative betas are exposures that are simply more subtle betas which do not show up in a regression but require a more complex tool kit than simple long exposure to asset classes. But these are what investors want. So some more effort is needed to extract the beauty and benefits of alternative beta. It is this effort that we will continue in the next chapters.

7

The Distributional Approach

7.1 BEING LESS AMBITIOUS

Next to the linear factor model approach to hedge fund replication which aims at mimicking the month-to-month (or at whatever frequency) returns of a chosen hedge fund return time series we can try to be less ambitious. What if the end investor was actually interested in having a replica that only matches the statistical properties of the long-term distribution of hedge fund returns instead of the month-to-month performance? This is much less than what we originally aimed at. In other words, we could try to reproduce only the desirable distributional characteristics of hedge funds their as described by volatility, skewness, kurtosis (i.e. the higher moments of the distribution) – and of course their mean return. The obtained replica return series would not match the exact time series of the original hedge fund index; in particular it will not match the correlation profile. But over time, the distribution of the replica time series would converge to the desired original hedge fund distribution. Evidently, this seems to be a less ambitious task as we give up on the point-to-point matching of the hedge fund return time series. We shall refer to this approach as the 'distributional replication' method. It finds its roots in the seminal work by P. Dybvig (who developed it, however, in a quite different context)[1] and has more recently been popularized by Harry Kat from the Cass Business School in numerous public appearances as well as in a series of 'Working Papers,'[2] none of which to my knowledge, however, have found their way into a peer-reviewed journal.[3]

Kat claims that this method provides reliable replication with returns that are often greater than the original hedge funds or hedge fund indices by matching their distributional characteristics through a daily trading process using a set of liquid futures and transaction-cost-efficient delta hedging schemes. The specific implementation of the distributional replication developed by him is a rather simple twofold process which involves bivariate distribution fitting using copulas to specify the desired dependence structure to a chosen target portfolio in a first step and the pricing of a calculated payout function using a standard option pricing framework in a second step. Despite some obvious severe implementational challenges of the method (e.g. multivariate copula fitting is by no means trivial, especially in a statistical environment with limited and questionable data sources), the designer claims the empirical results to show great robustness and argues that reliable replication of hedge fund returns can be obtained even by using models with rather astonishing minimal complexity.

So much has been written and discussed about this method and its capacity to replicate hedge fund returns in the popular press – specifically targeting a mathematically less-educated

---

[1] See P. Dybvig, 'Inefficient dynamic portfolio strategies or how to throw away a million dollars in the stock market' (1988).

[2] See the web page http://www.fundreplicator.com for a collection of these.

[3] Another recent paper – an extension and mathematically more sound adaptation of Dybvig's method – was published by N. Papageorgiou et al., 'Replicating the properties of hedge fund returns' (2007). However, I will not elaborate in detail on this paper which actually addresses some of the technical problems of Kat's method.

audience and, to a much lesser degree, peer-reviewed financial journals – that we cannot ignore it in our compendium on hedge fund replication. Further, so many strong claims about its miraculous results have been made publicly by its advocates that we cannot resist demystifying its merits and potentials. The reader may be warned that there is some mathematics involved, but I believe the general features of it can be described without great mathematical hocus pocus. This being said, I realize that some of the mathematical details of the method may be less well known by investors, and surely most participants in the hedge fund industry have quite a different association to the word 'copula' than it being a feature in statistical mathematics. But I claim that it is possible to provide a clear and appropriate overview on this method that is also readable by the less mathematically trained. This chapter is about giving a proof to this claim.

7.2   GENERAL PRINCIPLES OF THE DISTRIBUTIONAL APPROACH

The keystone of this approach is the insight that investors' benefit in being exposed to hedge fund returns is equivalent to acquiring a claim to a certain payoff distribution. And the goal is simply to replicate that respective payoff distribution through a particular trading strategy. If one is able to do that, the cost of that strategy could be compared to that of a direct investment in the hedge fund investment, and if lower its replication is worthwhile. This is why this approach is also referred to as 'payoff replication'.

The principle of payoff replication is inspired by derivative pricing theory, the principles of which go back to the 1970s. The underlying is a two-step process. In the first step we estimate the payoff function f that maps a chosen asset's return to the returns of a hedge fund or a hedge fund index. The second step consists of pricing that payoff function and deriving a dynamic replicating strategy, analogously to dynamic hedging, and thus replicating an option payoff priced by an option pricing formula, e.g. the Black–Scholes formula. In practice the second step is accomplished through a daily trading process that corresponds to dynamic option replication using delta hedging.

Let us go into the details. In the first step we transform the return distribution of a chosen investment, which is referred to as the 'reserve asset' or 'reserve portfolio', into the desired return distribution, as given, for example, by a hedge fund index. This transformation can consist of a variety of things like scaling returns (volatility), implementing a minimum performance, or increasing the skewness. The resulting payoff function is hereby created synthetically so as to match the given hedge fund return distribution (as opposed to it being exogenously given, for example by the Black–Scholes formula, in the case of a standard option pricing problem). In practice we have the cumulative return distributions of the hedge fund and the return distribution of the chosen reserve asset. The latter could be anything from T-bills, T-bonds, equity indices, currency rates or commodity indices. The payoff function is simply defined by the function that transforms the quantiles $F_{reserve}$ of the reserve asset distribution into the quantiles F_{HF} of the hedge fund distribution. This function can be simply estimated by mapping the percentiles to the percentiles.

Let us illustrate the construction of this function with an example illustrated graphically in Figure 7.1: we assume there is a 5% probability that the return of the chosen reserve asset over the time period of one month is higher than 20%, i.e. $F_{reserve}(20\%) = 0.95$. We then define the value of the payout function for 20%, i.e. $f(20\%)$, as the value that is such that the

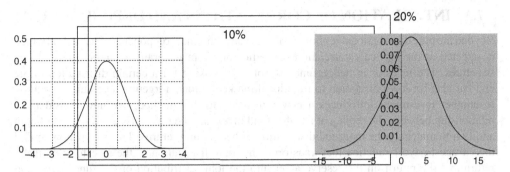

Figure 7.1   Construction of the 'payoff function'

hedge fund return to be replicated has only a 5% chance of being higher than that value, or in symbols: $f(20\%) = y$ such that $F_{HF}(y) = 0.95$. The particular value of y can then be looked up in the empirical percentiles of the hedge fund distribution. This process is then repeated for all values of the reserve asset's quantile function. This way we implicitly define the function f for all values of its range. Let me add that the payoff function of course depends ultimately on the chosen reserve asset.

Once the function f is derived, it can be priced (and dynamically replicated through delta hedging) with a suitable option pricing model. This provides the starting point of the dynamic trading strategy defined by the delta exposure to the reserve asset. In practice we can obtain the pricing function of the payout function using a simple Monte Carlo simulation of end-of-the-month values with the known drift and volatility for the reserve asset. The price of the payoff function is then obtained by discounting the average of the obtained payoffs corresponding to the simulated end-of-month index values. Finally, we estimate the necessary investment in the reserve asset corresponding to the delta of the option in accordance with the Merton replicating portfolio interpretation of the Black and Scholes formula. This delta is generated on a daily basis by a numerical approximation of the first derivative of the pricing function with respect to the underlying price of the reserve asset. And as a result we have the investment at that time for the replicating strategy. A variation of determining the appropriate trading strategy is offered by Papageorgiou et al.,[4] and in a more general context by M. Schweitzer.[5]

That is the simple version of the replication program which is actually quite straightforward to implement on a computer. One can use empirical distributions of returns for reserve asset and hedge fund index or parametric fits, whatever one defines as suitable. Evidently overly simple assumptions on the return distribution, such as using Gaussian distributions, induce biases in the resulting payoff function and its respective pricing, and ultimately in the replication strategy.

---

[4] N. Papageorgiou, B. Rémillard, and A. Hocquard, 'Replicating the properties of hedge fund returns' (2007).

[5] M. Schweitzer, 'Variance-optimal hedging in discrete time' (1995). This paper actually describes the problem of hedging in incomplete markets (i.e. markets in which not all arbitrage-free payout functions can be achieved with available instruments). This is one of the main technical problems of this method. The actual hedging error incurred is larger the less complete the markets are and the less suitable the instruments employed in the reserve assets are.

7.3   INTEGRATION OF CORRELATIONS AND DEPENDENCIES

Beyond the pure distributional replication there is an additional component to the method which is targeted at the replica's correlation properties or, more generally speaking, dependency structures. The investor in hedge funds is not only looking for a certain distribution in the end but also for low correlation to traditional market factors. Targeting a certain correlation to another investment introduces a new dimension to this method. We now consider the relationship between the replica of a hedge fund index and the investor's existing portfolio, in addition to matching the marginal distribution of hedge fund returns. The goal is now to find the cheapest payoff function that transforms the joint distribution of the investor's portfolio return and the return on the reserve asset into the joint distribution of the fund return and the investor's portfolio return. It is in principle nothing different than above, just that we are now looking at joint distributions. This is where the copulas come in. The general function describing the dependencies between two time series is called the 'copula'. More precisely, the copula is the function that describes the joint distribution of two random variables after their marginal distributions are considered individually. Copulas have been a research subject in the area of mathematical finance for many years. For a good introduction see the article by Embrechts et al.[6].

Again, two steps are involved, the first one consisting in pricing a payoff function and the second one in estimating the dynamic portfolio strategy in the investor's portfolio and the reserve asset that replicates it. The payoff function is now a function of two variables $f(x,y)$ as it maps the joint distribution of the reserve asset with the investor's portfolio into the joint distribution of the hedge fund index with the investor's portfolio. We describe these joint distributions now by copula functions (next to the individual marginal distributions). As two assets are involved in each distribution the situation now becomes a little more complex, and empirical estimates of the joint distributions are more difficult and chronically unstable. So, we often cannot escape making certain assumptions about the distributional properties, the individual distributions of reserve asset, the investor's portfolio, and the hedge fund index, as well as the copulas in the joint distribution. One has a choice between many different combinations of marginal distributions as well as copulas. Kat specifically uses the Normal, the Student-t and the Johnson SU distribution, as well as six bivariate copulas for integrating the dependence between hedge fund returns and the investor's existing portfolio (Normal, Student-t, Gumbel, Clayton, Frank, Symmetrized Joe-Clayton). All these allow for 54 combinations of joint distributions in the estimation process.

The objective is to find the best combination between marginal distributions and the dependence function to match the observed data considering symmetric/asymmetric, thin- and fat-tailed joint distributions. We then obtain the estimates for parameters by standard maximum likelihood processes. After we find the best combination of distribution, the calculation of the payoff function follows the description above. With the payoff function and a standard Monte Carlo simulation on period returns, now on the reserve asset as well as the investor's portfolio, one obtains the price and delta of the option for the replication strategy. We can also extend the method by using other multivariate option models which include transaction costs.

---

[6] P. Embrecht et al., *Correlation and Dependence in Risk Management. Properties and Pitfalls* (2002).

7.4   LIMITATIONS OF THE REPLICATION APPROACH

While the theory of the distributional approach is quite sound and might appear appealing at first sight it comes with some important practical limitations. The first one is that parameters of the true distribution are unknown and therefore have to be estimated. Mis-specifications, which are inevitable in an environment of sparse data as in the world of hedge funds, create severe biases on the obtained results. Making a choice out of 54 different distributions to calibrate the model and using 24 data points for this purpose (two years of data as suggested by Kat) seems ambitious to say the least. A possible and highly likely lack of stationarity in the returns of hedge funds (i.e. time-varying returns) and more importantly, heteroskedasticity in their return distribution (i.e. the clustering of volatility spikes) due to changing leverage employed by hedge funds would bias the parameter estimation further. A second problem comes up when we try to price the payout function. In most practical circumstances we are constrained to use a Black–Scholes framework to obtain its price and the corresponding option delta to obtain the dynamic trading strategy. This stands in contrast to the chosen original marginal return distributions of reserve asset and the investor portfolio which were explicitly modeled in a non-normal framework in order to avoid obvious biases due to tail mis-specifications. More generally, the desired payoff function often cannot be exactly generated in practice when the presence of market imperfections has to be accounted for. A third pitfall of the method is that the daily dynamic trading strategies are derived from a distribution of monthly returns. However, the properties of the estimated monthly distributions and the obtained dependence structure/copula functions cannot be broken down into the distributional properties of daily returns. As a result the replicating strategy will not be precise.

7.5   THE EMPIRICAL RESULTS OF THE DISTRIBUTIONAL METHOD

It is not surprising, given the above practical limitations of the distributional approach, that the empirical results of this method are far from convincing. We briefly summarize these results below.

Fitting the distribution

Empirical results reported in the literature imply that, even if one is willing to ignore the differences in mean returns (which are not explicitly modeled by this approach), not all hedge fund distributions can be matched with satisfaction.[7] Even for an out-of-sample period of eight years, the converging replication distribution does not match the original distribution in some cases. For an investor with less patience, the distribution method to hedge fund replication can lead to rather severe disappointments, as a reduction of the out-of-sample test period has a dramatic effect on the results, i.e. the quality of the obtained distribution as compared to the original hedge fund distribution.

---

[7] See the paper by W. Gehin *et al.*: 'The myths and limits of passive hedge fund replication', Edhec Research Paper (2007).

Matching the time series properties

While the distributional properties of the replica might be useful (to a varying degree depending on the strategy sector), the results on correlation properties are rather disappointing altogether. Out-of-sample correlation and R-squared values are typically extremely low. They range from zero to less than 50% averaging around some 30%.[8] Further, the correlation properties depend on the composite and the correlation properties of the reserve asset, i.e. the individual market factors and relative position sizes within the reserve portfolio. This strong dependency on the reserve asset bears analogy to the importance of choosing the right factors in the linear regression approach from the previous chapter.

Performance of the replication

It appears that while the method replicates distributional properties of hedge funds over long samples (with the notable exception of the mean return), it can lead to disappointing results from the perspective of replicating the time-series properties of actual hedge fund returns. As noted, the average return is an outcome of the method. Empirical results[9] indicate that mean returns from the replication process are dependent on the contents of the reserve portfolio, i.e. the market risk factors contained therein. The returns from the replication process are usually negative when the reserve asset returns are negative, and positive when the reserve asset returns are positive. A reserve portfolio with a high Sharpe ratio tends to produce a replica with a high Sharpe ratio, and a reserve portfolio with a low Sharpe ratio tends to produce a replica with a low Sharpe ratio.

Papageorgiou *et al.* (2007) conclude their above-cited paper with the following statement: 'The choice of the reserve asset only impacts the initial cost of investing in the replicating portfolio (and hence only impacts the return of the replicating strategy). This is not to say that the return generated by the model is not important, however it is not a measure of the model's success.'

7.6   CONCLUSION FOR THE DISTRIBUTIONAL APPROACH

A principal problem of the distributional approach is that the success of the method with respect to a possible replication can only be validated and confirmed over very long time horizon returns, as it does not replicate hedge funds' time-series properties directly. That means the investor has to be patient enough to be willing to wait up to eight years and more to see if his investment eventually behaves as it should on average. We know from reality that most investors' patience stretches over a significantly lower time period. My personal experience is actually that we can call ourselves lucky if an investor has eight months of patience with an investment that does not directly perform according to expectations.

There are serious concerns to be articulated over the robustness of the results, in particular those related to difference in average returns with respect to the choice of the reserve asset or sample period. The complexity in estimating the payout function leads to particular problems with respect to model stability and robustness as it involves the estimation of the optimal choice

---

[8] As reported by Gehin *et al.* (2007).

[9] See the paper by Northwater Capital Management Inc.: 'Northwater Capital Management's thoughts on hedge fund replication' for details on replication back-testing.

of a combination of dozens of distributions and copulas each with a multiple of parameters to be estimated, and all that on rather sparse data.

Notably, the most important aspect of the hedge fund return distribution, the average return, is not a well-defined output of the process but a complex and nonpredictable function of the choice of the reserve asset and its performance over the chosen period. This leads to the absurd situation that the investor himself is left with the question of choosing a suitable benchmark that could be used as a reserve asset in order to generate the best risk return of his choice. That is actually what the investor asks the hedge fund to perform for him. So, besides the numerous shortcomings of this method in the practical implementation, it does not really solve the original problem. On the contrary, the investor is left to solve it by himself. We clearly have to conclude, contrary to strong public claims made by its advocate(s), that the distributional method is not suitable for the task of hedge fund replication.

8

Bottom up: Extraction of Alternative Beta and 'Alternative Beta Strategies'

Having explored the limits of the 'top-down' factor model approach, let's move on to a newer, 'bottom-up' approach to hedge fund replication. This approach is distinctly different because it replicates individual strategies first, before then constructing composite portfolios from these individual replications. Although more complex to execute, the bottom-up approach has quickly gained support among many academics and market participants. New York University's Professor F. Whitelaw states that 'replicating individual strategies and then constructing composite portfolios from these individual replications, has several key advantages over replicating a composite index directly. These advantages include superior tracking, greater flexibility, and potentially improved performance characteristics.'[1]

Unless you randomly opened the book to this chapter, you no doubt realize the dilemma that providers of linear factor-based hedge fund replication face: these models work best on the hedge fund strategies for which investors need them least! Conversely, they break down in explaining the very strategies for which replication models are most needed.

Linear factor models – or related techniques that mimic past return time series and their statistical properties – have the most explanatory power for strategies in which the dominant explanatory factor is simple directional equity exposure.[2] Furthermore, basing replication efforts on broad hedge fund indices, rather than on individual hedge fund strategies, tends to dilute away the precious alternative beta in hedge funds altogether; leaving only equity beta. Because of these two limitations, RFS models have little more than 'traditional beta' to offer.

So, you might fairly ask, what is the point? Wasn't it 'alternative beta' that we are after when investing in hedge funds, and consequently when endeavoring to replicate their returns? It seems that replication models based on linear regressions of hedge fund indices are forced to give up on alternative beta.

The distributional approach faces these identical issues, as well as some additional technical problems. The choice of the reserve asset – most often some form of equity – determines almost entirely the obtained performance of the replication model.

8.1 THE RULE-BASED ALTERNATIVE

If nonlinearity, dependence on past data, and exclusive exposure to long-only equity factors limit the value of linear factor models, what approaches can we take to overcome these problems? Two paths seem to be open to us:

---

[1] Professor Robert F. Whitelaw of NYU Stern at the 'Hedge Fund Replication & Alternative Beta' Conference in New York on October 30 2007.
[2] For which the argument of fee savings holds, of course, too, even more. But the investor does not need anything that sounds like a hedge fund to obtain these exposures.

(1) Explicitly incorporate options and nonlinearities into the model.
(2) Implicitly create the desired nonlinearities through rule-based conditional trading models.

Explicitly incorporating options and nonlinearities into the model, in other words directly building in nonlinear factors, sounds much simpler than it actually is. In practice, including nonlinearity in models makes them much more mathematically intricate. And in following this path we are still forced to rely on past and chronically sparse data.

The second path enters nonlinearity through the back door, through rule-based conditional trading models. These models *implicitly* create the desired nonlinearities by providing non-stationary, contingent exposures to the risk factors. The trading design of this rule-based mechanical replication of hedge fund strategies relies little on past hedge fund data. Instead it relies on the available market prices of the traded assets. Therefore instead of fitting our exposure to past hedge fund (index) return data, this method takes a step away from the past data and digs deeper into the economic foundations of hedge funds' return generation.

In chemistry, molecules are described as combinations of individual atoms. One identifies the molecules based on the kind and number of atoms that comprise them. Analogously, it is the individual risk premium extraction schemes that eventually make up the hedge fund returns. It is these 'atoms' of hedge funds that we would aim at with the contingent rule-based risk premium extraction schemes.

This second route allows a more flexible adaptation to the dynamic nature of hedge fund strategies. Just as important, it lets us escape from the prison of hedge fund indices, and lets us make our own choices about which risks we like and which we don't. Finally, this approach brings us back to solid economic reasoning, instead of statistical data mining based on chronically sparse data.

Where do the nonlinearities and contingent return profiles of hedge funds come from? How come that hedge fund exposures change over time? Studying these questions leads us quickly to the very investment techniques hedge funds themselves employ.

Because the risk premia hedge funds earn are distinctly different from those underlying the returns of traditional investment funds – hence the term 'alternative beta' – some 'alternative investment' techniques are needed to extract them. These techniques include short selling, use of derivatives, and leverage. And it is mostly hedge funds that have the capability, experience and regulatory freedom to employ these techniques. It's not surprising then that simple factor models don't adequately reproduce hedge fund returns. They do not address the very return generation process of hedge funds, namely the employment of alternative investment techniques.

Let's look, for example, at the extraction of risk premia in merger transactions. Obviously, if we want to earn merger spreads, we need to invest in merger deals. However, there is no simple factor exposure that explains these types of returns. Broadening out from this example, in order to extract alternative beta in the global capital markets and thus replicate hedge fund returns, we need to employ the same alternative investment techniques that hedge funds do, in this case buy and sell short companies involved in merger transactions. These techniques are by their nature based on conditional trading rules rather than long-only 'buy and hold'. To replicate the returns of a hedge fund we must, in effect, trade like one.

I call this rule-based concept the 'bottom-up' approach, because it extracts each alternative beta individually before aggregating up to replicate the composite properties of a given hedge fund. Another name given to this approach is 'alternative beta strategies'.

The bottom-up approach enables us, and in fact requires us, to better understand the risks in hedge funds, including their contingencies and cyclicalities as expressed, for example, by 'flight to quality scenarios'. This approach is by its nature less rigidly defined. Therefore executing it requires more knowledge about what hedge funds actually do, and entails many more dimensions in the actual replication process. And formation of the desired composite portfolios also adds the important element of asset allocation. In exchange for these new tasks, however, the approach also brings new opportunities. It empowers us to define the precise risk profile we are seeking and hedge out more undesired risks, including more hidden tail risks.

Some of the actual steps in implementing the bottom-up approach contain information that its developers deem commercially proprietary. Furthermore, the larger flexibility of this approach comes with an extended set of extra degrees of freedom, which creates a whole spectrum of dimensions that we cannot all over here. However, I will go as deeply as possible into the bottom-up approach, revealing its basic principles and possible implementations. Along with numerous examples, this should give you a solid understanding of the approach and an appreciation of its merits.

8.2   WHAT HEDGE FUND INVESTORS REALLY WANT

But what do investors really want from hedge funds? It's not a question that Freud ever asked, but is certainly one that we should. The obvious goal of hedge fund replication is to produce, in a single investment product, the same returns and diversifying risk characteristics of hedge funds. And furthermore we would want to reproduce those characteristics without the inherent drawbacks of direct investment in hedge funds: illiquidity, idiosyncratic single-manager risk, and limited capacity.

But is that goal ambitious enough? It is mostly the diversifying properties of hedge funds that attract investors. But a closer look at the performance numbers of aggregated hedge fund indices of the most recent years exposes an inconvenient truth. Periods of weak hedge fund index performance coincide with the most dramatic equity downturns (October 2005, May/June 2006, February/March 2007, the summer of 2007, and finally the first half of 2008). We cannot deny that today the average hedge fund index displays a substantial correlation with the broad equity markets. Any hedge fund replication model based on these indices evidently must inherit that feature.[3]

This is not necessarily what investors are looking for. They want the good diversification properties that were promised them: return streams with low correlations to stocks. Achieving this task with replication requires a step beyond simply mimicking broad hedge fund indices. The 'copy' must be altered to strip out the equity exposure inherent in the original. The top-down approach is not flexible enough to allow this, because there is no existing time series to replicate. Asset allocation changes are not foreseen in this approach; therefore there is no way to alter the (nonpreferred equity) exposure profile.

Conversely the bottom-up approach frees us to change the asset allocation in any way we like. If the goal is to replicate the average hedge fund portfolio represented by hedge fund indices, then there is nothing wrong with sticking to that average asset allocation. But the bottom-up approach also opens the door to listening directly to different investors and delivering customized risk profiles. In the world of chemistry, there are many different molecules that can be assembled from the same basic atoms. This is why our world is as diverse as it is. Why not do the same with alternative betas? By putting together the alternative betas in a different

---

[3] This is maybe the reason why the development of hedge fund replication products by the investment banks largely came out of their *equity* derivatives groups.

way – for example stripping out the equity beta or others at the investor's request – we can create a portfolio with the return properties that the particular investor really wants.[4]

8.3   THE FIRST 'ALTERNATIVE BETA' STRATEGIES

A growing number of investment banks offer products designed to generate returns through mechanical trading rules which are similar to hedge fund investment. (These divisions have little to do with the replication teams in the same firms.) Some of the widely simple strategies to gain exposure to alternative betas include:

- currency carry indices, as provided by Deutsche Bank or Barclay's;
- the Fama–French factors (for equity strategies);
- mutual funds that specifically exploit the small-firm effect and book-to-market effects;
- long-only convertible funds;
- High Yield Bond Indices (e.g. CSFB HY Index or the CDS indices);
- passive futures strategies (including the sGFII[5] Index and the MLM index);[6]
- the CBOE Buy–Write Monthly Index[7] (for the covered call writing strategy);
- returns of a 'passive' Merger Arbitrage strategy (as presented by Mitchell and Pulvino).[8]

Figure 8.1 provides a first insight into how a combination of different simple 'alternative beta strategies' can track the performance of a hedge fund portfolio reasonably well. It displays the return of an equally weighted combination of three of these simple strategies, each tracking a different 'alternative beta':

(1) the 'sGFII Futures' trading scheme, a trend-following model on 25 liquid futures markets;
(2) the CBOE Buy–Write Monthly Index (BXM) Index;
(3) the Credit Suisse High Yield Bond Index.

There are no restrictions and only very limited fees for investing in these three strategies, and prices are readily available on information systems such as Bloomberg. Figure 8.1 also displays the returns of the HFR Composite Hedge Fund Index, a broad aggregate across all hedge fund strategies; the Hedge Fund Research Fund of Funds Index, which mirrors the performance of fund of funds managers; and finally the S&P 500 equity index. The return of this simple strategy combination over the 10-year period from 1994 to 2004 stands at 11.0%, with a volatility of 6.1% and a Sharpe ratio of 1.0. Compare this to a 12.0% return for the HFR Composite Index (volatility 8.0%, Sharpe ratio: 0.8) and 8.0% (volatility 6.2%, Sharpe ratio: 0.5) for the HFR Fund of Funds Index.

Surprisingly, the risk-adjusted performance of our simple strategy combination outperforms both hedge fund indices! It even fares better than the HFR Fund of Funds index on a total return basis, and has only marginally lower absolute returns than the HFR Composite Index. The fact

---

[4] Such portfolios often come with the popular but often unmerited name 'portable alpha' attached to them.

[5] See L. Jaeger, M. Jacquemai, P. Cittadini, 'Case study: The sGFI Futures Index', *The Journal of Alternative Investment* (Summer 2002). Bloomberg ticker: sgfii <Index>.

[6] See www.mountlucas.com

[7] The BXM index measures the performance of a simple strategy: long S&P 500 index and simultaneously writing (selling) a call on the index. This is economically equivalent to writing a put (put–call parity) plus return on cash. Bloomberg ticker: BXM <Index>.

[8] See the paper by M. Mitchel and M. T. Pulvino, 'Characteristics of risk in risk arbitrage' (2001).

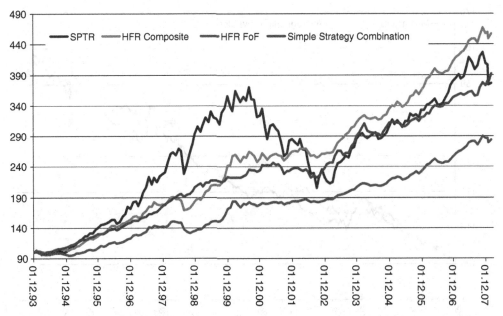

Figure 8.1 Performance of a combination of three simple 'alternative beta strategies' compared to standard hedge fund indices. (Data (until end of February 2008): Bloomberg)

that a combination of such simple strategies already beats hedge fund averages illustrates the key role of (alternative) risk premia in hedge fund returns overall.

Figure 8.2 displays a simple risk-weighted average of the following generic and publicly available 'alternative beta' strategies/factors: Deutsche Bank Carry Index, CDX High Yield Index, CRB Commodity Index, Value versus Growth Spread, Small cap versus large cap spread, BXM covered call writing (BXM Index − 0.5∗SPX Index), the Merger Arbitrage Fund (MERFX Index), and the spread between emerging market equity returns and developed equity markets (MSCI Emerging Markets − MSCI World). In the same graph we see the performance of the Merrill Lynch factor model, which, as discussed in Chapter 6, provides a very good proxy for the 'equity only component' in hedge fund returns. We see that alternative beta can yield similarly attractive results as the equity beta in hedge funds. This underlines that, even in a very benign period for equity directional strategies, alternative betas can add comparably good value to investors' portfolios. But how did the equity component of hedge funds perform when we include the bear market from March 2000 to March 2003? Figure 8.3 – which extends the same data as Figure 8.2 further into the past – makes it obvious that it did not do well. In contrast, the simple aggregate of alternative beta strategies made money despite heavy losses in the equity markets.

Fung and Hsieh introduced the idea of using conditional trading strategies to replicate the risk exposure of hedge funds in a 2001 paper on CTA strategies.[9] They modeled the performance of a generic trend-following strategy by using look-back straddles. Since then they and others have

---

[9] See W. Fung, D. Hsieh, 'The risk in hedge fund strategies: theory and evidence from trend followers' (2001).

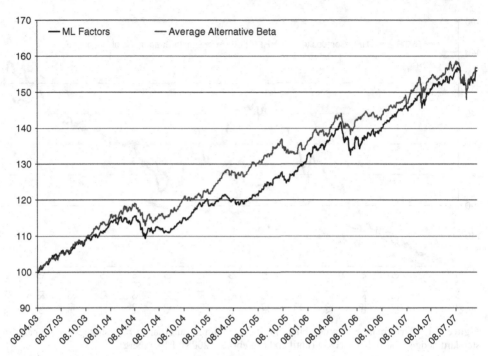

Figure 8.2 Performance of a risk-weighted average of alternative beta factors (see text for details) compared to the Merrill Lynch Factor model (a 'proxy for the equity component in hedge fund returns') for the bull market period 2003–2007. (Data source: Bloomberg)

applied this type of modeling to a variety of other hedge fund styles,[10] including Merger Arbitrage,[11] Fixed Income Arbitrage,[12] and Long Short Equity.[13] The hedge fund firm Bridgewater, for example, has conducted some simple but interesting research along these lines.[14] In most of these studies the authors used simple trading strategies to model Managed Futures, Long/Short Equity, Merger Arbitrage, Fixed Income Arbitrage, Distressed Securities, Emerging Markets, and Short Selling strategies. They generally reached surprisingly good correspondence with the broadly used hedge fund sub-indices for the corresponding strategy sector.

8.4 RELATING HEDGE FUND RETURNS AND RISK PREMIA: WHAT WE CAN MODEL

Table 8.1 provides a qualitative overview of what follows. It relates the various risk premia discussed in the previous chapter to the different hedge fund strategy sec-

---

[10] See W. Fung, D. Hsieh, 'The risk in hedge fund strategies: alternative alphas and alternative betas' in L. Jaeger (ed.), *The New Generation of Risk Management for Hedge Funds and Private Equity Investment* (2003).

[11] M. Mitchel, T. Pulvino, 'Characteristics of risk in risk arbitrage' (2001).

[12] W. Fung, D. Hsieh, 'The risk in fixed income hedge fund styles' (2002).

[13] W. Fung, D. Hsieh, 'The risk in Long/Short Equity hedge funds' (2004); V. Agarwal, N. Naik, 'Performance evaluation of hedge funds with option-based and buy-and-hold strategies' (2003).

[14] See the publication by G. Jensen and J. Rotenberg, 'Hedge funds selling beta as alpha' (2003).

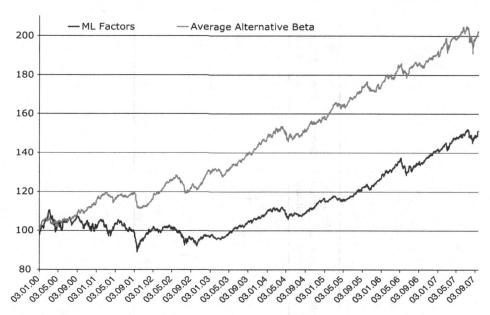

Figure 8.3 Performance of a risk-weighted average of alternative beta factors compared to the Merrill Lynch Factor model (a 'proxy for the equity component in hedge fund returns') including the bear market period 2000–2003. (Data source: Bloomberg; ML model: own calculation from 2000–2003)

tors according to a qualitative judgment based on their principal return generation characteristics.

8.5 ALTERNATIVE BETA STRATEGIES FOR INDIVIDUAL HEDGE FUND STYLES AND STRATEGY SECTORS

As we did in top-down models in Chapter 6, let's now examine how hedge fund return properties match up to risk premia under the bottom-up approach. The results show that bottom-up does not add much value in replicating strategies where the linear factor model yielded good results: directional biased Long/Short and Short Selling. On the other hand, the bottom-up approach proves essential for replicating most other strategies.

Long/Short Equity

As discussed in Chapter 6, linear factor models (RFS) provide a reasonable framework for describing and replicating Long/Short Equity hedge funds. Most managers have net long exposure to the broad equity market, and particularly to stocks of lower capitalization. These two factors explain the better part of Long/Short Equity managers' performance. For the more recent time period of 2005–2007, exposures to emerging markets and international equities need to be added to the factor set.

However, actual Long/Short Equity hedge funds often come with a nonlinear profile. This nonlinear exposure is reflected by the fact that a convertible bond index is a highly explanatory

Table 8.1 Exposure to systematic risk factors for the various hedge fund strategies

Premia	Long/Short Equity	Equity Market Neutral	Statistical Arbitrage	Merger Arbitrage	Fixed Income Arbitrage	Volatility Arbitrage	Convertible Arbitrage	Special Situation	Distressed Securities, Reg D.	Global Macro	Managed Futures
Equity risk	++			+				+	+	+	
Small firm risk (incl. equity risk)	++	+	++	+				+	++		
Corporate event risk	++	++	++	++				++	++		
Hedging demand risk										+	++
Short volatility/option risk			+		++	++					
Complexity or 'efficiency' risk		+	+		++	+	++	++	+	++	
Term structure risk					++				++	++	++
Credit risk					++		++	+	++		
FX carry risk										++	++
Convergence risk		+	++	+	++	++			++	+	
Liquidity risk					+		+	+	++	+	

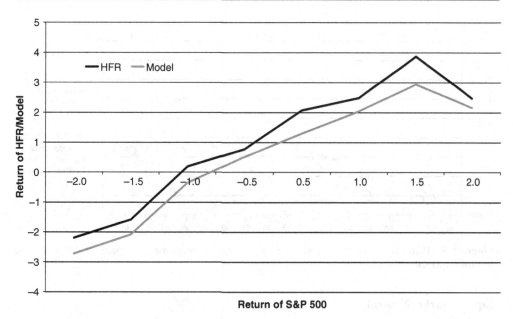

Figure 8.4   The Long/Short Equity exposure profile

independent variable in a regression.[15] Apparently, the inherent exposure profile of a convertible bond (displayed in Figure 8.4) accurately models the Long/Short Equity exposure profile: participation on the upside, protection on the downside to a certain point, but with more expressed losses in a severe downturn of the equity markets (when convertible bonds lose their bond floor). Thus, as shown in Table 6.2, substituting a convertible bond factor in place of an equity factor yields a better model.[16] However, convertible bonds themselves carry a rather complex dependency from equity, interest rate, and credit markets. Credit and interest rate factors individually do not enter into any linear model for Long/Short Equity strategies, so it is the equity dependence which we need to understand better. Hedge funds tend to decrease their exposure in falling equity markets and increase it in rising markets, similar to the 'Constant Proportion Portfolio Insurance' strategy often employed in capital-protected structures. We can simulate this behavior by including such a CPPI factor, based on the rolling 12-month performance of the S&P 500. A multilinear regression on the HFR Long/Short Equity index against these factors including the AR(1) term gives us an R^2 value of 86% – almost the same as the convertible bond factor with a lower value for alpha of 4.5% p.a. This is less than half of what was obtained with the simple equity factor model underlying Table 6.1. This indicates how better modeling of the nonlinear profile of Long/Short hedge funds uncovers systematic risk, which would otherwise remain hidden in fictively high alpha.

---

[15] The convertible bond index primarily serves as a proxy for high tech and small cap stocks. If we include the S&P 500 and Russell 2000 index a lot (but not all) of the explanatory power of the convertible bond index is substituted.

[16] However, it appears as if the significance of the convertible factor has declined in recent years.

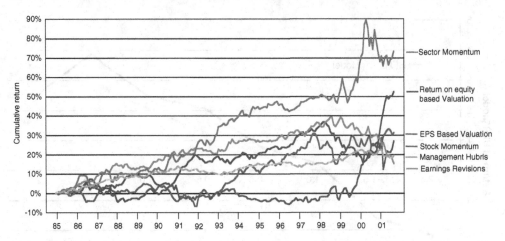

Figure 8.5 Performance of various generic value- and momentum-based strategies. (Source: Old Mutual Management)

Equity Market Neutral

Linear factor models such as the one displayed in Tables 6.1 and 6.2 show only a very small exposure to the broad equity markets, a characteristic which gives the strategy sector its name. But even with the statistically significant Fama–French factors in Table 6.2, the R^2 value of the regression comes out very low. In other words, linear models fall short of explaining the returns for this hedge fund style. In order to capture the return properties of this style, we need to develop rule-based strategies. To do this correctly, we must distinguish between two distinctly different sub-styles of this strategy: fundamental indicator (mostly value and momentum) based valuation models and 'Statistical Arbitrage' (pairs trading), see Chapter 3.

The Fama–French factors discussed in Chapter 5 generically capture a good part of the functional indicator style, although the model could still be further developed. Figure 8.5 shows the performance of various generic value- and momentum-based strategies. Not one of them yields impressive results. However, combining all of them into a portfolio and applying leverage can be quite interesting.

For the Statistical Arbitrage strategy, the research by Goetzman et al.[17] showed us the results of generic pairs trading. Figure 8.6 is an extract from this paper. Other variations of Equity Market Neutral strategies include the construction of minimum variance portfolios[18] or fundamental indexing.[19] These two approaches are quite extensively discussed in the academic literature. In the minimum-variance portfolio, far to the left on the efficient frontier, security weights are independent of their expected returns. Portfolios can be constructed using only the estimated security covariance matrix, without reference to equilibrium expected or actively forecasted returns. Numerous empirical results illustrate the practical value of this optimization using return-based covariance matrix estimation methodologies. These results reveal that

---

[17] W. Goetzman et al.,'Pairs trading: performance of a relative value arbitrage rule' (1998).

[18] See the paper by T. Schwartz, 'How to beat the S&P 500 with portfolio optimization', Working Paper, DePaul University (2000).

[19] See the paper by R. Arnott et al., 'Fundamental indexation' (2005).

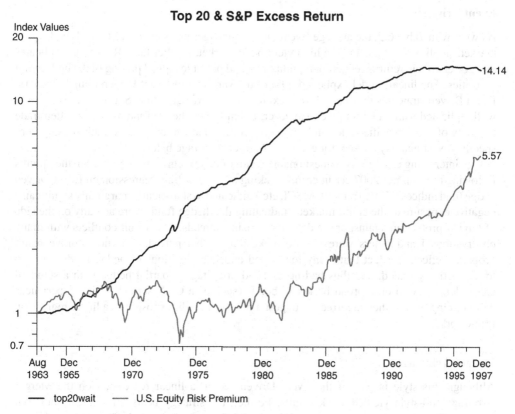

Figure 8.6 Performance of various pairs trading in a Statistical Arbitrage Strategy (from Goetzman *et al.* (1998))

the long-only minimum-variance portfolio has about three-fourths the realized risk of the capitalization-weighted market portfolio, with higher average returns.[20]

Short Selling

The exposure of a Short Selling strategy can be reasonably well modeled with linear factor models employing the equity factor – since the strategy's main exposure is obviously being short the equity market. The strategy further displays positive sensitivity to value stocks, as we saw in Chapter 6. Interestingly, if we include the Convertible Bond Index in the regression for Short Selling, it shows up as significantly as it did in the regression for Long/Short Equity. At the same time Short Selling is the strategy with the highest level of alpha. This appears to indicate that the short side does offer some actual profit opportunities, possibly explained in part by most investors being restricted from selling short.

---

[20] See also the paper by R. Clarke *et al.*, 'Minimum-variance portfolios in the U.S. equity market' (Fall 2006).

Event Driven

As we saw in Table 6.2, the average Event Driven manager takes exposure to the broad equity market, small cap stocks, and the high yield bond market. Further the AR(1) factor indicates autocorrelation in returns reflecting liquidity risk and possible lagged pricing of the underlying securities. The linear model explained 80% of the variation of Event Driven returns. Generic Event Driven strategies thus rank third (next to Long/Short Equity and Short Selling) in being well replicated using a RFS model. However, Event Driven hedge fund managers often trade a variety of more specific styles and exposure profiles that can only be mimicked using very specific investment styles, see, for example, Merger Arbitrage below.

One interesting example of a questionable result of linear regression occurred in the months following the summer 2007 credit crunch. Taking a 2-year rolling regression on Event Driven hedge fund indices (HFR, Tremont, MSCI, etc.) indicated a (statistically marginally significant) negative exposure to the credit markets; indicating that hedge funds were actually on the side of buying protection against credit defaults or rising spreads. This result conflicts with many observations I and others were able to make during that period. This nonintuitive result probably reflects the fact that many long bond and loan positions of hedge funds were no longer actively traded, and thus had no updated price tag. A partial hedge with a standard credit default swap on a broad basket of bonds (such as a CDX series), which experiences daily pricing, would then incorrectly suggest a net short credit exposure in a linear regression framework.

Merger Arbitrage

Although this style is part of the Event Driven sector, a linear regression on the Merger Arbitrage sub-style yielded weak results. Further, the strategy bears a nonlinear short put profile reflected in the significance of the BXM factor in Table 6.2. This is because the payout profile of Merger Arbitrage strategies corresponds directly to a sold put option on announced merger deals. Shorting put options provides limited upside but full participation on the downside (less the option premium). This argument extends beyond the immediate exposure to merger deals falling through: when the stock market falls sharply, merger deals broadly are more likely to break. The low explanatory power of linear factor models should not surprise us. After all, this style bears no direct directional exposure to the equity market, credit risk, or any other well-defined market exposures.

How can we improve our replication models for the Merger Arbitrage strategy? Knowing the underlying mechanics of the Merger Arbitrage investment style we must conclude that if we want to mimic Merger Arbitrage exposure profiles, there is simply no way around investing in actual merger transactions. In their seminal paper on the Merger Arbitrage strategy, Mitchel and Pulvino[21] describe a very simple strategy that can be summarized as 'invest in all mergers'. This strategy invests in every announced all-cash merger in the US market, with a prespecified entry and exit rule. They conducted this calculation for 4750 merger transactions from 1963 to 1998. The hedge fund manager Bridgewater performed a very similar study but constrained themselves to the 10 largest mergers at any point in time.[22] In both cases the resulting simulated

---

[21] See M. Mitchel and T. Pulvino, 'Characteristics of risk in risk arbitrage' (2001).

[22] See the publication by G. Jensen and J. Rotenberg 'Hedge funds selling beta as alpha' (2003), updated on February 13 2004, May 24 2005, and in December 2007.

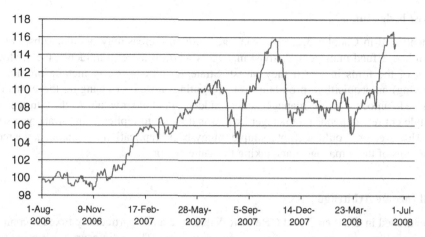

Figure 8.7 Performance of an 'all in' Merger Arbitrage Strategy (live trading results since August 2006 net of fees, no simulation)

returns came very close to the returns of the Merger Arbitrage hedge fund indices (HFR and Tremont).[23] Figure 8.7 provides our own live performance, net of fees, of such an 'invest in all mergers' strategy limited to the largest 30 mergers at a time.

Distressed Securities

The linear factor models showed that Distressed Securities strategies come with exposures to credit and equity, particularly small caps. The explanatory power of the linear model was rather low, with an R^2 value of around 60%. The factor bearing the largest sensitivity is the AR(1), reflecting the low degree of liquidity in Distressed Securities investing which in turn yields significant autocorrelation in the return streams. The return sources of partly illiquid strategies such as Distressed Securities closely resemble those of private equity investment. The investor provides an important funding source for companies without access to traditional capital sources, especially in times of distress. In contrast to investors in regular stocks, an investor in distressed debt or equity, like a private equity investor, might not have direct access to his capital for several years. He is further exposed to uncertainty about the size and timing of future cash flows. Eventually, the situation for the Distressed Securities strategies is similar to Merger Arbitrage: in order to capture its return profile we ultimately have to invest in actual distressed securities. But for Distressed Securities, the 'invest in all' approach might not be sufficient. The average performance of distressed bonds is rather lackluster compared to the top-performing fund managers in this field. As for Private Equity investment, the added value of manager skill is potentially very large, as shown by the significant alpha value in Table 6.2.

---

[23] There actually exists a mutual fund that focuses on investing exactly along the Mitchel/Pulvino study, the publicly available 'Merger Fund' (Bloomberg ticker: MERFX US Equity).

Activist hedge funds

As mentioned in Chapter 3, activist managers are an increasingly popular subset of Event Driven hedge fund managers. Activist managers work to directly influence the strategic direction of the firms in which they invest. Strategic influences can include promoting (or preventing) an acquisition, promoting (or preventing) a sale, or changing the firm's capital structure to unlock what the manager sees as hidden shareholder value. As the return profile of this style entirely depends on manager skill, it is difficult to replicate this strategy systematically. However, one could attempt a simple 'piggy-back' replication by looking at the required SEC filings of these managers and taking the same positions.

Fixed Income Arbitrage

As mentioned in Chapters 3 and 6 Relative Value strategies, particularly Fixed Income Arbitrage, have three general types of systematic exposures. These exposures are: price spreads between two or more related financial instruments (related to particular risks such as credit risk, interest rate term structure risk, liquidity risk, or exchange rate risk); liquidity and 'complexity' premia; and, finally, short volatility exposure.

The exposure of the Fixed Income Arbitrage strategy to combinations of liquidity, credit, and term structure risks expresses itself best as credit risk factor sensitivity in the linear factor models. The significance of the AR(1) term indicates autocorrelation in returns, which signals lagged pricing of the underlying securities and reflects liquidity risk. Linear models do a poor job in explaining the return pattern of this set of styles.

Fung and Hsieh[24] chose another – but similar – set of factors to model various Fixed Income Arbitrage trading styles. These included: long-only (standard fixed income benchmarks such as the CSFB Convertible Bond index return, the CSFB High-Yield Bond index return, the Lehman Mortgage-Backed index return, or the J.P. Morgan Emerging Market Bond index return) and passive spread trading (convertible bonds-minus-Treasury return, the mortgage bond-minus-Treasury return, the high-yield bond-minus-Treasury return, and the emerging market bond-minus-Treasury return). Further they included some dynamic factors in their model: trend-following (look-back straddle on the difference between two interest rates) and convergence trading (as convergence trading strategy is the opposite of the trend-following strategy they explain, the convergence trading strategy can be modeled as a short position in a look-back straddle). The last two factors in particular were derived from rule-based models mimicking various fixed-income hedge fund strategies and the underlying assets traded. The authors claim that the returns of these factors are highly correlated to the principal components of hedge fund returns drawn from qualitative style groupings. They obtained higher R^2 values than presented in our study in Chapter 6. Their and our results explain why the heaviest losses of this style occurred in 'flight to quality' scenarios. When credit spreads suddenly widen, liquidity evaporates and emerging bond and equity markets fall sharply. Events of the summers of 1998 and 2007 remind us that the strategy bears a risk profile similar to a short option, with the risk of significant losses but otherwise steady returns. It is inherently difficult to model exposure to these extreme 'black swan' events, to use Karl Popper's metaphor for unforeseen

---

[24] See W. Fung, D. Hsieh, 'The risk in fixed income hedge fund styles' (2002).

occurrences. They are so rare that their true likelihood is hard to calculate. However, the hedge fund investor should nevertheless keep this exposure in mind.

Convertible Arbitrage

We saw in Chapter 6 that linear factor models had limited success in describing the detailed features of Convertible Arbitrage hedge funds. To explain why this is the case and learn how we can better model this strategy sector, we must distinguish two distinctly different sub-styles. Option-based Convertible Arbitrage simply buys the convertible bond, sells short the underlying equity and frequently reestablishes a delta hedge. This technique is known as gamma-trading. This sub-style tries to hedge out credit risk as much as possible and thus cares little about the credit markets. The second style is credit-oriented, and therefore makes an explicit assessment of the issuer's creditworthiness and takes overpriced credit risk. Each style naturally has a different exposure to the credit markets. The credit-oriented sub-style carries a significant (and intentional) exposure to credit risk, while the option-based sub-style does not. Because credit risk is correlated with equity markets, the credit-oriented style has a less well-defined sensitivity to falling equities. Increasing volatility helps the strategy, but widening credit spreads hurt it. In contrast the option-based gamma trading style performs better in a volatile environment in which equities are falling, which explains the overall negative correlation of Convertible Arbitrage hedge funds to the equity markets shown in Table 6.2. Declining volatility drives down the performance of this strategy.

The dual nature of Convertible Arbitrage hedge funds led to an interesting development in 2003/2004 which confused some investors. In an environment of simultaneously rapidly declining credit spreads and equity volatility, credit-oriented Convertible Arbitrage strategies displayed stellar performance while the gamma traders displayed disappointing returns that hovered near zero. The difference between the two sub-styles is not reflected in the available hedge fund indices, which makes it more difficult for us to capture the generic sensitivities of the strategy sector.

To correctly evaluate these two variants of Convertible Arbitrage, we need to look separately at each. In a research paper,[25] V. Agarwal et al. separate the key risk factors in Convertible Arbitrage strategies: equity (and volatility) risk, credit risk, and interest rate risk. Consequently they designed what they called three 'primitive trading strategies' to explain the returns of the key exposures and risk premia captured by Convertible Arbitrage hedge funds. These were: positive carry ('synthetic put'), credit risk premium ('credit arbitrage') and gamma trading ('volatility arbitrage'). The mechanics of these strategies are simple and reflect the key characteristics of Convertible Arbitrage hedge funds (see also Chapter 3). The carry income is simply the combination of the coupon paid by the convertible bond combined with the short rebate on the short stock position. The combination of an in-the-money bond and a (high delta) short equity hedge creates a synthetic out-of-the-money put profile on the underlying stock. Credit risk is reflected by the spread between the convertible's yield and the risk-free government bond yield with equal maturity. Finally gamma trading is a dynamic strategy that captures the long gamma/long vega profile of the strategy as described in detail in Chapter 3.

---

[25] V. Agarwal, W. Fung, Y. Loon, N. Naik, 'Risks and return in Convertible Arbitrage: evidence from the convertible bond market' (2006).

While the second factor can be well described in the linear setting discussed in Chapter 6 (and, to a limited degree, the third, as long as the moneyness of the synthetic put does not change significantly, i.e. the price movements of the underlying stock are limited in size), there is absolutely no way to describe the highly nonlinear and dynamic gamma trading in the same context. To create the long gamma profile we have to directly engage in dynamic gamma trading involving the option/convertible and the underlying stock. We must buy the convertible, put a delta-neutral hedge on with a short position in the underlying stock, and re-hedge for delta neutrality at a chosen frequency (see Chapter 3 for details). As in Merger Arbitrage replication, there is no way to recreate the Convertible Arbitrage return profile except to make the same investments as Convertible Arbitrage funds. There is no static combination of securities that mimics the same. A serious replication effort rests on an 'invest in all convertibles' (and delta-hedge dynamically) approach.

Agarwal *et al.* investigated a combination of such an 'invest in all convertibles' approach with credit and carry in the US and Japanese market (see note 25). Their factors alone can explain up to 54% of the return variation of Convertible Arbitrage indices, which is nearly what the linear factor model from Chapter 6 can explain. Combining the two, the overall portion of Convertible Arbitrage strategy is likely to be well explained.

Global Macro

The only systematic exposure in a linear factor model we were able to detect for Global Macro managers was the bond markets. Other exposures modeled in a linear model (with partly nonlinear factors) are less obvious: exposure to the risk characteristic of trend-following strategies (the sGFI strategy factor) and some nonlinear exposure to the broad equity market (convertible bond factor). As we showed in Chapter 6, the R^2 value for a regression of Global Macro to linear factors came out quite low at 50%. Along with the heterogeneity of the strategy itself – covering as it does a wide range of different trading approaches – we can attribute that low explanatory power to the dynamic nature of the trading strategies Global Macro managers employ. These escape a linear modeling approach. The most prominent of these dynamic trading strategies is the 'carry trades', executed in the bond market as well as the global currency markets.[26] The mechanism of the bond carry trade is rather simple: the manager chooses those countries with the largest yield spread between long-duration government bonds and those of short duration. This spread is a direct reflection of the risk premium underlying changes in the level of interest rates. The FX carry trade is only slightly more complicated, and even more popular with Global Macro managers. Across a chosen set of currencies, the manager picks those that show the lowest yield as well as those with the highest. Investing in high-yield currencies financed by borrowing in a low-yield currency yields a static return in the form of the interest rate differential. This spread is nothing but the risk premium for assuming exposure to unexpected foreign exchange rate moves. The larger the chosen set of currencies, the more opportunities for returns and the better diversified the currency portfolio is. However, beyond G10 currencies hedge fund managers are likely to face some liquidity issues. Figure 8.8 provides the excess returns (over risk-free rate) of the most widely known 'FX carry index' as calculated by Deutsche Bank. This is based on the 10 most liquid currencies (G10). What we observed for other strategies, we see again here: carry trades

---

[26] The reader is referred to Chapter 3 for a more extended discussion of carry trades.

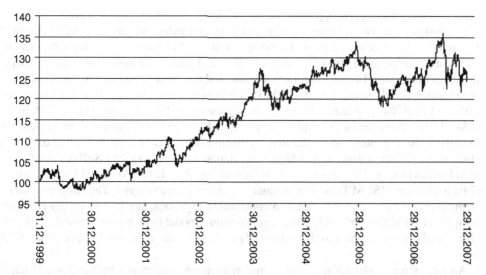

Figure 8.8 Performance of the Deutsche Bank Carry Index (excess returns over risk free rate)

cannot be modeled by static exposures because the extraction of the FX risk premium requires a trading strategy. Only by conducting our own carry trades can we hope to mimic this part of Global Macro returns.

An increasingly popular area of Global Macro investing, even outside the hedge fund realm, is referred to by asset allocators as 'Global Tactical Asset Allocation' (GTAA).[27] These strategies are also systematic, i.e. model-driven, in their nature. They often rely on value and momentum indicators on global asset classes such as equities, fixed income, and currencies. Rather than distinguishing the value or momentum of an individual security, the model applies these indicators to entire countries and regions. For example, it might evaluate the relative attractiveness of German stocks versus Japanese stocks, or UK gilts versus US government bonds. In order to model and replicate GTAA models we must come up with our own generic model. This is not too difficult because most GTAA models are actually quite similar in their basic structure.

In Chapter 3, we distinguished between two different categories of Global Macro hedge funds: systematic trading strategies and discretionary approaches. The returns of the discretionary approaches depend on the trading, timing, and security selection skills of the individual hedge fund manager. Therefore any replication approach finds its limit in trying to replicate discretionary hedge funds.

Managed Futures

Managed Futures hedge funds are the main speculative agents in the global futures markets, thus capturing what we referred to as the 'commodity hedging demand premium'. We saw in Chapter 6 that linear models fail completely in explaining CTA returns, because of the nonlinear V-shaped payout profile of the trend-following nature of CTAs. A simple

---

[27] See the book by D. Potjer and C. Gould, *Global Tactical Asset Allocation: Exploiting the Opportunity of Relative Movements across Asset Classes and Financial Markets* (2006), for more details on GTAA models.

trend-following trading rule applied to the major global futures markets, however, can capture a large part of these returns. Several different studies have independently obtained this result.[28] The sGFII index is designed to model the return of trend following strategies with a simple rule-based momentum approach. It is a volatility-weighted combination of trend-following strategies on 25 liquid futures contracts on commodities, bonds, and currencies. This index shows a 48% correlation with the CISDM Trendfollower index, and equally a 48% correlation with the CSFB-Tremont index. Based on the regression in Table 6.2 the average CTA in the CISDM Trendfollower index displays negative alpha. Schneeweis/Spurgin and Jensen and Rotenberg (Bridgewater) use similar trend-following indicators on a much more restricted set of contracts.[29] They obtain an even higher correlation coefficient to the CSFB-Tremont Managed Futures index (71% in the case of Bridgewater) or the CISDM Managed Futures Indices (79% against the CISDM Trendfollower index for Schneeweis/Spurgin). The lower correlation of the sGFII index is possibly due to a comparably high exposure to commodity contracts compared to Bridgewater's and Schneeweis/Spurgin's model (which overweight the complex of financial futures contracts as this is typically the case for the large multi-billion-dollar CTA funds).

An interesting model for trend-following strategies was proposed by Fung and Hsieh.[30] They constructed their trend-following factor using look-back straddle payout profiles on 26 liquid global futures contracts and the corresponding options. A look-back straddle pays the difference between the highest and lowest price of the reference asset in the period of time until maturity of the option, mimicking the payout of a trend-follower with perfect foresight. The degree of explanatory power of their model is around $R^2 = 48\%$, similar to all three models described above. However, translating this model into a real trading environment and actually investing in look-back straddle options is much more challenging.

8.6   NEW EXOTIC BETA

In recent years we can observe a significant flow of hedge fund capital into new and less liquid types of assets such as bank loans, mezzanine, insurance linked securities (ILS) or straight buyout (LBO) transaction.[31] Some of these investments are related to entirely new types of risks (such as ILS), others come with a liquidity risk premium (such as mezzanine or LBO transactions). Naturally the bottom-up approach needs to integrate these new types of betas into its overall scheme. Insurance-linked securities are a perfect example of these new exotic betas. These are a fixed income type of securities issued by reinsurance companies to transfer some of their catastrophe loss risks they insure their clients against, such as the risk of a hurricane, to the capital markets. Although the probability of such natural catastrophes occurring is very low – depending on the defined size of losses, they happen once every 20 to 200 years – the risks are generously covered by the reinsurance companies, offering an extra return to compensate investors who take them. This is a classic risk premium, but one

---

[28] See L. Jaeger et al., 'Case study: the sGFI Futures Index' (Summer 2002); G. Jensen, J. Rotenberg, 'Hedge funds selling beta as alpha' (2003); R. Spurgin, 'A benchmark on Commodity Trading Advisor performance' (1999).

[29] T. Schneeweis and R. Spurgin, 'Multifactor analysis of hedge funds, managed futures, and mutual fund returns and risk characteristics' (1998); G. Jensen and J. Rotenberg, 'Hedge funds selling beta as alpha' (2003).

[30] See W. Fung, D. Hsieh, 'The risk in hedge fund strategies: theory and evidence from trend followers' (2001).

[31] See the study 'The new power brokers: how oil, Asia, hedge funds and private equity are shaping global capital markets', McKinsey Institute (October 2007).

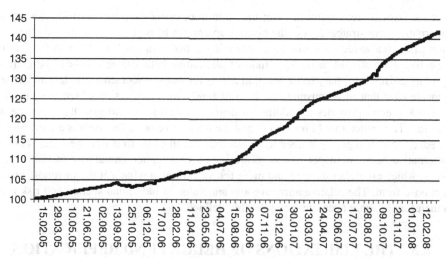

Figure 8.9   The performance of the Swiss Re BB Rated Cat Bond Total Return Index

entirely uncorrelated to the traditional equity or fixed income markets. The catastrophe bond (cat bond) is one of the security types most frequently used to transfer risk in this way. Figure 8.9 shows the performance of the broad Swiss Re BB Rated Cat Bond Total Return Index in the last three years. Data availability is rather low in prior periods due to the small size of the ILS market.

8.7   THE QUESTION OF ASSET ALLOCATION

The final goal after replicating the individual strategies and their individual exposure pieces is to establish an optimal risk/return and correlation profile for the overall portfolio. Thus, once the various risk premia are identified and replicated, the next step in the bottom-up approach is asset allocation. We need to construct the desired hedge fund 'molecules' out of the risk premium 'atoms'. Just as we could construct many molecules from relatively few atoms, we can build many possible portfolios from the alternative beta strategies. If we are slavishly replicating hedge funds, then our asset allocation should reflect that of the chosen hedge fund index. However, the bottom-up approach also enables us to go further and give the investor a custom risk/return/correlation profile.

Asset allocation actually occurs on two levels. On one level we determine the allocation of a particular hedge fund strategy sector to various risk premia. On the second level we mimic the desired asset allocation, e.g. the one we believe represents the global hedge fund industry. Here lies the crucial and yet unsolved part of hedge fund replication: there is as yet no unique method or systematic scheme for performing this task.[32] At this point the hedge fund replicator finds himself in essentially the same position as a fund of hedge funds manager. Both face the challenge of diversifying a portfolio across the various risk drivers.[33]

---

[32] We must therefore refer to this as the 'active element' in hedge fund replication.

[33] The crucial question of asset allocation across strategies and sectors is also important for the top-down approach. However, here the choice lies with the chosen index provider. This is problematic insofar as the compositions and

Let me issue a clear warning here: the definition, extraction, and portfolio management of alternative beta strategies (i.e. the bottom-up approach) requires more than mathematical optimization. It also requires sound understanding of hedge funds themselves. A fund of funds perspective – we should rather say 'fund of alternative beta strategies' – can be extremely helpful here. However, the asset allocation across alternative beta strategies has an important advantage over that of a conventional fund of funds: the atomization of return sources into single risk premia provides an additional degree of flexibility and granularity in the asset allocation. The reader should remember that the alternative betas themselves are the pieces of the hedge fund strategies that need to be put together in order to define the latter. The 'fund of alternative betas' manager has therefore access to a higher granularity of risk exposure profiles, which are better defined and more transparent than what a 'fund of funds' manager can choose from. The relative attractiveness and value in individual sectors and risk premia can therefore be more accurately and flexibly defined.

8.8   THE LIMITATIONS OF HEDGE FUND REPLICATION

Some hedge fund strategies such as Discretionary Global Macro managers or activist Event Driven managers do not lend themselves to successful replication because they rely, by their very nature, on skill or special market access rather than systematic exposure. They are opportunistic and highly variable in their directional exposure, as well as very selective in their selection of specific titles. Furthermore, there are managers in any strategy that have demonstrated an ability to generate alpha over time, even after taking into account the systematic risk exposure biases of their strategy. Evidently this part of the returns cannot be systematically replicated since if it could it would not be alpha. Furthermore, the hedge fund industry itself is very dynamic: new strategies emerge, others disappear. The emergence of Capital Structure Arbitrage hedge funds, which by their complex nature are difficult to replicate, is an example of the former. The disappearance of Equity Market Timing, once a prominent hedge fund strategy, is an example of the latter. The following Chapter 9 will discuss the implications of these limitations to hedge fund replication and thereby introduce a flexible combination between conventional 'fund of funds management' and 'fund of alternative beta' management.

8.9   A NOTE ON THE ISSUE OF LIQUIDITY

One other important issue with hedge fund replication has been surprisingly little addressed in discussions of replication. Up to now, we have implicitly assumed that the instruments employed to model and replicate hedge funds are liquid and easily traded in the global capital markets. However, this assumption does not hold across all hedge fund strategies. When the underlying hedge fund style is based on exposure to less liquid strategies, how can the replication approach involve only liquid instruments? Evidently, a liquidity mismatch is a warning sign that something does not add up in the replication. A significant AR(1) in the regression as we saw in Chapter 6 already provided a first indication in this direction.

---

index construction criteria of the underlying indices still depend more on 'committee decisions' than on objectively determined rules; see the discussion in Chapter 4 for more details.

In fact, more experienced hedge fund investors will note that the hedge fund industry has recently undergone some significant changes in the liquidity structure of the underlying instruments. With lower alpha return opportunities and risk premia in the liquid global capital markets, hedge funds have more and more moved into less liquid private markets. The popular press has repeatedly reported on large leveraged buyout transactions that involved hedge funds. In fact, private equity buyout firms specializing in those types of deals are complaining about hedge funds entering into their turf, competing with them on more beneficial terms (and ultimately driving down return expectations). But buyout deals are by their nature highly illiquid, requiring holding periods of five years and more. A 2007 study by McKinsey[34] provides yet another piece of evidence: it estimates that more than 30% of all bank loans were held by hedge funds (at the time of the study; this number is likely to be higher today). Private equity (leveraged buy-outs) and private debt (bank loans) are asset classes that are nowhere near as liquid as most of the instruments hedge funds were assumed to usually trade. It is difficult, if not impossible, to accurately model the corresponding returns with only liquid instruments.

If we want to include these new exposure profiles in our replication efforts, the only solution to this liquidity mismatch is to include illiquid instruments in our models. This is similar to the 'invest in all' approach introduced in the context of Merger Arbitrage, Distressed Securities, and Convertible Arbitrage above. In the case of the Distressed Securities strategies, a diversified set of distressed bonds can suit that purpose. Similarly, a (leveraged) diversified set of bank loans can help us to mimic and track the performance of Fixed Income Arbitrage and Event Driven hedge funds with such focus.

8.10 SUMMARY

The integration of nonlinearities and a solid understanding of the economic rationale of hedge fund returns are essential for properly describing hedge fund returns. Nevertheless, the method of choice for almost all hedge fund replication providers so far remains the trading model application of linear factor decompositions. But linear models yield satisfactory results for only a very few selected hedge fund strategies, namely those with well-defined and fairly static directional exposures such as Long/Short Equity hedge funds. And here directional equity market factors are all that is needed to explain returns. In other words, linear factor hedge fund replication works when investors need it least to work: in the directional equity space.

The bottom-up approach targets the replication of the particular hedge fund styles and strategies by gaining exposure to the individual alternative beta factors. The large majority of alternative beta can only be extracted by conditional trading rules directly aimed at benefiting from particular risk premia in the global capital markets, in much the same fashion as hedge fund managers themselves do. Instead of naively replicating past properties of doubtful (biased) time series with inappropriate (linear) models, it seems more appropriate to tackle the hedge fund risk premia/alternative betas one by one. We believe that the hedge fund investor is well advised to stay with the alternative beta returns rather than chase the 'pseudo hedge fund' returns of traditional beta. Hedge funds may be simpler than many investors have believed so

---

[34] McKinsey, 'The new power brokers: how oil, Asia, hedge funds and private equity are shaping global capital markets', McKinsey Institute (October 2007).

far, but they are not that simple. So the motto of the newly forming replication industry should be: 'Make the models as simple as possible *but not simpler*'.[35]

Proponents of replication suggest that most hedge fund strategies will eventually be replicated through the use of more complex market factors (despite the fact that the same people say that linear factor modeling might be an appropriate first step for replicating hedge fund returns). These factors then have to be represented by trading strategies that represent alternative risk premia expected to be profitable over longer time horizons. They might have formerly been considered as market inefficiencies, but as the underlying more exotic risks become more widely recognized they are no longer classified as alpha.

Furthermore, replication models should include proper asset allocation across risk factors and strategy sectors. Hedge fund replication is therefore not merely a simple 'job for the quants' but requires (a) the understanding of the concept of each strategy, (b) solid quantitative modeling, and (c) the 'fund of alternative betas approach' to portfolio management and asset allocation. We will now turn to this last element of hedge fund replication: the proper design of alternative beta strategies portfolios.

---

[35] A quote that ultimately goes back to Albert Einstein.

9

Hedge Fund Portfolio Management with Alternative Beta Strategies

Armed with new knowledge about the possibilities and limitations of hedge fund replication, let us now look at portfolio management with a special emphasis on the value replication can add. We'll start by outlining the basic tasks facing hedge fund portfolio managers – strategy sector allocation, investment selection and risk management. Then we will examine the effect of adding replication strategies, to replace parts of a conventional hedge fund portfolio. This naturally leads to a 'core–satellite approach' to hedge fund portfolio management, which cost-efficiently combines alternative beta with manager alpha.

9.1 THE TASKS OF THE HEDGE FUND PORTFOLIO MANAGER

Like a mutual fund, a fund of hedge funds allows investors to diversify idiosyncratic (manager) risk. The average fund of funds displays a volatility of 5–7%,[1] compared with the average 8–10% volatility of single hedge fund strategies or the 15–18% of the average equity mutual fund. In addition to the natural diversification inherent in combining several hedge funds, 'fund of funds' managers provide the following key added value services:

(1) *Sector allocation.* Top-down allocation to the various hedge fund strategies to allow investors to diversify across styles.
(2) *Manager allocation.* Bottom-up selection of the best managers.
(3) *Post-investment monitoring and risk management.* Monitoring the activities of hedge fund managers for unwanted risk.[2]

To deliver these services, the hedge fund portfolio manager must understand the return drivers and risk exposures of the various hedge fund strategies.

These services are particularly valuable for institutional investors, since the 'prudent man rule' requires them to diversify their investments. In effect, they can outsource a portion of their asset allocation responsibility to fund of funds managers. However this outsourcing does come with some costs and problems. First, another fee level is added on top of the already elevated fees charged by the individual hedge fund managers. Second, the larger the number of hedge fund managers the more their shared risk dominates the return profile of the overall portfolio. And naturally this risk is predominantly beta or systematic risk, a large part of which is actually traditional equity beta rather than the desired alternative beta. For fund of funds

---

[1] The HFR Fund of Funds index shows a standard deviation of 5.6% over the period from 1990 to 2007. However, this number is obviously lower than the average fund of funds due to diversification across funds of funds.
[2] See also the author's book *Risk Management in Alternative Investment Strategies* (2002) for a more detailed discussion on risk and risk management issues for hedge fund portfolios.

managers, hedge fund replication holds out the promise of constructing the desired portfolio at lower cost and with better control of the risk–return profile.

9.2   THE LURE OF SAVING FEES

The most widely discussed attraction of replicating hedge fund return profiles can be summarized in one word: fees! Traditional hedge fund managers charge their usual 2% management, 20% performance fees regardless of the origin of their returns. Yet surely beta, by definition a systematic risk, should be compensated less richly than alpha. Removing a good part of the 2%/20% fee for the beta portion of returns cuts about 2.5–3.5% p.a. from the total fund of funds fee burden.[3] Simply separating beta from alpha and compensating each appropriately creates considerable tailwind on the investor's *net* performance.

But replication techniques can also save another layer of fees that applies in funds of funds. I refer to this 'fee layer' as the 'diversification costs' in a hedge fund portfolio. Because the managers' performance is not netted on a portfolio level prior to the payout of a performance fee to the individual hedge fund managers, performance fees are asymmetric; the investor usually participates only 80% with the winning managers, but 100% with the losers. In effect, the individual hedge fund manager receives a free call on his own performance, leaving the investor short that call. The price of being short a portfolio of short calls is higher than being short a call on the entire portfolio. I estimate the price of such a portfolio of call options at between 0.4% and 0.8% per annum higher than the call on the portfolio. Replication therefore can save the investor this unfair difference.

Yet another fee level comes in an even more hidden form: financing costs for leverage. Inevitably some hedge funds employ external leverage, while others retain extra cash. For example CTAs use only small cash portions to fund their margin requirements, while, for example, a Convertible Arbitrage or a Fixed Income Arbitrage hedge fund uses, and must finance, considerable leverage. Leverage financing comes in at around Libor plus 60–80 bps,[4] while the credit on cash yields roughly Libor minus 20–30 bps. Because there is no way of netting the collateral across different hedge funds, the fund of funds investor pays the financing spread between these two values to the prime broker – a dead weight loss to the investor. Hedge fund replication is able to avoid these costs compared to a fund of funds, simply by trading futures and options on margin. In effect replication nets collateral across the various replicated strategy sectors. This saves the investor 40–80 bps p.a.: a 'fee retrocession' that comes right out of the pocket of the prime broker, or does not find its way there in the first place.

Saving fees is replication's most obvious contribution to solving one of the most nagging problems faced by the hedge fund industry today: decreasing net returns. In the heyday of the 1990s, manager gross performance ran 20–22% before any fees were deducted. This strong starting point drove net performance (after fees) of 11–13% at the fund of funds level: still reasonably attractive. However, current levels of realized and expected gross HF performance are lower, as risk premia in the global capital market declined drastically between 2003 and 2007 and numerous hedge funds are currently struggling to survive. A corresponding 10–15%

---

[3] In this simple calculation I assumed a gross performance of 9–18% on the manager level and an overall 1.5% fees for the replication.

[4] This number might have increased in the credit crisis that started in the summer of 2007 and, at the time of the writing of this book, had not yet found an end.

realized and expected gross performance translates into a net performance of only 5–8%. With lower absolute performance resulting from lower levels of risk premia in the global capital markets, the fee burden weighs more heavily on investors. If investors demand a net of all fees return of 10% p.a. (with contained volatility), the *average* underlying hedge fund manager has to generate a gross performance of 16–18% to cover their own and the fund of funds' fees. This is a difficult, if not impossible job when alpha is not in the equation and leverage is not the answer. For the fund of funds manager, using replication to save fees and passing on the savings to investors is a much more viable way to provide acceptable net returns.

9.3   THE LIMITATIONS OF HEDGE FUND REPLICATION

Let me say again that we cannot expect hedge fund replications to be as complete as their cousins in the traditional investment world. The alternative beta strategies approach described in Chapter 8 gives more complete risk premium coverage than factor models. But even this approach might not always adapt as quickly to newly available risk premia as traditional hedge funds. Hedge fund replication remains a moving target. The dynamic nature of this industry leaves any replication model chronically unfinished because hedge fund managers constantly explore new ways to gain risk exposures and make money. The recent flow of hedge funds into less liquid assets such as bank loans, mezzanine, insurance-linked securities (ILS), or private leveraged buy-out transactions, or the less recent move of hedge funds into the entire capital structures of companies (Capital Structure Arbitrage), illustrate how hard it is for replicators to keep up. We must therefore naturally expect that our replication models – bottom-up as well as top-down – will fall short of replicating the hedge fund industry in its entirety. There remain strategy sectors which are more difficult to mimic, and which we may only be starting to get our hands around. Again, a regression model will face the same problem as alternative beta strategies, but in a double fashion: recognizing the right factors plus the time lag due to the backward-looking bias exacerbate the challenge of keeping up.

Furthermore, there is a consensus across hedge fund investors that alpha does exist, even if it is rarer than was previously believed. That is, investors believe that some hedge fund managers do generate excess returns that are not (at least not entirely) correlated with systematic risk. Successful discretionary Global Macro or activist Event Driven investing for example does require greater skill by the very nature of the strategy. A number of the managers in these sectors have demonstrated their ability to generate alpha over time. In most other strategy sectors we can also find managers that (even after taking into account the systematic risk exposure biases of their strategy) have produced alpha outperformance.[5] Clearly if true alpha can be found, it still makes sense to include it in a hedge fund portfolio. The opportunity cost of leaving alpha out can exceed the fee savings of going all beta. However, since the amount of alpha in the global hedge fund industry has significantly decreased – and is often not persistent across managers – it is getting harder to find the 'right' hedge fund managers and stay with them. This makes it the more attractive to invest first in low-cost beta via replication, while at the same time constantly seeking out real (future) alpha managers whose returns can by no means be replicated.[6]

---

[5] This by itself is unfortunately no guarantee for future alpha returns, as we discussed in detail in earlier chapters.

[6] The reader is surely aware: the same applies to investing in traditional asset classes.

9.4   THE ROLE OF ASSET ALLOCATION

Portfolio construction is ultimately about spreading risk across various types of exposures. Fund of funds managers who realize the scarcity and idiosyncratic risks of true alpha can make alternative beta the foundation layer of their total portfolio. This does not in itself ensure proper asset allocation, but it does make such allocation possible. Properly constructed replications of specific return profiles enable the fund of funds manager to diversify into orthogonal risk factors by combining profiles in the desired mix. This asset allocation applies of course only to beta, since rational investors would normally want as much true alpha as they can get regardless of strategy sector. In other words, alpha does not need to be diversified, but rather kept by itself.

Bottom-up replication strategies prove best suited to flexible asset allocation. Top-down (RFS) replication simply assumes that proper asset allocation has already been determined by the provider of the chosen index,[7] thus it comes with neither portfolio management nor risk management. In contrast the bottom-up approach requires an additional process of asset allocation as the individual strategies are combined to create the desired composite profile. Consequently, rather than a 'passive index' we can look at the bottom-up approach as producing a 'fund of alternative betas'. As in conventional funds of hedge funds, asset allocation and portfolio management, including risk management are crucial to the overall investment process for 'fund of alternative betas'.

As challenging as this task is, it also comes with great opportunities. Most importantly it enables flexible construction of a desired risk profile. There is in many cases no need to replicate the average asset allocation of the entire hedge fund industry – if such a thing can be assessed in the first place. Instead the investor often wants a choice about what type of risk/return profile fits best for him – picking specific risk premia and leaving out others. The discussion on asset allocation in this chapter is therefore as relevant for a fund of alternative beta strategies as it is for a regular fund of hedge funds.

9.5   SEPARATION OF TASKS FOR THE FUND OF FUNDS MANAGERS

A fund of funds manager is responsible for two conflicting tasks: alpha selection and asset allocation. This same conflict shows up more generically in the history of traditional asset management as 'security selection' versus 'asset allocation'.

Her first job is to select and maintain capacity with skilled managers and thus provide her portfolio with alpha (i.e. return above the risk-free rate, free of any systematic risk). Her second task is to achieve a stable allocation across the various hedge fund strategy sectors balancing the diverse systematic risk factors in the portfolio. A conflict arises when the strategic balance in the asset allocation requires compromises on the alpha side. To be more precise, the need for strategy diversification can force investors into managers where their confidence in the managers' alpha generation potential is significantly lower than for other managers operating in different strategy sectors.

---

[7] The validity of this assumption must be questioned as I noted earlier, especially in light of the fact that different index providers' asset allocation varies substantially.

In this respect the hedge fund industry finds itself at a point where the traditional asset management industry was about 30 years ago, when in response to precisely the same challenge it invented a particular investment paradigm aiming at separating these two tasks: the 'core–satellite approach'. Such a core–satellite investment strategy is most appropriate for circumstances in which investors have only limited access to market inefficiencies, and they are uncertain about the persistence and quality of the overall alpha in the asset class. This is exactly the situation hedge fund investors are facing today. While it is by now widely accepted in traditional portfolio management that a large portion of the desired asset allocation should be represented by a generic type ('passive') exposure to the desired risk premia we should ask ourselves whether hedge fund investors facing the same challenge of separating strategic asset allocation (respectively, hedge fund strategy selection) from security (respectively manager) selection will find it equally beneficial to walk down that road.

9.6   THE IDEA OF A CORE–SATELLITE APPROACH TO HEDGE FUND INVESTING

A core–satellite approach to hedge fund portfolios would be based on the concepts of hedge fund replication and alternative beta strategies developed in this book which finally provides portfolio managers with a powerful tool to address one of the pitfalls of hedge fund investing, namely the fact that alpha and beta do not come separately to investors but in an uncontrolled and perhaps undesired and, last but not least, expensive, combination.

Generally in a core–satellite framework a significant part of the portfolio is dedicated to matching the 'benchmark' with low relative risk (tracking error) and low cost, while the rest is invested in actively managed, high-alpha funds, which make up the satellite element. Thus alpha generation and beta extraction are well separated – and differently compensated. The translation into the hedge fund world is quite simple: combine the hedge fund replication/alternative beta strategies techniques with the selection of alpha generating managers. I illustrate the concept in Figure 9.1.[8] The combination of both elements is potentially able to beat its benchmark in a risk-controlled manner, i.e. with a limited tracking error to a given asset class benchmark, in other words: limited idiosyncratic risk to the investor. This allows for:

- a better distinction between high-quality and lower-quality managers;
- strategic hedge fund asset allocation in the core portfolio and alpha generation in the satellite portfolio;
- greater overall cost-efficiency.

As mentioned before, there is another dimension in which in particular alternative beta strategies come in handy for the portfolio manager: granularity. The breakdown into risk premia versus entire strategy sectors provides the portfolio manager with a great deal of extra flexibility for her asset allocation: rather than allocating broadly to the strategy sector, let us say, Equity Market Neutral, a strategy sector which combines various risk premia such as exposure to value, small cap and momentum stocks, the portfolio manager is now in a position

---

[8] My personal preference lies in the analogy to the quantum world as the core–satellite approach can be illustrated by the structure of an atom. The model of massive bodies (planets) rotating around a center of gravity (sun) is equally illustrative, however.

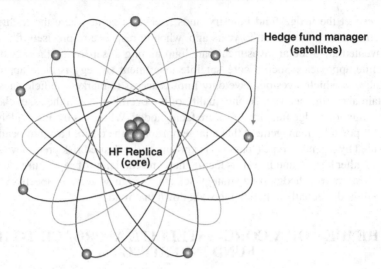

Figure 9.1 The core–satellite approach

to break down that exposure into the single atoms of risk exposure and thus fine-tune the exposure profile of the overall portfolio more granularly.

9.7   ISOLATING PURE ALPHA

The idea of hedge fund replication and alternative beta strategies gives birth to another exciting thought, equally not unknown to traditional asset managers: if hedge fund benchmarks based on replication techniques can deliver on their promises, hedge fund product providers may have found a way to isolate and extract the remaining (pure) alpha in hedge funds. The basic prerequisite of such endeavors would be that these benchmarks could be shorted, a possibility that, despite various efforts (and claims), is not possible as of today. If a particular fund manager's claim to produce alpha can be proven correct (with some justifiable confidence for future performance), why not take out the beta part of his returns with an active hedging overlay approach based on these benchmarks and keep the alpha only?[9]

9.8   THE FIRST PART IN THE INVESTMENT PROCESS: ALLOCATION TO STRATEGY SECTORS

The starting point of any investment process – be it in the traditional world or in the world of hedge fund investing – is a proper strategic asset allocation. As I emphasized before, this equally applies to a 'fund of alternative beta'. In contrast, regression-based replication models (RFS) stop short of any asset allocation questions (and will therefore not be considered further in the remainder of this chapter).

---

[9] This is what the marketing stories of hedge funds have phrased 'portable' alpha, a pleonasm in my view, as alpha is by definition 'portable', i.e. independent of any risk factor in any possible asset class.

Strategic asset allocation means allocating an acceptable level of risk across a spectrum of common different risk factors, irrespective of the specific risk-taking hedge fund managers. These risk factors are well-defined for alternative beta strategies but may be more opaque in the case of a portfolio of individual hedge fund managers.

Investors in traditional asset classes understand that strategic asset allocation determines a large part of their investment returns. Academic studies show that more than 90% of the performance in equity and bond portfolios is governed by strategic asset allocation.[10] While the number for hedge funds might not reach 90% as in the traditional world, allocation across different hedge fund strategy sectors is surely a key driver of hedge fund portfolio performance. This explains why the hedge fund portfolio manager cannot skip over sector allocation and diversify only by selecting the hedge fund managers he believes to be the best. Modern portfolio theory teaches us that risk should be diversified across investments that carry different risks. If hedge fund returns came exclusively from 'alpha', diversification across strategy (or style) sectors would not be necessary. The hedge fund portfolio manager would simply seek the 'alpha-est' managers regardless of the sector. But since we know by now that hedge fund returns come to a large extent from exposure to systematic risks (beta), portfolio managers must diversify by allocating across the various 'alternative betas' present within the different hedge fund strategy sectors. Inversely, the fact that hedge fund strategy selection is by most fund of funds managers considered one of the main keys to success indicates that the various hedge fund styles are exposed to common risks across the individual managers operating within one strategy sector, that is (alternative) beta risk.

The starting point of strategic sector allocation is proper risk analysis, in terms of both the risk characteristics of the sectors and the risk tolerance of the investor. The goal is to achieve the stable diversification across different return drivers (and their economic functions) and risk factors. By allocating to the various strategy sectors, respectively risk premia, the hedge fund portfolio manager not only specifies how much overall risk he will assume, but also how much of each kind of risk. Portfolio theory refers to the definition of the appropriate level and breakdown of risks as 'risk budgeting'. But within the risk budgeting process the hedge fund portfolio manager has much more freedom in his choices than managers in traditional asset classes. Traditional fund managers can only choose between the equity risk premium, the term structure (interest rates) risk premium, and possibly the credit risk premium. So while the manager of a traditional 'balanced portfolio' must strike the right balance between stocks and bonds, the hedge fund portfolio manager has a much larger spectrum of choices. He can choose from a dozen different systematic risks. Since many of these risks have a limited correlation to each other, these choices provide unmatched diversification potential. However, at the same time the wealth of choices also makes the strategic sector allocation in a hedge fund portfolio significantly more challenging.

Once the optimal allocation across systematic risk factors is defined, the next step is to map that risk budget onto an allocation breakdown across the strategy sectors (see Figure 9.2). Here the nature of the alternative beta strategies comes in handy: they are well-specified and transparent in terms of their precise exposure profile. The allocation to sectors requires both quantitative analysis and qualitative judgment. Past performance and correlation studies or regression models offer valuable guidelines for the portfolio manager, but she should also

---

[10] G. Brinson *et al.*,'Determinants of portfolio performance', *Financial Analysts Journal*, (July-August 1986).

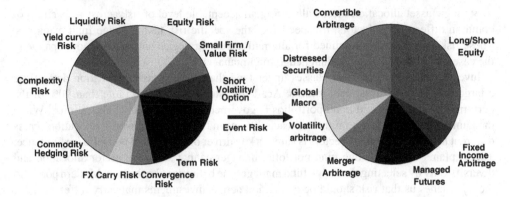

Figure 9.2   Projection of a risk budget onto a strategic asset allocation in a hedge fund portfolio

consider qualitative elements such as economic rationales of strategies as well as particularly hostile market environments for the individual strategy sectors and risk premia.

Pitfalls of quantitative analysis

For hedge fund asset allocation the situation is no different than for any investment portfolio: quantitative analysis is useful but comes with built-in dangers. Common methods such as mean–variance analysis have limitations if applied to the sort of aggregated historical manager data that is provided by hedge fund indices.[11] Here are a few of the pitfalls to watch out for when applying quantitative methods to sector allocation.

- Low available data. Performance histories for hedge funds are short, and data is usually only provided at monthly granularity. Statistical significance of the analysis is therefore generally low. These short histories mean that historical average returns are biased by the unusual market conditions of the 1990s and early 2000s.[12] Alternative beta strategies in contrast can be calculated for past periods much more reliably as their returns depend on publicly available data.[13]
- Mean–variance fails to capture all risks. Some hedge fund strategies have a sold option profile, which provides steady returns but is exposed to large losses in the case of big market moves. We saw that hedge funds often bear some of these hidden 'tail risks'. Some of these strategies may not have existed long enough to experience such a large move, similar to Europeans who had never seen a black swan before the 1940s and therefore claimed that 'all swans must be white'. Mean–variance-based portfolio optimization therefore tends to make these strategies look safer than they actually are, and recommends inappropriately large allocations to them. Conversely, mean–variance will allocate too little to strategies that are not subject to sudden unexpected shocks, such as those with a bought option profile.

---

[11] See also the discussion by W. Fung and D. Hsieh, 'Is mean–variance analysis applicable to hedge funds?' (1999).

[12] After 2008 we might have a few more data points to see what happens to hedge funds in so-called 'tail events'.

[13] In practice, however, it may not always be so easy to access these data, e.g. the statistics of mergers going back to the 1970s require detailed data research.

Mean–variance optimized portfolios will as a result be too exposed to nonconsidered risk, such as low liquidity by over-allocation to Distressed Debt or Regulation D strategies.[14]

- Variability is not captured in averages. Return and risk properties of strategy sectors vary substantially over time, across managers in the sector and across different market environments. This variability is not reflected in the average performance numbers for the sector. The dispersion of performance of individual managers within a strategy style is significantly higher than that of traditional asset managers.

Correctly applying quantitative optimization techniques to hedge fund strategy allocation therefore requires more than collecting past return data. In his seminal paper 'Portfolio selection', Markovitz noted the difficulty in determining the correct inputs for portfolio optimization:

> [We] must have procedures for finding reasonable [means] and [variances]. These procedures, I believe, should combine statistical techniques and the judgement of practical men. My feeling is that the statistical computations should be used to arrive at a tentative set of [means] and [variances]. Judgement should then be used in increasing or decreasing some of these [means] and [variances] not taken into account by the formal computation.[15]

Several methods have been proposed for patching the shortcomings of traditional mean–variance optimization for hedge fund portfolios, specifically on the question of the appropriate risk measure to choose in the optimization. One of them is taking estimates of higher moments (and cross-moments) into account, e.g. by using the Cornish–Fisher expansion. This entails substituting the standard deviation as a risk measure with a scaled standard variation, the commonly called z-sigma. In this case z is defined through using the first three cumulants of the Corner–Fisher expansion,[16] which explicitly consider the third moment (skew) and fourth moment (kurtosis) .[17] However, this extension tends to be unstable in the presence of high third moments, a fact most recent research results fail to mention.

Another approach ameliorates the shortcomings of estimating the covariance structure of hedge fund returns. It imposes some structure on the covariance matrix in order to reduce the numbers of parameters to be estimated. This can be done by a linear factor model on returns, either explicitly based on chosen independent factors or implicitly through principal component analysis.[18] Here again, alternative beta strategies come in handy: they provide much more stable covariance estimates than aggregates of past hedge fund (index) performance numbers.

Elements of successful strategic sector allocation

Having covered some of the pitfalls, let's now look at some of the types of analysis that should be considered for successful sector allocation:

---

[14] An interesting discussion of the optimization problem can be found in the article 'The dangers of historical hedge fund data', by A. Weismann and J. Abernathy in the book *Risk Budgeting: A New Approach to Investing*, ed. by L. Rahl, RISK (2000). A popular account of this and other fallacies when handling data is given by Nassim Taleb in the book *Fooled by Randomness: The Hidden Role of Chance in the Markets and in Life* (2001).

[15] H. Markowitz, 'Portfolio selection' (1952).

[16] See E. Cornish, R. Fisher, 'Moments and cumulants in the specifications of distributions', (1937), reprinted in Fisher, R., *Contributions to Mathematical Statistics*, John Wiley & Sons, Inc. (1950).

[17] See A. Signer, L. Favre, 'Mean-modified value-at-risk optimization with hedge funds' (2002).

[18] See the work by N. Amenc and L. Martellini, 'Portfolio optimization and hedge fund style allocation decisions' (2002).

- *General attractiveness of each strategy sector and risk premium*: The return drivers of the chosen risk premium should be examined, along with its underlying economic rationale.
- *Systematic risk factors of hedge funds*: The fund portfolio manager should understand the systematic risks of any hedge fund style and manager. Where possible she should quantify these risks and develop procedures for diversifying them. This is evidently much simpler for alternative beta strategies than for opaque hedge fund manager allocations.
- *Strategy sub-sectors.* Managers in the same strategy sector can have different focuses (e.g. sector, country, credit quality) and therefore different exposures to particular risk factors. For example, Long/Short Equity managers can vary widely in their exposure to different sectors or regions.
- *Market environment*: The hedge fund portfolio manager must understand how different strategies behave in different market environments. She should determine the specific favorable and unfavorable market conditions for each sector and alternative beta strategy, continuously follow developments in the global financial markets, and monitor key economic and financial variables that drive returns.
- *Past and anticipated future correlations and dependencies*: Correlations and dependencies across exposures determine diversification characteristics and therefore the optimal risk–return ratio within a portfolio. Strategy sectors and risk premia that behave differently from each other in particular market environments are obviously key to creating a diversified portfolio.

Many fund-of-funds managers and larger investors have developed quantitative tools to analyze these factors. We can easily integrate alternative beta strategies into a quantitative analysis, and they do not even require a mere linear approximation to their risk profile. The portfolio managers then integrate their macroeconomic outlook into these models and combine the results with qualitative judgment to allocate assets.

The winds of change – tactical sector allocation

It is important to understand that return drivers and risk premia of strategy sectors can change or even temporarily disappear over time. In traditional stock and bond funds, the manager of a 'balanced portfolio' constantly adjusts exposure to account for the changes in expected equity and bond returns. Asset allocation for a hedge fund portfolio should equally take into account the changing dynamics of risk in the global capital markets. A statically fixed asset allocation can result in widely fluctuating portfolio risk. So, like a skillful sailor, the fund portfolio manager must maintain a steady course by tacking in ever-changing winds. This means dynamically shifting asset allocation over time. This could potentially go as far as shifting exposures to risk due to sudden changes in the risk landscape of the global capital markets, which is usually a turf reserved for single hedge fund managers.

To do this, the fund manager endeavors to forecast shorter-term risk factor performance across financial markets, quite comparable to the task of a chief economist in the traditional asset management framework. Since it is impossible to effectively predict the time variation in the contribution from manager alpha, understanding the beta return sources of hedge funds is the only way to achieve a solid tactical allocation. Further, tactical allocation requires that the portfolio manager possesses the flexibility of switching across risks and has insights into the precise profile of the underlying beta exposures. The risk budget – once established in a strategic asset allocation process – needs to be rebalanced according to shifts in risk in the global capital markets. The risk budgeting process ultimately means that the dynamic nature of risk is accounted for, the risk structure in the portfolio is frequently reassessed and corrective measures are taken as needed in response to changes in the markets.

In a conventional fund-of-funds setting, the portfolio manager often lacks the required structural as well as informational infrastructure to perform this task:

- If liquidity terms for the underlying managers are yearly, quarterly or monthly with notice periods equally long, the time between tactical asset allocation shifts and their actual implementation exceeds the very time frame for which the shifts are foreseen in the first place. It can easily take a 'traditional' fund-of-hedge-funds portfolio manager six months and more to rebalance and reallocate within his portfolio, which is longer than the foreseen time frame of most of his tactical shifts. The process can take significantly longer in times of market distress, mostly likely the moment when flexibility is most needed.
- The manager often does not have detailed information about the actual exposures of the underlying hedge funds, neither the type nor the size.[19]

I will now discuss how a core–satellite approach can help to mitigate these problems of a conventional fund of funds by integrating alternative beta strategies to the portfolio. For that purpose we divide the hedge fund portfolio into two parts, a core allocation consisting of alternative beta strategies and an allocation to various hedge fund managers, referred to as 'satellite' managers (as graphically represented in Figure 9.1). However, the discussion presented on asset allocation in a core–satellite portfolio equally applies to a pure 'fund of alternative beta strategies'.

9.9 IMPLEMENTATION OF TACTICAL ASSET ALLOCATION IN A CORE–SATELLITE APPROACH TO HEDGE FUND PORTFOLIOS

The integration of liquid and transparent hedge fund replication in a core–satellite approach comes with two important advantages: flexibility and granularity. Acting on a necessary rebalancing and/or reallocation within a portfolio of hedge funds can take a significant amount of time due to the asset class's low transparency standards and inhibitive liquidity constraints. In a core–satellite approach the same task becomes a matter of days. Further, the breakdown into risk premia rather than strategy sectors allows the portfolio manager to fine-tune the asset allocation. The flexibility a portfolio manager obtains by integrating a core allocation to alternative beta strategies is thus a prerequisite of any systematic tactical asset allocation. The implementation of a tactical asset allocation with a fund of alternative betas is structurally straightforward.

After determining the strategic asset allocation as a starting point for further optimization based on given investors' views and return expectations of individual portfolio components, the most prominently chosen path towards systematically integrating the portfolio manager's views on return expectations of the individual portfolio components follows a Bayesian approach. The academic literature refers to this as the 'Black–Litterman' approach.[20] We will illustrate

---

[19] More and more fund managers have realized this problem. Many are happy with approximation to these exposures one can obtain by regression of the returns against standard risk factors. However, as we saw in Chapter 6, this comes with the problem of stationarity and backward-looking bias.

[20] The reader is referred to the original publications by F. Black and R. Litterman (1990, 1992).

how this optimization technique, originally developed in the world of traditional portfolio management to create stable, mean–variance efficient portfolios based on investors' views and insights, can be effectively applied to hedge fund portfolios. Unfortunately, we cannot avoid some mathematical detail in order to develop the underlying theory. The Black–Litterman approach consists of two steps. In a first step, we apply standard utility theory. Let P be a portfolio composed of a core portfolio C and a satellite portfolio of managers S. BM denotes the benchmark, e.g. the chosen strategic asset allocation. Then

$$P = \sum_i w(i)S(i) + \sum_j v(j)C(j) := \vec{w}\vec{S} + \vec{v}\vec{C},$$

where $\vec{w}$ denotes the weight vector in the satellite portfolio and correspondingly $w(i)$ the weight of the ith manager in the portfolio, $\vec{v}$ denotes the weight vector of strategies in the core portfolio and correspondingly $v(j)$ the weight of the jth strategy in the portfolio. The following holds:

$$W + V = \sum_i w(i) + \sum_j v(j) = 1$$

The tracking error TE and the information ratio IR with respect to a given benchmark asset allocation can then be defined as

$$TE(P) = \sqrt{\text{var}(P - BM)}$$
$$IR(P) = \frac{E(P - BM)}{\sqrt{\text{var}(P - BM)}}$$

The optimal total weight $\vec{w}^*$ of the satellite portfolio for an investor with a quadratic utility function taking the form

$$U(\vec{w}, \vec{v}) = E(\vec{w}, \vec{v}) - \frac{\lambda}{2}TE(\vec{w}, \vec{v})^2$$

given the risk aversion λ ($E[.]$ being the expected return operator) solves the following equations:

$$\frac{\partial U}{\partial \vec{w}}(\vec{w}^*) = 0, \quad \frac{\partial U}{\partial \vec{v}}(\vec{v}^*) = 0$$

Given that the investor is subject to linear constraints $A\vec{w} = \vec{c}$ and $A'v = \vec{c}'$ as represented by matrices A, and A' and vectors c and c', (such as, for example,

$$\sum_i w(i) + \sum_j v(j) = 1$$

above), the following optimality conditions apply (first-order conditions with Lagrange multipliers θ)

$$E(\vec{w}) - \lambda\frac{\partial \text{var}(P)}{\partial \vec{w}} + A^T\theta = 0$$
$$A\vec{w} = c$$
$$E(\vec{v}) - \lambda\frac{\partial \text{var}(P)}{\partial \vec{v}} + A'^T\theta' = 0$$
$$A'\vec{v} = c'$$

The weight vectors $\vec{w}^*$ and $\vec{v}^*$ provide the allocations to the individual portfolio components with no external investor views in a mean–variance framework.

Note: For a specific choice λ^{IR} (depending on the constraints imposed on the optimization) of the risk-aversion coefficient, the optimal portfolio corresponds to the information ratio optimal portfolio given by $\vec{w}^{IR}$ and $\vec{v}^{IR}$, i.e. the portfolio that maximizes the information ratio defined above. A more general target function could then be defined as the information ratio under the constraint that the tracking error must not be larger than a certain threshold. Based on this target function optimal core–satellite portfolios can be calculated.

The second step now consists of implementing the appropriate tactical asset allocation according to the investor's view. This can be performed in the above mentioned Black–Litterman-based Bayesian optimization approach. We recall that the Black–Litterman model was originally developed to overcome some major practical obstacles in the Markowitz model, i.e. the requirement to specify expected returns for every investment component of the relevant universe. A consequence of this problem is that when portfolio managers try to optimize using the Markowitz approach they usually find that the obtained portfolio weights take rather extreme values and are highly unstable with respect to small changes in the input of expected returns.[21] The Black–Litterman model in contrast uses the components' implied returns of a given allocation vector (referred to as the 'benchmark') as a starting point (the appropriate allocation vector would be the weights as determined by step one above). The implied returns are calculated through reverse optimization along the standard mean–variance optimization framework. We provide a quick outline to the Black–Litterman model and refer the reader to the literature on the details.[22]

The implied return vector Π of a given benchmark's portfolio weight vector ϖ_{BM} assuming an average investor risk aversion δ and the covariance matrix Ω of the portfolio components is given by

$$\Pi = \delta \Omega \varpi_{BM}$$

The Black–Litterman approach now combines these (*a priori*) neutral returns with a set of views and the respective levels of confidence, to integrated (*a posteriori*) returns $\mathbf{R}_{BL}$ ('Black–Litterman returns') employing Bayesian conditioning techniques. The Black–Litterman returns $\mathbf{R}_{BL}$ are given by the following optimization problem:

$$\min_{E(R)} \left\{ [E(R) - \Pi]^T \, \Omega^{-1} \, [E(R) - \Pi] \right\},$$

such that

$$PE(R) = V + \varepsilon, \varepsilon \propto N(0, \Sigma),$$

and

$$E(R) = \Pi + v, v \propto N(0, \Omega)$$

Here, the k views are expressed through the $k \times n$ matrix P and the k-dimensional vector V with a covariance of errors Σ.

---

[21] In his seminal paper 'Portfolio Selection', Markowitz noted the difficulty in determining the correct inputs for portfolio optimization. See the quotation given in the previous section 9.8.

[22] The paper by G. He and R. Litterman (1999) provides a good insight into the intuition behind the Black–Litterman model.

Using $\mathbf{R}_{BL}$, we can calculate the optimal portfolio weights ('Black–Litterman weights') ϖ_{BL} in a standard mean–variance optimization:

$$\varpi_{BL} = (1/\delta)\Omega^{-1}\mathbf{R}_{BL}$$

The final portfolio then results as the neutral portfolio plus a weighted sum of portfolios representing the investor's views. The weight on a portfolio representing a view is positive when the view is more bullish than the one implied by the neutral portfolio. The weight further increases as the investor becomes more confident about her view. With the modified weight vector ϖ_{BL} the portfolio manager has the necessary information to implement the optimal portfolio given her specific views. I emphasize once more that, without the flexibility and granularity in the core, tactical asset allocation in the Black–Litterman framework or any alternative (even possible nonsystematic) framework becomes inapplicable.

However, an important component of the overall portfolio construction process in a fund of funds portfolio – which obviously does not apply to a pure fund of alternative betas – remains the selection of the alpha-generating satellite hedge fund managers. I will dedicate the next section to this task.

9.10   THE SECOND ELEMENT: MANAGER SELECTION

Alpha is and will continue to be ultimately the most attractive sort of return, as it comes with no systematic risk and no correlation to other asset classes (albeit with idiosyncratic risk, e.g. the hedge fund blowing up). I discussed the potential flaws of wrongly classified alpha as well as the decline of the average hedge fund manager's alpha at the end of Chapter 5. Nevertheless the search for alpha continues even in the traditional investment world, where we must consider its average size to be significantly smaller compared to hedge fund alpha. So, there remains a great deal of appeal in the search for alpha. And as alpha is always based on the skill of individual investment managers it is the hedge fund portfolio manager's task to find these individuals. In other words, once sector allocation is in place, the fund portfolio manager must turn her attention to the selection of individual fund managers. Since performance of individual managers within a strategy is more dispersed than for traditional asset funds, manager selection is more important in hedge funds than in traditional investments. Due diligence should account for the fact that managers within the same strategy sector can differ with regards to strategy implementation, instrument diversification, hedging, use of derivatives, short selling, and the degree of leverage.

Investing in hedge funds without a proper due diligence is like throwing dice. Since not every potential investor has either the time or skill to conduct a proper due diligence on many different managers, expertise and dedication to this process is a value added of a fund of funds manager. Proper due diligence makes it much more likely one will end up with an alpha manager. Professional manager selection also reduces the need to jump from manager to manager, chasing last year's returns. Since individual hedge funds have substantial up-front or redemption fees, the fund portfolio manager can make up a good portion of her cost to investors simply by reducing the need to incur these costs. In the end the portfolio manager will have a very good idea of what objectively defined situations – not emotions – will cause her to pull her allocation out from the fund manager.

Some hedge funds managers are skillful and some are just lucky. Luck of course is not persistent, and Murphy's law predicts that a particular manager's luck runs out just after you have invested with that manager. Since there are a number of ways that managers can hide problems in their investments, it is important to uncover them before investing.

In analyzing a hedge fund manager's strategy, the portfolio manager should guide himself along a very simple route by key questions: Why does/did this fund make money? What proportion of returns derives from risk premia, exploiting market inefficiencies, or just plain luck? A comparison of performance to the appropriate alternative beta strategies can be very helpful here. There are more funds where past returns were generated on the basis of random chance than one might think. The rising stock markets in the 1990s or the years 2003–2007 have led more than one manager to the conclusion that he is an investment genius. To use a baseball metaphor, these managers were 'born on third base', but thought they hit a triple. Finding true investment skill which persists in changing market conditions is the key task of manager selection. The second most important question is: How does the hedge fund make money? This question aims at understanding the investment process, the strategies and systems used, and what risk is taken.

Quantitative analysis of the individual hedge fund's performance considers past returns, volatility, drawdowns, Sharpe ratio, and other performance measures,[23] as well as correlation studies, benchmark comparisons, and peer group analysis. However, the same problems that afflict quantitative analysis for sector allocation also apply when quantitative analysis is used to select managers. Many hedge funds have track records too short to separate the lucky survivors from the managers with a real edge, and many strategies and managers have not yet been tested by a stress event. So the portfolio manager must leaven quantitative analysis with a qualitative understanding of the individual hedge funds' performance characteristics. Qualitative aspects of the due diligence process involve understanding the manager's competitive edges, the investment style and attitude. The portfolio manager should also learn the details of the manager's investment decision-making processes, the organization and structure of the fund's operations, the trading facilities, and the character, quality, and background of key people.

It is easier to evaluate the performance of fund managers whose returns are based on an efficient collection of risk premia than those who genuinely exploit market inefficiencies. Since beta risk can be measured, the investor can benchmark their returns more easily, and peer group comparison is more accurate. It is harder to evaluate the performance of managers who claim to generate alpha returns, because it is more difficult to distinguish past performance that came from alpha from pure luck.

Manager selection steps

Much has been written about the details of the selection process,[24] and the fund of funds community has developed a consensus about the separate stages of manager selection.

---

[23] See also Chapter 27 in *Investment Analysis and Portfolio Management* by F. Reilly and K. Brown for a discussion of performance measures in traditional portfolios.

[24] For a more detailed discussion, see A. Dorsey, 'How to select a hedge fund of funds: pick the winners and avoid the losers' (2004) or the newer book by the same author: *Active Alpha: A Portfolio Approach to Selecting and Managing Alternative Investments* (2007).

Initial screening

This rough sort usually uses database searches to reduce the global manager universe to a manageable size. This stage does not necessarily require proprietary systems, so it is often done with commercially available databases of funds.

First contact

The portfolio manager or investor will contact the fund manager through personal references, conferences, manager sales visits, or prime brokers. One of the edges of a fund of funds manager is to be inside the 'information loop' of high-calibre managers.

Quantitative analysis

The portfolio manager will analyze the fund's performance, including return, volatility, drawdowns, and Sharpe ratio. He will also analyze the fund manager's correlation to other managers in the strategy sector and to other asset classes. In order to properly diversify, the portfolio manager will pay special attention to how the individual fund correlates to other funds in her overall portfolio.

A good track record is not a sufficient indicator of a high-quality trading and investment strategy. Poor strategies can come with excellent past performance obtained in favorable market environments. Database analysis of track record defines the starting point of manager selection, but funds can be vulnerable to market stress in ways that might not be apparent from historical returns. A good track record may not even be a necessary condition. If a manager uses a strategy that is exposed to certain risks due to external market conditions, he may do poorly even though he is true to his strategy and executes it well. If the fund of funds manager believes that macroeconomic factors are shifting to favor those risks, the fund may still be a better future investment than one that thrived in previous economic conditions.

Desk research

The beginning of the qualitative analysis includes reviewing the fund's legal documents, fee structure, assets under management, investment capacity, auditor statements, reference checks, and possibly a completed due diligence questionnaire.

For the sake of efficiency the investor might want to ask the manager to prepare a due diligence questionnaire before his onsite visit. This can be one of the most important sources of information for desk research. However, many managers are unwilling to complete extensive questionnaires and provide their own due diligence questionnaires. As long as key issues are discussed, there is no problem with accepting such a manager-prepared document.

On-site meetings

An onsite visit to the manager completes the qualitative due diligence process. It should include discussion with key personnel about investment approach, strategy implementation, risk management techniques. The visit should also include an assessment of infrastructure, including a review of operations and trade executions, an examination of back office structures, and an assessment of the firm's working atmosphere.

It is important to talk to the key people (trader, fund manager, CEO) directly instead of the marketing staff only. Generally, the latter do not know the strategy in sufficient detail. Onsite visits are the most important element of due diligence.

Due diligence has a strong subjective component. It is useful to visit and evaluate managers in a team, as several people observe more than one person by himself. A broad industry network can be helpful for discussing and evaluating managers.

Necessary background checks

Valuable information can be obtained from marketing and legal material (offering memorandum, historic letters to investors, audited track record, and annual reports, and any marketing material). This rather broadly composed material is usually of limited value in respect of the details of the investment process, but contains important information about fees, NAV calculation, biographies of key people, legal set-up, redemption periods, restrictions on leverage, counterparties, and disclosure policies.

Independent checks of the background of key personnel are a necessity. Many cases of fraud could have been detected early on, if investors had performed sufficient background checks.[25] Sources of information are ex-employers, auditors, administrators, prime brokers, other investors, and government agencies. Some funds of funds even hire private investigators. I believe even hedge fund managers have the right to keep their private sphere protected, though.

Areas of examination

During the above steps, the allocator must examine and apply her selection criteria to certain key aspects of the hedge fund under consideration. Some fund portfolio managers formalize this process using a points system, the fund is given a numeric score for each area of investigation and selection is made on a weighted average score. Others portfolio managers use a more qualitative approach. In either case the following areas, which I call the 'eight Ps' of manager evaluation, are the crucial areas that must be evaluated.

(1) *People*: Background, experience, integrity, attitude, and lifestyle of key people of the hedge fund. In addition to the named manager, other key employees should also be considered. Are any key employees likely to leave the firm? Whose departure could materially affect fund performance? Has a key person or director been subject to an investigation by a government regulatory agency?

(2) *Product*: Hedge fund characteristics such as target return and risk, investment instruments, level of diversification, position entry and exit criteria, hedging tools, time horizon, liquidity of traded instruments, leverage employed, use of derivatives, degree of short selling. Last but not least, what is the fee structure of the fund?

---

[25] See the article 'Hedge fund disasters: avoiding the next catastrophe' by D. Kramer in the *Alternative Investment Quarterly* (October 2001).

(3) *Process*: The key steps and people involved in making and executing investment decisions. Where investment decisions are based on a model, the investor should familiarize herself with the details of the model, including how it is developed and tested (e.g. distinction of in-sample and out-of-sample testing).[26]

(4) *Performance*: The past track record. The investor should request audited performance numbers of all relevant trading accounts of the manager. Performance presentation standards can vary among different managers, and the fund portfolio manager must make sure she understands the calculation assumptions and methods used.[27] Measures for risk are standard deviation, maximal drawdown, downside deviation, semi-variance, and leverage factors. Risk-adjusted performance measures are Sharpe ratios, Sortino ratios, Information Ratios, Park ratios, Treynor's measure, risk-adjusted return on capital ('RAROC'), 'effective return', and others.[28]

The intricate trade secrets and details about models are, for the most part, not that important for the fund portfolio manager. Nonconfidential information is generally much more informative than the details the manager is unwilling to disclose. More relevant information can be obtained by discussing the general approach, philosophy, and edge of the manager, which the manager should be more than comfortable discussing. The reader will by now be ready to classify the different possible sources of a hedge fund manager's returns and to apply them in a formal due diligence process.

(5) *Partnership*: The firm's legal and ownership structure. Incentive and compensation schemes within the firm can give important hints about the commitment of its employees, especially the dedication of key people. The location of the firm matters for attracting future investment talent. Hedge funds sometimes fail for pure business reasons such as employee turnover, partner disputes, or poor accounting. In many ways, a hedge fund is a business like any other. So the business infrastructure of the fund is just as important as the investment side. Are the managers good businessmen as well as smart investors?

(6) *Portfolio*: Diversification and portfolio management. Systematic model-based trading often occurs over a broad universe of different instruments and possibly asset classes, while discretionary approaches are more likely to be successful in a limited range of instruments. Manager-defined limits on positions in certain instruments and asset classes, if any, are a good indicator of concentration risk.

(7) *Peers*: The uniqueness of the hedge fund. How is this fund different from peers in the same strategy sector? The manager should be able to distinguish himself clearly from peers, either through high performance or through low risk and correlation.

(8) *Potential*: Capacity limits on the amount of assets the hedge fund can manage without diluting performance. Managers sometimes accept more money than they can efficiently invest. Managers who have reached capacity for their core strategy may offer other investment programs to capitalize on their reputation. But these additional programs may be outside their core competence. The fund portfolio manager should be careful about being

---

[26] In-sample testing refers to the optimization of the model's parameters on historical data, while out-of-sample testing means examining model performance on historical data that was not used during the optimization process.

[27] The Cfa Institute provides the GIPS standards aiming to define a well-accepted industry standard for performance presentation of money managers; see also http://www.cfainstitute.com/centre/codes/gips/index.html

[28] See the paper by M. Dacorogna *et al.*, 'Effective return, risk aversion and drawdowns', for a discussion of risk-adjusted performance measures; see also Chapter 27 in *Investment Analysis and Portfolio Management* by F. Reilly and K. Brown.

persuaded to invest in another program, when the original program of her choice is closed for further investments.

9.11   ACTIVE POST-INVESTMENT RISK MANAGEMENT

The final and most neglected step of hedge fund portfolio management is post-investment risk management. While one might learn a great deal during due diligence, only ongoing risk management can cope with the additional risk factors that inevitably emerge after investment with a particular hedge fund manager. Risk management is at least as challenging and time-consuming as strategy sector or manager selection.

Risk management can decrease the severity of investment losses by avoiding accidents and investment disasters. But risk management does not by itself lead to positive performance, nor does it prevent losses under all circumstances. For each investment strategy there exist hostile market environments that will lead to weak performance or losses. Risk management allocates and diversifies an acceptable level of measurable risk across hedge fund strategies and individual managers. Risk managers assess frequently whether the risk limits have been exceeded, and take corrective action. Risk management means taking the right kind and level of risk and is thus a central part of the asset-allocation process.

Risk management is both an art and a science. The science lies in quantitative measurement of changes in systematic risk, while the art applies experience and judgment to the factors that are not easily quantified. Risk management includes both measurement of changing risk and dynamic reallocation of assets among different strategy sectors and managers. The risk manager needs to take proactive steps as risk factors shift. By the time a crisis has arrived, it is often too late to make adjustments. Within a framework of active hedge fund risk management, there are various ways to manage risk and exercise control over trading managers.[29] These include regular conversations with managers, defined risk or exposure limits, defined stop-loss limits, requests for explanation of unusual positions, and firing of managers with 'issues'.

Portfolio versus manager risk

The risk manager must distinguish and monitor two different types of hedge fund risk:

(1) *Portfolio ('beta') risk*: These are the systematic risk factors in the global capital markets, i.e. the betas, which, as the reader has learnt, constitute the large part of performance drivers in hedge funds. Alternative beta strategies provide a cost-efficient, well-defined, and transparent exposure to these 'beta risks' without any manager-specific risks.
(2) *Manager-specific ('alpha') risk:* These are risks that arise from the individual manager's trading style, business set-up, leverage, etc. These risks include style drifts, operational problems, concentration in individual securities, fraud, and business risks such as the departure of key fund employees. I also refer to them as 'alpha risks' as alpha returns necessarily come with these risks as much as beta returns come with market-given risks. Ideally a satellite hedge fund manager should come with alpha risks only, and no beta risk.

---

[29] For more details, see the author's explications in 'The new generation of risk management for hedge funds and private equity investment,' Chapter 1 (2003) and 'Risk management in alternative investment strategies' (2002).

Any reader who has made it to this chapter will realize that style ('beta') risks are both necessary and systematic. They are a prerequisite for obtaining expected returns. It is the job of the portfolio fund manager to deal with them through diversification among strategy sectors that show their respective strengths and weaknesses in different market environments. While ongoing management of portfolio risk could be treated as part of post-investment risk management, it can also be viewed as ongoing tactical adjustment of strategy sector allocation. Since I have already treated the tactical asset allocation in the section on sector allocation, and it is the systematic component of return that we want to replicate and wrap in the core of the portfolio, I will focus on managing manager-specific risks and how to manage them here.

Unlike beta risk, manager-specific 'alpha risk' is unsystematic and therefore does not correspond to systematic return sources. In other words, this risk comes with no expected return if considered across all market participants (it is a 'zero sum game'). Generally, risk that remains uncompensated or is unintended, misunderstood, mismanaged, or mispriced should not be accepted by the investor. Consequently the risk manager must diligently monitor manager-specific risks.

Managing the managers

One way that fund portfolio managers limit manager-specific risk is to dilute it through sheer numbers. By selecting 50 to 100 different funds, they limit the impact of a single manager blow-up on their portfolio. The logic of this approach is obvious, as it applies basic diversification to manager risk. However, such large numbers can lead to over-diversification, due to the inclusion of 'dead weight' managers who would not be included in a more select group. Over-diversified alpha risk leads to the disappearance of alpha itself. This often causes mediocre performance and an undesired correlation to broad risk factors.[30]

The alternative to this 'shotgun' approach is active manager control. This approach can decrease manager risk significantly, and thus reduce the number of managers needed in the hedge fund portfolio. Active manager control consists of defining and enforcing risk limits, including permitted instruments and hedging techniques.

The prerequisites for monitoring and controlling manager-specific risk are transparency, liquidity, independent valuation, and quantitative risk analysis. As we will see, these elements are easily assembled in the framework of managed accounts.

Transparency

A risk manager cannot manage what he cannot see. So the traditionally low transparency of hedge funds represents the first serious barrier to independent risk management. Hedge funds have traditionally been reluctant to disclose details about their trading strategies and market exposure. But without transparency, risk analysis remains largely a guessing game. It is like trying to steer a car whose windshield has been painted black. Monthly returns, standard deviations, maximal drawdowns, and, in most cases, a monthly or quarterly letter to the investors, only scrape a tiny hole in that darkness. To make matters worse, this hole might even be at the wrong spot on the windshield, as past performance data come with an insufficient degree of statistical reliability and persistence. Much more thorough detail about the current

---

[30] See also S. Lhabitant, M. Learned, 'Hedge fund diversification: how much is enough?' (Winter 2002).

risk profile of a hedge fund is needed. But how much transparency does the risk manager need in order to fulfill his task properly? This is one of the most intensely discussed questions within the hedge fund industry.[31] The risk managers of proprietary trading operations, where the in-house hedge funds of the large investment banks are traded, show us one answer. In charge of overseeing the bank's capital at risk, they would never settle for anything less than full position disclosure.

But even complete transparency does not guarantee proper risk analysis. The 'art of transparency' involves integrating transparency into the risk-management infrastructure. This is a multilevel process that moves from collecting structural information about the hedge fund prior to investment, to efficiently dealing with the possibly thousands of single positions in hedge funds, appropriately valuing all instruments in the portfolio, and calculating the appropriate risk variables and the definition of necessary risk-management activities.

Valuation of hedge funds

Once the risk manager scrapes the paint off the windshield and achieves transparency, he must make his own judgment of the road ahead in the form of an independent valuation of the positions held in his portfolio. If the instruments in a hedge fund portfolio are not marked correctly, the risk manager might misjudge the level of risk. Further, valuations can affect the volatility of the reported returns. In its report from March 2007, the Alternative Investment Management Association (AIMA) provided a number of hedge fund valuation recommendations summarizing the industry's developing standards for proper valuation of hedge fund portfolios.[32] But risk managers are still often on their own when trying to find the appropriate rule for the valuation in order to avoid or mitigate potential conflicts of interest on the side of the individual fund manager. Regular disclosure of the hedge fund manager's exposure and transactions aids independent valuation. Since some of the securities traded by hedge funds are not regularly traded or valued by broadly accepted sources, risk managers must assemble their own resources in the form of data sources, pricing services, and valuation models. A working paper released by the Investor Risk Committee in September 2003 outlines the key concepts and issues involved in the valuation process for financial companies in general, and hedge funds in particular.[33] The summer of 2007 and subsequent developments in 2008 served as yet another reminder of how important the issue of hedge fund valuation is when many hedge funds and their administrators found themselves incapable of putting the appropriate price tag to their portfolio holdings in structured credit instruments. As a result numerous hedge fund managers closed their funds from further redemptions until market conditions improved and allowed more reliable estimations.

---

[31] See also the discussion in my book, *Managing Risk in Alternative Investment Strategies* (2002), and the book by L. Rahl, *Hedge Fund Transparency* (2003). Further, see the report by the Investor Risk Committee (IRC), 'Hedge fund disclosure for institutional investors', available on the IAFE Web-page: http://www.iafe.org, or on http://www.cmra.com. The report was amended in July 2001. The discussion within the IRC is ongoing. I am referring to the document published on July 27, 2001.

[32] See the report 'AIMA's guide to sound practices for hedge fund valuation', AIMA (2007).

[33] See the report by the Investor Risk Committee (IRC) of the International Association of Financial Engineers (IAFE), 'Valuation concepts for investment companies and financial institutions and their shareholders' (2003), available on http://www.iafe.org

The issue of liquidity

The benefits of transparency and independent valuation can only be realized if redemption periods allow the risk manager to act on his conclusions. Daily transparency is not actionable if the investors can only redeem their investments every six months. Therefore the risk manager should require redemption periods that correspond to the frequency of disclosure.

The traditionally long hedge fund redemption periods have become harder and harder for fund managers to justify. After all, most hedge funds operate in the most liquid stock, bond, currency, and futures markets (albeit more recently there has been an expressed move into less liquid instruments). Contrast the instant redemption capability of the instruments most hedge funds trade with the snail-like redemption periods they offer to their investors; they range from one month to several years (and can even be prolonged at their discretion). Until recently hedge fund managers have been neither willing nor operationally capable of providing shorter redemptions. Providing for frequent subscriptions and redemptions imposes a large back-office load, and most funds have very limited administrative resources. But if the hedge fund manager enjoys high liquidity in the instruments he uses to execute his strategy, why should the investor and third-party risk manager settle for less?[34]

Of course, not all hedge fund strategies are equally liquid and the liquidity features of certain strategies can be subject to change over time. Further, one limiting factor for better liquidity conditions to the investor can be the tendency of hedge funds to move into crowded trades, which entails many managers detecting the same opportunity and thus taking the same position (again the summer of 2007 with the 'quant crash' – model-driven equity hedge funds – illustrated what happens when trades become too crowded). The combination of leverage and crowdedness can lead to temporary illiquidity in otherwise liquid positions. So the risk manager must match his demands for redemption liquidity with the liquidity of the instruments and methods that underlie the specific fund strategy, and include that liquidity in his ongoing risk adjustments.

The liquidity of a given hedge fund has two parts: *instrument* liquidity and *funding* liquidity. Instrument liquidity is the ability of the fund to sell an investment without moving the price. Funding liquidity is the availability of financing for leverage. The risk manager should research both the liquidity of the instruments in which a strategy invests and the sources and reliability of leverage financing. The best liquidity indicator for a strategy is market liquidity of the traded instruments. Managed Futures, large cap Long/Short Equity, Equity Market Neutral, Global Macro, and Risk Arbitrage strategies involve highly liquid exchange-traded instruments, as do most arbitrage and Relative Value strategies.[35] In contrast, Distressed Debt and Regulation D strategies are by nature extremely illiquid, since liquidity premia constitute a major return source. Be aware though that the liquidity of securities can fluctuate rapidly over time, and can be especially low in turbulent markets. Liquidity tends to evaporate when it is most needed. An unprecedented example of previously unknown liquidity risk was the 'flight to quality'

---

[34] The rise in popularity of managed accounts (see discussion below) by funds of funds can change this. Managed accounts offer hedge fund liquidity to the level of the liquidity of the instruments traded, so it is in the hand of the funds of funds who employ managed accounts to structure products with the necessary liquidity.

[35] Convertible bonds are usually traded OTC as are swaps and other fixed income and credit derivatives. However, with the proliferation of these instruments liquidity has often reached high levels.

event in September 1998 that led to the failure of LTCM.[36] Another more recent example is the experience of asset-backed security hedge funds in the wake of the credit crisis in 2007/2008 when a combination of crowdedness in certain positions combined with the necessity to de-leverage due to prime brokers imposing higher haircuts, many hedge funds suffered losses they had never experienced before, and many had to close shop.

Resulting from the crisis in 2007/2008 one can observe an expressed concern by investors about the increasing complexity of the instruments hedge funds invest in today as well as their lower liquidity. One trend that can be observed amongst multistrategy hedge funds for example is the development of highly complex structures with multiple trading entities underneath the main master fund – expressed by the extent to which this web of subsidiaries invest in each other and provide cross-support and cross-guarantees in the event of margin calls or defaults. Maybe not entirely surprising came the re-experience of the notion of 'liquidity risk'. As the market for complexly structured asset-backed securities and related instruments dried up completely in the wake of the global credit crisis or niche markets that had soared just months before suddenly experienced drastic pull-backs (like the leveraged senior loan sector) hedge funds and other investors – in particular the Wall Street investment banks – went back and invented new 'mark-to-prayer' valuation schedules for the illiquid components of their book. There is a new 'urge for simplicity' by investors who want to avoid sudden surprises in their portfolio. The 'complexity risk premium' hedge funds have claimed for many years appears more and more expensive.

However, even in relatively calm markets, a single holding in a hedge fund manager's port-folio can become suddenly illiquid, especially when the manager holds a position of significant size compared to the trading volume of that security (and often traded it up himself building this position). This can be especially problematic when the position constitutes a large part of the manager's portfolio. Numerous Long/Short Equity managers, for example, hold single stocks in higher concentrations in their portfolio than their traditional counterparts, sometimes even in stocks of small capitalization, especially when they 'have fallen in love' with a particular stock. In some cases their trading activity itself had led to significant gains in the price of such stock. The risk manager needs to be aware of potential liquidity shortfalls in those holdings and assign appropriate liquidity measure to individual positions. A straightforward and appropriate mea-sure of such could be the ratio of position size and average daily trading volume of the security.

A final note on the issues of transparency and liquidity: in the end we are all trying to allocate capital to the smartest hedge funds out there. Unfortunately these are often 'too smart', knowing how to protect their capital base by requesting low liquidity terms and not providing much information about the details of what they are doing. So investors have to make a choice of what they really want. Transparency and liquidity are possible and no investor should forgo these if he can get them. He should put pressure on the hedge funds to provide a healthy balance of information and flexibility in their allocation process. If he thinks that low liquidity and long lock-ups is the only way to go for alpha – i.e. skill-based market-independent returns – what he has to live with then is idiosyncratic, i.e. manager-specific, risk which is just exacerbated by low transparency and liquidity terms. Once in a while this type of risk shows its ugly face.

[36] For a well-written and quite entertaining account of LTCM we recommend *When Genius Failed: The Rise and Fall of Long-Term Capital Management* by Roger Lowenstein (Random House, 2000); see also the report of the President's Working Group on Financial Markets, 'Hedge funds, leverage, and the lessons of Long-Term Capital Management' (April 1999), available on http://risk.ifci.ch/146530.htm

Quantitative elements of risk analysis

Given reasonable transparency and redemption periods short enough to allow the risk manager to act, there are several forms of quantitative analysis that will help him make the right choices. These are exposure analysis, value-at-risk, stress tests and scenario analysis.

Exposure analysis

Risk is a combination of exposure and uncertainty. Exposure and position analysis examines aggregate exposure of the level of the global portfolio, but also breaks down the exposure to different aggregation levels. It further includes monitoring of certain exposure ratios such as margin characteristics and leverage factors, credit quality, hedge ratios.

Value-at-risk (VaR)

VaR has introduced a new dimension of risk analysis in the 1990s and belongs today to the standard set of instruments in the risk management community. With VaR, risk can be quantified across different instrument and asset classes in a framework where correlations as well as volatilities are fully accounted for using a uniform and comparable measuring system for risk. But VaR provides only a very incomplete picture of the extreme left-tail region of the distribution. VaR therefore does not help us to forecast and prevent unacceptable losses. VaR also needs to be supplemented by other analytical tools, such as expected shortfall, in order to cope with extreme market conditions (e.g. stress tests).

Stress tests and scenario analysis

Stress tests apply extreme scenarios to the portfolio in order to ascertain the impact of extreme price changes in the market. Such tests give insight to the portfolio behavior under extreme, but plausible, market conditions.

Managed accounts for risk management

Managed accounts provide the best framework of liquidity and transparency for effective risk management. The hedge fund portfolio manager sets up a separate account in which the hedge fund manager has a special authority to execute his trading strategy, in most cases one-to-one with his fund (see Figure 9.3). Managed accounts provide the hedge fund portfolio or risk manager with full disclosure of the manager's trading activities together with the highest possible degree of liquidity. Further, the investor is in a position to select all involved counterparties including the prime broker, custodian, and auditor. This creates the ideal environment for proactive risk management.

Although the institutionalization of hedge funds and the increased importance of independent third-party risk management have made managed accounts popular, using one is not always practicable. The portfolio manager must be expert in setting up such an account, and trading in one requires the replication of the entire trading infrastructure of a hedge fund, including a range of operational and legal issues. This is quite complex, especially for managed accounts with top hedge fund managers not willing to compromise on their trading efficiency. Further the investor has to be willing and able to provide the manager with confidentiality

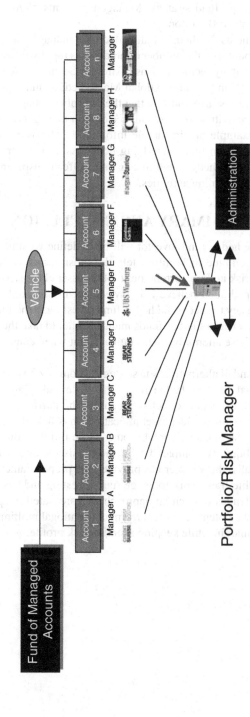

Figure 9.3 A managed account investment infrastructure

agreements. Finally the hedge fund investor should be in a position to allocate a significant amount of capital to the hedge fund strategy. Managed accounts often require a minimum investment of as much as $50–100 million.

Even with these requirements fulfilled, not all hedge fund managers agree to exercise their strategy via a managed account. But the number of holdouts is rapidly decreasing, and they are concentrated in particular strategy sectors such as Distressed Securities, Activist Event Driven, Multi-Strategy, Regulation D, and the large Global Macro hedge funds. And the absence of a managed account does not necessarily indicate that the portfolio manager remains completely in the black concerning the activities and performance of their managers at a higher frequency. Most funds of funds for example obtain sample information of positions and performance estimates on a weekly basis from their underlying hedge fund managers. It is increasingly considered a sign of quality for hedge fund managers to offer transparency with respect to their investment approach and trading activities.

9.12 SUMMARY AND CONCLUSION

The main task of the future hedge fund investor will be to define what he wants from hedge funds. Alpha is and will continue to be ultimately the most attractive sort of return, as it comes with no systematic risk and no correlation to other asset classes. While the search for alpha surely remains compelling, I believe it is investment in alternative betas which may become more and more the key to successful hedge fund investing in the future. A manager of portfolios of hedge funds such as a fund of funds manager, should take the new techniques of cost-efficiently extracting these alternative betas into account when constructing their overall portfolios.

The management of a 'fund of alternative beta strategies' comes with a variety of advantages compared to a conventional fund of hedge funds. High flexibility and granularity in the separation of particular risk exposures effectively enables the portfolio manager to perform an otherwise virtually impossible tactical asset allocation, thus flexibly reacting to changing market environments. The risk manager's job becomes more fulfilling due to the high degree of risk transparency and liquidity compared with the persistent opaqueness of traditional hedge fund portfolios. Finally, this chapter has provided the proper framework for a possible application of a core–satellite framework to hedge fund investing and has discussed some of the opportunities and challenges of such an approach. A core–satellite approach applied to hedge fund portfolios has the potential to outperform conventional multimanager hedge fund portfolios by a significant margin while keeping a similar risk profile.

10

Replication and the Future
of Hedge Funds

10.1 BEYOND ALPHA

Replication is only possible because beta predominates. Most hedge fund returns derive from risk premia rather than market inefficiencies. Surprisingly, this is actually good news for the industry. Because inefficiencies disappear as they are exploited, it is unlikely that there will be enough remaining inefficiencies in the market to indefinitely support the growth of hedge funds. On the other hand, the opportunities to develop new ways to identify and earn risk premia are almost unlimited. But both investors and fund managers must understand the difference.

The state of hedge fund research in the early twenty-first century is analogous to physics at the beginning of the twentieth. We have begun to understand the 'atoms' of hedge fund returns, their return sources. These in turn are being broken down into their elementary particles: beta, alpha, epsilon (the random term – in other words, luck). What we now observe is the emergence of an underlying fundamental theory for hedge fund returns. To stretch the physics analogy a bit further, what is emerging is a theory of 'quantum mechanics' for hedge funds. The hedge fund risk premia are more clearly revealed from behind the clouds of alpha. Applying this new understanding to the real world of investing can have effects as revolutionary as applying quantum mechanics did to the worlds of chemistry and industrial technology.

10.2 WHAT DO INVESTORS SAY SO FAR?

Even at this early stage of development, hedge fund replication has already found remarkably wide acceptance. According to a survey by AllAboutAlpha and Terrapin,[1] hedge fund replicators for the most part are seen as complementing hedge funds, though not replacing them (view of more than 70% of funds of hedge funds and long-only managers). The survey found that respondents overall considered alternative beta and hedge fund clones mostly as a tool for creating new products, while progressively smaller percentages valued them as a benchmark, a way to manage cash, for asset allocation, and for setting hurdle rates. The same study revealed that end-investors were much more likely than consultants to believe that hedge funds' returns are mostly the result of skill. Nearly 75% of end-investors say they are familiar with hedge fund replicators, though only 7% currently invest in them. But one-third say they plan to invest in them by the beginning of next year, indicating a coming surge in investment. More than half of end-investors say liquidity is the most attractive aspect of hedge fund clones, a portion that drops to about one-third of asset managers. Most striking, only 13% of respondents say they do not believe hedge fund returns can be replicated. This implies a major shift in investor understanding of the predominance of beta in hedge fund returns.

---

[1] See the web page http://allaboutalpha.com/blog/2008/02/18/ for details.

10.3   REPLICATION AND THE FOUR KEY CHALLENGES TO THE HEDGE FUND INDUSTRY

I have written previously that the future growth of hedge funds depends on whether the industry can address four key challenges: delivering attractive performance in difficult market environments, providing investors with a better understanding of their return sources, providing better transparency and independent risk management, and finding a fair compensation system that distinguishes between highly paid alpha returns and less costly beta. I continue to be among the optimists, because I observe that the needed changes have already begun. And while replication itself presents a challenge to the status quo, it also forces the industry to address these broader issues head-on.

Reducing the fee load of hedge funds is key to providing attractive returns in different economic cycles. The investor should not have to pay 'alpha fees' for beta returns. So separating beta from alpha and charging different fees for each could greatly improve funds of funds' value proposition. Since today's investable hedge fund indices are really funds of funds in disguise, they do not yet offer the cost benefit of passive investing. Real indexing and 'passive investing' requires a deeper digging into the roots of the hedge fund returns, namely the underlying risk premia. The emergence of 'hedge fund replication' and 'alternative beta strategies' products is a more promising development. Traditional index funds teach us that, net of fees, passive investment often offers the best returns. And just as 'passive investing' took off following the popularization of Bill Sharpe's capital asset pricing model (CAPM), I foresee a similar development in the hedge fund industry.

The industry is grappling with how to provide greater transparency and risk management, while still retaining trading flexibility. The new PR job of hedge funds is not to create market mystery, but to create market understanding. This means promoting hedge fund managers as among the best and most sophisticated risk managers on or off Wall Street, and explaining how the heterogeneity and internal diversification of hedge funds helps protect investors from the fallout of sudden and unforeseen events. The same growing knowledge of risk premia that underlies replication also helps meet this challenge. Hedge funds were surely less suitable for institutional investors before the academic research began revealing their return sources. Today, the sophisticated investor will find hedge funds challenging, but by no means mysterious. With some effort, he can comprehend the strategies. This insight allows the investor to navigate the return sources of hedge funds and their complex risk profiles. It enables him to better discern when managers are simply earning risk premia (beta) intelligently and when they are actually demonstrating superior skill by exploiting market inefficiencies (alpha). Because beta predominates, the investor's 'search for alpha' has to begin with the understanding of beta. And in some cases the hefty fee load of traditional hedge funds makes it best to call off the search entirely!

The two most dangerous risks for hedge fund investors are unwanted and/or unknown leveraged systematic risk and uncontrolled manager-specific risk. Once they understand that most hedge fund returns come from systematic risk, the skilled investor can choose from a universe of risk factors those he is willing to accept, and those he prefers to avoid.

When it comes to fairer compensation, funds of funds have a special role to play – either as part of the solution or as part of the problem! To add value, funds of funds must identify the various risk premia, execute a systematic risk budgeting, and actively manage that risk. Hedge fund portfolio managers must realize that their job extends well beyond picking managers. If they mistake beta for alpha, then they will pay too much for it and simply add another layer of fees to risk premia that are already too expensive. If they incorrectly identify the beta sources in their portfolio, they will not be able to balance them.

On the other hand, replication actually gives funds of funds the opportunity to play a powerful role in bringing investor cost down. With a fee burden that can exceed the average alpha of hedge funds, the fund of funds manager will have to reexamine their value proposition. A core–satellite approach that includes replication products could enable funds of funds to take up the task of layering expensive alpha on top of cheaper beta at a lower total cost. This would not only be more cost-efficient for investors, it would also provide them with a more flexible and more granular asset allocation.

By helping to meet these four challenges, replication products have the potential to attract both disgruntled HF investors, and those who have stayed out of alternatives because of the issues raised (high fees, double fee layer, and low transparency). Replication therefore constitutes an important step in the maturation and institutionalization of the hedge fund industry.

10.4 REPLICATION IN REALITY

Of course replication can only help meet the above challenges to the extent that it actually works, that is, accurately reproduces the returns of hedge funds. And available replication products still have a long way to go. Various product providers have just started to test the academic concept of hedge fund replication through linear factor models in a real trading environment. However, as we discovered in earlier chapters, simple linear factor analysis is insufficient to model the broad universe of hedge fund strategies. Early academic work had already demonstrated that the integration of nonlinearities is essential for properly describing hedge fund returns. Further, linear factor model-based hedge fund replication is not really about replicating hedge funds, it is about replicating hedge fund *indices*. Since today's hedge fund indices simply combine hedge funds into an over-priced portfolio, many typical hedge fund features just diversify away – leaving mostly traditional beta driven by equity risk. With precious little alternative beta actually present in a diversified hedge fund index, the main problem when replicating it via commercial hedge fund indices is that it is being shadowed by traditional beta. Therefore even if linear factor models successfully replicated hedge fund indices, most of the alternative beta that makes hedge funds attractive would still be lost. To be genuinely useful to investors, replication models should feature the attractive hedge fund properties. While it is not reasonable to expect alpha from a passive investment, replication models should provide alternative beta, i.e. provide returns with little correlation to traditional risk premia. Simple linear factor models fail this test.

Where they work – such as in the space of directional equity exposure taken by the hedge funds – linear factor models can be useful for replication. But overall, instead of naively replicating past properties of doubtful (biased) time series with inappropriate (linear) models, it makes more sense to tackle the hedge fund risk premia one by one. More sophisticated replication models that attempt to do just that will lead in turn to investment products that more accurately deliver the desired alternative beta. Interestingly such alternative beta strategies have already been around for many years, but in disguised format – as hedge funds – and with a hefty fee burden.

Finally, I believe that hedge fund replication should include a proper asset allocation across (alternative) risk factors and strategy sectors. Hedge fund replication is therefore not merely a simple 'job for the quants' but requires (a) the understanding of the concept of each strategy, (b) solid quantitative modeling and (c) the 'fund of funds approach' to portfolio management and asset allocation.

10.5   REPLICATION AND HEDGE FUND GROWTH

Can the booming growth that has made hedge funds a multi-trillion-dollar industry continue? Yes and no.

Yes, the investment level can continue to grow. Despite some disappointments and widely publicized blow-ups, hedge funds have still offered an attractive (albeit lower) performance record in recent years. Ironically, the current credit crisis that began in 2007 has actually helped dispel one negative myth about hedge funds: the myth that speculators operating through hedge funds are the main threat to the architecture of global capitalism. I recently overheard someone at a dinner say, 'It was not the hedge funds that blew up the financial world, it was the banks!' And indeed the hedge fund industry as a whole has escaped large losses in the credit crisis – at least as of finalizing this writing in late March 2008.

The influx of institutional investors provides a new and considerably larger potential asset pool. Better investor understanding, along with improved transparency and risk management give comfort to these more mainstream investors, and improve the credibility of hedge funds with both press and public. Risk-management techniques have become much more sophisticated. The 'cowboy mentality' of hedge funds has given way and will continue to give way to investment managers who are better and more professional risk managers, and thus more credible in the eyes of the investor. At the same time the demystification of hedge funds will lead to an increased incorporation of hedge fund investment techniques in investors' global investment portfolios as replication techniques for the extraction of global risk premia emerge.

And no, the old status quo of fat hedge fund fees for (in some cases) illusory alpha cannot grow indefinitely. In an economic downturn, the institutional investors who have powered recent growth will be even less willing to drop billions into an over-priced black box and hope for the best. The mystique of a wizardly 'manager skill' and supposed unique trading methodology might once have attracted investors. But today obscuring return sources has the opposite effect: it impedes mainstream acceptance. Institutional investors naturally regard investments they do not understand as risky, if not shady. Historical returns show that hedge funds offer these investors a very attractive risk profile. But it is up to the industry to open up the black box and help investors understand this profile. Early individual hedge fund investors may have been looking for the 'Wizard of Oz'. But today's institutional investors want to meet the real man behind the curtain and understand in detail what he does and how it fits into their portfolio. Therefore, hedge fund reputation, as well as hedge fund replication requires that we understand and disclose the nature of our return sources.

Of course this very openness raises legitimate questions about fund fees and the possibility of replicating hedge fund returns at lower cost. So no wonder replication has become the new buzzword in the hedge fund industry – despite the limitations of the models that drive many of the investable replication products so far. Hedge fund replication is the practical application of the emerging theoretical knowledge about hedge fund return sources; as that knowledge improves, so will the products that apply it. With further product offerings and increased levels of modeling sophistication, replication could become an entirely new paradigm in hedge fund investing – one that could turn the alternative asset management industry upside-down as thoroughly as innovations such as index funds did the traditional investment industry years ago.

Hedge funds, using the term broadly, will continue to grow; but an increasing share of that growth will come outside of the traditional 'black box' model. A currently small, but rapidly growing portion of alternative investment will go to replication products, just as a large share of mutual fund investment in equities migrated to lower-cost index funds. The theory and modeling techniques that will power these 'alternative alternative' investment vehicles are still in their infancy. But, as those products better track the returns of hedge funds strategies, their cost and transparency advantages will encourage additional investment. More and more investors will include replication products in their portfolios.

So I believe that hedge funds are here to stay, but not here to stay the same! Replication is simply the most tangible part of a much larger trend toward blurring the line between traditional and alternative finance. As the hedge fund industry matures, investors obtain a better assessment of their real opportunities and risks. Hedge funds will exert a broader intellectual influence on world financial markets, the academics who study those markets, and the practitioners who trade in them. The traditional asset management industry will learn from hedge funds and will adopt and incorporate some of their investment strategies as replication techniques for extracting global risk premia emerge. Competition will heat up and the compensation scheme for hedge funds will change fundamentally. The hedge fund replication techniques and alternative beta strategies discussed in this book are about to accelerate this process. Far from impeding industry growth, replication techniques expand the investor pool to help hedge funds continue as one of the most intellectually challenging and financially rewarding disciplines of modern finance.

10.6 HEDGE FUNDS IN THE BROADER CONTEXT: THE FUTURE OF ABSOLUTE RETURN INVESTMENT

I noted in this book that in recent years we can observe a significant flow of hedge fund capital into new and less liquid types of assets such as bank loans, mezzanine, insurance linked securities (ILS) or straight buyout (LBO) transactions. Combining two important insights – the increased participation of hedge funds in the private markets and the 'beta nature' of their returns – we should revisit their overall investment case. Rather than being pure alpha generators for the investor's portfolio in the liquid capital markets the association of hedge funds with 'alternative beta', as well as their exposure to the private markets, provides through an old concept a new foundation to a widely used name for hedge funds. It is by the well known idea of diversification that hedge funds can earn back their name 'absolute return investments'. What does all this mean for investors? The flippant, however appropriate, answer is: their search and request for 'absolute return' should continue. But we must supplement and partly replace the traditional claim of hedge funds for achieving this by investing in talent with the notion of constructing robust portfolios that diversify over a full spectrum of return sources and corresponding risk exposures.

The consequences of this new line of thinking can be more dramatic than they appear to be at first sight. It is the renaissance of the 'all weather portfolio': a portfolio that weathers any storm in the global capital market and is yet not affected by the occasional unpredictable thunderstorms of a manager blowing up. The two most important elements of constructing such a portfolio is a) being highly cost conscious, avoiding paying alpha-fees for beta-return and b) employing 'hedges that have a positive expected return'. The magic of the latter is – again – diversification: combining different types of financial assets with uncorrelated return sources yields more efficient portfolios. The more uncorrelated return sources included, the more diversified the resulting portfolio is, and the more 'absolute return'-like its performance will end up being.

In practice, the investor often starts off by expanding the traditional balanced portfolio with exposure to non-traditional, i.e. alternative betas. The resulting efficiency increases are constituted by the well popularized diversification benefit of hedge funds. But he then has to naturally ask himself how far the diversification benefits can go. Why stop at the liquid spectrum of risk exposures most hedge funds have been seeking until recently? He should include further risk exposures from the private markets to the portfolio mix (such as venture capital, private equity, senior loans, mezzanine, etc.), and he will quickly see that the benefits of diversification play out even more strongly.

Based on this understanding we can justify a conceptual shift in asset allocation: rather than thinking of alternatives as asset classes that should be added to an already existing portfolio of traditional equity and fixed-income assets, we could view alternatives as the core assets to which equities and fixed income are added to achieve the desired overall set of portfolio characteristics, i.e. expected risk and return. Generating 'absolute returns' – the ultimate goal of any alternative asset manager – clearly goes beyond traditional asset classes but also beyond conventional hedge funds in their search for often spurious alpha. It is the most sophisticated asset managers in the world, such as the often cited US super-endowment funds, that follow precisely a concept of the 'all weather' portfolio being thereby able to constantly generate double digit returns even in the most severe bear markets. Naturally we should ask: why not give the broader investor access to such optimal 'absolute return portfolios' and thereby extend his access to the sources of return on capital?

In his seminal book *Against the Gods*,[2] Peter Bernstein introduces the mastery of risk as 'the revolutionary idea that defines the boundary between modern times and the past'. He shows how the great philosophers, mathematicians, and scientists of the past two and a half millennia 'have transformed the perception of risk from chance of loss into opportunity for gain, from FATE and ORIGINAL DESIGN to sophisticated, probability-based forecasts of the future, and from helplessness to choice'. I mentioned in one of my previous books that hedge funds and their contribution to mastering risk merit another, perhaps final, chapter in his book. But it is always hubris to claim that any chapter in such a complex story is final. Replication in turn now represents a still newer chapter in the story of risk. As it drives deeper understanding of the true sources of hedge fund returns, replication will help dispel helplessness and further expand investor choice. Whether you are still searching for alpha, or are looking to replication for more efficient extraction of alternative beta, happy hunting!

---

[2] Peter Bernstein, *Against the Gods: The Remarkable Story of Risk*, New York, John Wiley & Sons, Inc. (1996).

References and Bibliography

Ackermann, C., McEnally, D., Ravenscraft, R., 'The performance of hedge funds: risk return, and incentives', *Journal of Finance*, 2 (1999)

Agarwal, V., Naik, N., 'Multi-period performance persistence analysis of hedge funds', *Journal of Financial and Quantitative Analysis*, 35, 2 (2000)

Agarwal, V., Naik, N., 'On taking the "alternative" route: the risks, rewards, and performance persistence of hedge funds', *The Journal of Alternative Investments* (Spring 2000)

Agarwal, V., Naik, N., 'Performance evaluation of hedge funds with option-based and buy-and-hold strategies'; Working Paper (September 2000)

Agarwal, V., Naik, N., 'Performance evaluation of hedge funds with option-based and buy-and-hold strategies', Working Paper (2001); published under the title: 'Risks and portfolio decisions involving hedge funds', *Review of Financial Studies*, 17, p. 63 (2004)

Agarwal, V., Naveen, D., Naik, N., 'Flows, performance, and managerial incentives in hedge funds', London Business School Working Paper (2004)

Agarwal, V., Fung, W., Loon, Y., Naik, N., 'Risks and return in Convertible Arbitrage: evidence from the convertible bond market', Working Paper, London Business School (2006)

AIMA 'AIMA's guide to sound practices for hedge fund valuation', AIMA (2007). The reader can download the executive summary from the AIMA homepage: www.aima.org; http://www.aima.org/uploads/ExecSummaryAIMAGuideSPforHFValuation2007.pdf

Alexander, C., Giblin, I., Weddington, W., 'Cointegration and asset allocation', *Research in International Business and Finance*, 16, p. 65, (2002)

Alexander, G., 'Efficient sets, short-selling, and estimation risk', *Journal of Portfolio Management*, (Winter 1995)

Amenc, N., El Bied, S., Martellini, L., 'Evidence of predictability in hedge fund returns and multi-style multi-class tactical style allocation decisions', USC Marshal School of Business, Working Paper (2002)

Amenc, N., Martellini, L., 'Portfolio optimization and hedge fund style allocation decisions', *Journal of Alternative Investments* (Fall 2002)

Amenc, N., Martellini, L., Vaissie, M., 'Benefits and risks of alternative investment strategies', *Journal of Asset Management* (July 2003)

Amenc, N., El Bied, S., Martellini, L., 'Predictability in hedge fund returns', *Financial Analysts Journal* (September/October 2003)

Amin G., Kat, H., 'Hedge fund performance 1990–2000: Do the money machines really add value?', Cass Business School Research Paper (May 2001)

Amin, G., Kat, H., 'Stocks, bonds, and hedge funds: not a free lunch!' ISMA Centre Working Paper (April 2002)

Amin, G., Kat, H., 'Welcome to the dark side: hedge fund attrition and survivorship bias over the period 1994–2001', *Journal of Alternative Investments*, 6, 1, pp. 57–73 (2003)

Anson, M., *Handbook of Alternative Assets*, John Wiley & Sons, Ltd (2005)

Aristotle, *The Politics*, Cambridge University Press (1988)

Arnott, R., Pham, T., 'Tactical currency allocation', *Financial Analysts Journal*, May, pp. 47 (1993)

Arnott, R., Hsu, J., Moore, P., 'Fundamental indexation', *Financial Analysts Journal*, 61, 2, pp. 83–99 (2005)

Asness, C., 'An alternative future, I & II', *Journal of Portfolio Management* (Fall 2004)

Asness, C., Krail, R., Liew, J., 'Do hedge funds hedge?', *Journal of Portfolio Management*, 28, 1 (Fall 2001); also available on http://www.aqrcapital.com

Bachelier, L., *Theory of Speculation*, Gauthier-Villars, Paris (1900)

Bailey, J., 'Are manager universes acceptable performance benchmarks', *The Journal of Portfolio Management* (Spring 1992)

Bailey, J., Richards, T., Tierney, D., 'Benchmark portfolios and the manager/plan sponsor relationship', *Journal of Corporate Finance* (Winter 1988)

Bank of England, *Financial Stability Review* (June 2004)

Banz, R., 'The relationship between returns and market value of common stocks', *Journal of Financial Economics*, 9 (1981)

Barra Strategic Consulting Group, 'Fund of hedge funds – rethinking resource requirements', Market Survey (2001)

Bernstein, P., *Capital Ideas: The Improbable Origin of Wall Street*, New York, John Wiley & Sons, Inc. (1993)

Bernstein, P., 'Risk as a history of ideas', *Financial Analysts Journal*, 51, 1 (1995)

Bernstein, P., *Against the Gods: The Remarkable Story of Risk*, New York, John Wiley & Co., Inc. (1996)

Bing, L., 'On the performance of hedge funds', *Financial Analysts Journal*, 55, pp. 72–85 (1999)

Bing, L., 'Hedge fund performance: 1990–1999', *Financial Analysts Journal*, pp. 11–18 (January/February 2001)

Black, F., Litterman, R., 'Asset allocation: combining investor views with market equilibrium', Goldman, Sachs & Co., Fixed Income Research (September 1990)

Black, F., Litterman, R., 'Asset global portfolio optimization', *Financial Analysts Journal* (September 1992)

Bollerslev, T., Chou, R., Kroner, K., 'Arch modeling in finance', *Journal of Econometrics*, 52, pp. 5–59 (1992)

Brinson, G., Hood, R., Beebower, G., 'Determinants of portfolio performance', *Financial Analysts Journal* (July-August 1986)

Brooks, C., Kat, H., 'The statistical properties of hedge fund index returns and their implications for investors', *The Journal of Alternative Investment* (Spring 2002).

Brown, S., Goetzmann, W., 'Hedge funds with style', *Journal of Portfolio Management*, 29, pp. 101–112 (2003)

Brown, S., Goetzmann, W., Ibbotson, R., Ross, S., 'Survivorship bias in performance studies', *Review in Financial Studies*, 5, 4 (1992)

Brown, S., Goetzmann, W., Ibbotson, R., 'Offshore hedge funds: survival and performance 1989–1995', *Journal of Business*, 92 (1999)

Brown, S., Goetzmann, W., Park, J., 'Hedge funds and the Asian currency crisis', *Journal of Portfolio Management*, 26, 4, p. 95 (2000)

Buffet, W., Speech at the shareholder meeting of his investment company Berkshire Hathaway (2004)

Cagnati, R., 'PG hedge fund strategy paper – Global Macro', Partners Group Research (May 2006)

Cagnati, R., Connors, M., 'PG hedge fund strategy paper – Relative Value', Partners Group Research (April 2007)

Caldwell, T., Kirkpatrick, T., *A Primer on Hedge Funds*, Lookout Mountain Capital, Inc. (1995)

Capocci, D., Hübner, G., 'Analysis of hedge fund performance', *Journal of Empirical Finance*, 11 (2004)

Carhart, M., 'On persistence in mutual fund performance', *Journal of Finance*, 52 (1997)

Chalmers, J., Edelen, R., Kadlec, G., 'The wildcard option in transacting mutual-fund shares', Wharton School of Finance (2000)

Chan, L., Lakonishok, J., 'Value and growth investing: review and update', *Financial Analysts Journal* (2004)

Chordia, T., Shivakumar, L., 'Momentum, business cycle, and time-varying expected returns', *Journal of Finance*, 57 (2002)

Clarke, R., de Silva, H., Thorley, S., 'Minimum-variance portfolios in the U.S. Equity Market', *The Journal of Portfolio Management* (Fall 2006)

Connolly, K., *Pricing Convertible Bonds*, John Wiley & Sons, Ltd (2000)

Conrad, J., Kaul, G., 'An anatomy of trading strategies', *Review of Financial Studies*, 11 (1998)

Cornish, E., Fisher, R., 'Moments and cumulants in the specifications of distributions', *Review of the International Statistical Institute* (1937), reprinted in Fisher, R., *Contributions to Mathematical Statistics*, John Wiley & Sons, Inc. (1950)

Crowder, G., Hennessee, L., 'Hedge fund indices', *Journal of Alternative Investments*, Summer (2001)

Dacorogna, M., Gencay, R., Müller, U., Pictet, O., 'Effective return, risk aversion and drawdowns', *Physica A*, 289, pp. 229–248 (2001)

Daniel, K., Hirshleifer, D., Subrahmanyam, A., 'Investor psychology and security market under and overreactions', *Journal of Finance*, 53 (1998)

Davis, A., Huang, X., 'The stock performance of firms emerging from Chapter 11 and accidental bankruptcy', Preprint, Queen's School of Business (January 2004)

DeFusco, R., McLeavey, D., Pinto, J., Runkle, D., *Quantitative Methods for Investment Analysis*, AIMR Publications (2001)

Dimson, E., Marsh, P., Staunton, M., *Triumph of the Optimists: 101 Years of Global Investment Returns*, Princeton University Press (2002)

Dorsey, A., *How to select a hedge fund of funds: pick the winners and avoid the losers*, New York, Institutional Investor Books (2004); Euromoney Publications (2004)

Dorsey, A., *Active Alpha: A Portfolio Approach to Selecting and Managing Alternative Investments*, John Wiley & Sons, Ltd (2007)

Dybvig, P., 'Inefficient dynamic portfolio strategies or how to throw away a million dollars in the stock market', *Review of Financial Studies*, 1, 1 (1988)

Eberhardt, A., Altman, E., Aggarwal, R., 'The equity performance of firms emerging out of bankruptcy', *Journal of Finance*, 14, 5 (1999)

The Economist, 'The benchmarking bane', p. 67 (September 1 2001)

The Economist, 'The latest bubble', p. 59 (September 1 2001)

EDHEC, 'EDHEC alternative indices', EDHEC Risk and Asset Management Research Center (January 2003)

Edwards, F., Caglayan, M., 'Hedge fund performance and manager skill', Working Paper, Columbia University and JPMorganChase Securities (May 2001)

Eibl, A., 'Risk and return properties of hedge funds', Diploma Thesis, University of Karlsruhe (2004)

Eichel, H., 'The dangers of hedge funds', Personal view column, *Financial Times* (February 7 2002)

Embrecht, P., Klüppelberg, C., Mikosch, T., *Modelling Extremal Events*, Heidelberg, Springer (1999)

Embrecht, P., McNeil, A., Straumann, D., 'Correlation and dependence in risk management. Properties and pitfalls', in *Risk Management: Value and Risk and Beyond*, ed. by M. Dempster, Cambridge University Press (2002)

Engle, R., Granger, C., 'Co-integration and error correction: representation, estimation, and testing', *Econometrica*, 55, 2, p. 251 (1987)

Erb, C., Harvey, C., 'The tactical and strategic value of commodity futures', Preprint, Duke University (February 2005)

European Central Bank, *Financial Stability Review of the European Central Bank* (December 2004)

Fabozzi, F., *Fixed Income Analysis*, New Hope, PA, Frank J. Fabozzi Associates (2000)

Fama, E., 'Efficient capital markets: a review of theory and empirical work', *Journal of Finance*, 25, 2, p. 383 (May 1970)

Fama, E., 'Efficient capital markets: II', *Journal of Finance*, 46, 5, p. 1575 (December 1991)

Fama, E., 'Market efficiency, long term returns and behavioral finance', *Journal of Financial Economics*, 49, 3 (1998)

Fama, E., French, K., 'The cross section of expected stock returns', *Journal of Finance*, 47, 2, p. 427 (1992)

Fama, E., French, K., 'Common risk factors in the return of stocks and bonds', *Journal of Financial Economics*, 33 (1993)

Fama, E., French, K., 'Size and book-to-market factors in earnings and returns', *Journal of Finance*, 50, 1, p. 131 (March 1995)

Fama, E., French, K., 'Multifactor explanations of asset pricing anomalies', *Journal of Finance*, 51, p. 55 (1996)

Finger, C. (ed.), 'CreditGrades – technical document', RiskMetrics Document (2002)

Forbes Magazine, 'The $500 billion hedge fund folly' (August 6 2001)

Forbes Magazine, 'The sleaziest show on Earth: how hedge funds are robbing investors' (May 24 2004)

FSA Newsletter, 'Short selling – feedback on DP17' (April 2003); available on http://www.fsa.gov.uk/pubs/discussion/fs_newsletter.pdf

Fung, W., Hsieh, D., 'Empirical characteristics of dynamic trading strategies: the case of hedge funds', *The Review of Financial Studies*, 10, 2 (1997)

Fung, W., Hsieh, D., 'A primer on hedge funds', *Journal of Empirical Finance*, 6, pp. 309–331 (1999)

Fung, W., Hsieh, D., 'Is mean–variance analysis applicable to hedge funds?', *Economic Letters*, 62 (1999)

Fung, W., Hsieh, D., 'Measuring the market impact of hedge funds', *Journal of Empirical Finance*, 7, pp. 1–36 (2000) (can be downloaded on: http://faculty.fuqua.duke.edu/~dah7/vitae.htm)

Fung, W., Hsieh, D., 'Performance characteristics of hedge funds and commodity funds: natural versus spurious biases', *Journal of Financial and Quantitative Analysis* (2000)

Fung, W., Hsieh, D., 'Asset-based hedge fund styles and portfolio diversification', Duke University School of Business Working Paper (October 2001)

Fung, W., Hsieh, D., 'The risk in hedge fund strategies: theory and evidence from trend followers', *Review of Financial Studies*, 41, pp. 313–341 (2001)

Fung, W., Hsieh, D., 'Asset-based style factors for hedge funds', *Financial Analysts Journal*, 58, 5, pp. 16–27 (September/October 2002)

Fung, W., Hsieh, D., 'The risk in fixed income hedge fund styles', *Journal of Fixed Income*, 12, 2 (2002)

Fung, W., Hsieh, D., 'The risk in hedge fund strategies: alternative alphas and alternative betas'in Jaeger, L. (ed.), *The New Generation of Risk Management for Hedge Funds and Private Equity Investment*, Euromoney (2003)

Fung, W., Hsieh, D., 'Benchmarks of hedge fund performance: information content and measurement biases', *Financial Analysts Journal* 58, pp. 22–34 (2004)

Fung, W., Hsieh, D., 'Extracting portable alpha from equity long/short hedge funds', *Journal of Investment Management*, 2, 4, pp. 1–19 (2004)

Fung, W., Hsieh, D., 'Hedge fund benchmarks: a risk based approach', *Financial Analysts Journal*, (September/October 2004)

Fung, W., Hsieh, D., 'The risk in long/short equity hedge funds', Working Paper, London Business School, Duke University (2004)

Fung, W., Hsieh, D., Naik, N., Ramadorai, T., 'Hedge fund: performance, risk and capital formation', BNP Paribas Hedge Fund Centre Working Paper, Series HF-025, London Business School (2007)

Gatev, E., Goetzmann, W., Rouwenhorst, K., 'Pairs trading: performance of a relative value arbitrage rule', NBER Working Paper, 1999

Gehin, W., Vaissié, M., 'Lighthouses or tricks of light? An in-depth look at creating a quality hedge fund benchmark', *The Journal of Indexes* (May/June 2005)

Gehin, W., Martellini, L., Meyfredi, J., 'The myths and limits of passive hedge fund replication', Edhec Research Paper (2007)

Getmansky, M., Lo, A. W., Makarov, I., 'An econometric model of serial correlation and illiquidity in hedge fund returns', *Journal of Financial Economics*, 74, 3, pp. 529–610 (2004)

Goetzmann, W., Gatev, E., Rouwenhorst, K., 'Pairs trading: performance of a relative value arbitrage rule', Yale School of Management Working Papers ysm109, Yale School of Management (1998)

Goetzmann, W., Ingersoll, M., Spiegel, M., Welch, I., 'Portfolio performance manipulation and manipulation-proof performance measures', *Review of Financial Studies*, 20, 5, pp. 1503–1546 (2007)

Gross, B., *Pimco Investment Outlook* (April 2003)

Gross, B., *Pimco Investment Outlook* (August 2004)

Grossman, S., Stiglitz, J., 'On the impossibility of informationally efficient markets', *American Economic Review*, 70 (1980)

Gruber, M., 'Another puzzle: the growth in actively managed mutual funds', *Journal of Finance* (1996)

Hasanhodzic, J., Lo, A., 'Can hedge fund returns be replicated? The linear case', *Journal of Investment Management*, 5, 2, p. 5 (2007)

He, G., Litterman, R., 'The intuition behind Black–Litterman model portfolios', Goldman, Sachs & Co. (December 1999)

Hedge Fund Research, Inc., *Market Neutral and Hedged Strategies* (August 2000)

Hong, H., Stein, J., 'A unified theory of underreaction, momentum trading, and overreaction in asset markets', *Journal of Finance*, 54 (1999)

Hull, J., *Options, Futures, and Other Derivatives*, 4th edition, Prentice Hall (1999)

Ineichen, A., 'In Search of Alpha: Investing in Hedge Funds', UBS Warburg, London (October 2000)

Ineichen, A., 'The search for alpha continues: Do "fund of hedge fund" managers add value?', UBS Warburg (September 2001)

Ineichen, A., *Absolute Returns*, John Wiley & Sons, Ltd (2002)

Ineichen, A., *The Critique of Pure Alpha*, Zurich, UBS Research (March 2005)

Ineichen, A., *Asymmetric Returns*, John Wiley & Sons, Ltd (2007)

International Association of Financial Engineers Investor Risk Committee, 'Hedge fund disclosure for institutional investors' (2001); available on http://www.iafe.org

International Association of Financial Engineers, Investor Risk Committee, 'Valuation concepts for investment companies and financial institutions and their shareholders' (2003); available on http://www.iafe.org

ISI publications, *The Capital Guide to Alternative Investments* (2001)

ISI publications, *The Capital Guide to Alternative Investments* (2002)

Jacobs, B., Levy, K., '20 myths about enhanced active 120–20 strategies', *Financial Analysts Journal*, 63, 4 (2007)

Jaeger, L., 'Monitor transparency', *Global Pensions*, p. 10 (2002)

Jaeger, L., *Peering into the Black Box*, IPE Publications, p. 12 (September 2002)

Jaeger, L., 'Return sources of hedge funds', in *The Capital Guide to Hedge Funds*, ISI Publications (2002)

Jaeger, L., '*Risk Management in Alternative Investment Strategies*', Financial Times/Prentice Hall (2002)

Jaeger, L., 'The trouble with the bubble theory', *Risk and Reward* (April 2002)

Jaeger, L., 'Risk management and transparency in the construction and monitoring of a fund of hedge funds portfolio' in *The New Generation of Risk Management for Hedge Funds and Private Equity Investment*, Euromoney (2003)

Jaeger, L., 'The benefits of alternative investment strategies in the global investment portfolio', Partners Group Research Publication (2003); available on http://www.partnersgroup.net

Jaeger, L., (ed.), *The New Generation of Risk Management for Hedge Funds and Private Equity Investment*, Euromoney (2003)

Jaeger, L., 'Hedge fund indices – a new way to invest in absolute returns strategies?', *AIMA Newsletter* (June 2004)

Jaeger, L., *Through the Alpha Smokescreen: A Guide to Hedge Fund Return Sources*, Institutional Investor (2005).

Jaeger, L., Müller, St., 'Return sources of hedge funds', in *The Capital Guide to Hedge Funds*, ISI Publications (2004)

Jaeger, L., Wagner, C., 'Factor modelling and benchmarking of hedge funds: Can passive investments in hedge fund strategies deliver?', *Journal of Alternative Investments* (Winter 2005)

Jaeger, L., Jacquemai, M., Cittadini, P., 'Case study: the sGFI Futures Index', *The Journal of Alternative Investment* (Summer 2002)

Jaeger, L., Jacquemai, M., Cittadini, P., 'Hedge Funds in Marktturbulenzen', *Neue Zürcher Zeitung* (January 8 2002)

Jaeger, L., Jacquemai, M., 'Return sources of hedge funds I & II', *AIMA Newsletter* (September and November 2002)

Jaffer, S. (ed.), *Fund of Hedge Funds for Professional Investors and Managers*, Euromoney (2003)

Jegadesh, N., Titman, S., 'Returns to buying winners and selling losers: implication for stock market efficiency', *Journal of Finance*, 45 (1993)

Jegadesh, N., Titman, S., 'Profitability of momentum strategies: an evaluation of alternative explanation', *Journal of Finance*, 56 (2001)

Jensen, G., Rotenberg, J., 'Hedge funds selling beta as alpha', Working Paper, Bridgewater Associates Inc. (2003)

Jensen, G., Rotenberg, J., 'Hedge funds selling beta as alpha – an update', Working Paper, Bridgewater Associates Inc. (February 13 2004)

Jensen, G., Rotenberg, J., 'Hedge funds selling beta as alpha', Working Paper, Bridgewater Associates Inc. (May 24 2005)

Kahneman, D., Tversky, A., 'Prospect theory: an analysis of decision making under risk', *Econometrica*, 47, 2 (1979)

Kahneman, D., Slovic, P., Tversky, A., *Judgment under Uncertainty: Heuristics and Biases*, New York, Cambridge University Press (1982)

Kant, I., *The Critique of Pure Reason* (German original: *Die Kritik der reinen Vernunft*), Riga (1781)

Keynes, J. M., *A Treatise on Money*, Vol. II. New York, Macmillan & Co. (1930)

Kohler, A., 'Hedge fund indexing: a square peg in a round hole', State Street Global Advisors (2003)

Kramer, D., 'Hedge fund disasters: avoiding the next catastrophe', *Alternative Investment Quarterly* (October 2001)

Kung, E., Pohlman, L., 'Portable alpha – philosophy, process and performance', *Journal of Portfolio Management* (Spring 2004)

Lake, R. (ed.), *Evaluating and Implementing Hedge Fund Strategies*, Euromoney Books (1996)

Lakonishok, J., Shleifer, A., Vishny, R., 'Contrarian investment, extrapolation, and risk', *Journal of Finance*, 49, 5 (1994)

Lederman, J., Klein, R., *Hedge Funds: Investment and Portfolio Strategies for the Institutional Investor*, New York, Irwin Professional Publishing (1995)

Lefevre, E., *Reminiscences of a Stocks Operator*, John Wiley & Sons, Ltd (republished 1994; first published 1923)

Lhabitant, S., *Hedge fund myths*, John Wiley & Sons, Ltd (2002)

Lhabitant, S., *Hedge Funds: Quantitative Insights*, John Wiley & Sons, Ltd (2004)

Lhabitant, S., Learned, M., 'Hedge fund diversification: how much is enough?', *Journal of Alternative Investment* (Winter 2002)

Liang, B., 'On the performance of hedgefunds', Association for Investment Management and Research (July/August 1999)

Liang, B., 'Hedge fund performance: 1990–1999', *Financial Analysts Journal*, 57, 1 (January/February 2001)

Lo, A., MacKinlay, A., 'When are contrarian profits due to stock market overreaction?', *Review of Financial Studies*, 3 (1990)

Longstaff, F., Schwartz, E., 'A simple approach to valuing risky fixed and floating rate debt', *Journal of Finance*, 50, pp. 449–470 (1998)

Loomis, C., 'The Jones nobody keeps up with', *Fortune Magazine*, p. 237 (April 1966)

Lowenstein, R., *When Genius Failed: The Rise and Fall of Long-Term Capital Management*, Random House (2000)

Malkiel, B., *A Random Walk down Wall Street*, W.W. Norton & Co., 1st edition (1973), 7th edition (2000)

Malkiel, B., Saha, A., 'Hedge funds: risk and return', Working Paper (2004)

Markowitz, H., 'Portfolio Selection', *Journal of Finance*, 7, 1, p. 77 (1952)

Markowitz, H., *Portfolio selection – Efficient Diversification of Investment*, New York, John Wiley & Sons, Inc. (1959)

Mauldin, J., *Analysing Global Macro Funds*, Millennium Wave Investments (2005)

McFall Lamm Jr., R., 'Portfolios of alternative assets: why not 100% hedge funds?' *Journal of Alternative Investments* (Winter 1999)

McKinsey, 'The new power brokers: how oil, Asia, hedge funds and private equity are shaping global capital markets', McKinsey Institute (October 2007)

Merton, R., 'On the price of corporate debt: the risk structure of interest rates', *Journal of Finance*, 29, pp. 440–470 (1974)

Merton, R., 'On market timing and investment performance I: An equilibrium theory to value for market forecasts', *Journal of Business*, 54 (July 1981)

Miller, M., 'Behavioral rationality in finance: the case of dividends', *Journal of Business*, 59, 4 (1986)

Mitchel, M., Pulvino, T., 'Characteristics of risk in risk arbitrage', *Journal of Finance*, 56, 6, p. 2135 (2001)

Moore, K. M., *Risk Arbitrage: An Investor's Guide*, New York, John Wiley & Sons, Inc., 1999

Moskowitz, T., Grinblatt, M., 'Do industries explain momentum?', *Journal of Finance*, 54 (1999)

Northwater Capital Management Inc., 'Northwater Capital Management's thoughts on hedge fund replication' (May 2007)

Odean, T., 'Do investors trade too much?', *American Economic Review*, 89 (1999)

Odean, T., Barber, B., 'The courage of misguided convictions: the trading behavior of individual investors', *Financial Analysts Journal* (November 1999)

Odean, T., Barber, B., 'Trading is hazardous to your wealth: the common stock performance of individual investors', *Journal of Finance*, 55 (2000)

Papageorgiou, N., Remillard, B., Hocquard, A., 'Replicating the properties of hedge fund returns', Preprint, HEC Montreal (2007)

Parker, V. R. (ed.), *Managing Hedge Fund Risk*, London, Risk Books (2001)

Patel, N., 'Flow business booms: credit derivative survey', *Risk Magazine* (February 2003)

Pitaro, R., *Deals, Deals, and More Deals*, Gabelli University Press (1999)

Popper, K., *The Logic of Scientific Discovery*, German original: *Die Logik der Forschung* (1933)

Potjer, D., Gould, C., *Global Tactical Asset Allocation: Exploiting the Opportunity of Relative Movements Across Asset Classes and Financial Markets*, Risk Books (2007)

President's Working Group on Financial Markets, 'Hedge funds, leverage, and the lessons of Long-Term Capital Management' (April 1999), available on http://risk.ifci.ch/146530.htm

Rahl, L. (ed.), *Risk Budgeting: A New Approach to Investing*, Risk Books (2000)

Rahl, L., *Hedge Fund Transparency*, Risk Books (2003)

Reilly, F., Brown, K., *Investment Analysis and Portfolio Management*, 5th edition, The Dryden Press (1997)

Rohrer, J., 'The red hot world of Julian Robertson', *Institutional Investors Magazine*, p. 86 (May 1986)

Rosenberg, B., Reid, K., French, K., 'Persuasive evidence on market inefficiencies', *Journal of Portfolio Management* 11, 3, p. 9, (spring 1985)

Ross, S., 'The arbitrage theory of capital asset pricing', *Journal of Economic Theory*, 13, 2, p. 341 (December 1976)

Schenk, C., 'Convertible arb funds turn to default swaps', *Risk Magazine*, p. 14, (July 2001)

Schneeweis, T., Kazemi, H., 'Conditional performance of hedge funds', CISDM Working Paper (2003)

Schneeweis, T., Martin, G., *The Benefits of Hedge Funds*, Lehman Brothers Publications (August 2000)

Schneeweis, T., Spurgin, R., 'Multifactor analysis of hedge funds, managed futures, and mutual fund returns and risk characteristics', *Journal of Alternative Investments* (Fall 1998)

Schneeweis, T., Kazemi, H., Martin, G., *Understanding Hedge Fund Performance: Research Results and Rules of Thumb for the Institutional Investor*, Lehman Brothers Publications (December 2001)

Schneeweis Partners, 'A review of alternative hedge fund indices' (2001)

Schwartz, T., 'How to beat the S&P 500 with portfolio optimization', Working Paper, DePaul University (2000)

Schweitzer, M., 'Variance-optimal hedging in discrete time', *Mathematics of Operational Research*, 20, 1, p. 470 (1995)

Sharpe, W., 'Capital asset prices: a theory of market equilibrium under conditions of risk', *Journal of Finance*, 19, 3, p. 425 (September 1964)

Sharpe, W., 'Mutual fund performance', *Journal of Business*, 39, p. 119 (1966)

Sharpe, W., 'Asset allocation: management style and performance measurement', *Journal of Portfolio Management*, 18, 2, pp. 7–19 (1992)

Shefrin, H., *Beyond Greed and Fear: Understanding Behavioral Finance*, Boston, Harvard Business School Press, (1999); revised version: Oxford University Press (2002)

Shiller, R., 'Human behavior and the efficiency of the financial system', in *Handbook of Macroeconomics*, ed. by Taylor, J., Woodford, M., North-Holland (1999)

Shiller, R., *Irrational Exuberance*, 2nd edition, Princeton University Press (2005)

Signer, A., Favre, L., 'The difficulties of measuring the benefits of hedge funds', *The Journal of Alternative Investment* (Summer 2002)

Signer, A., Favre, L., 'Mean-modified value-at-risk optimization with hedge funds', *The Journal of Alternative Investment* (Spring 2002)

Soros, G., *The Alchemy of Finance: Reading the Mind of the Market*, New York, John Wiley & Sons, Inc. (1987)

Spurgin, R., 'A benchmark on Commodity Trading Advisor performance', *Journal of Alternative Investments* (Fall 1999)

Strachmann, D., *Julian Robertson – A Tiger in the Land of Bulls and Bears*, John Wiley & Sons, Inc. (2004)

Stratman, M., 'Behavioural finance: past battles and future engagements', *Financial Analysts Journal* (November/December 1999)

Talib, N., *Fooled by Randomness: The Hidden Role of Chance in the Markets and in Life*, Texere Publishing (2001)

Talib, N., 'Bleed or blowup. On the preference for negative skewness', *Journal of Behavioral Finance*, 5, p. 8 (2004)

Tavakoli, J., *Credit Derivatives: A Guide to Instruments and Applications*, 2nd edition, John Wiley & Sons, Ltd (2001)

Till, H., 'The capacity implications of the search of alpha', *AIMA Newsletter* (2004)

Tremont, Partners, Inc., and TASS Investment Research, Inc., 'The case for hedge funds' (1999)

Tversky, A., 'The psychology of decision making', in *Behavioral Finance and Decision Theory in Investment Management*, Charlottesville, AIMR Publication (1995)

Umlauf, S., Bowler B., 'Merrill Lynch Factor Index: a new approach to diversified hedge fund investing', presented at the Hedge Fund Replication and Alternative Beta Conference, London (February 2007)

Uryasev, S., Rockafellar, T., 'Optimization of conditional value-at-risk', *The Journal of Risk*, 2, 3, pp. 21–41 (2000); also available on http://www.ise.ufl.edu/uryasev/roc.pdf

U.S. Securities and Exchange Commission, 'Implications of the growth of hedge funds', Staff Report to the Securities Exchange Commission, Washington, DC (2003)

Watterson, P., 'Offering private investment funds in the capital markets', *Alternative Investment Quarterly*, p. 43 (October 2001)

Zhong, Z., 'Why does hedge fund alpha decrease over time? Evidence from individual hedge funds', (January 2008); available at SSRN: http://ssrn.com/abstract=1108817

Index

Printed in the United States
By Bookmasters